T0305273

Study on the Auditing System of Socialism with Chinese Characteristics

Founded in 1807, John Wiley & Sons is the oldest independent publishing company in the United States. With offices in North America, Europe, Asia, and Australia, Wiley is globally committed to developing and marketing print and electronic products and services for our customers' professional and personal knowledge and understanding.

The Wiley Corporate F&A series provides information, tools, and insights to corporate professionals responsible for issues affecting the profitability of their company, from accounting and finance to internal controls and performance management.

Study on the Auditing System of Socialism with Chinese Characteristics

CHIEF EDITOR

LIU JIAYI

WILEY

Library of Congress Cataloging-in-Publication Data:

ISBN 9781119324706 (Hardcover)
ISBN 9781119328322 (ePDF)
ISBN 9781119328315 (ePub)

Printed in the United States of America

10 9 8 7 6 5 4 3 2 1

Contents

Preface

OW DOES STATE AUDIT COME INTO BEING? What is its role in the national political system? What role does it play in national governance? How can the national auditing system better guarantee audit to play the fullest role? The answers to these questions determine the development course of state audit, and these are questions to which the audit organs of various countries must seek answers. The *Lima Declaration of Guidelines on Auditing Precepts* and the *Beijing Declaration on Promotion of Good Governance by Supreme Audit Institutions*, both released by the International Organization of Supreme Audit Institutions (INTOSAI), reflect a growing understanding of the importance of state audit and transformation from merely stressing independence to recognizing its essential role in achieving good national governance through supreme audit institutions. China has made its due contribution to this through its innovative practices in state audit. Under the leadership of the CPC, and with the guidance of the theory of socialism with Chinese characteristics, a state auditing system of socialism with Chinese characteristics has emerged reflecting these principles to guide state audit to become full of vigor and innovative vitality and plays an important role in promoting national governance and guaranteeing the healthy development of the national economy and society. Some of my international colleagues, who are also my friends, speak highly of the achievements China has made in this regard, including Mr. Josef Moser, former Secretary General of the International Organization of Supreme Audit Institutions (INTOSAI) and former President of Austrian Court of Audit, and Mr. Gene Dodaro, former Comptroller General of the United States. They have also urged me to sum up and tell them more about China's state audit, including the theory, system, methods and experience. In accordance with the "mutually beneficial experience shared by all" concept upheld by the INTOSAI, my Chinese colleagues and I have tried to work on a book entitled *Study on the Auditing System of Socialism with Chinese Characteristics* based on research, study and practice of our auditing system for better communication. Hereby, I am writing this prologue for the book.

System, a product of the development of human civilization, undoubtedly is a foundation for building up the relationship of human society in regard to politics, economy, culture, etc., under certain historical conditions. The history of the development of human society is, in a sense, a witness to continuous efforts featuring constant exploration, repeated tests of ways and means for addressing errors that invariably appear in work, and bold reforms, with the ultimate aim being introduction of a new system conducive to further self-development. China has made great achievements since the reform and opening up, a program introduced in late 1978, thanks to the innovation in its system. The auditing system of socialism with Chinese characteristics, an important part of the overall socialist system with Chinese characteristics, developed from scratch and has gone on to achieve full maturity. During this process, China's state audit has developed to cover public funds, state-owned assets, state-owned resources, and leading officials' economic performance. As a result, the potential risks, outstanding problems and institutional obstacles are revealed in a timely way and dealt with effectively. All these point up to the fact that state audit has become an important force in promoting and improving national governance, becoming the cornerstone and important guarantee for the modernization of the national system of governance and its associated capabilities.

The state auditing system of socialism with Chinese characteristics is based on national conditions, hence reflecting distinctive national characteristics of the times. It came into being and saw various improvements on the basis of China's historical heritage, cultural traditions, and economic and social development and endogenous evolution over a long period. It is well adapted to China's national situation and fundamental political and economic systems. The theoretical system of socialism with Chinese characteristics provides an appropriate theoretical basis for the introduction, development and further improvement of the auditing system. The socialist system with Chinese characteristics constitutes a systemic basis for the introduction and development of the current audit structure, and determines the mode of China's auditing system. Meanwhile, China's excellent traditional culture and socialist core values combine to serve as the necessary cultural basis. From this, one sees that the auditing system of socialism with Chinese characteristics is rooted in confidence in the road adopted in regard to theory, system, culture and practice, ensuring continued strong vitality.

The auditing system of socialism with Chinese characteristics originates from practice, and is the condensation and sublimation of audit practices stretching over a long period. China's auditing system has a history of over 3,000 years, and auditing has been conducted under the leadership of the

Communist Party of China for nearly 100 years and the auditing system of the People's Republic of China has been established for almost 40 years. Its great practical experience involves rich thought and profound rules. A careful study shows that national governance has created different needs to meet the demands of the goals and changing modes in different periods, with the business scope of state audit, institutions and work functions determined and adjusted based on the objective need of national governance; no matter what it has done, it has effective national governance as its clear goal. Judging from the basic elements of national governance, this calls for comprehensive exploitation, management and control of people, money, materials and events, with power and responsibility reflected in each element. State audit, as an important tool in national governance, is conducted always with a strong sense of audit responsibility, a work attitude involving "things, officials and capital, all open to auditing". In other words, auditing should be conducted to ensure it can play its due role in "exercising power, choosing the right person for the right position, and managing money matters", and to achieve national governance and safeguard public interests through supervising and restricting the exercise of power. The formation of the auditing system of socialism with Chinese characteristics is a result of the self-reflection of China, and especially the valuable experience China has gained in the transformation of its economic system, and the auditing system is also based on summarizing and abstracting valuable experience indispensable for auditing, and filtering elements unsuited to the auditing system and, on this basis, further improving its ability to benefit national governance through innovation.

The auditing system of socialism with Chinese characteristics pays attention to the historical inheritance and absorption and reference ensuring an open and inclusive system. All rivers run into sea, and tolerance is a virtue. Chinese people have, since ancient times, been advocating "self-examination", "emulating those better than oneself", and "learning from the strong points of others and making up for one's own weakness". For a nation, system consciousness is of special significance. In the introduction and improvement of its auditing system, China never forgets to learn, with an open mind, from the successful auditing experiences of other countries, and traditional thinking of rich ideals and value and information reflected in other country's systems and theories. Meanwhile, China works hard to monitor the latest auditing practice of major developed countries so as to learn from their successful experience for use in improving our own auditing system unique to the nation. From this we see China has traversed a road featuring absorbing anything and everything, independence, and scientific development.

This book is divided into five chapters: The Birth and Development of the Auditing System of Socialism with Chinese Characteristics; Foundation of the Auditing System of Socialism with Chinese Characteristics; Basic Framework of the Auditing System of Socialism with Chinese Characteristics; Features, Effects and Experience of the Auditing System of Socialism with Chinese Characteristics; and Development of the Auditing System of Socialism with Chinese Characteristics and Prospects. It comprehensively tells how the auditing system of socialism with Chinese characteristics was introduced and developed, and the way it has involved historical law and logic; the purpose is to make a profound and systematic analysis of China's auditing system at the time when China is in the transitional period of its economy and society. It also outlines the blueprint concerning auditing system reform in a period when China is working hard to deepen its reforms and implement the rule of law. This is a sister book to the *Study on the Auditing Theory of Socialism with Chinese Characteristics*. Both have been created on the basis of understanding of the essence of China's state audit; they come down in one continuous line, and complement each other. With different study objects, they meet in the auditing system of socialism with Chinese characteristics.

This book was written, but revised several times, over three years. During this period, we profoundly sought knowledge of the historical process concerning the introduction and development of the auditing system of socialism with Chinese characteristics so as to create a book of great value to the lofty mission of the state audit, and thus making due contribution to the modernization of the national governance system and capabilities.

In this colorful and exciting world of ours today, we dedicate this book to all my dear fellow auditors.

October, 2016

Introduction

THE AUDITING SYSTEM OF A COUNTRY, as an integral part of its institutional framework, is closely related to its history, culture, politics, and economy, as well as social development level and the soundness of its national governance. Under the leadership of the Communist Party of China (CPC), the auditing system of socialism with Chinese characteristics has been established and developed based on long-time Chinese and foreign audit experience and the experience of other countries, while adapting to the needs of reform and opening up, scientific socioeconomic development, democracy and rule of law, and the modernization of the national governance system and expansion of capacity. As a component of socialist system with Chinese characteristics, the auditing system has a wealth of connotations and historical characteristics.

1. ABOUT THE SYSTEMS

A system can be viewed in both broad and narrow senses. In a broad sense, it refers to a normative system of politics, economy, society and culture forming under certain historic conditions, that is, political system, economic system, social management system, and so forth. In a narrow sense, it refers to work procedures or action guidelines by which all parties should abide. As Karl Marx pointed out in *Capital*, a social system is a political instrument of a specific ruling class. It is a social structural framework of productive relations in a particular period, and also a fundamental rule of people's economic actions at a specific productivity level. The fundamental driving force for system evolution comes from the development of productive forces. Some scholars, however, defined system from different perspectives. For example, Douglass C. North has argued that a system involves the game rule of a society. Theodore William Schultz saw it as a code of conduct governing the acts of a society, its politics, and its economy. John

Rawls defined it as a kind of social system of norms, and so forth. Despite these different definitions, it can be concluded that a system has three basic features.

First, *system* has a historical feature. The generation of systems is not different from other products of human civilization. Systems did not exist intrinsically but were products of the development of human society at a certain historical stage. Marxism thought that the form, model, and level of systems were adaptable to the development level of productive forces, that is, "Production and subsequent exchange of products are the foundation of all social systems"[1]; "There will be particular social systems, families, classes or class organizations at a certain development stage of production, exchange and consumption."[2] Development and changes of systems reveal they are also reforming and adapting to the development of human society. "No system can come out of nothing abruptly. A system is gradually developed based on the original source. A system will never disappear without any reason, and there must be changes. A system would be gradually deteriorating and changing before its disappearance. Only in such a manner can we seize the truth of all systems."[3] To judge a system, we "must also know the opinions of all related parties during implementation," and these are referred to as *historical opinions.*[4]

Second, *system* is a term covering social relations. Systems are normative criteria that regulate the social relationships and determine the rights and obligations of relationships among people, and among organizations. Along with the development of the economy and the society, individuals hardly realized the desired effect by themselves alone. Accordingly, the subjects of communication presented a diversity whereby the communication scope was extended from individuals to communities, organizations, ethnic groups, and countries. Especially in a modern society, the communication among communities goes far beyond individuals. This process gives birth to systems. In this sense, *systems* refers to standardization achieved during production and communication, formed according to cultural traditions and historical experience, to safeguard the order of production and social development, meet common social needs and coordinate the behavioral relations among humans and with society. "Understanding of systems in an era must be inseparable from deep cognition of humans."[5]

---

[1] Engels: *Socialism: Utopian and Scientific. Marx Engels Selected Works*, 2nd ed., Vol. 3. Beijing: People's Publishing House, June 1995, pp. 740–741.
[2] *Complete Works of Marx and Engels*, Vol. 4. Beijing: People's Publishing House, June 1995, pp. 320–321.
[3] Chien Mu, *China's Rise and Fall*, 1st ed., New Revision. Beijing: Jiuzhou Press, 2012, p. 2.
[4] Ibid.
[5] Ibid., p. 1.

Third, a system has a hierarchical feature. The literature of institutional economics presents a different understanding to the composition of systems. Some have argued that a system involves an institutional environment, institutional arrangements and implementation mechanisms. Some believe a system consists of a constitutional environment, institutional arrangements, and implementation mechanisms. Others divide a system into three types, namely, official and unofficial rules and their execution mechanisms. The official rules include social systems, laws, rules and regulations, code of ethics, disciplines, and so forth; unofficial rules refer to the established codes of conduct formed through long-term social communication of people, and publicly recognized as norms to be jointly abided by, including values, manners and customs, cultural traditions, ethics, ideologies, and so on. Although without the dominant executive force and binding force, the unofficial rules constitute a theoretical foundation and the supreme principle of official institutional arrangements (or official restrictions) in the forms of "guiding principle," "guideline," "principle," and so on. Oliver Williamson divided the general institutional framework into four interrelated levels: the first covers the history and the culture of a country, including traditional customs, code of ethics, and so forth. These are "unofficial rules"[6] proposed by Douglass C. North; the second level covers the basic institutional environment, including the Constitution, and the fundamental systems, and so on of a country; the third level involves various governance mechanisms; and the fourth refers to a short-term resource distribution system. Each level is subject to the higher.[7] It can be said that systems are closely related to economic and social development. To understand a system thoroughly, we need to analyze the logic of various rules and essentials, and also need to make in-depth analysis on the history of its generation and development, as well as the background of the times and the basic institutional environment.

2. ABOUT THE AUDITING SYSTEM

The auditing system is a normative scheme relating to audit formed under the particular historic conditions, and a sum of work procedures or action guidelines relating to acts of auditing. According to such elements as audit subjects,

---

[6] (U.S.) Douglass C. North, "New Institutional Economics and Development," in *Transition, Rules and Institutional Choice*, edited by Sun Kuanping. Beijing: Social Sciences Academic Press, 2004, pp. 3–4. ("North" mentioned in this paragraph remains consistent with the commonly used expressions hereof.)

[7] Paul L. Joskow, *New Institutional Economics: A Report Card*. June 2, 2004; Oliver Williamson, a representative personage of new institutional economics. About systems levels, refer to Joskow.

functional localization, objectives, and roles, auditing is divided into government auditing, internal auditing, and CPA auditing (also known as independent auditing). The auditing system mentioned herein means the government auditing system. Government auditing refers only to actions whereby national professional audit institutions supervise public funds, State-owned assets, and State-owned resources independently according to law. In nature, it is an endogenous "immune system"[8] within the overall system of national governance, with functions of exposure, resistance, and prevention. "No system may be isolated. All systems must interact with each other, forming a complete set."[9] A country's auditing system, as an important part of the national political system, must be determined by its fundamental political system, social nature, and economic system. We can analyze the connotations of a government auditing system as well as the chosen mode and arrangement design from three aspects.

First is analysis of the relationship between the auditing system and national governance. National governance is the process of controlling and managing State affairs and social affairs and providing services by configuring and exercising State powers, so as to ensure national security, safeguard national interests and the people's interests, maintain social stability, and realize scientific development.[10] The generation and development of countries shows that, despite the differences in historical and cultural traditions and socioeconomic development, all must configure State power to achieve a reasonable division, form the corresponding power structure, and establish a mechanism for mutual balance and restriction among different powers, so as to prevent abuse of power. Under the modern constitutional system, the function of separation of powers never means negatively restricting State power, but dividing various State powers and functions proactively and specifying responsibilities and procedures.[11] The design of an auditing system is, in nature, a specific distribution of State audit powers in the national governance system. Government audit emerged to satisfy the need for governing a nation, national governance objectives determine the direction of government audit, and the national governance mode determines the system and form of government audit.[12] In addition, the power restriction mode of the national governance system directly determines the framework, mode, and operation mechanism of auditing system.

---

[8] Liu Jiayi, "National Governance and State Audit." *Social Sciences in China*, No. 6, 2012, p. 60.
[9] Chien, p. 2.
[10] Liu Jiayi (chief editor), *Study on the Auditing Theory of Socialism with Chinese Characteristics* (Rev. ed.). Beijing: Commercial Press, China Modern Economic Publishing House, 2015, p. 8.
[11] Han Dayuan, "Formal Meaning and Material Significance of 'A Country under Rule of Law. *Procuratorial Daily*, January 14, 2014.
[12] Liu, p. 13.

International practice shows a division into structural power restriction mode and functional power restriction mode.[13] Under the former, State power is divided into those of legislation, administration, and jurisdiction, which are separated and restrained mutually, and auxiliary means such as multiparty competition, open election and judicial independence, and so on are adopted, so as to achieve the goal of establishing a capitalist constitutional system and to manifest the nature of the political system. The functional power restriction mode involves the distribution of decision-making power, executive power, and supervisory power generated against the expansion of administrative power, reflecting the quality of the political system through functional division and setting of the operational level and operation mechanism of the political system. Adapting to national governance modes and power restriction modes, the government auditing systems of various countries also have their own characteristics. Audit institutions in some countries are independent from the legislative, judicial, and administrative organs but are responsible to legislative bodies; audit institutions in some other countries are independent from the legislative and administrative organs but have certain rights of judicial decision and are responsible to the legislative bodies. There are countries where audit institutions practice an integrated audit and supervision system; there are countries where audit institutions come under government departments; for example, the Chinese National Audit Office (CNAO), as a government department, independently exercises the audit power according to law under the premier's guidance and reports its work to the National People's Congress upon government entrustment.[14] The core of any auditing system is to guarantee the independent exercise of audit power according to law, and to effectively give full play to the role of government auditing as the bedrock and important guarantee for national governance.

Second is analysis of the relationship between government auditing and other aspects of national governance. If we regard national governance as a large system, government auditing belongs to the scope of supervision and control, serving the decision-making organs and playing a role of monitoring and restraining the executive organs.[15] Compared with other aspects of national governance, government auditing has a unique status. First, it is independent. Among national governance agencies, government audit institutions undertake their audit responsibilities objectively and independently,

---

[13] For relevant arguments, see Tang Yalin, *Theoretical Investigation*, Issue No. 3, 2015.

[14] Scientific Research Institute of the China National Audit Office, *Introduction to Foreign Audit Supervision System*. Beijing: China Modern Economic Publishing House, 2013, p. 4.

[15] For relevant arguments, see Liu.

without specific functions of decision making and management; however, a vast majority of countries also explicitly require legally safeguarding the independent exercise of audit power in accordance with the law, without any intervention. Such role design and institutional guarantee determine that government audit institutions are not tied to the interests of any institution, organization, or individual and can reveal problems, report realities, audit, and offer recommendations objectively and fairly based on the overall situation of national governance so as to safeguard the interests of the State and the general public. Second, it is comprehensive. Government auditing is a regular control system covering all public funds, State-owned assets, and State-owned resources. The wide-ranging audit targets and contents involve many fields of national governance, including a number of institutions and participating personnel. The exertion of audit role is also comprehensive, that is, government auditing can promote duty performance, use of power, and wealth management through auditing the use of public funds, exercise of public powers, and duty performance of public sectors, and improve the corresponding institutional mechanism. Third, it is specialized. As government auditing is highly professional and policy based, auditors should have adequate professional knowledge, rich practical experience, and good organizational and coordination skills, including the skills and knowledge for checking accounts, handling financial affairs, and managing business. By checking audited units in regard to capital, business, material, and information flows, audit institutions can understand the real situation, reveal potential risks, identify prominent issues, act appropriately, and analyze all collected materials relating to the problems precisely so as to put forward audit recommendations. Fourth, it is objective. Audit institutions must adhere to the basic principle of auditing according to the facts and the law. Audit institutions have to detect the source, reveal problems, and analyze causes in a practical manner and make evaluation and recommendations in an objective and fair way, so as to reveal and solve problems on the strength of precise evidence. This is the professional habit and professional ethic of auditing. It is observed that these essential attributes and unique advantages of government auditing determine the relationship between government auditing and other aspects of national governance. That is to say, by independently and fairly reviewing the truthfulness, compliance, and performance of various economic activities concerning national governance, government audit institutions can understand the real situation, reveal hidden risks, reflect prominent problems, and analyze systemic obstacles and defects, so as to solve the problems in a timely and effective manner. In this way, the government auditing plays an "immune system" role of preventing, revealing, and resisting and provides a bedrock and assurance role for standardized, efficient national governance in other aspects.

In view of the above features, to give full play to the role of government auditing as the bedrock of and important guarantee for effective state governance, various countries adopt some common practices. First, most supreme audit institutions (SAIs) are constitutional institutions. As mentioned earlier, a majority of countries stipulate the legal status, responsible person, organizational framework, protective mechanism, and the like, of SAIs in the Constitution, and no adjustment is allowed unless it is made via a constitutional amendment. Second, the independent exercise of audit power in accordance with the law is explicitly specified in the law. Third, legality of auditing authority is emphasized; that is, in the process of fulfilling their supervisory duties, SAIs are generally given the authority of inspection, investigation, reporting, transferring, and, in some cases, temporary handling of major matters, as well as audit disposal and punishment and judicial decision making. Fourth, audit results announcement is emphasized. That is, audit results must be made public. Fifth, exerting the constructive role of audit is highlighted. All of these endow SAIs with the authority to specifically put forward warnings and recommendations.[16]

Third is analysis of the relationship between auditing system and system functions. A system, in general terms, is characterized by normative and relative stability. Its core function is to improve the order and basically regulate coordinated relationships, work development, operations management, restrictions, and incentives. In brief, the function of a government auditing system is to meet the demand of external systems for government auditing through coordinating the internal operations of the government auditing system, which are mainly specified as follows:

(1) *Providing the fundamental methods and approaches for government auditing to serve national governance.* A government auditing system is generated in conformity with the needs of national governance. "To discuss a system, we should certainly attach importance to the 'nature of the times' and 'territoriality,'" "a system established and well implemented in a country or region is not necessarily effective in another country or region."[17] To meet the needs of national governance and operation mechanism, various

---

[16] For relevant situation, see Scientific Research Institute of the China National Audit Office, p. 4.
[17] Chien, p. 4.

countries adopt different design modes of auditing, define the basic duties and authorities of auditing in their national governance system, and stipulate the basic methods, approaches, and working modes to exert the functional roles of auditing. The more scientific and reasonable auditing system will better meet the needs of national governance, and the role of government auditing in national governance will be greater.

(2) *Providing the legal and compulsory foundation for audit supervisory power.* Endowed by national laws, the power of supervision through auditing has legality and a mandatory nature, which is mainly reflected in three aspects. First, SAIs should audit in strict accordance with authorities endowed by laws. Second, SAIs should effectively exercise their supervisory power through auditing, and any random waiver is prohibited. Third, audit targets, other units, and individuals must not refuse or hinder audit institutions from legally enforcing their audit power, or they should bear the legal consequences. Audit on the basis of public acceptance and conviction will enjoy much authority and enforceability, and can thus better play its role. By specifying the allocation pattern of audit power, the auditing system can regulate and adjust the relationships among auditors, audit institutions, audited units, and other institutions or organizations, which provides a foundation for legality and enforcement.

(3) *Specifying the organizational structure and operating rules of auditing.* Organizations and rules are elements of a system. Organizations function as the carriers to exercise the power and also the principals to exert the role of systems; rules mean the elaborated relations between procedures and standards. The auditing system defines the space to exercise the audit power in aspects of auditing organization structure and rules of exercise. To be specific, audit institutions, as a material part of the auditing system, are the carriers to implement the auditing system and safeguard audit order and constitute a relatively static space for the execution of audit power. Auditing rules provide a dynamic space for the exercise and development of audit power, and stipulate various procedures and rules on the authorities, restrictions, and responsibilities of audit subjects and auditees. These two spaces constitute two basic dimensions that regulate and restrain every aspect of exercise of audit power.

(4) *Stipulating the operation mechanism and responsibilities of audit power.* Audit supervisory power stems from the powers and responsibilities of audit endowed or entrusted by people to the State through the national political system, while the State, in turn, endows such powers and responsibilities to audit institutions in a legal format. The auditing system provides a

basis and guarantee for audit institutions to exercise their power of audit through defining the basic functions, basic properties, statutory authorities, and business boundaries of the government auditing. Meanwhile, the auditing system restricts and restrains the audit power in aspects of normal operation mechanism and power role, so as to balance the audit power and safeguard auditing according to the law and in compliance with the law.

Hence, from the perspective of system functions, the specific contents of an auditing system are designed around the functions of the auditing system, reflecting the requirements of the State and the public for government auditing. In this regard, the contents of the world's auditing systems are by and large the same, mainly covering audit management system, institutional setting, audit staffing and management, audit duties and authorities, audit targets, audit scope, and audit operation mechanisms. Accordingly, the audit results are the realistic achievements of implementation and exertion of auditing powers. Audit relations mainly include internal relations among audit institutions at higher and lower levels, and between auditors and audit institutions, audit institutions and external institutions or individuals such as other supervision and inspection organs, procuratorial agencies, and auditees.

The preceding analysis concludes that the first two aspects, as the basis of establishment of auditing system, determine the type and design base of the auditing system. Generally speaking, the auditing system is a design and arrangement made through combining the requirements in the first two aspects with the features of auditing, while the specific contents of the auditing system mentioned in the third aspect must embody the requirements for combination. Therefore, the auditing system is a standard system and mechanism, featuring legality and enforceability, established by the State to regulate audit relations. Accordingly, we must design the auditing system based on the requirements of national governance for auditing, and the need to exert the role and functions of auditing, and regulate and standardize all audit relations, in a vision to provide a foundation and guarantee for effective audit activities.

3. ABOUT THE AUDITING SYSTEM OF SOCIALISM WITH CHINESE CHARACTERISTICS

The auditing system of socialism with Chinese characteristics, a general designation of relevant government audit standards in the socialist system with Chinese characteristics, accurately reflects all interrelated work procedures or action guidelines formed through practice. The auditing system of socialism with Chinese characteristics is a specific institutional system of socialism with Chinese characteristics, with the fundamental political system as the highest guide and the basic political, economic, and social systems as the basis. It involves the audit law system and audit system, as well as various specific audit standards conducive to implementation. Three basic concepts should be highlighted.

First, the fundamental characteristics of the auditing system of socialism with Chinese characteristics are to adhere to the CPC's leadership and to independently exercise audit power according to law. The CPC is the leadership core of the cause of socialism with Chinese characteristics. Adherence to CPC's leadership is the primary political precondition for establishment and improvement of the auditing system. This determines that government auditing is an integral part of the supervision system of the Party and the State, so its fundamental objective is to safeguard the fundamental interests of the masses; this also determines the definition, reason, and object of auditing, and ensures that audit work always adheres to the correct political direction. Adhering to CPC leadership over audit work means specifying the objective, direction, and emphasis of auditing in line with the central tasks of the Party and the State, strengthening the ideological and political attainments of audit institutions, leadership and cadre system development, the construction of a clean and honest government, and the building of grassroots organizations around the strategic layout of comprehensively building a moderately prosperous society, comprehensively deepening reform, comprehensively implementing the rule of law, and comprehensively strengthening Party discipline building, so as to continually advance audit work. The independent exercise of audit power in accordance with the law is a basic principle determining the subjects, contents, and ways of audit. The *Constitution of the PRC*, the *Audit Law of the PRC*, and other laws define the responsibilities, authority, procedures, behavior, and results of audit, safeguarding the independence of audit plans, implementation, institutions, auditors, and funds. These are the main system contents.

Second, the auditing system of socialism with Chinese characteristics is generated and developed during the construction of socialism with Chinese characteristics; hence, it must always stick to and improve the latter. The auditing system of socialism with Chinese characteristics consists of socialism with Chinese characteristics and the auditing system, of which the former specifies the foundation and environment for generation of the auditing system, and the latter makes clear the function of the system, that is, supervision through auditing. As noted by General Secretary Xi Jinping, "The key for what kind of ism a country implements, is to look at whether or not that ism can resolve the historical issues this country faces."[18] Socialism with Chinese characteristics is the fundamental achievement of the Party and Chinese people made through over 90 years of struggle, creation, and accumulation, and also a scientific summary of great practice of reform and opening up over the past 30 years or so. It embodies the painstaking exploration of the Party and Chinese people in the first 30 years of reform and opening up, and is a concentrated embodiment of the beautiful expectation and unremitting pursuit of Chinese people for socialism since the modern time.[19] Due to a unique historical destiny, cultural traditions, and fundamental realities, China must stick to a development path suited to its own characteristics, and must always adhere to and develop socialism with Chinese characteristics. This consists of the road, theories, and systems that lead to realization of the goals guided by the theories and guaranteed by the systems. They are united in the great practice of socialism with Chinese characteristics. Guided by the theories of socialism with Chinese characteristics, the auditing system must be developed and improved based on past practice and firmly following the road of socialism with Chinese characteristics.

Third, the auditing system of socialism with Chinese characteristics specifies the mechanism for government auditing to play its role in national governance, and helps to enhance the pertinence and timeliness of auditing. Existing in the entire design of the national political system, the auditing system of socialism with Chinese characteristics has both the general properties of systems and the peculiarities of auditing. It stipulates such contents as the legal status of audit institutions, affiliations, leadership among audit institutions at different levels, and audit institution system, standardizes relations between audit institutions and individual auditors, between audit institutions and audited units, and between audit institutions and the Chinese National People's Congress, the government, and other institutions or organizations, and reflects the objectives, needs, and operation mechanism of national governance during the construction of socialism with Chinese characteristics. From the perspective of system, government audit institutions have the administrative establishment nature, but the law prescribes the independence of audit. Audit institutions must report results to the Party committees and governments at all levels and relevant departments and the audited units, as well as

---

[18] Xi Jinping, "Unswervingly Adhering to and Developing Socialism with Chinese Characteristics." In *The Governance of China*, 1st ed. Edited by Xi Jinping. Beijing: Foreign Languages Press, October 2014), p. 22.
[19] China Steering Committee of Compiling and Reviewing Cadre Training Materials, *Uphold and Develop Socialism with Chinese Characteristics*. Beijing: People's Publishing House, 2015, p. 1.

to the public. On the one hand, the system design is conducive to the pertinence of audit and helps auditing to better focus on the central tasks and serve the overall interests; on the other hand, it helps to enhance the timeliness of audit to enable relevant departments to make decisions on treatment and punishment of relevant responsible persons and units according to audit situation, to correct uncovered problems in a timely way, and ensure audit reports and recommendations play an important reference role for decision making in a timely manner.

4. ABOUT THE SIGNIFICANCE OF STUDYING THE AUDITING SYSTEM OF SOCIALISM WITH CHINESE CHARACTERISTICS

The significance of studying the auditing system of socialism with Chinese characteristics is mainly reflected in three aspects.

First is helping to deepen cognition to the principle of development of auditing of socialism with Chinese characteristics. Principles are the inherent, essential and necessary linkages for things, phenomena, and processes. Systems are the important results and represent the intellectual achievements of human practice. China has a long history of over 3,000 years in audit practice producing a wealth of ideas and profound laws. Combined with human cognition, some of these objective principles were developed into auditing theories or guiding principles, and some are further materialized into various auditing systems. The systematic and in-depth study on the auditing system of socialism with Chinese characteristics contributes to deepening our cognition to the objective laws of auditing, to understanding and applying these laws, and to making clear the road and direction of future development, so as to promote the continuous audit improvement.

Second is helping to enhance institutional self-confidence of the auditing system of socialism with Chinese characteristics. Various countries have their unique government auditing systems due to the differences in history, culture, political and economic systems, and national governance modes. Adapting to China's national conditions and basic political and economic systems, the auditing system of socialism with Chinese characteristics is a product of long-term development, progressive improvement, and endogenous evolution based on the historical legacy, cultural traditions, and economic and social development. Judging from the role of the auditing system, China's government audit institutions in recent years have performed their duties in the national governance in an all-round manner by firmly stressing "jurisdictional control, employment of talents and wealth management," playing an important role in ensuring the implementation of major policies, safeguarding economic and financial order, promoting clean government, and so forth, and become the bedrock and important assurance for national governance. Through in-depth and systematic study, we can fully recognize its necessity and intrinsic advantages, strengthen our confidence in the auditing system of socialism with Chinese characteristics, and become more conscious and determined to consolidate, develop, and improve this system.

Third is helping to promote continuous development and improvement of the auditing system of socialism with Chinese characteristics. Auditing system represents a relatively fixed form and specification of audit practice, which, for innovation and development, inevitably requires the continuous improvement of the auditing system, so as to better meet development needs. Now China has entered a new period featured by a new normal of social and economic development. The strategic layout and requirements for comprehensively building a moderately prosperous society, comprehensively deepening the reform, comprehensively implementing the rule of law, and comprehensively strengthening the Party discipline building, as proposed by General Secretary Xi Jinping, make clear the strategic direction of China's future development. In line with the situation and needs of national governance, the auditing system of socialism with Chinese characteristics must be developed and improved through continuous reform and innovation according to the requirements of national governance modernization, and enable itself to better exert its functions in the national governance. Through in-depth and systematic study, we can objectively realize and analyze the weak links of development and improvement of the existing auditing system according to the needs of national governance as well as the new situation and new requirements of socioeconomic development; make appropriate adjustment and continuous optimization in an innovative, reform-driven manner during national governance modernization; accelerate the development and improvement of the auditing system of socialism with Chinese characteristics; and continuously improve the level and capacity of government auditing in promoting the modernization of national governance.

CHAPTER ONE

The Birth and Development of the Auditing System of Socialism with Chinese Characteristics

"HISTORY IS THE ROOT OF REALITY."[1] China has a time-honored history of auditing. To embark on any study of it, we need first to clarify the historical origins of the People's Republic of China's (PRC) government auditing system and the development course of the auditing system of socialism with Chinese characteristics established on the basis of past experiences. Only in this way can we have a profound understanding of the internal relation between government auditing and national governance, the development trend of government auditing and how the auditing system of socialism with Chinese characteristics will be further advanced.

 ## 1. HISTORY OF THE CHINESE AUDITING SYSTEM

Government auditing in China has a long history. Ancient Chinese used words such as *investigating, listening, counting, checking, comparing,* and so on to describe "audit" activities. The contemporary Chinese term for *audit* first appeared in the *Foreword to Sun-Tzu*, written by Cao Cao (155–220), a major warlord in the

---

[1] Xi Jinping's speech at the College of Europe in Bruges, April 1, 2014.

Three Kingdoms period, who proposed, "Audit, as a well-planned action, should be precise and profound, without any misrepresentation." The first government institution using the term *audit* was the Court of Auditors established in 1127 during the Southern Song Dynasty (1127–1279). Documentary resources appearing at different stages reveal the features and history of auditing system.

(1) Official Auditing System[2] during the Shang and Zhou Dynasties

The Official Counting System and Administrative Report System in the Shang and Zhou Dynasties were collectively referred to as the Official Auditing System. A great number of tribute activities were recorded in the Yin Ruins' Oracle-Bone Inscriptions of the Shang Dynasty (1600–1046 BC), and the tortoise shell-bridge inscription, with records of tributes on the right bridge and verification words on the left bridge, is regarded as the earliest verifiable records of audit activities. After King Wu had overthrown the Shang Dynasty, Ji Zi, an aristocrat of the former dynasty wrote the *Great Plan*, summarizing the experience of the ousted dynasty in country administration, and presented it to King Wu. According to the *Great Plan*, the supreme ruler should insist that government officials give top priority to the "Eight Government Affairs" including the administration of the people's food and wealth as well as the five critical factors of ruling the nation, including "Listening," and not seeking private benefits and tyrannically abusing their power. "Listening," meaning "Listening and Accounting," covered the administrative performance of officials and the careful maintenance of financial records. Through proper listening, the supreme ruler can ensure officials are honest and never engage in fraud by applying supervisory tools such as accounting, auditing, and the like. Hence, the audit supervision connotation contained in "listening" is the same anywhere and at any time. In Chinese history, audit was always described as "Listening and Accounting" or "monthly and yearly accounts by listening to differences." Both *audit* in English and *audition* in French were originated from *audier* in Latin. In the fourteenth century, the audit work of the United Kingdom was carried out by hearing a statement of the accounts.[3] Even today, State organs exercise their

---

[2] In some studies of audit history, the auditing of this period was called *official auditing*, which was a designation relative to the "social (nongovernmental) auditing." There was no "non-governmental auditing" in the Shang and Zhou Dynasties. To summarize the features of auditing system during this period more precisely, this book uses *official auditing*.

[3] Wen Shuo, *The World History of Auditing*, Rev. ed. Beijing: Enterprise Management Publishing House, 1996.

important powers of economic supervision by listening to budget and audit reports.

The official ranks system of the Western Zhou Dynasty (1046–771 BC) was a political system used to appraise and supervise the administrative performance of officials in regard to finance and the economy. This took the form of accounting annually or every three years. The head of the accounting department undertook overall responsibility for the national finances and their accounting, and for related auditing; Zaifu (an official taking charge of the qualification assessment of all the officials and reporting the results to the monarch) mainly inspected and supervised decrees, policies and financial revenues and expenditures under the control of all officials. In the bureaucratic system of the Western Zhou Dynasty, Taizai (official rank), the head of six major ministers, took charge of national events, while Zaifu was affiliated to Xiaozai (official rank) under Taizai. According to the literature, such as the *Rites of Zhou*, Zaifu was responsible for supervising the implementation of decrees and rites, that is, to supervise the authority and the rankings of the king, ministers, and officials; conduct national governance and investigate offenders; report on governance performance and effect and achievements in finance and economy to the imperial court; audit and review government officials; recheck the accounts of income and expenditure; and report offenders found to be involved in document forging, manipulation of accounts, extravagant waste, and improper expenditure to the Taizai for punishment according to the laws and regulations. On the positive side, the recommended rewards for persons who saved on expenditure, sufficiently protected the treasury reserves and managed money well. The Zaifu could report any problems to the Taizai or even directly to the king of Zhou.[4] In summary, the Zaifu mainly performed the duties of "guiding the methods of managing State affairs and formulating the laws governing the actions of officials" and achieved the governance goal of "defining the authority and rank of the king, ministers and officials" by audit supervision, which played an important role in maintaining the structure and capacity of national governance. Professor Michael Chatfield, an expert on the history of accounting and auditing in America, wrote in his book *A History of Accounting Thought:* "In the aspect of internal management, budgets and audit procedures, the Western Zhou Dynasty was unsurpassed in the ancient world."[5]

---

[4] Li Jinhua (chief editor), *The History of Audit in China*, Vol. 1. Beijing: China Modern Economic Publishing House, 2004.
[5] (U.S.) Michael Chatfield, *A History of Accounting Thought*, translated by Wen Shuo, Dong Xiaobo, et al. Beijing: China Commerce and Trade Press, 1989.

The Spring and Autumn Period (770–476 BC) and the Warring States Period (476–221 BC) witnessed changes in the system of public land into private ownership with taxation on land and the system of enfeoffment changed into the system of prefectures and counties, while a hereditary system regarding appointments changed into one of recruitment and dismissal. To meet the needs of national governance, the official rank system was replaced by the System of Administrative Reports. Accordingly, local officials were supervised and restricted. They or personnel sent in their place had to regularly report to the imperial seat the situation regarding any changes in the revenue and expenditure related to households, farmlands, taxes, property, and so on within their jurisdiction, while such officials as Chuanji (official rank), Neishi (clerk of the capital), minister, and counselor-in-chief assisted the ruler in investigating, assessing, and meting out rewards and punishments. In the development of the auditing system, the Administrative Reports System made great progress in three aspects.

First, certain important auditing concepts appeared. Guan Zhong (c. 720–645 BC), a legalist chancellor, wrote in the book *Guanzi Youguan*, "If a country is dedicated to developing agriculture, industry and commerce, it will get rich; if a country can establish a legal system, develop common rules, scrutinize its policies, and cultivate competent officials, it will enjoy prolonged stability." That is to say, auditing should not only verify and examine financial bookkeeping but also investigate and appraise decrees and policies.

Second, the *Law of Verifying the Properties of Government Departments* and other codified laws directly related to audit supervision were formulated. During this period, audit supervision and the dispersion of the results were widely mentioned in statute laws such as the *Canon of Laws* by the Wei Kingdom, *Law of the State of Qin* by the Qin Kingdom, the Royal Orders by the Chu Kingdom, the *Monograph on Criminal Law* by the Han Kingdom, *Law of the State* by the Zhao Kingdom, and so forth. Among them, the *Law of Verifying the Properties of Government Departments* in the *Law of the State of Qin* was specifically designed for audit supervision and imposition of penalties in regard to finance, economy, and discipline. It pointed out in the "Decrees for Checking Officials in the Capital and Counties" that "The excess or shortage of supplies and properties should be subject to evaluation, and penalties imposed according to the highest value therein."[6] It also prescribed that "If any problem is discovered in properties, supplies and account books, the person in charge of administration and accounting and other involved officials involved should be liable for the indemnification against the insufficiency."

---

[6] Edited by the Editorial Office of Zhonghua Book Company Gao Heng, "Several Issues about Officials in the Bamboo Slips of the Qin Dynasty," In *Studies on Bamboo Slips of the Qin State from Yunmeng*. Beijing: Zhonghua Book Company, 1981. P207

Third, the idea that "chaos originates from the ruler's arbitrary listening and accounting" came into existence. Up to the middle and later period of the Eastern Zhou Dynasty (770–256 BC), slackness in the laws and disciplinaries measures led to the decay of the Administrative Reports System. The *Book of Lord Shang: Interdicts and Encouragements* pointed out limitations in the Administrative Reports System for local officials and the ruler's arbitrary listening and accounting. In detail, as local officials remained far from the royal seat, they made decisions at their own discretion, which might have easily resulted in fraud, data misrepresentation, and unfaithful reporting, but the king could hardly discover the problems existing in many of the reports during the short period of the annual listening and accounting. Even if the ruler could find some problems, it was hard to investigate and make a judgment due to insufficient evidence. It was in order to solve such problems that Han Fei-tzu (280–233 BC) proposed the concept that "chaos originates from the ruler's arbitrary listening and accounting." He stressed that the king should rule by virtue of "Laws" and "Kingcraft" and should audit and supervise officials rather than the people. Besides, he also proposed methods such as "matching the items of accounts with real objects, collecting evidence on a wide range, and soliciting opinions from all walks of life" to address the existing problems and improve the system of "Listening and Accounting." To sum up, audit should be conducted in such a manner as to ensure accuracy between cash in hand and the accounting ledger, and make comparison in a fair and public manner.

(2) Censorate Auditing System during the Qin and Han Dynasties

Following the successful national unification, the Qin Dynasty launched a centralized system under which the official ranks of Chengxiang counselor-in-chief, Taiwei commander-in-chief, and Yushi Dafu censor-in-chief were established to respectively handle administrative, military, and supervisory power, forming a political layout of separation of the three powers with mutual checks and balances. This was further consolidated during the Han Dynasty (206 BC–220 AD). As recorded in the *History of the Former Han*, the emperor set the official rank of Jianmu (supervisor) to supervise and detect any ministerial misconduct, and Sicha (auditor) to rectify the performance of supervision.[7] Hence, a surveillance system with full authority came into being.

---

[7] *Yan Kejun, All Three States Articles (Complete Collection of Literature from the Ancient Past through the Six Dynasties, Vol. 1), Vol. 21: Discussion on Politics by Xiahou Xuan, quoted from Records of Wei: Biography of Xiahou Xuan. Beijing: Zhonghua Book Company, 1965*

On the one hand, the Qin and Han Dynasties carried on the Administrative Reports System and formulated the *Law of Administrative Reports System* under which the counselor-in-chief should serve as the head of the Administrative Reports Institution; on the other hand, a censor auditing mode of "comprehensive supervision and investigation, and united supervision and examination" was developed. The Censor Prefecture and the Prefecture of Counsellor-in-chief were collectively referred to as the "Two Prefectures." The censor-in-chief was obliged to "enforce laws, give reference, lead and supervise all officials," and the Censor Prefecture could directly participate in administrative reporting presided over by counselor-in-chief.[8] The Censor could directly exercise supervision over the site of administrative reporting, investigate the gains and losses resulting from the decrees issued by the chief, magistrate, and assistant officers, and verify whether "books of accounts" and other economic accounts were true.[9] Besides, the Censor could also inspect the local government authorities at various levels and carry out on-site auditing. The Han Dynasty also successively promulgated the *Nine Articles of Supervisory Censor* and *Six Articles for the Prefectural Governor*, in which the Supervisory Censor and Prefectural Governor were authorized to supervise local officials, review the financial ledgers, and report, investigate, and impeach offenders who levied unfair taxes and engaged in corruption, according to laws.

The auditing system was further improved during the Cao Wei Dynasties (220–265). The term *audit* in comtemporary Chinese first appeared in *Foreword to Sun-Tzu* written by Cao Cao (155–220) for annotations to *The Art of War*. He proposed that "Audit, as a well-planned action should be precise and profound, without any misrepresentation." Political strategy, military stratagems, and records of finance and military supplies were covered. The opening of Chapter 2, *Conducting Operations*, of the *Art of War*, reads, "In the operations of war, where there are in the field a thousand swift chariots, as many heavy chariots, and a hundred thousand mail-clad soldiers, with army provisions enough to carry them several hundred miles, the expenditure at home and at the front, including entertainment of guests, small items such as glue and paint, and sums spent on chariots and armor, will reach the total of a thousand ounces of silver per day. Such is the cost of raising an army of 100,000 men." In this period, the establishment of Bibu (Court of Auditors) was the most significant development, replacing the Administrative Reports System.

---

[8] Yan Shigu (Tang Dynasty) and Ban Gu (Han Dynasty), *The History of the Former Han*, Vol. 83: *Biography of Zhu Bo*. Beijing: Zhonghua Book Company
[9] Li Jinhua (ed.), *The History of Audit in China*, Vol. 1. Beijing: China Modern Economic Publishing House, 2004.

(3) Bibu (Court of Auditors) Auditing System during the Tang and Song Dynasties

In the Tang Dynasty, the auditing system was developed based on the experience of previous dynasties, and the system of "unity of special audit, concurrent audit, and internal audit by different departments respectively" was formed.

First, Bibu—a professional audit institution—was set up. In Chinese, the character *Bi* means checking, examination, appraisal, evaluation, and so forth, which vividly generalizes audit work. Bibu, initiated in the Cao Wei Dynasties, was later affiliated with the Ministry of Justice in the Tang Dynasty and served as an institution specializing in auditing with a certain jurisdiction. As recorded in the *New Book of Tang: Records of Officials* and *Institutional History of Tang*, Bibu took charge of auditing and examining the revenues and expenditures of the central government, local authorities, military towns, and imperial family.[10] The wide range of auditing and the details of audited items were unprecedented. The *Legislative Articles of Bibu* and *Conventions of Bibu* formulated by the Tang Dynasty were special audit laws elaborating on the scope, contents, procedures, timing, means, and results of the Bibu's auditing, and thus occupied an important position in the ancient audit laws. Bibu played an important role in national governance at this time. Yang Yan (727–781), counselor-in-chief of the Tang Dynasty, pointed out, "In the beginning, the country followed the old system and all properties were stored in the Left National Treasury; the Taifu (Ministry of Imperial Supplies) conducted accounting on a quarterly basis, and reported it to Bibu for rechecking. No loss was incurred."[11] In the later period of the Tang Dynasty, most of the old systems of Bibu's auditing were abolished; accordingly, Bibu officials were made idle, which greatly impaired national finance.

Second, the audit functions of the Censorate were strengthened. According to the official system of the Tang Dynasty, the Censorate, apart from the Department of State Affairs, Department of Supervision, and the Central Secretariat, should also be subject to the emperor's direct supervision. The Censorate Auditing System that originated from the Qin and Han Dynasties was further developed in the Tang Dynasty. The *Collections of Liu Zongyuan* recorded that, in the 14th year of the Dali period (779), an administrative office for the two capitals (Chang'an and the Eastern Capital of Luoyang) was set up, consisting

---

[10] Zhang Shuo, Zhang Jiuling, et al. *The Six Statutes of the Tang Dynasty*, Vol. 6: *Ministerial Directors and Vice Directors of Bibu*, Beijing: Zhonghua Book Company.

[11] Liu Xu, et al. (Later Jin Dynasty), *Old Book of the Tang*, Vol. 118, *Biography of Yang Yan*, Beijing: Zhonghua Book Company.

of a censor, five officers, and two clerks. The administrative office took charge of "accounting the expenses of these two stations, auditing and supervising whether the revenues and expenditures accrued thereof complied with the system at the end of each month and quarter."[12] After the Bibu's audit function weakened in the later period of the Tang Dynasty, the Censorate strengthened its supervision and inspection over national finances, and gave top priority to financial revenues and expenditures among all supervision of local and central organs. In this regard, Shu Yuanyu (791–835) alleged in the *New Creation of the Censorate: Records of the Imperial Secretariat Ministry* that the Censorate was "the place of accounting in the world."[13]

Third, the system of internal auditing by the Ministry of Civil Affairs, the, Financial Revenue and Expenditure Ministry, and the Salt and Iron Management Ministry was established. The Tang Dynasty conducted internal and external auditing of financial revenues and expenditures. At the end of each month, all departments would prepare their account books recording revenues and expenditures, and conduct reconciliation on a monthly, quarterly, and annual basis. Therefore, fiscal institutions represented by the Ministry of Civil Affairs, Financial Revenue and Expenditure Ministry, and Salt and Iron Management Ministry were also required to conduct internal auditing of the administrative organizations, while Bibu and the Censorate conducted external auditing. Under the official system at that time, commissioners and vice commissioners of the three ministries served as the general leaders of internal auditing; a judge and patrol officer were in charge of reviewing different sectors; other officials like Shixia (official title), Liuhou (an official agent when the post of administrator or supervisor was vacant), Xunyuan (touring salt brokerage) and Jianguan (supervisor) were in charge of examining and reviewing the financial revenues and expenditures of all places. Internal auditing promoted standardized financial control. Han Huang (723–787), Minister of Financial Revenue and Expenditure Ministry, Liu Yan (715/716–780) and Pei Xiu (791–864), Forwarding Magistrates of the Salt and Iron Management Ministry, and so forth, were well known for their "proficiency in review and examination and resistance to offenders and consumption of public finance."

This auditing mode of "unity of special audit, concurrent audit, and internal audit by different departments respectively" in general was inherited by the Song Dynasty (960–1279); however, the name and affiliations of audit institutions

---

[12] Shang Yongliang and Hong Yinghua, *The Collections of Liu Zongyuan*, Vol. 26: *Records of Administrative Offices*, Beijing: The Commercial Press, p. 704.
[13] Li Fang, Song Bai, and Xu Xuan, *Best Literary Works*, Vol. 807, *The New Creation of Censorate: Records of Imperial Secretariat Ministry*. Beijing: Zhonghua Book Company

were changed in many cases. In the Southern Song Dynasty, the Court of Auditors had significant influence in the history of audit. Before the reform in the Yuanfeng's regime of the Northern Song Dynasty (960–1127), such organs as the Sanbugou Office, Dumokan Office, Mabujun Office, and Dupingyou Office under the three Ministries also had audit functions. Among them, the Sanbugou Office, as a professional audit institution under the Central Government, "took charge of reviewing and auditing the account books to observe the difference and prevent errors and malfeasance."[14] However, the Sanbugou Office was affiliated to the three ministries, so it generally lacked auditing independence. Sometimes, it even faced retaliation of different sorts. As recorded in Volume 40 of *Extended Continuation to Zizhi Tongjian*, Liu Shi (949–997), the head of the Sanbugou Office, was framed by Li Weiqing (943–998), Minister of the Salt and Iron Management Ministry, and others as he disclosed through auditing that Li Weiqing's son-in-law had embezzled hundreds of thousands in governmental funds. The system of Three Councils and Six Boards was restored among the reforms made during Yuanfeng's regime. Accordingly, the three ministries of the State financial commission were deposed, and most of the audit work was reassigned to the Bibu under the Ministry of Justice. Thus, audit independence was enhanced. Besides, the rewards for audit officials were much highlighted in the reign of Emperor Yuanfeng, which is proved in the record of "an official who disclosed the embezzlement of public funds will be rewarded with three percent of the value involved."[15] Afterwards, the audit functions of Bibu and censor were gradually weakened when the imperial seat of the Song Dynasty migrated to the southern region; however, some achievements were made in respect of professionalization of audit institutions. In the first year of the Jianyan Era of the Southern Song Dynasty (1127), the Zhuangou Department was renamed as the "Audit Department," also known as the Court of Auditors and collectively referred to as the Six Courts together with Court of Inspection, the Court of Capital Liaison, Court of Litigation, and so on. It was the first institution in the history of China specializing in auditing and using the contemporary term *audit* in its name. According to the *Inscriptions of All Departments by Supervisory Censor Wu Bogu*, Volume 8 of the *Xianchun Lin'an Zhi* ("Records about Lin'an from the Xianchun reign [1265–1274]"), "at the very beginning, the Court of Auditors was separated to take charge of accounting in relation to cavalry and infantry. In the second Yuanfeng year, these two courts were integrated under uniform leadership.

---

[14] Li Tao, *Extended Continuation to Zizhi Tongjian*, Vol. 99. Beijing: Zhonghua Book Company
[15] Tuotuo and Alutu, *The History of Song Dynasty*, Vol. 179: *Shihuo Zhi I*. Beijing: Zhonghua Book Company

Any official earning a salary must accept audit. Offenders should be judged according to the laws. All books of accounts in every aspect should be submitted to Danong (a government office in charge of tax incomes and expenditures). The Court of Auditors should provide the decision-making and consultation services while formulating any policies in relation to regulations on economy and plans of financial revenues and expenditures."

The preceding historical materials account for the evolution and duties of the Court of Auditors in the Southern Song Dynasty and its duties, which are helpful in further understanding of the nature, functions, and operation mechanism of audit. The major features of the Court of Auditors are: (1) The decision-making and consultation function of audit was taken seriously and strengthened. In this case, the Court of Auditors should provide the decision-making and consultation services while making any policies in relation to economic regulation and plans of financial revenues and expenditures. (2) The range of audited entities became largely extended. Army, imperial family, and government officials should be audited. (3) The professionalization level of audit increased. Account books of revenues and expenditures, all taxes, and budgets for revenues and expenditures should be audited pursuant to the emperor's orders, laws, legislative articles, conventions, and so on.

(4) Kedao Audit Supervising System during the Ming and Qing Dynasties

In the 13th year of the Hongwu Era (1380) of the Ming Dynasty (1368–1644), Emperor Zhu Yuanzhang deposed his counselor-in-chief and decentralized the powers of the Imperial Secretariat and counselor-in-chief to the Six Ministries whose heads directly reported to the emperor. Two years later, the Censorate was set up. Audit functions were mainly manifested in the following three aspects: (1) to expose misdeeds in government offices and identify officials who took bribes, bent the law, and violated the decrees of finance and economy; (2) to appraise the administrative performance of officials over the economy; (3) to manage the Supervisory Censors from the Court of Censors in charge of auditing. As recorded in *The History of Ming* the latter were responsible for "investigating misdeeds of officials, auditing the account books, and checking the treasury, salaries, warehouse inventories, money, grain, salt, water transportation, tea and horses."[16] In addition, the Ming Dynasty assigned the

---

[16] Zhang Tingyu, *The History of Ming*, Vol. 73: The Treatises on State Offices (Zhiguan Zhi) II. Beijing: Zhonghua Book Company

task to the Jishizhong (an imperial attendant) of the Six Ministries (Ministry of Official Personnel Affairs, Ministry of Revenue, Ministry of Rites, Ministry of War, Ministry of Punishments, and Ministry of Works), which directly reported to the emperor instead of the Censorate and other organs. *The History of Ming* recorded that Jishizhong was responsible for auditing on administrative control, supplement, appropriate and audit ministerial affairs at all levels.[17] The Jishizhong could participate in government affairs, discuss politics and suggest persons to be given an official rank and dismissed, and also take charge of audit supervision over a wide range of activities.

The Supervisory Censors from the Court of Censors and the Jishizhong from the Six Ministries were collectively referred to as "Kedaoguan" (supervisory officials), exercising independent audit powers under mutual coordination and restraint. However, the Ming Dynasty encouraged the two sides to monitor and report on each other, to prevent Kedaoguan from deceiving the emperor. Consequently, this resulted in endless disputes and abuses of power. After the reign of emperors Jiajing and Wanli, the increasing factional strife aggravated this situation. "In the reign of emperor Shizong, the restrictions on public opinion were much relaxed, resulting in different arguments. It was a worry that some arguments were excessive and inapplicable. As they often bore ill wills more opinions would mean nothing but more chaos."[18]

The Qing Dynasty (1644–1912) basically followed this auditing system. The system of combining supervision and examination was introduced. In the first year of emperor Yongzheng's reign (1723), the Six Ministries were incorporated into the Censorate, thereby reducing their power to make remonstration and deliberation. On the other hand, this strengthened the efforts of the Censorate to investigate, report, and rectify the acts of all departments and related officials. In the Censorate, the Six Ministries, Fifteen Departments, Imperial Office of Censor, and Censor Office of Imperial Household Supervision Department had audit power.[19] The Six Ministries were to "verify all government affairs," "investigate and interrogate the official business to write off official papers," and so forth. Despite the different audit fields, the Six Ministries were jointly responsible for inspecting warehouses, water transportation, and provisions, as well as salt-related matters, where audit powers were mostly assigned to

---

[17] Zhang Tingyu, *The History of Ming*, Vol. 74: *The Treatises on State Offices (Zhiguan Zhi) III*. Beijing: Zhonghua Book Company

[18] Zhang Tingyu, *The History of Ming*, Vol. 215: *Collective Biographies 130*. Beijing: Zhonghua Book Company

[19] Qing Emperor Gaozong, *The Total Annals of the Qing Dynasty*, Vol. 65: *State Offices*. Beijing: The Commercial Press

the Ministry of Revenue and Ministry of Works. The Fifteen Departments exercised certain audit power.[20] According to the *Wenxian Tongkao of the Qing Dynasty* (Comprehensive Investigations based on Literary and Documentary Sources), "Supervisory Censors from the Fifteen Departments were responsible for investigating the misdeeds of all officials, checking the records of lawsuits by all government offices, inspecting the capital garrisons, supervising all levels of examinations, and inspecting departments, courts and offices; externally, they were responsible for supervising the affairs relating to salt, transportation, warehousing and schools." Among them, checking the records, supervising salt, and transportation were specifically related to the audit function.

The Kedao Audit Supervising System of combining supervision and examination was introduced in the Ming and expanded in the Qing Dynasty, to meet the needs of centralism under imperial power. On the whole, the system of "unity of special audit, concurrent audit and internal audit by different departments respectively" had been abolished, though it was a beneficial exploration in auditing. Accordingly, the Kedao Audit Supervising System was inevitably downgraded to a tool of imperial autocracy and rule by man. For example, in the Censor Office of the Imperial Household Supervision Department under the Censorate, "all revenues and expenditures of the Imperial Household Department shall be checked and compared by the censor in accordance with the budget of the Capital Province, in order to check the records of lawsuits by all government offices."[21] However, the Imperial Household Department, with more than 3,000 officials and tens of thousands of personnel under its jurisdiction, directly served the imperial family. On the contrary, the Censorate only assigned two 7-grade part-time officials and three 9-grade inferior officials to examine and audit the Imperial Household Department, making the work a mere rubber stamp. As a matter of fact, the Censorate was responsible for write-off, that is, to legitimize the expenditures of the imperial family and corruption of powerful ministers, which led to it being given the title of "the worst least useful government office of the Qing Dynasty."

(5) Auditing System in the Early Days of the Republic of China and Nanjing KMT Government Period

From the early days of the Republic of China to the Nanjing Kuomintang (KMT) government period (from April 18, 1927, to May 20, 1948), the Court of

---

[20] Zhao Erxun and Ke Shaomin, *The Draft History of Qing*, Vol. 115: *State Offices II*. Beijing: Zhonghua Book Company

[21] The Palace Museum, *Qinding Taigui*, Vol. 32: *Verification IV*. Haikou, Hainan Publishing House

Auditors was set up in parallel with the Executive Yuan (Ministry), the Supervisory Institute the Supreme Court, the Board of Examination, and other ministries, and then restructured into a subsidiary body of the Supervisory Institute. The system of combining supervision and examination was thus introduced. Under the five-chamber political system, the audit offices of the Republic of China were independent of the fiscal administration and government administrative systems, possessing certain independence. The auditing system had the features as set out below.

First, audit institutions were mandated by the Constitution. The legal status of auditing and duties of audit institutions were specified in the *Provisional Constitution of the Republic of China* promulgated in 1914, the *Constitution of the Republic of China* released in 1923, the *Draft Constitution of the Republic of China* unveiled in 1936, the *Constitution of the Republic of China* announced in 1947, and so forth. Correspondingly, four audit laws were promulgated successively.

Second, audit methods were flexible and diverse. Due to constant wars, heavy debts, and a weak financial position in this period, the audit institutions made great efforts to rectify the economic and financial order, so as to safeguard stability. They turned to ex ante audit, random investigation, field audit, travelling audit, off-office audit, and other methods, reflecting a strong trend of innovation and flexibility.

Third, the pilot project of a publicity system of audit results was carried out. The audit communique was prepared and printed by the audit institutions on a regular basis and made public. The announced contents were mainly associated with government decisions, laws and decrees on audit work, important instruments of audit business, disclosure of specific audit cases, and introduction of audit results.

Fourth, the professional quality of audit officials was emphasized. The special laws including the *Establishment Law of the Court of Auditors*, *Law of the Court of Auditors on Organization*, and *Law of Penalties on Audit Officials* provide a firm regulatory basis covering job requirements, qualifications for selection, salary and professional ethics, and so forth. In 1946, half of auditors in the Court of Auditors had a university degree, which was very rare among government institutions at that time.

Audit supervision played a certain role in consolidating financial discipline, combating corruption, increasing revenue and reducing expenditure, and assuring government operations. However, due to the corrupted political system and official system, the limitless abuse of power by a privileged class and financial chaos, different men and institutions in power, such as tycoons manipulating the economic lifeline and the military sectors that consumed a huge of funds, repeatedly refused to accept audit supervision. As a result of long-term wars, it became increasingly difficult for auditing to play an effective role, and it remained in name only, which was an important factor in the growing decline and fall of the Nanjing KMT Regime.

2. AUDITING SYSTEM DURING THE NEW DEMOCRATIC REVOLUTION LED BY THE COMMUNIST PARTY OF CHINA

This period witnessed the founding of the Communist Party of China and the Great Revolution, the Agrarian Revolutionary War, the War of Resistance against Japanese Aggression, and the Liberation War. The specific forms and contents of the auditing system varied in each period, but audit supervision also played an important role.

(1) Auditing Exploration during the Establishment of the Communist Party of China and the Great Revolution Period

The Examination Department of Economic Committee incorporated by the Anyuan Railway and Mine Workers Club was the earliest audit supervisory institution to appear after the founding of the Communist Party of China (CPC). Established in May 1922, the Anyuan Railway and Mine Workers Club raised a large amount of funds through membership dues and subsidies from the bureaus of railway and mines. In April 1923, the Club set up an Economic Committee directly attached to the supreme congress. This was responsible for examining all economic revenues and expenditures of the Club and verifying the books of accounting shares each month. The audit results would be made public to all members. Yu Hanhua served as the First Director of the Examination Department. In the second election, in August 1924, the Club decided to separate the Examination Department from the Economic Committee and individually set up the Economic Review Committee, specializing in economic examination.

After the "May Thirtieth Movement (1925)," the CPC set up the Canton-Hong Kong Strike Committee, consisting of an Audit Bureau working in parallel with such administrative institutions as the Financial Committee, Bureau of Legislative Affairs, and Bureau of Directors. This was the first Chinese institution incorporated with the term *audit* in its name under the leadership of the CPC, and Huang Wenshao served as its first director. On March 29, 1926, the Canton-Hong Kong Strike Committee issued the *Organization Law of the Audit Bureau* to stipulate the staffing and duties of the Audit Bureau.[22] Through direct affiliation, the Audit Bureau was entitled to conduct audit on all current expenditures of all organs under the Canton-Hong Kong Strike Committee. The funding expenditures were effectively monitored through audit, which thus provided an effective assurance for the strike campaign led by the CPC.

During this period, the audit work was going through an exploratory stage. It not only played an important role in implementing the CPC's resolutions and safeguarding the implementation of its policies, but also accumulated experiences in auditing by the Chinese Soviet areas under CPC leadership during the Agrarian Revolutionary War Period.

(2) Auditing during the Agrarian Revolutionary War Period

In April 1927, the CPC Central Leadership initiated the position of the Central Audit Commissioner after the 5th CPC National Congress, with Ruan Xiaoxian taking the post. In July 1928, the *Constitution of the Communist Party of China* adopted at the 6th CPC National Congress made specific stipulations: "In order to supervise the finance, accounting and performance of all organs of the CPC, the CPC Congresses, at national, provinces, counties and citie levels should set up Financial Review Boards at the central, provincial, city or county level." Accordingly, the Congress established the Central Review Board where Liu Shaoqi, member of the CPC Central Committee, served as Secretary and Sun Jinchuan, Ruan Xiaoxian, and Zhang Kundi served as commissioners. In August 1932, the *Interim Organizational Guidelines of the Ministry of Finance*[23] was adopted at the 22nd Executive Meeting of the Central People's Committee. The Audit Department with Ruan Xiaoxian as Director was set up under the Central Financial Committee, and Audit Offices set up under Provincial Financial Departments. The Audit Department took charge of examining national overall budgets and final accounts, checking the bookkeeping, and reviewing matters concerning preparatory expenditures and the treasury's cash and deposits. In order to strengthen audit supervision on inner-party funding, the Fifth Plenary Session of the 6th CPC Central Committee held in January 1934

---

[22] China Audit Society and Scientific Research Institute of the China National Audit Office: *Compilation of the History of China's Revolutionary Base Areas*. Beijing: Beijing University of Technology Publishing House, 1990, p. 204.
[23] China Audit Society and Scientific Research Institute of the China National Audit Office: *Compilation of the History of China's Revolutionary Base Areas*. Beijing: Beijing University of Technology Publishing House, 1990, p. 205.

set up the Central Review Board of the CPC, with Lin Boqu, Ruan Xiaoxian, and Teng Daiyuan as commissioners and Lin Boqu as Central Audit Commissioner.

In September 1933, the 49th Meeting of the Central People's Committee decided to establish an Audit Committee directly subordinate to it and independent of the department of finance. In February 1934, the First Session of the 2nd Meeting of the Central Executive Committee decided to assign the power of review and approval for budgets and final accounts to the Central Executive Committee with the subordinate body of the Central Audit Committee in parallel with the Central People's Committee, Central Revolutionary Military Affairs Committee, and Provisional Supreme Court,[24] with Ruan Xiaoxian as First Director. Meanwhile, Chairman Mao Zedong approved the promulgation of the *Audit Regulations of the Executive Committee of Central Government of Chinese Soviet Republic*,[25] which became the first audit law of the regime under CPC leadership. Consisting of 19 articles, the Regulations covered the auditing authority, auditing system, audit scope and task, audit work reporting system, audit procedures, audit disposition, reconsideration measures, delegated review, and so forth. During this period, the Central Audit Committee audited the budgets and final accounts, which strengthened audit of the financial expenditures of state-owned enterprises and mass organizations, leading to the exposure of some major corruption cases. Some audit results were published by newspapers in the Soviet area, reflecting the high transparency of audit work.

All revolutionary base areas positively implemented the regulations of the Provisional Central Government for establishing the auditing system. The revolutionary base areas such as Hubei-Henan-Anhui, Sichuan-Shaanxi, Zuojiang, and Youjiang Region and Hunan-Western Hubei set up specialized audit institutions or supervision and examination institutions with audit power. Some base areas also formulated the work requirements and regulations on the audit work according to their respective actuality, and audited the fiscal spending, economic activities, and related institutions, thus ensuring the construction of base areas and the corresponding military struggles.

During this period, the auditing system had become an important part of power building of the CPC. The Party always carried out audits in line with the

---

[24] In 1934, the *Law of the Central Government of Chinese Soviet Republic on the Organization of Chinese Soviet Republic* issued by the Temporary Central Government of the Chinese Soviet Republic stipulated, the Central Executive Committee would set up the Central Audit Committee in parallel with the Central People's Committee, Central Revolutionary Military Affair Committee and Provisional Supreme Court, taking charge of auditing the financial revenues and expenditures and supervising the implementation of State budgets.

[25] *Audit Regulations of the Executive Committee of Central Government of Chinese Soviet Republic*, Red China, Issue 153, 5th and 6th eds., March 22, 1934.

economic construction and military needs of the anti-encirclement struggle of the revolutionary base areas by means of on-site audit, audit through submitted documentaries, mandated audit, commissioned audit, and the like, all of which had far-reaching influence in improving the auditing system of socialism with Chinese characteristics.

(3) Auditing during the Period of the National War of Resistance against Japanese Aggression

In February 1937, the Provisional Central Government of the Chinese Soviet Republic set up the Auditing Commission headed by Xie Juezai. The army and local governments at various revolutionary base areas established their own audit institutions in succession. The anti-Japanese bases led by the Communist Party of China fought behind enemy lines under tough conditions. They were required not only to resist the Japanese invaders but also to maintain effective strength for the longer struggle. To this end, it became increasingly important to maintain basic financial supply, to strictly control the fiscal budget, financial revenues, and expenditures, and to abide by fiscal discipline. In its guidance of audit work and the construction of an auditing system of such bases as those in Shaanxi-Gansu-Ningxia, Shanxi-Chahar-Hebei, Shanxi-Hebei-Shandong-Henan, Shandong, and Central China, the CPC insisted on the basic principle of meeting the demands of war and ensuring logistic supply. Audit institutions were mostly established in the financial departments. For example, the audit institutions under the government of the Shaanxi-Gansu-Ningxia border region restored the system of audit office under the financial department in July 1942, after making multiple changes along the way. Meanwhile, the changes of war also caused instability in the work of audit institutions, and some were revoked and then rebuilt. To comply with the political structure unifying the CPC, government, military, and the people in all the anti-Japanese bases, personnel from the CPC, government, and military institutions also joined the audit institutions, which were not only able to adapt to the needs of a highly unified organizational system in wartime but also facilitated close cooperation.

During this period, all anti-Japanese revolutionary base areas formulated the specialized audit laws or others that covered audit; for example, in January 1942, the *Interim Organizational Regulations of the Government of the Shaanxi-Gansu-Ningxia Border Region* were issued stipulating the establishment of audit institutions and the necessary audit assignments; on February 20, 1943, the financial department of Administrative Committee of Shanxi-Chahar-Hebei

Border Region issued the *Rules of Procedures for Auditors*,[26] making specific provisions on the work of all dispatched specialist auditors; on April 1, 1944, the Shanxi-Suiyuan Border Region issued the *Audit Regulations* on the procedures for auditing the organization and authority, budgets and final accounts, army provisions, quilts, and clothing, representing a relatively complete audit law among those emerging in all the base areas[27] and so forth. The contents of these audit laws showed that the financial revenues and expenditures, budgets, and final accounts were mostly incorporated into the objective of audit supervision, and the regulations covered the audit methods, audit institutions, procedures for budgets and final accounts, and audit of the treasury. (See Table 1.1.)

(4) Auditing during the Liberation War of China

Despite different audit institutions and auditing systems, all liberated areas established their respective auditing systems according to the conditions in terms of political, military affairs, and economic situations. Quite a few liberated areas set up an Auditing Commission consisting of principals from military institutions, government, and the Party to serve as the actual leading authority of audit work.[28] However, it was a common practice to set up audit institutions within the financial department in view of the fact that the work was relatively simple and there were few qualified personnel available at that time, which not only facilitated the cooperation of financial and audit practices, but also kept down the operating costs. For example, the North China People's Government was established officially in September 1948. The *Organizational Regulations on All Departments of the North China People's Government* implemented in October prescribed that the North China Financial and Economic Committee, separated from the Ministry of Finance, was authorized to take charge of auditing; however, in reality, subject matters were still handled by the Ministry of Finance. In May 1949, it further specified that the audit institution of the North China People's Government was the Audit Department under the Ministry of Finance.

During this period, all liberated areas continued to improve laws and regulations in accordance with the targets of the liberated areas and their central tasks,

---

[26] China Audit Society and Scientific Research Institute of the China National Audit Office, *Compilation of the History of China's Revolutionary Base Areas*. Beijing: Beijing University of Technology Publishing House, 1990, p. 89.

[27] Compiling Group of Financial and Economic History of Shanxi-Suiyuan Border Region, *Selections from the Financial and Economic History of Shanxi-Suiyuan Border Region*. Taiyuan: Shanxi People's Publishing House, 1986, pp. 141–145.

[28] Li Jinhua (chief editor): *The History of Audit in China*. Vol. 2. Beijing: China Modern Economic Publishing House, 2004, p. 371.

TABLE 1-1 Establishment of Auditing System in All Border Regions during the National War of Resistance against Japanese Aggression

Audit Institution	Main Responsibilities	Leadings Officials	Main Laws and Regulations
The Shaanxi-Gansu-Ningxia Border Region: There were two types of audit institutions: Auditing Commission like the Auditing Commission established by the Provisional Central Government of the Chinese Soviet Republic; and Audit Departments, Branches, and Audit Offices set up by all levels of governments of the border regions.	To examine the compliance and use of outlays by all organs and the army, approve fiscal budgets and final accounts for financial revenues and expenditures, etc.	Xie Juezai served as Chairman of Auditing Commission of the Central Government.	*Interim Organizational Regulations of the Government of the Shaanxi-Gansu-Ningxia Border Region, Decision of the Central Committee on Strictly Establishing the Financial and Economic System, Notice on Outlays of All Organs, etc.*
The Shanxi-Chahar-Hebei Border Region: Auditing commissions at the level of border region and special region were established in 1942; namely, "Auditing Commission of the Shanxi-Chahar-Hebei Border Region" for the border region, "Auditing Commission of Central Hebei Province of the Shanxi-Chahar-Hebei Border Region" for the Central Hebei Province, and "Auditing Commission of No. X Region of Shanxi-Chahar-Hebei Border Region (Special Region No.)" for the special region.	To audit the budgets and final accounts for money and provisions of military departments, check and impeach the extravagantness, corruption, and other matters at all levels of military departments, etc. To understand the staffing of all units, examine the budgets and final accounts for money and army provisions check production revenues and expenditures, and impeach anyone guilty of extravagance, corruption, and other related matter.	Xiao Ke served as the Director of Auditing Commission of the Shanxi-Chahar-Hebei Border Region; Zhao Erlu, Gao Peng, Luo Yuanfa, Wang Ping, Liu Daosheng, and Xiao Wenjiu served as the Directors of Auditing Commission of the First, Second, Third, Fourth, Fifth, and Sixth Special Regions, respectively. Xiao Tong, Zhang Yejian, Wang Zhuozhi, Li Xin, Li Jirong, and Chen Guanghan served as auditors of financial departments of these six Special Regions.	*Rules of Procedures for Auditors*

(continued)

TABLE 1-1 (*continued*)

Audit Institution	Main Responsibilities	Leadings Officials	Main Laws and Regulations
United Auditing Commission in 1943. In 1945, auditing commissions at the level of border region, administrative office, special region and county were established.	To take charge of examining and approving the budgets and final accounts on army provisions, quilts and clothing, funds construction, as well as foreign exchange and acceptance of donations of all organs, troops and schools of the Party, the government, and the army.	The Auditing Commission of organs directly under the Party, government, and military of the Border Region consisted of Tang Yanjie, Pan Zili, Wu Xian'en, Cheng Hongyi, and Yao Yilin, with Tang Yanjie serving as the Chairman.	Audit Regulations
Shanxi-Suiyuan Border Region: Auditing Commission			
The Shanxi-Hebei-Shandong-Henan Border Region introduced institutions and personnels including Auditing Commission, Audit Department, Audit Office, and auditors.	Auditing is a mandated by law as a part of financial administration. No revenues should be collected unless approved through audit. Expenditures shall be rejected unless approved through audit. Offenders regarded as guilty of corruption.	Lv Zhengcao served as the Chairman, and Wang Dacheng, Bai Rubing, Chen Manyuan, Chen Xiyun, etc. served as commissioners; Wang De, Sun Zhiyuan, Sun Chaoqun, Luo Guibo, and Yao Zhe served as chairmen of Auditing Branches of all subregions.	Auditing Procedures, Interim Auditing System

Source: Li Jinhua (chief editor), *The History of Audit in China*, Vol. 2. Beijing: China Modern Economic Publishing House, 2004, pp. 298-314.

and promoting the continuous improvement in the auditing system. For example, the Draft Constitution of Autonomy for the Shaanxi-Gansu-Ningxia Border Region proposed to strictly implement an auditing system in September 1946; Shanxi-Suiyuan and Shaanxi-Gansu-Ningxia Border Regions promulgated the *Provisional Auditing Stipulations for the Shanxi-Suiyuan and Shaanxi-Gansu-Ningxia Border Regions (Draft)* in March 1948, and the *Provisional Auditing Regulations of the Shanxi-Suiyuan and Shaanxi-Gansu-Ningxia Border Regions* in October; the Shanxi-Hebei-Shandong-Henan Border Region released the *Auditing System of the Party, Government, People and Academia at the Border Region Level* in February 1948; the Government of Shanxi-Hebei-Shandong-Henan Border Region and Shanxi-Chahar-Hebei Administrative Office of the Shanxi-Chahar-Hebei Administrative Committee promulgated the *Auditing Regulations (Draft)* in July; the North China People's Government issued the *Provisional Auditing Procedures of North China* in March 1949 and the *Rules for Implementation of Provisional Auditing Procedures of North China (Draft)* in May; the *Auditing Procedures of North China* was officially issued and implemented in July. These regulations guided and standardized auditing procedures most effectively.

During this period, the audit work of liberated areas had to be adjusted to the needs of unifying the administration of financial revenues and expenditures, strengthening fiscal administration and strictly enforcing economic discipline in wartime. As the financial revenues and expenditures were mainly used for the war of liberation and for administrative affairs, the liberated areas closely supervised the implementation of regulations on expenditures and the financial systems of governments at all levels, organs, schools, and the army, with a focus on auditing the expenditure budgets and final accounts, and strengthening prior approval, real-time examination, and post-auditing, in the form of unified law enforcement and examination in collaboration with the departments of financial revenues and expenditures, public sector entities, military audit departments, and others. This played a positive role in stabilizing and boosting the economy of liberated areas, supporting the war of liberation, preventing corruption and extravagance, and maintaining the spirit of being honest in performing official duties.

3. ESTABLISHMENT AND DEVELOPMENT OF THE AUDITING SYSTEM OF SOCIALISM WITH CHINESE CHARACTERISTICS

Audit methods of the revolutionary base areas and liberated areas were carried over in the early days after the founding of the People's Republic of China in 1949. The Central Government and local finance departments also set up audit institutions within their jurisdiction. After the implementation of the planned economy system, audit supervision was executed by supervisory or management bodies of the finance department respectively, in combination with the fiscal administration. In December 1982, the *Constitution of the People's Republic of China* was adopted at the Fifth Session of the 5th CPC National Congress. It officially specified the implementation of the audit supervision system and initiated new approach to Chinese audit.

(1) Establishment of the Auditing System in the Early Days of the Reform and Opening-up Period

The period 1978 to 1985 witnessed the early stage of Chinese reform and opening up. In 1978, the Third Plenary Session of the 11th CPC Central Committee made the strategic decision to shift the focus of work to economic construction, including the tasks to further promote socialist democracy and improve the socialist legal system. In 1982, the 12th CPC National Congress put forward the important concept of building socialism with Chinese characteristics and establishing strategic objectives, focuses, steps, and guidelines and policies needed for economic construction. In October 1984, the Third Plenary Session of the 12th CPC Central Committee adopted the *Decision of the CPC Central Committee on Economic System Reform* to enhance the policy of invigorating the domestic economy and opening up, and speeding up economic restructuring with cities as the core. Catering to requirements of enhancing financial and economic management, establishment and improvement of the economic supervisory system, strong maintenance of national financial and economic discipline, and assurance of reform and opening up and sound development of the overall economy, the government auditing system emerged at this historic moment as a result.

1) Government Audit System Stipulated by the Constitution

In May 1981, Yao Yilin, then vice premier of the State Council, pointed out at a National Fiscal Work Symposium that it was quite necessary to strengthen financial supervision and prevent tax evasion fraud, corruption, and extravagance. Financial discipline should be strictly executed and the effective system adopted before should be resumed and enhanced. On January 12, 1982, Hu Qiaomu, then Secretary of the Secretariat of the CPC Central Committee, stated in his letter to Finance Minister Wang Bingqian that China needed to set up an audit institution (named either Audit Bureau or Court of Auditors) under the State Council during the ongoing adjustment of national institutions. From

February to March 1982, Hu Qiaomu, entrusted by Peng Zhen, Vice Chairman of the Standing Committee of the National People's Congress and Vice Chairman of the Constitutional Amendment Committee, stressed the importance of setting up audit institutions, establishing their mandate and ensuring the independence of auditing while explaining the *Draft Amendments to the Constitution (Exposure Draft)* to the Constitutional Amendment Committee on two occasions. According to him, audit independence was a general practice of most countries, therefore audit institutions should be subordinated only to law and independently exercised the right of financial supervision, without any interference from administrative organs. In April 1982, the *Draft Amendments to the Constitution* was published to solicit public opinions, including the implementation of the audit supervision system and establishment of audit institutions. In December 1982, the new Constitution was adopted at the Fifth Session of the 5th CPC National Congress. It defined the main responsibilities of the auditing system and the audit institutions and set out basic principles of audit supervision. This marked the establishment of the auditing system of socialism with Chinese characteristics as one of China's fundamental institutional arrangements.

2) Establishment of Audit Institutions

In June 1981, the Ministry of Finance submitted the *Suggestions on Setting up National Audit Institutions to the Standing Committee of the National People's Congress*, suggesting that affiliated agencies should be established under it to independently exercise audit supervisory power. Local audit institutions at all levels should accept inspection and supervision from the budget committee of the National People's Congress at the same level. With about 500,000 personnel, all levels of audit institutions nationwide took charge of regular, comprehensive and direct audit supervision of budgets, revenue and expenditures, and economic and financial activities of all regions and units. In July 1981, the State Council proposed to set up an audit institution under financial departments for the purpose of strengthening financial supervision. In October 1981, the Ministry of Finance submitted a report entitled *Opinions on Establishing National Audit Institutions (Exposure Draft)* to the State Council, proposing three programs: (1) Establishing the National Court of Auditors or Auditing Commission under the leadership of the Standing Committee of the National People's Congress. Its major leaders should be directly appointed by the NPC, and local branches should be established under the vertical leadership of the headquarters. (2) Establishing the National Ministry of Audit or National General Administration of Audit under State Council leadership. Its major leaders should be directly appointed by the State Council, and local branches should be established under the vertical leadership of the headquarters. (3) Establishing the General Administration of Audit under the leadership of the Ministry of Finance. Local branches should be established and audit work should be subject to the vertical leadership of the headquarters. In June 1982, the Preparatory Group of Audit Institutions under the Ministry of Finance issued a *Report on Preparation and Building of Audit Institutions Submitted to the State Council*, proposing that the State Council should establish the national court of auditors, while provinces, autonomous regions and municipalities should establish the court of auditors with branches in counties and cities. Afterwards, the term *national court of auditors* was mentioned repeatedly in various documents, such as the *Notice on Recruiting Cadres for the National Court of Auditors* issued by the Organization Department of the CPC in January 1983. In March 1983, the *Notice on Issues Concerning Establishment and Staffing at All Levels of Local Audit Institutions* issued by the State Council pointed out that "in accordance with the provisions of the Constitution, the State Council should establish the China National Audit Office (CNAO) of the People's Republic of China, and the people's governments of provinces, autonomous regions and municipalities should establish an Audit Bureau." Henceforth, the CNAO and Audit Bureau were formally established respectively as audit institutions under the State Council and the people's governments above county level. In June 1983, the First Session of the 6th CPC National Congress appointed Yu Mingtao as Auditor General of the CNAO, and it was founded on September 15, 1983. In more than two years thereafter, the local people's governments above county level generally established their own audit institutions. In March 1985, the 10th Session of the 6th NPC Standing Committee decided and appointed Lu Peijian as Auditor General of the CNAO. By the end of 1985, there were 3,007 audit institutions nationwide with a total of 27,900 auditors.

3) Thereafter, Audit Work Was Positively Explored and Carried Out

Following the policy of "working while establishing" released by the State Council to centralize economic work, the CNAO mainly audited the use of extra budgetary funds, losses by State enterprises, losses and waste incurred in production and operation, and major violations of financial disciplines, aiming to increase revenues, reduce expenditures and ensure basic balance in the that year. Meanwhile, audit pilots were launched focusing on financial revenues and expenditures, specific industrial sectors, special funds, special cases and economic benefits, which marked the first significant step of audit supervision. For example, the CNAO conducted a trial audit on Tianjin Iron Plant, Huaihai

Cement Plant, Hubei Jianli Foods Company, and Beijing Shuanqiao State Farm in 1983, becoming the first examination of industrial enterprises, capital projects, merchandising business, and agricultural enterprises since the CNAO's establishment. In April 1984, to ensure better management and use of foreign capital, the CNAO supported six cities including Beijing and Shanghai to audit dairy projects in collaboration with the World Food Program, which was the first foreign-assisted audit project undertaken by State audit institutions. In order to explore the most feasible auditing method on final statements of local governments, the CNAO organized the trial audit on the general financial accounts of Liaoning Province from August to September 1984. Audit on financial institutions also started at this time. In 1985, the CNAO audited the financial revenues and expenditures and final settlement of the Agricultural Bank of China, covering the headquarters, branches, and over 1,330 grassroots units. A total of 890 million yuan was identified as being involved in violations. Some local audit institutions also tried to carry out the regular documentary audit of administrative institutions. In 1985, the experience of Hubei Xiangfan Audit Bureau was replicated in 17 provinces, autonomous regions, and municipalities. Based on the pilot audit, they preliminarily established the system of regular audit on financial revenues and expenditures of administrative institutions, the accountability audit of factory directors leaving their posts, contract operation responsibility audit, self-financing infrastructure funding audit, and other regular auditing systems, which were beneficial in realizing the regularization and institutionalization of audit work.

In more than two years from 1983 to the end of 1985, audit institutions at all levels audited 81,300 sectors and units, and investigated activities violating financial regulations involving around 13.7 billion yuan, including around 3.4 billion yuan duly turned over to the fiscal authority. In detail, in 1985, the audit verified 544 major violations of rules each involving an amount over one million yuan and 158 cases of corruption involving an amount over 10,000 yuan. A total of 1,114 persons were subject to disciplinary action or criminal punishment. Audit supervision played an active role in strictly observing financial and economic discipline, rooting out improper conduct in various trades, promoting and improving management, enhancing economic efficiency and strengthening macro control and management.

4) Standardization of Audit Work

In August 1983, the State Council approved the *Application of the China National Audit Office for Instruction on Several Issues concerning Audit Work*, which specified policies, management principles, tasks, and powers at the stage of establishment of audit institutions, the relationship between local audit institutions and the people's government at the corresponding and superior levels, and the relationship between internal auditing and government audit. In August 1985, the State Council promulgated the *Provisional Regulations on Government Audit Work* defining the establishment of audit institutions, reporting system, tasks, powers, internal auditing, social auditing as well as audit procedures, audit reports, audit conclusions and decisions, application for review, and other contents. During this period, the CNAO successively developed some administrative rules of auditing in combination with audit practice, in accordance with the *Application of the China National Audit Office for Instruction on Several Issues Concerning Audit Work Approved and Distributed by the State Council* and the *Provisional Regulations on Government Audit Work*, including following four aspects. First, the *Notice on Audit Supervision of Financial Insurance Institutions* specified the jurisdictional scope of audit on financial institutions issued in May 1984. Second, the *Procedures for Trials in Audit Work* stipulated on the auditing procedures of audit institutions as well as work contents, requirements, and formats of audit documents in each step issued in October 1985. Third, in order to exercise the rights of disposal and punishment of audit institutions under the *Provisional Regulations on Government Audit Work*, the CNAO, the Ministry of Finance and the People's Bank of China jointly released the *Notice for Enforcing Audit Institution Decision on Handling Payments, Deductions, Suspension of Financial Appropriation, and Bank Loans* in December 1985. Fourth, in order to deal with certain specific problems during the implementation of the *Provisional Regulations of the State Council on Government Audit Work*, the CNAO issued the *Notice on Several Issues Concerning the Enforcement of Provisional Regulations of the State Council on Government Audit Work* to further specify the principles of auditing activities at all levels according to law and emphasize that all local audit bureaus were under the dual leadership of the people's government at the same and superior levels.

(2) Auditing System in the Period of Transition from the Planned Economy to Socialist Market Economy

From 1986 to 1993, China's economic system was gradually transformed from central-planned to socialist market economy. During this period, objectives and tasks of the Party and the State in regard to socialist construction, economic system reform improvement, and rectification influenced a lot on the formation and adjustment of audit policy, the deepening of audit practice, and improvement of the auditing system. In April 1986, the Fourth Session of the 6th CPC

National Congress approved the *Seventh Five-Year Plan of the People's Republic of China for National Economic and Social Development* drawn up by the State Council. This was a key period of transformation from old to new in China's economic development strategy. In October 1987, the theory of the "primary stage of socialism" was systematically elaborated on at the 13th CPC National Congress. It proposed the basic line of taking economic development as the central task, adhering to the "Four Cardinal Principles" and persevering in reform and opening up, and further specified and stressed the objectives, focal points, and emphasis of the overall economic development strategy. In September 1988, the Third Plenary Session of the 13th CPC Central Committee proposed the guiding principle of regulating the economic environment and economic order and comprehensively deepening reform. In November 1989, the Fifth Plenary Session of the 13th CPC Central Committee decided on further improvement, rectification, and deepening reform. In October 1992, the 14th CPC National Congress explicitly proposed that the objective of China's economic system reform was to build a socialist market economic system. According to the instructions of the CPC and the State Council, audit institutions were required to adhere to the working guidelines and guiding principles of "stressing essentials and enhancing the foundations"; "positive development and gradual improvement"; and so forth. This was to be the vision to continuously improve the audit framework, enrich and deepen audit contents, and promote the construction of legality and standardization of audit work. It played an important role in strictly observing financial and economic discipline, promoting the improvement and rectification, and ensuring the smooth development of economic system reform.

1) Continuous Improvement of the Audit Institution System

Audit institutions saw continuous improvement along with the development of the audit work. The State Council introduced two institutional reforms to adjust the functions of the CNAO and internal institutions. In particular, affiliated agencies of audit institutions were established. First, to strengthen supervision of the central enterprises and institutions across the country, the CNAO established affiliated audit offices in large- and medium-sized cities where subordinate bodies of central enterprises and institutions run. With approval from State Council, the CNAO established resident audit officers for a trial run in Shanghai, Shenyang, Wuhan, and Guangzhou, respectively, in 1986, and assigned directors general to take charge. Those resident audit offices performed their duty under the authorization of CNAO. The primary mission was to conduct audit supervision on the financial revenues and expenditures of subordinate bodies of Central Governemnt departments at provincial and municipal level as well as surrounding areas. The supervision went further on the monetary efficiency of large-scale capital construction projects in previous statement. By 1994, 16 out of 18 planned CNAO resident audit offices had been established. Second, CNAO's attached audit offices were established in all departments of the State Council. This was a product of Chinese Government institutional reform. At that time, considering that such reforms of the State Council might nullify the internal audit institutions and weaken audit forces, the CNAO proposed to restructure the internal audit institutions of all departments into the CNAO's attached audit institutions to bolster this newly established audit team. In 1988, the CNAO set up attached audit offices in 41 departments under the State Council after the completion of the institutional reform process. The attached audit offices mainly took charge of auditing financial revenues and expenditures and the economic benefits of enterprises and institutions of all departments in Beijing, assisting in the industry management of relevant departments, and organizing and guiding their internal audit work. The attached audit offices implemented a dual leadership system both by the CNAO and the corresponding department. The staffing and funding were allocated by the CNAO, while the logistics support was undertaken by the relevant departments.

During this period, the government audit team kept expanding. In April 1988, in collaboration with the Ministry of Labor and Personnel and the Ministry of Finance, the CNAO issued the *Notice on Headcount Increase and Redeployment at All Levels of Audit Institutions*, which stipulated an increase of 50,000 personnel for audit institutions within five years, including 5,000 personnel to be assigned to relevant departments and regions. By the end of 1988, there were 100,000 personnel in audit institutions across the country. The CNAO had a total of 6,269 staff members (including 5,300 in resident audit offices and 414 assigned to attached audit offices). By the end of 1993, there were 3,179 audit institutions with 81,000 staff members actually at the level of county and above, representing a 2.8-fold increase from early 1986.

2) Establishing Professional Auditing System of Various Industries

During this period, the State Council required audit institutions to "gradually exercise regular audit supervision in lieu of an annual general check-up on financial work,"[29] "conduct audit work on important issues, especially in terms of the public economy and at all levels of fiscal and financial auditing," "play a role in the

---

[29] National Audit Office of the People's Republic of China, *Selections of Important Files of Audit Work*. Beijing: China Audit Publishing House, September 1993, p. 187.

high-level macro control and supervision,"[30] and so forth. On August 31, 1985, Auditor General Lu Peijian presented his *Work Report of Audit Institutions since Establishment* at the 12th Session of the Standing Committee of the 6th National People's Congress, which was the first work report delivered since the establishment of the CNAO. By the end of 1991, the CNAO promulgated and implemented the *National Audit Work Outline (1991–1995)* as the country's first medium-term audit plan, which guided and provided necessary concepts for the development of the auditing system of socialism with Chinese characteristics. By focusing on major issues, including improving the economic environment and regulating the economic order, audit institutions launched industry auditing, special fund auditing, and audit investigations in a planned way, and gradually formed a regular auditing system. Afterwards, auditing expanded from enterprises to government departments, financial institutions, infrastructure investment, agricultural funds, and the utilization of foreign capital. Based on micro perspective, audit institutions highlighted the authenticity and legitimacy of audit, thus resulting in better improved management and higher efficiency. During economic system transformation, the auditing system of socialism with Chinese characteristics was positively explored and developed mainly in the following seven aspects.

First, establishing an accountability audit system for persons in charge of State-owned enterprises when leaving their posts. In September 1986, the CPC Central Committee and the State Council promulgated the *Work Regulations on Factory Directors of Industrial Enterprises Owned by the Whole People*, which specified that "before a factory director leaves his/her post, competent authorities of enterprises should (or in collaboration with the administrative organ of cadres) request audit institutions to conduct an accountability audit of the said factory director." In December 1986, the CNAO issued the *Notice on Several Issues Concerning the Accountability Audit of Factory Directors Leaving Their Posts*, defining the scope, contents, procedures, and methods involved. This was the earliest documented regulation on the accountability audit. The audit institutions in many places conducted the contract operation responsibility audit, and some local governments also stipulated "contract once audited" and "cash in once audited." In February 1988, the State Council issued the *Provisional Regulations on the Contractual Management Responsibility System of Industrial Enterprises Owned by the Whole People*, which stated that "for the contractual management responsibility system, the government audit offices and other authorized audit institutions should audit contract parties and business operators."

---

[30] National Audit Office of the People's Republic of China: *Selections of Important Files of Audit Work*. Beijing: China Audit Publishing House, September 1993, p. 251.

Second, establishing a regular auditing mechanism on financial revenues and expenditures for the Party and government organs and institutions. In 1987, the CNAO made an announcement on the regular auditing system of the above-mentioned issues. In 1989, the *Regular Auditing System of Administrative Units* was promulgated. At that time, it attached great importance to opening up a new prospect of auditing and building up the authority of audit supervision.

Third, establishing the auditing system on financial revenues and expenditures for local governments. From 1990, audit institutions independently supervised the revenues and expenditures of people's governments at lower levels according to the *Audit Regulations of the PRC*. Henceforth, public finance audit was no longer combined with the tax inspection. In 1990, the CNAO organized audit institutions nationwide to audit the revenues and expenditures on 31 provinces, autonomous regions, municipalities and municipalities with independent planning status. In 1991, it defined the objective to "promote the process of institutionalization, legalization and standardization to gradually realize the goal of 'auditing once every two years with a two-year duration each time' and enlarge the audit coverage to around one-third" for public finance audits.

Fourth, implementing system on fixed assets investment prior to the commencement of construction. The mechanism of "examination before approval" for self-financing infrastructure capital was gradually implemented from 1987. The sources of funds were audited before the approval of self-financing infrastructure plans. The audit results served as a basis of approval by the planning departments. In 1992, the CNAO, the former State Planning Commission, and the former Ministry of Construction jointly released the *Provisional Measures for Auditing of Fixed Assets Investment Prior to the Commencement of Construction*. In 1998, audit institutions suspended their checks on fixed asset investment prior to commencement of construction in order to thoroughly execute the audit laws meet the requirements of investment and financing system reform, lay stress on key auditing points, and prevent auditing risks.

Fifth, establishing the regular auditing system on financial revenues and expenditures for the State-owned financial institutions. The system of auditing by rotation was introduced in 1986. Specifically, audit institutions audited one or two State-owned financial institutions, focusing on violations of laws and regulations. In 1990, auditing on State-owned financial institutions was set as the norm. The audit covers revenues and expenditures, safety of credit funds, and implementation of the "Three Provisions"[31] by financial institutions.

---

[31] In 1993, the Central Committee issued a document which proposed the improvement and rectification of the financial order and required financial institutions not calling in loans in violation of regulations, investing in self-operated entities and improving the deposit and loan interest rate, which were called the "Three Provisions."

Sixth, establishing an auditing system for Chinese-foreign equity and contractual joint ventures. Complying with the continuous expansion and requirements for the utilization of foreign capital, China issued the *Audit Regulations of the PRC* in 1988, defining the auditing system of Chinese-foreign equity and contractual joint ventures with State-owned assets. In 1993, the CNAO released the *Auditing Measures for Chinese-Foreign Equity and Contractual Joint Ventures*, which advanced and standardized the corresponding audit work.

Seventh, establishing the auditing system on assets, liabilities, profits and losses of the State-owned enterprises. From its inception, the CNAO attached importance to business audits, with a focus on unreasonable losses, general loss and wastage, poor management, and other prominent issues. In 1986, the CNAO organized the first audit on 3,700 material enterprises across the county, uncovering financial funds of 660 million yuan to be reclaimed. From 1987 to 1988, it organized an audit on 1,500 agricultural enterprises above the county level, and the audit was extended to more than 1,800 grassroots supply and marketing cooperatives. This curbed embezzlement and speculative selling of agricultural products by abusing management powers, and offered suggestions on improving the agricultural exclusive operations and correcting improper conduct in trades. In 1991, the CNAO conducted the "Two-extension"[32] pilots in 67 large- and medium-sized enterprises, which contributed to an increase of economic benefits totaling 270 million yuan that year after they adopted the opinions on improving business management. In 1993, the CNAO, the former State Commission for Economic Restructuring and the former State Economic and Trade Commission jointly distributed the *Regulations for Audit Supervision on the Operational Conversion Mechanism of Industrial Enterprises Owned by the Whole People*, which further specified the auditing of assets, liabilities, profits, and losses as key points of a business audit. In the same year, an audit was conducted on 969 Chinese-foreign equities and contractual joint ventures in 24 provinces, municipalities, and autonomous regions including Sichuan, Tianjin, and Xinjiang. It uncovered an aggregate deficit of 3.37 billion yuan, latent losses of 410 million yuan, and investment losses of 1.84 billion yuan to be paid back to the State.

3) Promoting Framework Building of Audit Laws and Regulations

In November 1988, the State Council published the *Audit Regulations of the PRC* (Audit Regulations), implemented from January 1, 1989. It elaborated regulations stipulated by the Constitution, which laid a solid foundation for

---

[32] Work Conference proposed that audit institutions at all levels should determine a batch of large- and medium-sized enterprises to conduct regular audits. They not only audited the authenticity and legality of financial revenue and expenditure, but also extended the examinations to relevant internal control systems and economic benefits (the "Two-extensions" for short, as an exploration of effective audit).

achieving its legalization, institutionalization, and standardization. Three principles of audit supervision were stipulated as follows. First, auditing according to law, which means that the activities of audit supervision must be conducted according to the legal requirements. Second, independent audit, which means that audit supervisory power, a power of government economic supervision, should be exercised by all levels of audit institutions independently and according to the law, without any interference by any other administrative organ, social organization, or individual. Third, dual leadership, which means that audit institutions are supervised by both the government at the corresponding level and the superior audit institution from administrative perspective, and audit work is led by the superior audit institution from professional perspective. In accordance with the Audit Regulations, supervision covers State administrative organs, financial institutions, enterprises and institutions owned by the whole people and infrastructure units, other units entitled to State financial allocations or subsidies, Chinese-foreign equity and contractual joint ventures involving national assets, domestic affiliated businesses, and other enterprises. Mainly targeting truthfulness, compliance, and performance in regard to financial revenues and expenditures, the Audit Regulations explicitly stipulated the specific contents of audit supervision, and described the principal powers of audit institutions as supervision and checking, economic processing, administrative processing, and application for judicial sanction. In order to ensure that audit institutions exercise their audit supervisory power according to the law, and that audit institutions and auditors duly perform their duties. Audit Regulations also stipulated punishments for units and individuals (including auditors) violating the regulations. The specific provisions on audit work procedures included: determining the focus of audit work, drafting of audit plans, clarifying the relationship between audit institutions and audited units, regulating audit reporting mechanism making audit conclusions and implementing audit decisions, rechecking and dealing with complaints, and so forth.

To implement the Audit Regulations, the CNAO formulated the general rules and regulations on audit work, that is, the *Rules for Implementation of Audit Regulations of the People's Republic of China*, the *Provisions of the National Audit Office on the Implementation of Audit Work Procedures*, as well as specialized rules and regulations on finance, banking, fixed asset investment, enterprises, administrative affairs, agriculture, and foreign capital auditing. In compliance with requirements of the 14th CPC National Congress for "strengthening audit and economic supervision and improving the rational macro management system," in December 1992, the CNAO issued the *Opinions of National Audit Office of*

China on Strengthening Audit Supervision. It emphasized that audit supervision, as a high-level comprehensive supervision on finance and economy, should fully exert its role in macro management and serve socialist market economic system building. At the same time, local governments at various levels and audit institutions should positively promote the improvement of audit regulations according to local conditions. Some places formulated relevant rules and regulations for audit work in the aspect of the contract operation responsibility audit, off-term directors (managers) auditing, economic benefit auditing, and so on, in combination with the requirements of reform, opening up, and economic development.

(3) Auditing System at the Establishment of the Socialist Market Economic System

The years 1993 to 2002 marked a period of initial establishment of the socialist market economic system. In November 1993, the *Decision of the Central Committee of the Communist Party of China on Some Issues Concerning the Establishment of the Socialist Market Economic System* was adopted at the Third Plenary Session of the 14th CPC Central Committee. It specified the basic framework of socialist market economic system, and the related major issues. In March 1996, the Fourth Session of the 8th CPC National Congress adopted the *Ninth Five-Year Plan of the People's Republic of China for National Economic and Social Development and Outlines of Objectives in Perspective of the Year 2010*, the first medium- and long-term plan formulated in developing a socialist market economy. In September 1997, the 15th CPC National Congress put forward and discussed the basic program of the Party at the primary stage of socialism systematically and completely. It made a strategic deployment for the cross-century socialist modernization, and also proposed to accelerate the pace of building a socialist country under the rule of law. In November 2002, the 16th CPC National Congress systematically summarized the former experience of reform and opening up and modernization after the Fourth Plenary Session of the 13th CPC Central Committee. It comprehensively elaborated the fundamental requirements of the important thought of the "Three Represents," explicitly putting forward the objective of building a well-off society in an all-round way, and made an all-round deployment for economic, political and cultural reconstruction with corresponding reforms. The basic strategy of building the socialist market economic system and ruling the country by law provided a more favorable environment for further improvement of the auditing system. In 1994, the *Audit Law of the*

People's Republic of China was implemented, which witnessed audit work has entered into a regulated and legal framework, as a result great progress was made in developing auditing system of socialism with Chinese characteristics.

1) Adjusting the Institutional Setting and Reinforcing Audit Independence

In May 1994, the Seventh Session of the 8th NPC Standing Committee decided to appoint Guo Zhenqian as Auditor General of the National Audit Office. In March 1998, the First Session of the 9th CPC National Congress decided to appoint Li Jinhua to the post. In 1998, part of the functions and institutions of the CNAO were adjusted during the institutional restructuring of the State Council. First, assigning the CNAO's function of managing social audit to the Ministry of Finance but reserving the duties to supervise the quality of audit reports by social audit institutions. Second, assigning the function of management and supervision of internal audit to China Institute of Internal Audit, but reserving the guidance duties. Third, adding the function of organizing the accountability audit of the Party and government cadres and leaders. Fourth, adjusting the administrative status of attached audit offices as part of CNAO and under its direct leadership instead of the then dual leadership. Therefore, those attached audit offices didn't function as internal audit units of relevant departments any more. Fifth, streamlining administrative departments of CNAO and adjusting the audit scope of different fieldwork units according to different industries, such as public finance, financial institutions, and enterprise audits, so as to reduce overlapping and fragmentation.

2) Preliminary Establishment of the Audit Law System

During this period, a relatively complete system of audit laws was established in accordance with the Constitution, with the *Audit Law of the People's Republic of China* and its Rules of Implementation as the subject based on audit standards.

(a) In August 1994, the *Audit Law of the People's Republic of China* was adopted at the Ninth Plenary Session of the 8th NPC Standing Committee. To meet the requirements for building a socialist market economic system, the Audit Law extracted valuable experiences of audit practice and stated in a legal format. The Audit Law stipulated audit supervision of budget performance, submission of audit reports to people's governments at corresponding levels, and submission of audit reports to the National People's Congress upon entrustment by the Government, notification, or promulgation of audit results, and so forth. This not only incorporated the budget execution audit as an indispensable link in the State's fiscal administration mechanism, but also had far-reaching influence on the audit work in the long run.

Based on the *Audit Regulations of the PRC* promulgated by the State Council in 1988, the Audit Law also made explicit provisions on some fundamental issues that existed in practice over several years. First, audit institutions could examine revenues and expenditures under the management of the finance department at the same level. Second, audit institutions could submit audit reports of budget execution to the corresponding people's government, and the audit reports of budget execution and other financial revenues and expenditures to the NPC Standing Committee upon government entrustment. Third, audit institutions were entitled to conduct a special audit investigation of relevant specified matters related to national financial revenues and expenditures. Fourth, an avoidance system of personnels was adopted for the seeking of audit independence. Fifth, audit institutions were required to notify the relevant government departments or make public the audit results. Sixth, audit opinions and decisions were to be generally applied. Seventh, audit funds were to be revealed, and so forth. The contents saw much change. First, among the duties of audit institutions, that related to major State-owned businesses was given top priority. Second, among legal liabilities, acts related to fiscal and financial revenues and expenditures violating the national provisions were clearly highlighted to strengthen disposal and punishment. Third, audit procedures specified the rights and obligations of audit institutions and the audit targets, simplified the compilation of audit work plans, audit documents on file, and other internal management procedures. Fourth, the regulations on internal audit and social audit were revised from a special chapter to a single article, with major content adjustment. Fifth, the regulation that audit institutions might entrust matters within the scope of the audit to internal audit institutions and social audit institutions was deleted. Sixth, the regulation that "audit institutions can notify the bank regarding the withholding the corresponding payments" was revised into "apply to a people's court for compulsory execution." Seventh, the funds necessary for performance of duties of audit institutions should be incorporated into the financial budget ensured by the corresponding people's government.

(b) Two provisional regulations for the accountability audit were formulated. In May 1999, the General Office of the CPC Central Committee and the General Office of the State Council issued the *Provisional Regulations Concerning Below-County-Level Party and Government Leading Cadres' Economic Accountability Audit* and the *Provisional Regulations Concerning Leading Personnel of State-Owned Enterprises and State Holding Enterprises in Regard to the Economic Accountability Audit during Their Term of Office*. Later, the CNAO developed relevant implementation rules. This provided the fundamental basis for audit institutions to conduct an accountability audit. In October 1999, the Central Commission for Discipline Inspection, the Organization Department of the CPC Central Committee, the former Ministry of Personnel, the Ministry of Supervision, and the CNAO established the "Economic Accountability Audit Joint Meeting," and a Joint Meeting Office was set up within the CNAO. In 1999, the General Office of the CNAO set up the Administrative Office of Economic Accountability Audit and Audit Techniques. In 2001, it began using the signboard of the Office of Economic Accountability Audit, taking charge of relevant coordination.

(c) In October 1997, the State Council issued the *Regulations for the Implementation of the Audit Law of the People's Republic of China*. Maintaining consistency with the Audit Laws in contents, it elaborated the basic requirements of the auditing system established according to the Audit Law, explained the provisions therein, and explicitly defined issues prone to dispute. Additionally, it also specified the matters covered by State Council stipulation, further improving the audit laws and regulations.

(d) In July 1995, the State Council issued the *Interim Measures for Audit Supervision of Central Budget Implementation*. It stipulated the main contents of audit supervision on central budget implementation and other financial revenues and expenditures, time of audit implementation reporting procedures, that materials should be proposed to CNAO by the finance and tax authorities of the State Council and other central departments, principles of audit disposal and related legal liability, and so on. Upon the implementation of the Measures, local governments formulated adaptable measures for audit supervision on local budget performance within their jurisdiction. These regulations guaranteed the audit supervision on corresponding levels' budget performance and other financial revenues and expenditures.

(e) In 1996, the CNAO issued 38 audit standards including the *Basic Principles of Government Audit*, implemented on January 1, 1997. In 1998, the CNAO revised, supplemented, and improved these 38 auditing standards. In November of that year, the CNAO set up the Draft Argumentation and Revision Committee of Auditing Standards System that divided the system into basic auditing standards, specific auditing standards, and professional audit guidelines. By 2003, 20 single auditing standards had been formulated in succession.

(f) The "Eight Restrictions" for auditing were implemented. To practice the spirit enunciated by then Premier Zhu Rongji for achieving strict management of audit teams, the CNAO issued the *National Audit Office's Provisions on Strengthening Audit Discipline Inspection* in January 2000. It stipulated that auditors should have no economic ties with any person or organization being audited, and practically maintain audit work independence. Local audit institutions formulated relevant measures successively in light of actual conditions.

3) Continuously Enhancing Audit Supervision

(a) Strengthening the budget implementation audit. Before the promulgation of the Audit Law, the public finance audit was mainly subject to the approach of "lower-level audited by higher-level"; that is, the higher-level audit institution audited the financial revenues and expenditures of the lower-level government. The Audit Law proposed to conduct same-level public finance audit and establish the system of submitting audit reports to the NPC Standing Committee, which enriched the socialist audit supervision system. From October 1995 to April 1996, the CNAO audited the central budget implementations of the previous year, which was the first such audit carried out. It then submitted an audit report to the State Council. On July 3, 1996, Auditor General Guo Zhenqian was entrusted by the State Council to present the *Audit Report on the Central Budget Implementation in 1995* to the Twelfth Session of the 8th NPC Standing Committee, which was the CNAO's first audit report of central budget implementation to a standing committee of the State's supreme authority in accordance with the laws and regulations. Since then, such documents are respectively submitted to the State Council and the NPC Standing Committee in the form of audit result report and audit work report every year. It is also a statutory requirement for the NPC Standing Committee to hear and deliberate on the audit work report every year, which has energetically brought into play the role of audit in promoting budget management and financial reform. For example, the CNAO has continuously suggested to standardize and elaborate budgets in its audit work report submitted to the NPC Standing Committee ever since 1996. In 1999, the State Council decided to conduct budget reform in central departments from year 2000 according to the resolution made by the NPC Standing Committee.

Adapting to tax-distribution reforms introduced in 1994 while strengthening the budget execution audit, the CNAO, respectively, in October 1995 and March 1996, organized a phased audit on the central tax revenue collection of 17 provinces, autonomous regions, and municipalities. Afterwards, CNAO conducted audit investigation and extended the audit to taxation departments at the prefecture (city) and county levels. Strengthening audit on tax collection administrative departments became an important function of auditing, considering the budget performance at various administrative levels. Additionally, the CNAO also organized and conducted the audit on budget funds collected and allocated by the treasury system, extending the audit scope to the budget implementation and drafting of final accounts of departments and units.

(b) Strengthening the special audit. This mainly covered the audit of financial statements of people's governments at lower levels, audit on financial revenues and expenditures of administrative institutions, and special fund audits. Specifically, in 1995, the CNAO organized its resident offices to audit the 1994 financial statements of 16 provinces, autonomous regions, and municipalities including Heilongjiang and Shanghai. Priority was given to the special audit investigation on the authenticity of deficits in financial statements, the raising and use of funds from the central government for supporting rural development, as well as the set-up and use of extra budgetary special funds. A total of 70 capital construction projects were audited. Besides, local audit institutions audited the financial revenues and expenditures of 3,276 judicial and public security organs above county level in 1994, including the funds for handling cases, fines and confiscation, and charges, as well as the agricultural funds invested by 202 counties of 20 provinces in 1993–1994. In 1996, CNAO organized its resident offices and attached audit offices and local audit institutions at various levels, to conduct an audit on the pension insurance fund and the unemployment insurance fund for national enterprise employees, and the financial revenues and expenditures, as well as the pension insurance fund of enterprise employees from 11 departments (i.e., the Ministry of Railways and the Ministry of Communications) under the integrated system in 1995.

(c) Strengthening the audit of financial institutions. To meet the goal of safeguarding the financial order and promoting financial reform, this period saw a focus on exploring and improving the new way of auditing the assets, liabilities, profits and losses of financial institutions. In 1995, the CNAO conducted the audit investigation on the losses of some State-owned financial institutions. In 1996, it organized local audit institutions and resident audit offices to audit the assets, liabilities, profits, and losses of the Agricultural Bank of China, Bank of China, China Construction Bank, and China International Trust and Investment Corporation and their affiliates during the fiscal year of 1995. To rectify the financial order and maintain the stability of financial position, the CPC Central Committee and the State Council required a joint audit carried out by the People's Bank of China and the CNAO on non-banking financial institutions across the country in 1997. The CNAO organized audits on 110 trust investment companies nationwide, and submitted two special reports to the State Council in succession. The CNAO proposed suggestions on the settlement of existing issues concerning violations of financial regulations and the way to control economic risks of trust investment companies. Meanwhile, audit supervision of the application of foreign funds was further strengthened. Every year, the CNAO audited the aid and loan projects of such international organizations as the World Bank and Asian Development Bank.

(d) **Strengthening audit on important enterprises.** With a view to macro-regulatory services, audit institutions checked the assets, liabilities, profits, and losses of key enterprises according to law, with a focus on State-owned assets supervision. The industry audit received priority. The audit revealed the existing problems of the whole industry during the operation of State-owned assets, providing a basis for government macro control. From 1995 to 1997, audit institutions checked the industries of grain, posts and telecommunications, transportation, medicines, tobacco, and so forth. In accordance with the arrangement of the State Council, the CNAO, in May 1998, organized over 50,000 auditors to spend over half a year auditing the source and application of credit funds of the Head Office of the Agricultural Development Bank of China and its 2,499 branches in the first five months of 1997 and 1998, in collaboration with the Ministry of Finance and the former State Planning Commission. They audited 30,850 grain collection and storage enterprises for newly increased on-record financial accounts and other irrational handling of loans of the Agricultural Development Bank of China from April 1, 1992, to May 31, 1998. Meanwhile, they also carried out the special audit or audit investigation on 2,681 competent departments of grain and 2,594 financial departments. Audit institutions found out 1,181 violations of laws and regulations, such as major misappropriation of acquisition funds, severe damage due to disorderly management, illegal acquirement of public funds, and individual embezzlement of public funds, and so on. This had a great influence on society. Later, the CNAO presented the *Audit Report on Grain Inventory* and the *Report of Suggestions on Deepening the Reform of Grain Distribution System*. In 2000, it organized an investigation of 1,290 enterprises that discovered 78 clues of major and serious cases, and helped put forward suggestions on further deepening enterprise reform and speeding up the establishment and improvement of a modern corporate system and market withdrawal mechanism.

(4) Auditing System during Improvement of the Socialist Market Economic System

In 2003, the *Decision of the Central Committee of the Communist Party of China on Some Issues Concerning Improvement of the Socialist Market Economic System* was adopted at the Third Plenary Session of the 16th CPC Central Committee.

It proposed the objective of improving the socialist market economic system and the guiding ideology and principles involved in deepening economic system reform. Thus, the reform and opening up entered a new period involving improvement of the socialist market economic system. In September 2004, the Fourth Plenary Session of the 16th CPC Central Committee adopted the *Decision of the Central Committee of the Communist Party of China on Enhancing the Party's Governing Capacity*, which stressed, "We will tighten supervision and oversight on the exercise of State power to ensure that the powers bestowed by the people are used for the benefit of the people." During this period, audit institutions proposed an audit policy of "conducting audit according to law, serving the overall situation, focusing on the central task, highlighting the key points and being realistic and pragmatic." This also involved formulating the *National Audit Work Plan (2003–2007)* to further specify objectives and orientation of audit work, by taking the opportunity of comprehensively implementing the Audit Law and focusing on improving the audit quality and audit performance. Through maintaining a basis of truthfulness, and exposing distorted or wrong accounting information as the focus, audit institutions intensified their investigation and punishment of major violations of laws and regulations involving economic crimes, strengthened their restrictions and supervision over the exercise of power, promoted audit result announcement, and enhanced the work on the performance audit. They continued to improve the fiscal, financial, and business audits; actively explored ways to expand the efficiency of the accountability audit; and built the "3 + 1" audit pattern. They also focused on strengthening talents, methods, and technologies, improving audit criteria and the overall quality of audit teams, promoting rapid adoption of modernized audit technical means. Audit supervision played a positive role in maintaining the economic order, deepening reform and development, strengthening restrictions on the exercise of power, and promoting democracy.

1) Defining Guidelines for Audit Work

After the 15th CPC National Congress, the CNAO's Party Group conscientiously summed up the achievements and experience of audit institutions over the 15 years since its establishment, researched audit tasks, and proposed the guidelines of "conducting audit according to the law, serving the overall situation, focusing on the central task, highlighting the key points, and being realistic and pragmatic."

- **Auditing according to the law** means to conscientiously implement the CPC Central Committee's strategy of building a socialist country under the rule of law, and comprehensively perform duties in accordance with provisions of the Constitution and the Audit Law. It requires to strengthen audit supervision from the perspective of maintaining the sanctity of the law, ensure audited units strictly abide by financial and economic discipline, and perform their duties and obligations according to law. It highlights the truthfulness, compliance, and performance in regard to handling financial revenues and expenditures.

- **Serving the overall situation** means to support reforms, promote development, and maintain stability of the overall situation. Catering to the guideline, auditing should strengthen comprehensive analysis, pay attention to research into universality and various global trends through audit, create more high-level audit results, and serve the goal of strengthening macro control and improving national policies and regulations.

- **Focusing on the central task** means to conduct audits by focusing on economic construction and determine the objectives and tasks of auditing according to State Council requirements.

- **Highlighting the key points** means to strengthen audit supervision of key funds, projects, and units.

- **Being realistic and pragmatic** means first to set standards for all work, specify responsibilities, and ensure practical results; and second, carry out the basic audit work effectively, further implement and improve audit standards, and improve the quality and level of audit work. The principle played an important guiding role in the development of the audit cause.

2) Building the "3 + 1" Audit Pattern

To meet the requirements of building a socialist market economic system, the CNAO integrated and adjusted the originally scattered business layout into a "3 + 1" audit pattern (public finance audit, audit on financial institutions, enterprises audits, and accountability audit), stressing resource integration in terms of key projects, audit plan, audit work plan and organizational strength, and highlighting work emphases.

(a) Public finance audit. The public finance audit gradually shifted from previous equal attention to financial revenues and expenditures to the focus on these aspects to reveal problems. Through auditing and audit investigation, the CNAO made suggestions on strengthening budget control and improving budget regulations overall, thus promoting reform of the budgetary system. Meanwhile, the CNAO positively explored the government performance audit, promoted the establishment and improvement of the government performance control system, and explored an "integrated" approach to the public finance audit to improve efficiency and results.

(b) Audit on financial institutions. Following the main objective of preventing and defusing financial risks, the CNAO focused on "risk, efficiency, and management" and gave priority to key issues, especially gathering evidence in major cases. Statistics show that, from 1998 to 2007, the CNAO discovered and transferred evidence in more than 470 major cases investigated by related institutions through audit of financial institutions, involving more than 67 billion yuan and more than 920 officials. This brought a tremendous shock in the financial sector and society, playing an important role in preventing financial risk.

(c) Enterprise audits. By "exposing distorted or wrong accounting information" in the financial fields, the CNAO established the working principle of "relying on truthfulness and making in-depth disclosure to promote development." Evidence in a number of major cases was uncovered, which promoted the gradual improvement in the corporate governance structure of large- and medium-sized State-owned enterprises. As the State-owned enterprises supervision system improved, the audit emphasis shifted from the audit of general financial revenues and expenditures to the accountability audit of corporate leaders. By these means, audit institutions combined the audit of financial revenues and expenditures and the performance audit, and bore equal attention to supervision and services.

(d) Accountability audit. By the end of 2003, a total of 31 provinces (autonomous regions and municipalities) set up the Economic Accountability Audit Joint Meeting or Leading Group. Some of them also set up the Economic Accountability Work Leading Group involving major leaders of the Party Committee and government. Audit institutions at various levels and nearly 2,000 county-level audit institutions of over 400 prefectures and cities set up professional agencies of accountability audit. In 2005, the accountability audit of Party and government cadres was extended from at and below the county level to the prefectural level. In 2006, the revised Audit Law incorporated the contents of accountability audit, specifying its legal status. In the same year, the Organization Department of the CPC issued the *Trial Measures for Comprehensive Assessment and Evaluation of the Local Party and Government Leading Team and Leading Cadres in Conformity with the Scientific Outlook on Development*, which incorporated the conclusions and evaluation opinions of the accountability audit into the organization departments' overall investigation and evaluation of leading cadres, providing a basis for effective application of audit results.

3) Improving Talents Capacity, Legal Framework, and Technologies

When auditing leading officials and the legal system, auditing methods and technologies become the key factor in auditing, and they also serve as the basis and guarantee of continuous audit development. Since its establishment, the CNAO has given top priority to developing a "solid foundation." In 1998, the CNAO's Party Group summarized this aspect as the development of "talents, legal framework, and measures." Premier Zhu Rongji modified "measures" to "technologies" after listening to the CNAO's work report. The development of "talents, legal framework, and technologies" was determined thereafter. Following the people-oriented concept, this reflected the principle of building a socialist country under the rule of law and auditing according to the law and keeping up with the times, thus providing a solid guarantee for sustainable development of the audit cause.

(a) *Talents* **refer to team building.** During this period, audit institutions strengthened leadership and team building in an all-round way, deepened reform of the personnel system, optimized the personnel structure and made efforts to train multiskilled personnels, improve vocational education of audit cadres, strengthen the building of clean government and achieve stricter management of the audit teams. To solve problems in department staffing and auditors' status, the CNAO reduced the total number of resident audit offices from 5,050 to 2,710, and began to emphasize administrative staffing in March 2006, in accordance with the *Approval of the State Commission Office for Public Sector Reform for Transferring the Staffing of the CNAO's Resident Audit Offices to Administrative Staffing.*

(b) *Legal framework* **refers to legal enhancement.** During this period, audit institutions strived to efficiently revise audit laws and regulations, and established the audit quality control system to conduct whole-process quality control of audited projects, improve various audit standards and further regulate audit management and audit behavior.

(c) *Technologies* **refer to skills and techniques.** During this period, priority was given to strengthening planning, management, organization, and coordination of information-based construction of the auditing system. Audit institutions accelerated the construction of the "Golden Auditing Project," realized office system informationization, promoted computer-aided audits, and made great efforts to promote and improve audit sampling, internal control evaluation, risk assessment and other audit methods.

We will mainly introduce the building of legal framework of audit, covering two important aspects.

First, the Audit Law was revised. In February 2006, the 20th Session of the 10th NPC Standing Committee adopted amendments to the Audit Law. The following four aspects were revised:

(a) The audit supervision mechanism was further improved. This was mainly reflected as follows. First, defining the legal basis with which audit institutions conduct audit evaluation and make audit decisions in conformity with other laws and regulations on financial revenues and expenditures. Second, strengthening guidance and supervision of the NPC and its Standing Committee on audit work, and promoting the organic combination of audit supervision and NPC supervision; carefully putting forward requirements for rectification of issues and reports made by audited units and related departments. Third, stipulating the duties and management of branches of audit institutions and the appointment and removal of principals of local audit institutions at various levels.

(b) Audit supervision responsibilities were further defined. This was mainly reflected as follows. First, clarifying that audit institutions are obligated to conduct audit supervision on financial revenues and expenditures of the national institutions and other organizations using supplied funds, and on budget performance and final accounts of projects invested in and supported by government investment. Second, stipulating that audit institutions should conduct the accountability audit of the Party and government leading cadres and State-owned enterprise leaders during their term of office, and specifying the legal status of audit institutions in the accountability audit. Third, defining the duties of audit institutions to guide and supervise internal audit work and verify the relevant audit reports issued by social audit institutions.

(c) The means of audit supervision were further strengthened. This was mainly reflected as follows. First, clearly differentiating audit responsibilities and accounting responsibilities, empowering audit institutions to use electronic data and necessary computer technical documentation and other materials of financial revenues and expenditures stored and processed by the audited units via computer. Second, empowering audit institutions to inquire into the accounts of audited units at financial institutions and individual deposits therein, upon approval. Third, specifying the power of audit institutions to take compulsory measures against any behavior of transferring, concealing, altering, and damaging related data, and transferring and concealing illegal assets. Fourth, specifying the right of audit institutions to request the organs of public security, supervision, finance, taxation, customs, price, industry, and commerce administration to assist in performing the audit supervision responsibilities. Fifth, stipulating that audited units should execute the audit decision.

(d) Behavior in regard to audit supervision were further regulated. This was mainly reflected as follows. First, not issuing auditor's opinions and changing audit reports as internal instruments of audit offices to published reports with free access to the public with legal force. Second, strengthening hierarchical supervision of audit institutions at a higher level over those below, and stipulating that the former can order the latter to alter or revoke any audit decision made in violation of national relevant regulations, and also can make a decision on alteration or revocation if necessary. Third, further specifying the legal action on audit reconsideration and designing different remedy channels for audit decisions on the fiscal and financial revenues and expenditures. Fourth, defining the legal responsibilities for auditors' disclosure of national secrets and business secrets they may have acquired.

Second, auditing standards were revised and improved. In 2003, the CNAO formulated the *Measures for the Quality Control of Audit Projects of Audit Offices (Trial)*, consisting of 100 articles. It respectively prescribed the quality control of auditing program, audit evidence, audit report, auditing files, and other aspects, specified the corresponding responsibilities of quality control and required implementing the quality responsibility evaluation system for audit projects.

4) Building the System of Announcement of Audit Findings

In 2001, Premier Zhu Rongji instructed audit institutions to draw on the U.S. experience to build the system of announcement of audit findings, after he had met with U.S. Auditor General David Walker. To this end, in 2002, the CNAO successively published the *Trial Measures of National Audit Office of China Announcement on Audit Findings* and the *Provisions of National Audit Office of China on Announcement of Audit Findings*, to specify the implementation of the system of announcement on audit findings. Except for specific announcements involving the national secrets or other special cases, all audit results of projects under the unified organization of the CNAO should, in principle, be reported to the general public. Meanwhile, the main contents of the announcement were stipulated, including the audit results of central budget implementation and other financial revenues and expenditures, fiscal and financial revenues and expenditures organized by government departments or enterprises and institutions of the State, relevant industries or special funds, and corresponding economic accountability during a term of office. In 2003, the CNAO made public the "Announcement of National Audit Office of China on Audit Results of Special Funds and Social Donations for Preventing and Controlling SARS." The audit results announcement system raises higher requirements for quality work by audit institutions, further mobilizes society to participate in supervision, and plays a positive role in promoting the disclosure of budget and government information.

(5) Auditing System during the Overall Building of a Well-Off Society in the New Period

In October 2007, the 17th CPC National Congress proposed that we should (1) insist upon comprehensive, coordinated and sustainable economic and social development; (2) advance all-round economic, political, cultural, and social development; (3) coordinate all links and aspects of our modernization drive; and (4) build a resource-saving and environment-friendly society that coordinates growth rate with the economic structure, quality, and efficiency, and harmonizes economic growth with the population, resources, and the environment, so that our people can live and work under sound ecological and environmental conditions and our economy and society can develop in a sustainable way. We should focus on strengthening oversight on leading officials and especially principal ones, over the management of human resources, financial and material resources, and key positions. We should improve the systems of inquiry, accountability, accountability audit, resignation, and recall to make them more effective. In February 2008, the *Opinions on Deepening the Reform of Administrative System* adopted at the Second Plenary Session of the 17th CPC Central Committee explicitly proposed, "We should improve the supervision system for the exercise of power. The governments at various levels must actively accept the supervision by people's congresses and their standing committees at their respective administrative level, accept the supervision system of the Chinese People's Political Consultative Conference, and fully exert the role of specialized supervision, i.e., inspection and auditing." In 2012, the 18th CPC National Congress proposed the goal of (1) building a moderately prosperous society in all respects and deepening reform and opening up in an all-around way; (2) making overall arrangements for stimulating socialist economic, political, cultural, social and ecological advancement in an all-around way; and (3) comprehensively improving the rational level of Party building. The congress emphasized that we must unswervingly follow the path of socialism with Chinese characteristics and must have every confidence in our path, in our theories and in our system. In November 2012, the *Decision of the CPC Central Committee on Several Important Issues of Comprehensively Deepening Reform* adopted at the Third Plenary Session of the 18th CPC Central Committee proposed that the overall goal of deepening reform comprehensively was to improve and develop socialism with Chinese characteristics, and to promote the modernization of the national governance system and capacity. In addition, it expounded on the significance and future trend of deepening reform comprehensively and made detailed deployment plans for the strategic emphasis and means of deepening the reform. In 2014, the *Decision of the CPC Central Committee on Some Major Issues Concerning Comprehensively Promoting the Rule of Law*, adopted at the Fourth Plenary Session of the 18th CPC Central Committee, proposed that the general target was to establish a system serving "the socialist rule of law with Chinese characteristics" and build a country under "the socialist rule of law," and specially proposed to strengthen the national supervision, including inner-party supervision, NPC supervision, democratic supervision, administrative supervision, judicial supervision, audit supervision, social supervision, and public opinion supervision, so as to form the scientific and effective restriction and supervision system of power operation and make it more effective. Specifically, it gave explicit deployment plans for improving the auditing system and safeguarding the independent exercise of audit supervisory power in accordance with the law. Checking by audit institutions should fully cover public funds, State-owned assets, State-owned resources, and leading cadres' performance of their economic accountabilities. Additionally, it highlighted that higher-level audit institutions must enhance the leadership of lower-level audit institutions and explore the unified management of audit institutions below the province level in human resources and financial and material resources, so as to promote the construction of audit professionalization. In August 2014, the newly revised Budget Law put forward new requirements for audit work. The *Opinions of the State Council on Strengthening Audit Work*, issued in October of that year, put forward the requirements for fully exerting the guaranteed role of audits in promoting the national major decision-making deployment and strengthening the role of audit supervision in the new period. In December 2014, General Secretary Xi Jinping put forward the strategic layout of "Four Comprehensives" (comprehensively building a moderately prosperous society, comprehensively deepening the reform, comprehensively implementing the rule of law, and comprehensively strengthening Party self-discipline), and specified the strategic direction, key fields, and main objectives of the undertakings of the Party and the State.

During this period, guided by the socialist theoretical system with Chinese characteristics, audit institutions treated the rule of law and improving livelihood for the people through reform and development as the starting point and supreme goal, seriously investigated the major issues of violating laws and disciplines as well as economic cases. Audit work also focused on revealing problems at the institutional level and strived to safeguard national security. It concerned more on further advanced audit work concerning fiscal affairs, finance, business, economic accountability, resources and environment, and foreign capital. Audit offices positively explored the real-time audit and working hard to further improve the audit system of socialism with Chinese characteristics by undertaking five fundamental tasks—audit teams, rule of law, informationization, theory, and culture.

1) Improving the Government Audit Pattern

In March 2008, the First Session of the 11th CPC National Congress decided to appoint Liu Jiayi as the Auditor General of the CNAO. During this period, in line with the overall layout of "Five-in-One" covering the political, economic, cultural, social, and ecological civilization, China's government audit pattern was further developed and improved, and the six major audit patterns, including public finance audit, audit of financial institutions, enterprise audit, accountability audits, resources and environment audit, and overseas audits were formed. Basically covering the key fields of government auditing, these audit patterns complied with the requirements of national governance for government audit and promoted the national auditing playing a role in national governance. Among them, public finance audit is the basic responsibility and eternal theme of government auditing, which is recognized by all countries. Auditing on the State-owned financial institutions and State-owned enterprises is adapting to China's basic economic system of keeping public ownership as the mainstay of the economy and allowing diverse forms of ownership to develop side by side. The accountability audit is one with Chinese characteristics and complying with China's supervision system of cadres. It means audit offices should inspect and evaluate the fulfillment of the duty of leading officials, which was entrusted by corresponding departments. Conducting the audit on resources and environment and promote the ecological civilization building and sustainable development is a common concern of audit institutions throughout the world and it also forms an important responsibility of the government auditing. Adapting to the development strategy of "bringing in" and "going global," the audit on the management and utilization of foreign capitals, overseas investment of State-owned enterprises, and other foreign matters is an important means for government auditing to promote the reform and opening up.

2) *Exploring and Innovating the Audit Methods and Ways*[33]

The audit methods and ways affect the efficiency and effect of audit supervision. During this period, the audit methods and ways were mainly innovated and explored as follows on the basis of regular auditing.

(a) **Explore the comprehensive audit methods.** With the deepening reform, the macro perspective and overall importance of audit work were further strengthened, and the audit objective had been shifted from single projects to the combined multiple projects. Hence, the combination and complementary advantages of all professional audits were highlighted. Audit institutions set forth the "Five Unified" principle (i.e., financial audits should stick to a unified audit plan, unified audit program, unified audit implementation, unified audit report, and unified audit handling), and insisted upon the "Six Combinations" (i.e., the combination of "same-level audit" with "lower-level audited by higher-level," the combination of fiscal audits with special audits enterprises and economic accountability audit, the combination of audit, with audit investigation, and combination of regular audit with real-time audits, the combination of the audit on authenticity and legitimacy with the performance audit, the combination of revealing the problems with promoting rectification), positively exploring how to promote the integration of the audits of business and resources.

(b) **Explore the real-time audit methods.** Real-time audit refers to the involvement of audit institutions at a certain key link during the course of handling the audited matter, and also a kind of persistent dynamic supervision activity following the progress of the audited matter.[34] The *CNAO Program for the Development of Audit Work 2008–2012* clearly set forth the following rules that real-time audit shall be conducted in the entire process of major construction projects concerning the people's livelihood, particular resource development and environmental protection, major emergencies relating to public matters, and the implementation of major state policies and measures. During this period, audit institutions successively implemented the total real-time audit on national major investment projects like the Beijing-Shanghai High-Speed Railway; the second line of the West-East natural gas transmission project and the Three Gorges Project; the anti-earthquake and relief work after

---

[33] Liu Jiayi (chief editor), *Study on the Auditing Theory of Socialism with Chinese Characteristics* (Rev. ed.). Beijing: The Commercial Press, China Modern Economic Publishing House, 2015, pp. 107–150.

[34] Liu Jiayi (chief editor): *Study on the Auditing Theory of Socialism with Chinese Characteristics* (Revised Edition). Beijing: The Commercial Press, China Modern Economic Publishing House, 2015, p.119.

the Wenchuan, Yushu, and Zhouqu earthquakes; post-disaster reconstruction; and major public projects such as the Beijing Olympic Games, Shanghai World Expo, and the Asian Games. Those audit practices effectively guaranteed the vigorous and orderly implementation of major projects, post-disaster reconstruction, and also ensured the smooth and complete success of major events and meetings. Audit institutions also organized the real-time audit on the implementation of major policies and measures. For instance, to promote the implementation of major policies and measures of the Central Committee for expanding domestic demands, the CNAO concentrated efforts to conduct audits and special audit investigations on the implementation effects of the Central Committee's policies and measures for expanding domestic demand and promoting the steady and rapid economic development in 17 provinces, autonomous regions and municipalities and relevant units since September 2009. In order to promote the implementation of policies for stabilizing growth, promoting reform, adjusting structure, and benefiting people's livelihood, the CNAO carried out real-time audits on the implementation of the above policies since August 2014. To do the real-time work well, the CNAO concentrated efforts and broke the boundary of different departments and sections to develop the audit ways involving multiple professions.

(c) **Innovate modes for unified audit of large-scale projects.** In view of difficulties, major issues, and matters concerned by the society, the audit institutions at higher levels organized a number of audit offices at the lower levels to jointly conduct the comprehensive auditing from three dimensions and from multiple angles, so as to know the base number, expose problems, analyze their causes at the mechanism and system level, make suggestions, and better provide reference and basis for decision making. For instance, in accordance with the arrangements and requirements of the State Council, the CNAO organized the audit institutions nationwide to conduct all-round auditing on the debts of local governments at provincial, city, and county levels, according to the principle of "conducting the audit by transaction and item on the basis of inspecting involved personnel, accounts, and objects in person," respectively, in 2011 and 2013. In 2012, the CNAO organized audit institutions nationwide to conduct all-round auditing on the national social security funds. And in 2014, audit institutions were mobilized to carry out the all-round audit on revenues and expenditures of land leasing and farmland protection.

The selection of a unified audit mode for large projects focused on the integration of resources, and aimed at safeguarding audit independence, exerting a joint force of supervision and fostering the concept of "one game of chess" by adhering to the "Five Unified" principle (i.e., financial audits should be subject to unified design, unified planning, unified implementation, unified reporting, and unified handling). In light of the different features of audit projects, the mode of flat management, that is, unified planning, hierarchical responsibility, or breaking of level restrictions, could be adopted for specific organizations and implementations. For instance, the mode of unified implementation and hierarchical responsibility was adopted for the audit of governmental debts and social security funds. The CNAO built a unified audit group to conduct auditing within its jurisdiction, and all regions adopted the way of "lower-level audited by the higher-level" and "cross audit" or built a unified audit group to conduct auditing. When the CNAO audited revenues and expenditures of land transfers and farmland protection, they adopted the flat management mode featured by a large audit group at the country level and a comprehensive group for each provincial audit group, instead of leadership organizations at all prefectural audit groups any longer. The CNAO's personnel could serve as the group leaders of all audit groups at various provincial and prefectural levels, and the deputy positions and division heads of provincial audit institutions and directors of prefectural audit institutions, respectively, served as the deputy group leaders. The audit teams dispatched by all prefectural audit groups to districts and counties shall be subject to the unified agreement of the CNAO. Under the direct command of the CNAO, all prefectural audit groups assigned certain auditors report to the CNAO and give feedback to when encountering difficulties and issues. While replying to all prefectural audit groups, the CNAO would provide feedback to all provincial comprehensive groups synchronously. Audit groups were required to report clues of major cases to a higher-level audit group with a copy submitted to the CNAO. The particularly significant matters shall be directly reported to the CNAO. Such scheduling and organization and reasonable redeployment of audit forces could effectively exert the joint forces of audit supervision and enhance the integrity of audit work from the macro perspective.

(d) **Explore digital audit methods.** During this period, through the construction of "Golden Auditing Project," phase I and phase II and application practice, the overall framework of the national audit informatization was basically established, which consisted of an application system meeting the needs of audit services and audit management, a set of data resources supporting audit services and audit management, a network system achieving interconnection and information sharing, a safeguard system maintaining information security and system operation, a service system safeguarding system maintenance and application promotion, and an audit team satisfying real-time informational needs. It provided the technical support for audit informatization and digitization. The audit management, the audit management system (OA), the on-site auditing system (AO), and the online auditing system as the subject were widely applied during the audit implementation, audit management and handling of office affairs. Meanwhile, audit forces positively conducted the information system audit, and explored the digital auditing of "overall analysis, doubt discovery, dispersion verification, and systematic research." The audit capability and technical level were continuously improved.

The said digital audit mode was to make the overall analysis of the situation or data acquired through audit, find an appropriate method for overall data analysis by summarizing audit experience, so as to precisely guide auditors in the field to verify the key points, eventually to summarize audit findings, systematically analyze causes, and make recommendations. This new mode of audit institution could greatly reduce the uncertainty for auditors in the audit field, enhancing the orientation and efficiency of auditing. With the audit data platform as the basis, the data analysis team as the support, and the audit informatization system as the guarantee, many audit institutions positively explored the new mode of audit groups under the guidance of the Headquarters (Head Office and Corporation) and with the interaction among different levels and the explicit division of labor, strengthening the supervision on the trans-market, cross-industrial, and cross-sector large-value transactions and fund flows. They not only realized the routine supervision and appropriate feedback of hot issues during the economic operations, but also improved the level of reporting issues and accelerated the pace of revealing problems. Good achievements were obtained. It is estimated that, on the condition that the staffing of audit institutions nationwide remained basically unchanged, the number of audited units increased by 15 percent. By means of IT technology, audit institutions had jointly improved revenues and reduced losses by 300 percent, and increased the number of transferred clues of major violations of laws and rules by 100 percent, with a great improvement in system maintenance. As a result, the application of information technology, especially the exploration of digital audit methods, was an important and foundational factor.

3) Improving the Audit Law System

(a) **Revise the Rules for the Implementation of the Audit Law.** In accordance with the newly revised Audit Law, the 100th Executive Meeting of the State Council deliberated and adopted the new Rules for the Implementation of the Audit Law in February 2010. The following four aspects were revised.

First, the revisions for improving the audit supervision mechanism and strengthening audit supervision, are mainly as follows: (1) further specify the legal basis for affiliated audit offices to carry out audit work; (2) require the principal of audited units to make written commitments on the authenticity and integrity of the provided materials; (3) empower audit institutions to punish the relevant principals of audited units violating the Audit Law or national regulations on financial revenues and expenditures; (4) empower audit institutions to suggest the punishment imposed on the principals who default in fulfillment of an audit decision; (5) stipulate that the masses have the right to report cases to audit institutions, which in turn shall handle them according to the law in time.

Second, the revisions for explicitly defining the audit responsibilities and fully exerting the role of audit supervision, are mainly as follows: (1) further specify the duties and authority of the audits of financial revenues and expenditures; (2) explicitly require audit institutions to conduct audit supervision on enterprises and financial institutions whose State-owned capital accounts for over 50 percent or below 50 percent of the total capital (capital stock) of the enterprises and financial institutions, but the State-owned investment subjects control actual right; (3) further define the scope of construction projects invested and supported by government, and adjust the scope and way of supervision on relevant units under the government-invested projects; (4) further determine the scope of auditing on social security fund and social donation funds; (5) further define the scope of special audit investigation; (6) clarify the legal status of internal audit self-discipline organization, specific ways of guiding and supervising the internal audit work by audit institutions, and ways of verification and handling of relevant audit reports issued for social audit institutions.

Third, the revisions for standardizing the audit behaviors and maintaining the lawful rights and interests of audited units, are mainly as follow: (1) remove the original restrictions on the scope of audit matters in published audit results and make special regulations on the results of audit reports from audit firms and the procedures for audit results of listed companies; (2) specify that audit institutions have the obligation to inform audit plans to audited entities where State-owned assets occupy a holding or leading position; (3) formulate regulations on the procedures of an audit hearing.

Fourth, the revisions for improving the audit procedures and ensuring the quality of auditing, are mainly as follows: (1) specify the requirement that an audit institution should carefully prepare an audit plan before the auditing; (2) stipulate that audit institutions can directly carry out the audit on the strength of an audit notice in a special case; (3) explicitly stipulate the audit review system; (4) standardize the behavior of proposing audit reports, making audit decisions and handling the transfer issue of auditing; (5) specify the procedures for handling the violations of laws and rules during the special audit investigation; (6) improve the mode of serving the audit instruments, and define the way of confirmation of delivery date; (7) further improve the way of handling the audit decisions violating relevant state provisions made by the audit institutions at the lower levels.

(b) **Improve the system of the accountability audit.** In October 2010, the General Affairs Office of the CPC Central Committee and the General Affairs Office of the State Council issued the *Regulations Concerning accountability Audit for Leading Officials of the Party and Government and Leaders of State-Owned Enterprises* (hereinafter, the Regulations), which specified auditees, audit plans, organization and coordination, audit contents, audit implementation, audit evaluation, definition of responsibilities, application of results and so forth. In May 2011, the Central Commission for Discipline Inspection, the Organization Department of the CPC Central Committee, the Ministry of Supervision, the Ministry of Human Resources and Social Security, the National Audit Office of China, and the State-Owned Assets Supervision and Administration Commission of the State Council jointly issued the opinions on implementation of the above regulations. In July 2014, the Central Commission for Discipline Inspection, the Organization Department of the CPC Central Committee, the State Commission Office for Public Sector Reform, the Ministry of Supervision, the Ministry of Human Resources and Social Security, the China National Audit Office, and the State-Owned Assets Supervision and Administration Commission of the State Council printed and distributed the *Rules for Implementation of the Regulations Concerning Accountability Audit for Leading Officials of the Party and Government and Leaders of State-Owned Enterprises*. These documents further improved the legal system of accountability audits and laid a solid legal foundation for promoting the rational progress of accountability audits.

(c) **Forming an appropriate government auditing system.** In July 2010, in view of various practical development and changes, the CNAO integrated the former audit standards, and incorporated the former basic principles of government auditing and general audit standards into the *National Auditing Standards of the PRC* (hereinafter, the Standards), forming a unified auditing system that was implemented from January 1, 2011. Inheriting the mature regulations of the original version, this stressed a rational audit concept and use of advanced audit technologies, systematically summarized effective approaches from years of audit practice, and drew on useful lessons from the international community, with the sense of Chinese characteristics and high applicability. Meanwhile, the single audit guide was gradually formed according to the new audit standards, and a national system with a clear structure and detailed regulations came into being. Throughout the Standards, there has been a strong emphasis on the great importance of improving China's auditing system and realizing its standardization.

The establishment and development course of the auditing system of socialism with Chinese characteristics shows that the system was established in conformity with the needs of national governance in the context of reform and opening up, and continuously developed and improved within the overall auditing needs. This is a process that continuously converts and incorporates successful experiences with a theoretical approach, and it is also a process of continuously creating a better institutional environment for audit development through institutional innovation.

4. CONCLUSION AND ENLIGHTENMENT

We can draw the following basic conclusions by reviewing the above contents.

First, the mode of national governance determines the system and form of government auditing. The system and practice of governance are the fundamental issues concerning the nature and competitiveness of a country.[35] The evolutionary history of China's government auditing shows that government auditing emerged and developed to meet the demand of national governance and it has always been related to it. As the goals of national governance changed in accordance with different historical periods, requirements for government auditing differ as well. Functions and roles, institutional setting, and functional positioning of government auditing must always adapt to the objective needs of national governance. For instance, the Zhou Dynasty (1046–256 BC) advocated the "rule by rites," and the governance goal of "defining the authority and ranks of the king, ministers and officials," with the Zaifu required to perform the duties. In the Qin and Han dynasties, rulers advocated "grand unification" and an auditing mode of "supervising all officials, rectifying from every aspect and achieving the integration between supervision and auditing" by the censor. This embodied the orientation of strengthening centralized governance. The Tang Dynasty adopted the governance mode of Three Councils and Six Boards, forming the auditing system of "unity of special audit, concurrent audit and internal audit by different departments respectively."

---

[35] Commentary Department of the People's Daily, *Learning and Reading of 'Four Comprehensives,* 1st ed. Beijing: People's Publishing House, March 2015, p. 123.

In history, the prosperity of a dynasty and stability of a regime are closely linked with the performance of national supervision system, including national audit. Generally speaking, a period of great prosperity and well-developed politics attached importance to supervisory tools, which usually ensured the powers of decision making, execution, and supervision were well balanced and coordinated, giving better play to the role of national governance. However, in a period of a declining dynasty and political corruption, the supervisory system, including auditing, would generally be on the decline first, and thus normally could not play a proper role serving national governance. In this aspect, Han Feizi proposed that "chaos existed at the beginning of emperor's arbitrary listening and accounting."[36] The Western Zhou Dynasty was relatively advanced in its budget and auditing system in ancient times, and its national governance was also appraised by Confucius and others. The Tang Dynasty executed the audit of "unity of special audit, concurrent audit and internal audit by different departments respectively," which played an important role at that time and was closely associated with Tang's well-known prosperity. However, in sharp contrast, the Censor Office of the Imperial Household Supervision Department declined to "the worst Yamen (government office) of the Qing Dynasty" in the later period of the Qing Dynasty. After the Nanjing Nationalist Government came to power, financial tycoons refused to accept audit supervision. In this sense, we may say that national governance reflects the level of government auditing to a great extent, while the capacity of government auditing also embodies national governance ability to a certain degree.

Second, government auditing is a fundamental institutional arrangement for China's national governance, serving as its bedrock and important guarantee. The development history of auditing reveals that historical periods with a relatively perfect auditing system considered this as a fundamental institutional arrangement and made corresponding provisions in the fundamental law or special laws, where the auditing system was endowed with certain authority and responsibilities, becoming an important and indispensable "institutional infrastructure"[37] of national governance. For example, the *Rites of Zhou* in the Western Zhou Dynasty, *Law of Qin* in the Qin Dynasty, *Legislative Articles of Bibu* and *Conventions of Bibu* in the Tang Dynasty made provision in regard to the

---

[36] Mr. Yang Shizhan, a contemporary accounting and auditing expert, also proposed the thought—"a ruler should firstly manage accounting and auditing to govern the country well."

[37] Hu Angang, "The Essence of Governance Modernization is Institutional Modernization." *People's Tribune*. November 2013, p. 20; Wang Shaoguang, "National Governance and Basic National Capacity." *Journal of Huazhong University of Science and Technology, Social Science Edition*, No. 3, 2014. Special Edition, P3

auditing system. The auditing system of socialism with Chinese characteristics was established and developed according to the *Constitution of the PRC*. The stability, coerciveness, and authority of government auditing determine its role as the bedrock and important guarantee of national governance.

Judging from the functions and roles of government auditing, it is like the "immune system" of the human body and plays a similar role in national governance system by safeguarding the healthy development of the national economy and society. Since the establishment and development of the auditing system of socialism with Chinese characteristics more than 30 years ago, and adapting to the needs of different periods, audit institutions always consciously consider overall economic and social development when tackling the central tasks, and make continued efforts to improve the overall system and its operational mechanism, perfect audit laws and regulations, and adjust audit duties and authority, thus playing an important role in safeguarding the economic and financial order, improving the effective use of financial funds and promoting China's healthy economic and social development.

Third, the scope of duties and role of government auditing are mainly defined on the principle of "jurisdictional control, employment of talents and wealth management." From "centralized governance" to "well-planned action," "establishing a legal system and common rules and scrutinizing its policies," "formulating any policies in relation to economic regulation and plans of financial revenues and expenditures," the scope of duties throughout auditing is mainly determined by three key considerations, the officials to be audited, their actions, and the funds involved. To a great extent, the evolution of auditing system was based on the politics, economy, and culture prevailing at a specific time, and became an arrangement and adjustment to bring into full play the role of auditing in "jurisdictional control, employment of talents, and wealth management."

National governance involves elements such as labor, finance, and material resources (assets). Governance refers to the integrated use, management, and control of these elements, while powers and responsibilities are reflected by them all. The political scientist E. A. Rees has proposed that the center of all studies on a political system is concerned with the issues of the nature of a State, while the focus of studies on the State rests with control and accountability.[38] As an important part of national governance, government auditing is required to supervise and constrain the State's execution of power execution through the audit activities of checking and supervising losses and risks, so as to realize the

---

[38] E. A. Rees, *State Control in Soviet Russia*. New York, NY: Macmillan Press, 1987, p. 1.

governance goal of "defining the authority and ranks of the king, ministers, and officials," promote good national governance and safeguard public interests.

Fourth, an important aspect of the auditing system is to maintain its independence and authority. The vicissitudes of China's political system and evolution of auditing system show that the authority and independence are mainly safeguarded by the following three measures.

(a) Audit institutions are authorized legally. In different periods in history, the establishment of the government auditing system and authorization of audit institutions were under the rule of law. For example, "defining the authority" in the *Rites of Zhou* written by Zaifu in the Zhou Dynasty, *Law of Administrative Reports System* in the Han Dynasty, *Legislative Articles of Bibu* in the Wei and Jin Dynasties, procuratorate auditing system incorporated into the *Constitution of the Republic of China* during the period of the Nanjing Nationalist Government, the government auditing system incorporated in the *Constitution of the PRC* upon the founding of new China, all embodied the concept that laws serve as a guarantee for the independence and authority of audit.

(b) Audit institutions reported to the most senior decision makers. In the course of history, the affiliations of audit institutions were mostly changed, leading to different ranks of auditors, but all should report to the most senior decision makers (rulers).

(c) Professional audit institutions were established independently. Audit institutions, fiscal institutions, and supervisory organs suffered vicissitudes during thousands of years of development course. However, on the whole, the more independent and professional the audit institutions could be, the stronger government auditing became, along with a higher level in serving the cause of national governance.

General Secretary Xi Jinping has pointed out: "Today's China is developing based on the past. To govern today's China, we should have a profound understanding of the history and traditional cultures of China, and also positively summarize the ancient explorations and wisdom in ruling and administering the country."[39] Only by integrated analysis of the course of government auditing can we understand and effectively steer the development, historical law and future trend from a more comprehensive and objective perspective. Thousands of years of development of China's government auditing have helped to accumulate abundant historical experience for establishing and improving the auditing system of socialism with Chinese characteristics.

---

[39] Xi Jinping, "Keep Firmly in Mind the Historical Experience, Lessons and Cautions—A Speech at the 18th Collective Learning of the Political Bureau of the CPC Central Committee." *Xinhua Daily Telegraph*, October 14, 2014.

CHAPTER TWO

Foundation of the Auditing System of Socialism with Chinese Characteristics

"A SYSTEM SHOULD BE SUPPORTED BY RELEVANT theories and thoughts. No system can come out of nothing."[1] These theories and thoughts, also called the core of a system, are the foundational elements of a system, and determine its intrinsic basic properties and features during the continuous development and evolution with changing times. To study the rules of development of the government auditing system, we first need to grasp its developmental foundation. This chapter analyzes and studies the theoretical foundation, institutional foundation, and cultural foundation of the socialist system with Chinese characteristics, so as to better understand and grasp the basic properties and major features of the auditing system of socialism with Chinese characteristics.

1. THEORETICAL FOUNDATION OF THE AUDITING SYSTEM OF SOCIALISM WITH CHINESE CHARACTERISTICS

The establishment and improvement of a system depend on practice, but the system relies more on theories for ideological guidance and key references. For a state, the objectives and ways of its government auditing during a specific period depend on its theoretical basis and political attitude during that period, to a great extent.

---

[1] Chien Mu, *China's Rise and Fall*, New rev. Beijing: Jiuzhou Press, 2012, p. 49.

The 18th Communist Party of China (CPC) National Congress clearly pointed out that the path of socialism with Chinese characteristics is the way to reach the goal, the theories of socialism with Chinese characteristics offer a guide to action, and the socialist system with Chinese characteristics provides a fundamental guarantee. The three functions are integrated in the great practice of building socialism with Chinese characteristics, which is the salient feature formed through the long-term endeavors of the Communist Party of China leading people in building socialism.[2] Socialism with Chinese characteristics fosters the ultimate dream of realizing a great rejuvenation of the Chinese nation in modern times, and also manifests the beautiful vision and unremitting exploration of the Chinese people regarding socialism. Since the start of reform and opening up, the theoretical basis and political attitude of national governance have been epitomized as the dynamic and developmental theories of socialism with Chinese characteristics.

The theories of socialism with Chinese characteristics scientifically shed light on the ideological line, development path, development stage, basic task, development drive, development strategy, supporting forces, international strategy, and leadership. Those theories are systematic and scientific, which link up such fields as Marxist philosophy, political economics, and scientific socialism and cover economy, politics, culture, society, national defense, diplomacy, united front, national reunification, Party building, and so forth. Summarizing the correct theoretical principles and experience of building, consolidating, and developing socialism, which are proven in practice, the theories of socialism with Chinese characteristics systematically make clear a series of important issues on socialism in China, a big developing country with a population of more than one billion, that is, the kind of socialism to be built, ways of building socialism, the kind of Party to be built, ways of Party building, desired development, ways of development, and so forth. Guided by the theories of socialism with Chinese characteristics, a series of systems of socialism building and Party building and development have come into existence and constitute the system of socialism with Chinese characteristics.

The theories of socialism with Chinese characteristics are the ideological foundation and action guideline of building socialism with Chinese characteristics and also the fundamental guideline for advancing various socialist causes. The auditing system is an important system of socialism with Chinese characteristics. Hence, in essence, the theories of socialism with Chinese characteristics offer the ideological line and theoretical basis for establishing and improving the auditing system of socialism with Chinese characteristics.

---

[2] Hu Jintao, *Firmly March on the Path of Socialism with Chinese Characteristics and Strive to Complete the Building of A Moderately Prosperous Society in all Respects: Report of Hu Jintao to the 18th CPC National Congress*. Beijing: People's Publishing House, November 8, 2012, pp. 12–13.

Terminology 1: The Theoretical System of Socialism with Chinese Characteristics

The report at the 18th CPC National Congress pointed out that the theoretical system of socialism with Chinese characteristics is a system of scientific theories including Deng Xiaoping Theory, the important thought of "Three Represents" and the Scientific Outlook on Development, representing the Party's adherence to and development of Marxism-Leninism and Mao Zedong Thought. It embodies the wisdom and hard efforts of several generations of Chinese Communists leading officials in their tireless exploration and practice. It is the latest achievement of Marxism in China, the Party's invaluable political and intellectual asset, and the common ideological foundation of the concerted endeavor of people of all ethnic groups. As the open system constantly improves, it reflects the Party's adherence to and development of Marxism-Leninism and Mao Zedong Thought. The theoretical system of socialism with Chinese characteristics covers ideological line, basic task, development stage and development strategy, development drive, ultimate purpose, core of leadership and supporting forces, as well as over ten main aspects, that is, politics, economy, culture, society, national defense and army, diplomacy, and international strategy.

Ideological Line of Socialism with Chinese Characteristics

We must persevere in emancipating the mind, seeking truth from facts and keeping up with the times, always proceed from reality, combine theory with practice, integrate theory with practice, verify and develop the truth through practice. That is the essence of the theories of socialism with Chinese characteristics and also the soul of Deng Xiaoping Theory, the important thought of the "Three Represents" and the Scientific Outlook on Development.

Essence of Socialism with Chinese Characteristics

We must gradually achieve the goal of common prosperity, continuously meet people's growing material and cultural needs, improve people's ability and capability, and promote the overall development of the people based on the continuous development of productivity.

Basic Tasks of Socialism with Chinese Characteristics

We must emancipate and develop productive forces and continuously improve people's living standards.

(continued)

Development Stage and Development Strategy of Socialism with Chinese Characteristics

China is still at the primary stage of socialism and will remain so for a long time. Our mission is to build a moderately prosperous society in all respects by the time the Communist Party of China celebrates its centenary in 2021, and to turn China into a modern socialist country that is prosperous, strong, democratic, culturally advanced, and harmonious by the time the People's Republic of China celebrates its centenary in 2049.

Development Drive of Socialism with Chinese Characteristics

Reform and opening up is crucial to adhering to and developing socialism with Chinese characteristics. We must always apply the spirit of reform and innovation to all aspects of governance, and continuously promote the self-improvement of China's socialist system.

Fundamental Purpose of Socialism with Chinese Characteristics

We must stick to the principle of putting people first and always ensure that development is for the people, by the people and with the people sharing in its fruits.

Economic Development of Socialism with Chinese Characteristics

We must adhere to and improve the basic economic system with public ownership playing a dominant role and different economic sectors developing side by side; we must adhere to and improve the system in which distribution on the basis of labor remains as the predominant mode and coexists with various other modes.

Political Development of Socialism with Chinese Characteristics

We must integrate the leadership of the Party, the status of the people as masters of the country, and the rule of law. We must uphold and improve the system of people's congresses, the system of multi party cooperation and political consultation under the leadership of the CPC, regional ethnic autonomy, and self-governance at the primary level of society.

Cultural Development of Socialism with Chinese Characteristics

We must keep to the orientation of advanced socialist culture, build the system of socialist core values and improve socialist core values, and develop balanced socialist culture that is inclusive of all ethnic groups, embraces modernization, the world, and the future, and puts people first.

Social Development of Socialism with Chinese Characteristics

Social harmony is an inherent attribute of socialism with Chinese characteristics. We must give high priority to safeguarding and improving people's well-being while strengthening the social development, and strive to create a situation in which all people do their best, find their proper positions in society, and live together in harmony.

Ecological Development of Socialism with Chinese Characteristics

We must enhance our ecological awareness of respecting, adapting to and protecting nature. We must give top priority to making ecological progress, incorporating it into all aspects and the whole process of advancing economic, political, cultural, and social progress, and work hard to build a beautiful country and achieve the lasting and sustainable development of the Chinese nation.

National Defense and Army Building of Socialism with Chinese Characteristics

We must persevere in the Party's absolute leadership over the army, insist upon the fundamental purpose of the armed forces serving the people, and build a strong national defense and powerful armed forces which are compatible with China's international standing, and adapted to security needs and development interests.

Supporting Forces of Socialism with Chinese Characteristics

The people are the creators of history. We must persist in the dominant position of public ownership, bring all positive factors into full play and rally all the forces available.

Advancing the Great Cause of Achieving National Reunification

We will unwaveringly implement the policy of "one country, two systems," promote the long-term prosperity and stability of Hong Kong and Macao, firmly keep to the theme of peaceful development of cross-Straits relations, and safeguard national sovereignty and territorial integrity, so as to finally achieve complete national reunification.

Diplomacy and International Strategy of Socialism with Chinese Characteristics

We must adhere to the path of peaceful development, pursue an independent foreign policy of peace, and carry forward the Five Principles of Peaceful Coexistence to enhance friendship and cooperation among peoples of various countries.

(continued)

> **Core of Leadership of Socialism with Chinese Characteristics**
> We must comprehensively promote Party building in the spirit of reform and innovative and make Party building more scientific in all respects, and build the Party into an innovative, service-oriented, Marxist, governing party good at learning to ensure that the Party is always the firm core leadership guiding the cause of socialism with Chinese characteristics.
>
> ———————————
> *Source:* China Steering Committee of Compiling and Reviewing Cadre Training Materials, *Uphold and Develop Socialism with Chinese Characteristics.* Beijing: People's Publishing House and Party Building Books Publishing House, 2015, pp. 29–31.

A system bridges theory and practice. Advances made in theories, practices, and institutions constitute a unified process. The theoretical system of socialism with Chinese characteristics not only functions as an integrated theory but also has the periodical characteristics of development stage, reflecting the mutual promotion between theoretical innovation and practical development. The auditing system of socialism with Chinese characteristics is established and developed under the guidance of theories of socialism with Chinese characteristics and based on the audit practice. The theoretical system of socialism with Chinese characteristics offers a theoretical foundation for the establishment and improvement of the auditing system of socialism with Chinese characteristics, arms our minds, and guides our practice and work. That is mainly reflected as follows: (1) it provides the ideological foundation and theoretical basis for the establishment and improvement of the auditing system of socialism with Chinese characteristics; and (2) it offers a guide to the continuous exploration and innovation in the auditing system of socialism with Chinese characteristics and the construction of a theoretical system, so as to guide and promote the improvement of the auditing system. Their interrelation is briefed in Figure 2-1.

Specifically, it can be understood from the following four aspects.

(1) The Theoretical System of Socialism with Chinese Characteristics Provides the Ideological Foundation for the Establishment and Development of the Auditing System of Socialism with Chinese Characteristics

A common ideological foundation is the prerequisite for the existence and development of a Party, a State, and its ethnic groups. Socialism, as a new social system, is not only a social practice but also a pursuit of ideals and values. The

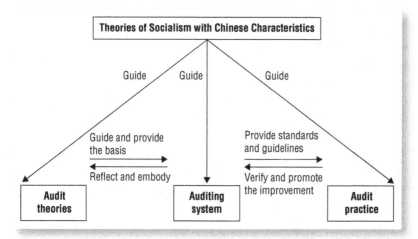

FIGURE 2-1 Logical relation between the theoretical system of socialism with Chinese characteristics and the auditing system of socialism with Chinese characteristics

theoretical system of socialism with Chinese characteristics functions as the common ideological foundation for the united struggle of the Chinese people, and also the ideological foundation of establishing and improving the auditing system of socialism with Chinese characteristics. Audit institutions and individual auditors must stick to their ideals and convictions, resolutely adhere to the Marxist standpoint and methodology, have every confidence in the path of socialism with Chinese characteristics, its theories and system, remain loyal to the Party, the State and the people, abide by laws, respect history and stay committed to the audit cause. They must earnestly perform their audit supervision responsibilities, and promote the establishment and improvement of the auditing system of socialism with Chinese characteristics.

(2) The Theoretical System of Socialism with Chinese Characteristics Guides the Establishment and Development of the Auditing System of Socialism with Chinese Characteristics

Auditing is a highly political, professional, and policy-oriented work. The political nature determines the life of audit work. Audit institutions must always focus tightly on the centers of activity set by the Party and the State, and the auditing system must always seek the correct political direction for improvement. Based on national conditions, the auditing system of socialism with Chinese characteristics is always developed and improved in such a manner that the advanced experience of other countries' government auditing acquired through research and adoption is incorporated into China's actuality, and that practice and innovation are in line with the requirements of economic and social development of the times. It manifests the ideas and methods of socialism with Chinese characteristics, including the philosophic thoughts of historical materialism, the ideological line of emancipating the mind, seeking truth from facts and keeping up with the times, the essence of socialism and its law of development, and so on. Guided by the theories of Chinese socialism, the auditing system of socialism with Chinese characteristics always develops in the right direction and forges ahead.

(3) The Theoretical System of Socialism with Chinese Characteristics Provides the Practical and Theoretical Foundation for the Contents and Arrangements of the Auditing System of Socialism with Chinese Characteristics

The principal arrangement of the auditing system of socialism with Chinese characteristics specified in the Constitution, Audit Law, and its Regulations for Implementation; the establishment of the auditing system; the setting up of audit institutions; the definition of auditing duties and responsibilities, and the design of auditing procedures all follow the Party's leadership and follow the basic concept of upholding the interests of the people. All the work stems from a scientific understanding of the development stage, basic task, and development drive, and complies with the development strategy of socialist economic, political, cultural, social, and ecological progress with Chinese characteristics. The auditing system established and improved on a socialist ideological foundation suits China's conditions, plays an important role in the development of socialism with Chinese characteristics, and demonstrates its institutional advantages and great vitality.

(4) The Theoretical System of Socialism with Chinese Characteristics Leads the Continuous Exploration and Innovation of the Auditing System of Socialism with Chinese Characteristics, and Guides and Promotes the Development and Improvement of the Auditing System

Through over 30 years of improvement, the auditing system of socialism with Chinese characteristics has witnessed the practical exploration and advancement of socialist audit theories with many improvements. Progress in theory, practice, and system has always been achieved under the guidance of the theories of socialism with Chinese characteristics.

At the early stage of the reform and opening up in 1982, China initiated the audit supervision system of socialism with Chinese characteristics to meet the needs of economic system restructuring and financial and economic supervision. At the early stage, audit institutions followed the policy of "working while establishing" and explored for ways to develop good practice while focusing on centers of economic activity and adopting some foreign audit experiences. They conducted a great number of audit pilot projects. Audited entities included enterprises, administrative institutions, fiscal departments, financial institutions, special funds, foreign-funded projects, and so forth. During this period, in association with audit practice, audit institutions gained an initial understanding of audit development, audit institutionalization, the leadership system, audit function, relationship between audit institutions and audited entities, relations among government auditing, internal auditing and auditing by accounting firms, and so forth, by introducing and learning from foreign audit experience and theories.

As China's economic system gradually shifted from the planned economy to a socialist market economy, the audit work was based on the working guidelines of "stressing the essentials and laying the foundations"; "positive development and gradual enhancement"; "consolidation, improvement, development and enhancement"; aiming to enforce financial and economic discipline, promote improvement and rectification, and safeguard smooth systemic reform. Audit institutions firmly stressed economic growth continuously expanded the audit scope. Correspondingly, the audit focus gradually changed from enterprises to public finance, banking, key construction projects, and so on. During this period, audit institutions deepened their understanding of the audit definition, audit functions, internal control, how audit serves macro-management, and how to strengthen audit legislation, institution, and standards.

The basic strategy of building a socialist market economic system and the rule of law provides a favorable environment for further improvement of the auditing system. The Audit Law implemented in 1995 marked the point when the audit supervision system embarked on a legal track. Firmly stressing the requirements for economic growth and Party building, audit institutions conscientiously implemented the Audit Law, put forward and adhered to the guideline of "auditing according to law, serving the overall situation, focusing on the central tasks, highlighting the priorities and being realistic and pragmatic." Through focusing on truthfulness as the basis, and disclosure of distorted or wrong accounting information as the focus, audit institutions have investigated major violations of laws and rules as well as economic criminal cases, and proactively conducted accountability audits, striving to strengthen "auditors, legislation, and methodologies," to open a new prospect for auditing. Through a period of exploration and practice, further understanding was gained of the nature of auditing, so that the definition of audit changed from "independent economic supervision" to "tool of the democratic rule of law." Basic understanding emerged on the relationship between audit and fiduciary responsibilities, and between auditing and democratic rule of law, audit system, and audit operation. The auditing theoretical system of socialism with Chinese characteristics was thus established in a preliminary way.

New audit requirements have been put forward for the following aspects: the establishment of a series of significant strategic concepts about implementing the Scientific Outlook on Development; building a harmonious socialist society; building a moderately well-off society, realizing the China Dream for the great rejuvenation of the Chinese nation and so forth; the establishment of the "Five-in-One" overall layout of socialism with Chinese characteristics covering political, economic, cultural, social, and ecological progress; and the definition of the strategic layout of the "Four Comprehensives" (comprehensively building a moderately prosperous society, comprehensively deepening reform, comprehensively implementing the rule of law, and comprehensively strengthening Party self-discipline). To adapt to these requirements, audit institutions have taken a scientific outlook on development as their guiding force, firmly adopted the rule of law and improved livelihood for people through reform and development as the starting point and supreme goal, seriously investigated major violations of the laws and regulations as well as economic criminal cases, and promoted the in-depth advancement of the performance audit. More emphasis has been given to exposing problems, analyzing their causes, and making recommendations at the institutional, mechanism, and systemic levels. Accordingly, audit institutions have promoted the implementation of policies and measures of the central government; worked for steady, rapid economic growth; safeguarded national economic security; positively promoted the institutional and systemic innovation, democracy, and legal construction; and punished corruption, giving full play to the function of audit as an "immune system" in safeguarding the healthy operation of the national economy and society. It is safe to say that the scientific outlook on auditing has further enriched the connotations of the auditing theory of socialism with Chinese characteristics. Guided by this concept, cognition of the auditing nature has further deepened. Government auditing functions have become an endogenous "immune system" of the national governance system. Auditors have further established a series of viewpoints on audit functions and objectives and basic audit features, and so on. These interrelated concepts, ideas, and viewpoints ran through all aspects of the auditing of socialism with Chinese characteristics and enriched and expanded the contents of the auditing system of socialism with Chinese characteristics.

The auditing theory of socialism with Chinese characteristics was formed on the basis of improvement of audit practice and theoretical exploration previously mentioned. Based on the theories of socialism with Chinese characteristics, audit theories make clear that government auditing is an integral part of the socialist political system with Chinese characteristics, and is an institutional arrangement to supervise and restrict power in accordance with the law. In nature, as already mentioned, auditing is an "immune system" with the functions of exposure, resistance, and prevention within the scope of the national governance system and is the bedrock and important guarantee of national governance. It explicitly proposes that the first requirement is to safeguard the fundamental interests of the people, the realistic objective is to promote rule of law, to safeguard people's livelihood, and to promote reform and development. The direct objective is to monitor and evaluate the reality, legality, and effectiveness of the financial revenues and expenditures of audited entities; the primary task is to safeguard national security, especially economic security; ensure smooth policy implementation; promote democracy and rule of law, as well as the anticorruption campaign; and accelerate the deepening of reform and scientific progress. All of the work should be based on openness, initiative, service and understanding the overall situation, and insisting on criticalness, supervision, micro investigation and disclosure, adaptability, and independence, which are five major features of the current government auditing. The latter must follow the guideline of "auditing according to law, serving the overall situation, focusing on the central tasks, highlighting the priorities, and being realistic and pragmatic." Auditing is the staunch "defender" of national interests, the "guardian" of public funds, the "supervisor" of the exercise of power, the "sharp sword" of anticorruption, the "catalyst" of deepened reform, the "monitor" of economic development, and "supervisor" of policy implementation. These theoretical views are the specific reflection and application of theories of socialism with Chinese characteristics in the field of auditing.[3] Guided by these audit thoughts and theories, the audit community has

---

[3] With regard to the argumentations about the socialist audit theories with Chinese characteristics, refer to: Liu Jiayi (Cchief Eeditor), *Study on the Auditing Theory of Socialism with Chinese Characteristics*, (Rev. ed. Beijing: The Commercial Press, China Modern Economic Publishing House, 2015.

summed up experiences, and formulated and issued a series of new audit laws, rules, and regulations in line with objective laws and development needs. Thus, the auditing system has been further improved.

To further improve the auditing system of socialism with Chinese characteristics under new historical conditions, it is vital to always adhere to guidance by the theories of socialism with Chinese characteristics, insist upon and expand socialist audit practice with Chinese characteristics, and pay close attention to the guiding role of audit theories of socialism to improve the overall auditing system. As long as we continue to insist upon and improve our self-consciousness and conviction in the auditing system of socialism with Chinese characteristics and ensure it can continue improving along with the development of audit practice and socialist audit theories with Chinese characteristics, the necessary institutional guarantee for the development and progress of the modern Chinese audit cause will stay firm. Accordingly, we can continue to explore the audit cause.

2. INSTITUTIONAL FOUNDATION OF THE AUDITING SYSTEM OF SOCIALISM WITH CHINESE CHARACTERISTICS

There are neither identical systems nor an institutional mode applicable to all countries. Each has its unique system formed through long-term development, progressive improvement, and endogenous evolution based on its historical legacy, cultural traditions, and economic and social development. The socialist system with Chinese characteristics is rooted in the reform and opening up and the vivid practice of socialist modernization, with distinctive characteristics and unique superiorities. As noted by the General Secretary Xi Jinping, "The socialist system with Chinese characteristics upholds the organic unity of the fundamental and basic political and economic systems and various institutional mechanisms, the organic unity of the national and grassroots democratic systems, and the unity of the Party's leadership, people's status as masters, and rule of law. It complies with the Chinese situation, and fully embodies the distinctive features and strengths of socialism with Chinese characteristics, thus constituting a fundamental institutional guarantee for development and progress of contemporary China." The socialist system with Chinese characteristics, as the systemic foundation for the establishment and improvement of the auditing system, determines the audit mode.

Terminology 2: Institutional System of Socialism with Chinese Characteristics

The socialist system with Chinese characteristics is a complete set of interconnected and interrelated systems, consisting of systems at the fundamental, basic, and specific levels as well as socialist system of laws with Chinese characteristics. Different levels are endowed with a different status and functions in the institutional system of socialism with Chinese characteristics. This is a fundamental institutional guarantee for development and progress of contemporary China and fully embodies the distinctive features and strengths of socialism with Chinese characteristics.

The fundamental system with a decisive role in the institutional system reflects its essential contents and fundamental characteristics and embodies its "qualitative determinant." It is an outstanding feature distinguishing the institutional system from others. In the institutional system of socialism with Chinese characteristics, the system of people's congresses as a fundamental political system reflects the State's nature and essence of the socialist system with Chinese characteristics.

The basic institutional systems have a major influence on the economic and social development of a state. In the institutional system of socialism with Chinese characteristics, this includes the basic political system and basic economic system, and specifies the basic principles of political life and economic life of the State. The basic political systems include the system of multiparty cooperation and political consultation under the leadership of the CPC, the system of regional ethnic autonomy, and the system of self-governance at the primary level of society, and so forth. The basic economic system means the system with the public ownership playing a dominant role and diverse forms of ownership developing side by side.

The specific system derives from systems at the fundamental and basic levels, and is the specific form of manifestation and realization of the latter. In the institutional system of socialism with Chinese characteristics, specific systems refer to the economic, political, cultural, and social systems, and the like, which are established on the basis of fundamental political system, basic political system, and basic economic system.

The legal system of socialism with Chinese characteristics provides a good legal environment for the implementation of systems at different levels through various laws and specifications. With the Constitution playing the fundamental role, with laws as the mainstay and with administrative regulations and local regulations as major components, the legal system of socialism with Chinese characteristics ensures that there are

(continued)

laws to abide by in economic, political, cultural, and social development, as well as in ecological progress. The systems established through legislation are of high authority and stability.

Sources: China Steering Committee of Compiling and Reviewing Cadre Training Materials, *Uphold and Develop Socialism with Chinese Characteristics*. Beijing: People's Publishing House and Party Building Books Publishing House, 2015, pp. 42–46; Ren Lixuan, "The Fundamental Institutional Guarantee for the Development and Progress of Modern China: Thinking about the Adherence and Improvement of Socialist System with Chinese Characteristics." *People's Daily*, June 13, 2013.

(1) State Political System Determines the Political Nature of the Auditing System

"Two basic functions of a system, namely definition of jurisdictional scope and execution of sanctions, involve the fundamental aspects of politics. Hence, a system is naturally associated with politics."[4] Political system covers laws, the institutional framework, rules, and normal practice that standardize a series of fundamental issues such as State power, governmental system, the relationship between the State and society, and so forth. The socialist political system with Chinese characteristics involves the system of people's congresses, regional ethnic autonomy, self-governance at the primary level of society, and multiparty cooperation and political consultation under the leadership of the CPC, all of which establish the basic principles of Chinese political life. The government auditing system is an important national political system, in turn determining the nature and political orientation of the government auditing system.

1) CPC Leadership Is the Primary Political Precondition for the Establishment and Improvement of the Audit System of Socialism with Chinese Characteristics

Article 1 of the Constitution makes clear the State system adopted by the People's Republic of China. It is a socialist state under the people's democratic dictatorship led by the working class and based on an alliance of workers and farmers.[5] The leadership of the working class is realized through its political party. The Communist Party of China is the vanguard both of the working class and of the Chinese people and nation. It is the core of leadership for the cause of socialism with Chinese characteristics and represents the development trend of China's advanced productive forces, the orientation of its advanced culture, and the fundamental

---

[4] (U.S.) Talcott Parsons, *Structure and Process in Modern Societies*, translated by Liang Xiangyang. Beijing: Guangming Daily Publishing House, 1988, p. 155.
[5] *The Constitution of the People's Republic of China* adopted at the Fifth Session of the 5th CPC National Congress, December 1982.

interests of the overwhelming majority of the Chinese people.[6] As noted by the Preamble to the Constitution, the victory in China's New-Democratic Revolution and the successes achieved in the socialist cause have been achieved by people of all ethnic groups, under CPC leadership by surmounting numerous difficulties and hardships. The people will continue to comprehensively advance the cause of socialism with Chinese characteristics and ensure that China becomes a prosperous, strong, democratic, culturally advanced, and harmonious modern socialist country under CPC leadership. All of this determines the status of the CPC as the core of leadership in regard to the cause of socialism with Chinese characteristics.

Since the establishment of audit institutions, the various CPC congresses and other important meetings have raised clear requirements for strengthening the audit cause, economic supervision, and the restrictions on and supervision of the use of power. The 13th CPC National Congress proposed to conduct the necessary supervisory management, consolidate and strengthen financial and economic discipline, strengthen audit institutions, and so forth. The Fifth, Seventh, and Eighth Plenary Sessions of the 13th CPC Central Committee required the strengthening of auditing and supervision of various economic activities, promoting improvements in audit work, and establishing a strict management system of finance, auditing, supervision, and so forth. The 14th CPC National Congress stressed strengthening audit and supervision, improving the system and methodology of rational macro management, and developing accounting and auditing consultancy. The Third and Fifth Plenary Sessions of the 14th CPC Central Committee stressed strengthening the work of the disciplinary inspection organs and judiciary, supervision, and auditing departments of the Party; strict enforcement of economic discipline; and promotion of audit supervision. The 15th CPC National Congress focused on strengthening the law enforcement and supervision departments and promoting their supervision of cadres at all levels, especially leading leaders. The Fourth Plenary Session of the 15th CPC Central Committee required efforts to strengthen the audit and supervision of enterprises' economic activities and conduct the accountability audit of heads of State-owned enterprises and State holding enterprise leading officials during their term of office. The 16th CPC National Congress proposed to strengthen the restrictions on and supervision of the use of power, and give full play to the role of judicial, administrative supervision, and audit institutions and other functional departments. The Third and Fourth Plenary Sessions of the 16th CPC Central Committee focused on the reform of the budgeting system, improving the balance between budget preparation and execution, and strengthening audit supervision; establishing and improving the systems of

---

[6] The *Constitution of the Communist Party of China*, revised and adopted by the 18th CPC National Congress, November 14, 2012.

reporting significant personal affairs and reporting performance, democratic appraisal, persuasion, and admonition, and accountability audit on the part of leaders, and implementing the system of inquiry, accountability, and dismissal according to law. The 17th CPC National Congress proposed to focus on tightening oversight over leading officials, and especially that of the principal ones, the management and use of human, financial, and material resources; and over key positions, and improve the systems of inquiry, accountability, accountability audit, resignation and dismissal, and so forth. According to the Second and Fourth Plenary Sessions of the 17th CPC Central Committee, it was necessary to strengthen supervision at all levels of government; fully exert the role of dedicated supervision, that is, inspection and auditing; improve the accountability audit of leading officials of the Party, government, and State-owned enterprises; and promote audits of financial funds and major investment projects. The 18th CPC National Congress proposed to improve the systems of inquiry, accountability, accountability audit, resignation, and dismissal. As required by the Third Plenary Session of the 18th CPC Central Committee, the most important aspect was to strengthen and improve the restriction and supervision of the exercise of power by the principal leaders, and strengthen administrative supervision and audit supervision; improve the strict systems of financial budgeting, approving, and auditing; and conduct auditing of natural resources and assets at the end of the terms of the leading officials involved. The Fourth Plenary Session of the 18th CPC Central Committee stressed improvements on the systems of inner-party supervision, National People's Congress (NPC) supervision, democratic supervision, administrative supervision, judicial supervision, audit supervision, social supervision, and public opinion supervision, so as to form a scientific and effective restriction and supervisory system regarding the operation of power and increase synergy and outcomes; improve the auditing system and protect the right to exercise audit oversight independently; conduct comprehensive audits of public funds, State-owned assets, State-owned resources, and the accountability of leading officials; intensify the leadership of audit institutions at the next higher level; explore unified management of audit institutions below provincial level in regard to human, financial, and material resources; and promote audit professionalization. The requirements mentioned above not only indicate the direction for the development of the audit cause but also show that strengthening of audit supervision is important in advancing all Party activities and promoting Party building.

We can fully realize the following three aspects through analyzing the establishment and improvement of the auditing system of socialism with Chinese characteristics.

First, adherence to the CPC's leadership guarantees the political orientation for this task. Government auditing is an important cause of socialism with Chinese characteristics, so we must regard the adherence to the CPC's leadership as the basic principle and primary political precondition. Since the audit supervision system was established according to the Constitution, audit institutions at all levels have always adhered to Marxism, Leninism, and Mao Zedong Thought and the theories of socialism with Chinese characteristics as the guide, and followed the correct political direction; in action, they have firmly stressed Party and government work and have performed their audit supervision responsibilities in accordance with law, and maintained the fundamental interests of the masses as a prime objective; besides, through the institutional arrangement, audit institutions have extended the audit scope to cover implementation of various guidelines and policies, and fulfillment of accountability of Party leaders, thus strengthening the restrictions on and supervision of power, positively supervising the building of a clean and honest government, and contributed to running the Party strictly and strengthening its construction.

Second, the management of audit institutions and the organization and development of audit work is conducted under Party leadership. In both thinking and action, audit institutions absolutely obey the decisions and deployments of the Party committees at all levels, and are consistent with the line of the Central Party Committee. In the process of practice, audit institutions at all levels as well as individual auditors have energetically promoted the implementation of the Party lines, principles, and policies in all its departments, regions, and fields, as well as the rule of law, safeguarded people's livelihood, and advanced reform and development and maintained the fundamental interests of the public. The Party organizations of audit institutions at all levels always research and design their work while firmly stressing the Party's major decisions, and have made contributions to the realization of development strategies and development goals of the Party in various historic periods; they always emphasize the Party building in their institutions and give full practical play to the "fortress" role of grassroots party organizations and the exemplary vanguard role of Party members.

Third, the Party building of audit institutions offers a powerful ideological and organizational guarantee for the development of audit work. Since the establishment, under the leadership of the Central Party Committee, local Party committees and the Party organizations of audit institutions, the latter have always armed Party members and cadres with scientific theories, intensified the training of Party members, strengthened theoretical study, and closely combined this with the handling of actual problems, thus improving the theoretical and ideological level of Party members and cadres. They have always emphasized the construction of Party branches and strengthened the autonomous activities of the branches, Party members' management and organization thus enhancing the cohesion force and effectiveness of the Party organizations. They have also persevered in the Party building while focusing on the political, economic, and audit work of the Party and the State, thus fully exerting the role of the Party organizations as the political guarantee; they have always insisted upon exploring the new paths of Party building, strengthened and improved the ideological and political work, and cultivated a favorable style of audit, all of which not only give full play to the role of the departments of labor unions, youth, and women's organizations as the bridge and link, but also maintain the vigor and vitality of the Party organizations. Especially in recent years, the China National Audit Office (CNAO) and audit institutions at various levels have carried out the education and practice activities on the Party's mass line and "Three Stricts and Three Honests" special education, adhering to the objective of serving the people wholeheartedly, striving to seek benefits for the people, and staying pragmatic and incorruptible. They have worked hard to develop the "Competing for Excellence" activity, further strengthening the construction of learning grassroots Party organizations to further enhance the ideological and political awareness of Party members and cadres. They have positively advanced the openness management of Party affairs, ensuring the democratic rights of Party members in a better way. They have thoroughly promoted the construction of a clean and honest government and always insisted upon auditing according to law in an independent and incorruptible way, and made efforts to build clean and honest party organizations in audit institutions, practice the core values of auditors, and carry forward the audit spirit. Party building of audit institutions constitutes a powerful ideological and organizational guarantee for the development of audit cause.

Meanwhile, we should also realize that the system of multiparty cooperation and political consultation under CPC leadership is a basic political system of the nation, a political party system of socialism with Chinese characteristics, and also an important form of promoting socialist democracy in political life. To adapt to it, audit institutions established the system of "special auditors," which is an important embodiment and specific measure for adhering to and improving the system of multiparty cooperation and political consultation under CPC leadership, fully bringing into play the functions of democratic parties' and nonparty personages' participation in government affairs and deliberation over governmental affairs and democratic supervision. Since the CNAO and the United Front Work Department of the CPC published the *Opinions on Appointing Democratic Party Members and Non-party Personages as Special Auditors* in 1991, audit institutions nationwide successively appointed over 5,000 democratic party members and nonparty personages to this post, basically forming the system of special auditors with rational contents, standard procedures, and effective management. The special auditors are experts in relevant fields covering public finance, banking, public administration, resources and environmental protection, social security, science and technology, statistics, laws, and other aspects. An open employment and appointment procedure upon the recommendation of the united front departments and the assessment of audit institutions has been established. Accordingly, measures relating to the duties, powers, work processes, and organizational management for special auditors were also formulated. An annual working program specifies the timing, contents, methodologies, responsible units, and persons in charge of special auditors participating in audit work to ensure smooth operation. Considering that special auditors have many other responsibilities and are scattered across the country, the CNAO established a consultation, notification, and work meeting system of special auditors. Moreover, special auditors were organized to participate in the survey and consultation on some important audit work, lay stress on exerting the advantages and expertise of special auditors, and offer advice and suggestions to audit work. For instance, the CNAO invites special auditors to attend the executive meetings, audit meetings, or other relevant meetings, to get involved in discussion and study of important laws and regulations like Audit Law and its Rules of Implementation, auditing standards and five-year work plan of audit development, as well as work arrangements, to offer advice and suggestions at important meetings every year, like the National Audit Work Conference and Special Auditors Workshop, to report the opinions and suggestions of all walks of life on audit work and give full play to the role of consultation. They were also invited to jointly carry out the real-time audit of post-disaster reconstruction after the Wenchuan earthquake and a series of key audit projects, such as the nationwide social security audit, the audit of energy conservation and emission reduction, the audit of the final accounts of completed Three Gorges Project, accountability audit, and so forth, through NPC recommendations, Chinese People's Political Consultative Conference (CPPCC) motions, media interviews, and other channels, the special auditors fully exert their function as a bridge for strengthening and improving audit work and expanding the effects of audit. Additionally, the CNAO also invited special auditors to review the budget execution of its headquarters, to issue and publish the results, so as to fully play their role of democratic supervision.

2) The System of People's Congresses Is an Institutional Guarantee of the Establishment and Improvement of the Auditing System of Socialism with Chinese Characteristics

The system of people's congresses is a fundamental political system and way of governance of the PRC. It is an organizational form of political power established according to the Marxist theory on State in combination with Chinese conditions, and is commensurate with the system of people's democratic dictatorship led by the working class, based on the alliance of workers and farmers. The people's democratic dictatorship is a means by which all powers in the PRC belong to the people.[7] The people's status as masters is one of important features of democratic politics of socialism with Chinese characteristics. The people exercise State power through voting for delegates to the people's congresses. When exercising power, the people's congresses and their delegates are responsible to and accept supervision of the people. The people's congresses are the organs of State power. The National People's Congress and its Standing Committee, as the supreme organs of State power, mainly exercise legislative power; elect or remove the heads of State organs; examine and approve the national economic and social development plan, State budgets and final accounts, and the establishment of provincial administrative division and special administrative regions; and choose plenipotentiary representatives sent abroad to conclude treaties with foreign countries, the national mobilization or introduction of a state of emergency, and such important powers as free pardon and conduct of war or peace. Local people's congresses at various levels and their standing committees are local organs of State power, exercising their powers within their jurisdiction. All administrative, judicial, and procuratorial organs of the State are set up by people's congresses by which they are supervised. The people's congresses and their standing committees supervise the work of these State organs; cancel inappropriate provisions, decisions, and orders; and carry out inquiries for their work.

The system of people's congresses is the foundation of legitimacy in the establishment and improvement of the auditing system of socialism with Chinese characteristics. Since the audit supervision system was established according to the Constitution, the heads of audit institutions at all levels have been chosen by people's congresses and their standing committees. Audit institutions are directly responsible to the governments at the corresponding level, and ultimately responsible to people's congresses and their standing committees at the corresponding level. Audit institutions should accept supervision from people's congresses and their standing committees at the corresponding level. Since the implementation of the Audit Law, audit institutions at various levels always report their work and related rectification

---

[7] The *Constitution of the People's Republic of China* adopted at the Fifth Session of the 5th CPC National Congress, December 1982.

of budget execution and other financial revenues and expenditures to the people's congress at the corresponding level, so that the latter's standing committee can perform the duties of approving budgets and supervising the government's budget execution and so on, and strengthen its guidance and supervision of audit work.

3) The Unitary State Structure Is the Organizational Foundation of the Establishment and Improvement of Auditing System of Socialism with Chinese Characteristics

The Constitution stipulates that, "The People's Republic of China is a unitary multinational state created jointly by the people of all its ethnic groups."[8] Paragraph 4 of Article 3 specifies that, "The division of functions and powers between the central and local State organs is guided by the principle of giving full scope to the initiative and enthusiasm of the local authorities under the unified leadership of the central authorities." The above provisions indicate that China's state structure is a unitary system. China's unitary system takes on the following two features due to special national conditions. One is to solve ethnic minority issues under the unitary system through the regional ethnic autonomy system; the other is to solve the problems left over from history under the unitary system through the establishment of the special administrative region system.[9]

Terminology 3: Unitary State Structure

A unified system is a form of State structure, which is a system of unified sovereignty consisting of a number of general administrative regions and units without independent sovereignty. A unitary system and federal system are two key forms of contemporary State structure. China is a unitary state. Most countries in the world also adopt this approach, such as the United Kingdom, France, Japan, Italy, South Korea and North Korea, and so on. Unitary states feature the following aspects. In view of the legal system, a state has only one Constitution under which laws are formulated by the unified legislature of the Central Government; a state only has a supreme legislature, a central government, and one complete judicial system. According to the power division of central government and local authorities, under the centralization of authority, local governments are empowered by and accept the unified leadership of the Central Government, which in turn exercises hierarchical control and is entitled to revoke any local government for inappropriate administrative acts, but a certain degree of regional local self-government is allowed.

(continued)

---

[8] The *Constitution of the People's Republic of China* adopted at the Fifth Session of the 5th CPC National Congress, December 1982.

[9] Zhu Yong (chief editor), *Chinese Law*, p. 46. Beijing: China University of Politic Science and Law Press, 2012.

The Central Government uniformly exercises its power of diplomacy, while local government organs have no external independence.

Under the unitary state structure, China handles State affairs on the principle of unified central leadership of the Central Government, with specific responsibilities assigned to different levels of local governments. It is a State system of administrative control. The State Council, as the highest administrative organ, conduct unified leadership of local administrative organs at all levels. Local people's governments administrate work within their jurisdiction, and leading subordinate departments and people's governments at the next lower level.

To adapt to this unitary state structure and the State administrative management system of unified leadership and management at different levels decided by it, China has formed a sound organizational system of audit institutions covering both central and local governments. The State Council sets up the National Audit Office of China, and people's governments at county level and above set up their own audit institutions respectively, which determines the features of unity and multilevel features of the audit system. In the audit leadership system, the CNAO is responsible for national audit work under the premier's guidance. Local audit institutions at all levels are responsible for audit work within their jurisdiction under the guidance of the executive heads of the people's government at the corresponding level and audit institutions at the next higher level. Accordingly, there is a dual leadership whereby local audit institutions at various levels are accountable to and report on their work to people's government at the same level and to audit institutions at the next higher level, with the audit work subject to leadership by audit institutions at the next higher level.

To adapt to its unitary state structure, China has established a unified but multilevel legislative system with Chinese characteristics. It has formed a socialist legal system with Chinese characteristics guided by the Constitution that features the organic unity of laws, administrative regulations, local laws and regulations, rules, and other laws and regulations at various levels.[10] Accordingly, a multilayered but inherently coordinated system of socialist audit laws with Chinese characteristics on the basis of the Constitution, with the Audit Law and Implementation Rules as the core, supplemented by local audit laws and regulations, has been established.

(2) State Economic System Determines the Duties and Responsibilities of the Auditing System

Marxism believes that "production and exchange of products developed accordingly are the foundation of all social systems."[11] The emergence of a system not

---

[10] The White Paper of the *Socialist System of Laws with Chinese Characteristics* published by State Council Information Office, October 2011.

[11] Friedrich Engels, *Socialism: Utopian and Scientific. Complete Works of Marx and Engels*, 2nd ed., Vol. 3. Beijing: People's Publishing House, June 1995, pp. 740–741.

only pertains to the laws and ethics of a social universal will, but also is a product of productivity growth at a certain stage. It is derived from the productive relations or fundamental social system, and determined by the economic foundations.[12] Economic system refers to the combination of rules, principles and policies of various basic economic relations adjusted according to the Constitution and laws, including the ownership of the means of production, interrelation of various economic sectors and their constitutional status, the basic policy of national economic development, basic policies of national economic management, and so forth.

The basic national economic system refers to various basic economic relations established by the State, with the ownership of the means of production as the core. As an important aspect of national governance, the basic national economic system, especially the status, role, and ways of the functions of government and market during resource allocation, determines the duties and functions of the government auditing system during economic and social operations.

1) The Basic Economic System with Public Ownership as the Mainstay Determines the Audit Scope and Audited Entities

The Constitution specifies that, at the primary stage of socialism, the State should adhere to a basic economic system, with the public ownership playing a dominant role and diverse forms of ownership developing side by side. It reflects the nature of socialist economic system and the requirements for development of productive forces, and functions as the basic economic system for the establishment of an auditing system of socialism with Chinese characteristics.

The public sector involves the state economy, collective economy, as well as State-owned elements or collectively owned elements in the mixed sector of the economy. Diversified public ownership covers proprietorial enterprises, shareholding cooperative system, and cooperatives joint-stock companies, which reflect the operational mode and organizational form of socialized mass production. There are provisions in regard to both quantity and the essence of the public sector. From the perspective of quantity, the dominant role of the public sector of the economy is generally evidenced by the overwhelming majority of public-owned assets in the total social assets. Judged from its essence, the dominant role of the public sector should be reflected especially in the control of the State economy over the lifelines of the national economy and the guiding role in economic development. Hence, the 18th CPC National Congress determined to consolidate and develop the public sector of the economy, allow public ownership to take diverse forms, deepen the reform of State-owned enterprises, improve the mechanisms for managing all types of State assets, and invest more

---

[12] Friedrich Engels: *A Letter to J. Bloch, An Introduction to Marxism Philosophy*. Shanghai: Shanghai People's Publishing House, 1990, p. 226.

State capital in major industries and key fields that comprise the lifeline of the economy and are vital to national security.

The basic economic system with public ownership as the mainstay determines the wide-ranging audit scope and audited entities. The *Decision of the CPC Central Committee on Some Major Issues concerning Comprehensively Promoting the Rule of Law* and the *Opinions of the State Council on Strengthening Audit Work* adopted at the Fourth Plenary Session of the 18th CPC Central Committee specified that auditing should fully cover public funds, State-owned assets and resources, and the leading officials' economic accountability. According to the requirement, audit supervision not only covers revenues and expenditures as well as other public funds at all levels of governments, State-owned financial institutions, enterprises and institutions, and State-owned assets and resources, but also involves heads of the Party, Governments at all levels, and State-owned enterprises, which are mainly classified into the following four categories. First are public funds, including all revenues and expenditures, funds under control of government departments or other units upon the commission of the government, and relevant economic activities. Second are State-owned assets, which covers domestic and foreign State-owned assets controlled, used, and operated by administrative institutions, and State-owned enterprises and those in which State capital plays a controlling or dominant role (including financial enterprises). Third are State-owned resources, including State-owned natural resources such as urban land, minerals, rivers, forests, grasslands, waters, and so on; State-owned intangible resources like franchise and pollutant discharge rights; and other resources owned by the State as specified in laws and regulations. Fourth is leading officials' performance of economic accountability covering government officials and heads of State-owned enterprises.

2) Government Functions under the Socialist Market Economy System Determine Audit Functions

Economic system refers to the specific economic organizational form and economic management system adopted according to the social economic system or productive relations. A socialist market economy first has the general characteristics of a market economy, that is, the market plays a dominant role in resources allocation. Besides, it has three distinct aspects: (1) public ownership plays a dominant role and diverse forms of ownership developing side by side; (2) distribution according to work functions as mainstay and a variety of modes of distribution coexistent; and (3) government macro control is more conscious and powerful.

Government functions are mainly divided into three categories in the socialist market economy system. The first is social management Government, as the administrator, should achieve the goal of upholding territorial integrity and State sovereignty, protecting the security and freedom of citizens, maintaining social stability and legal order, and so forth. This function mainly applies to the social activities of administrative organizations at lower levels, and groups and citizens within the administrative regions, and serves the needs of building a harmonious socialist society. Specifically, the government controls this function according to political power and implements administrative directives through the administrative mechanism. Second is economic management. Government, as the economic regulator, should achieve the economic policy objectives concerning economic growth, price stability, sufficient employment, and so forth. This function applies to the entire national economy and indirectly realizes the economic policy objectives mainly through market intermediaries (such as instruments of fiscal control and monetary policy tools). Third is the ownership function. Government, on behalf of the State, exercises the right of ownership over State-owned enterprises, to achieve an increase in value and prevent losses, and maximize owner's equity. This function is mainly exercised by the management departments of State-owned assets, and acts directly on State-owned enterprises. Through separating government administration from enterprise management, the management departments of State-owned assets ensure State-owned enterprises become players of market competition and legal entities independent and responsible for their own profits and losses. To establish and improve the socialist market economy system, it is necessary to rationalize the relationship between the government and the market, separate the three functions above, thoroughly promote the separation of government functions from enterprises, investment, social undertakings, and communities, to build a well-structured, clean, efficient, and service-oriented government that has defined functions, meets the people's expectations. The transformation of government functions that can help create a favorable environment for development, provide quality public services, and safeguard social fairness and justice shall be promoted.

Under the socialist market economy system, the transformation of government functions, and rationalization of the relationship between the government and the market have a significant impact on the audit assignments. It is mainly reflected as follows:

First, social construction and ecological progress have been boosted, in particular, audit of projects and funds for improving the people's livelihood. As government functions in social management, ecological environmental protection, and other aspects are intensified, the State gradually increases government investment in public services, social development, scientific innovation, ecological environmental protection, and so forth. As the scope and scale of fiscal expenditures expand, it is necessary to strengthen the corresponding audit. In recent years, audit institutions have gradually strengthened the special audits concerning the three issues (i.e., agriculture, rural areas, and farmers), social security, major emergencies relating to public welfare, science and technology, education, health care, cultural construction, ecological progress, environmental protection, and other aspects. Much importance has been attached to the implementation of policies and measures and the efficiency of fund use, in order to promote the continuous improvement and effective implementation of relevant policies and systems, facilitate the government's fulfillment of its social management functions, and promote scientific development and social harmony.

Second, the real-time audit of the implementation of major State policies and measures has become an important task. Audit institutions not only conduct audit supervision on the authenticity, legality, and benefit of fiscal and financial revenues and expenditures of the audited units, but also continuously organize the real-time audit of the deployment and implementation of key national policies and measures as well as macro-regulation deployments. They should strengthen the supervision and inspection of specific deployments, progress in execution and actual results, and other aspects involving all regions and all departments in implementing polices and measures. In particular, priority should be given to the implementation of major projects, major funds, and administrative streamlining and decentralization, so as to promptly discover and rectify behaviors such as disobeying orders and defying prohibition, timely reflect new circumstances and new issues during the execution of policies, and promote the implementation and improvement of policies and measures and develop countermeasures.

Third, audit institutions need to audit foreign loans and grants, foreign aid, overseas investments, and institutions stationed abroad. The trend of economic globalization and openness of the socialist market system determine that foreign-related audits should become as one of the important responsibilities of government auditing. Audit institutions should promote the positive, rational, and effective utilization of foreign funds through audit supervision on the projects involving foreign loans and grants, and strengthen the audit of overseas investments and institutions stationed abroad, so as to maintain the security of overseas State-owned assets, promote the gradual development of large transnational corporations and financial institutions, and improve the level of internationalized operation. By strengthening the auditing of China's foreign aid, the effective use and management of funds shall be enhanced.

Fourth, audit institutions are obligated to conduct audits of the assets, liabilities, profits and losses of State-owned enterprises, and State-owned financial institutions' officials' accountability audit during their terms of office, which are the main forms for audit institutions to serve the government and exercise the owner's function as part of government departments. The aim is to maintain the security of State-owned assets and achieve increases in value and prevent losses, to make leading officials comply with laws, disciplines, and regulations and fulfill responsibilities, and to promote the implementation of guidelines, policies, laws, and regulations, as well as the comprehensive, systematic, and strategic transformation of the State economy and its rational progress.

Fifth, audit institutions should always adhere to the principle of "grasping two key links at the same time." On the one hand, audit institutions should detect major violations of laws and regulations, significant losses and waste, significant potential risks, and poor performance of duties; on the other hand, they should promote the deepening of reform and the rule of law, and improve performance. They should reveal and investigate the striking problems and evidence of major violations of laws and rules during the execution of major decision making and deployment; maintain financial and economic discipline and promote the construction of a clean government; report outstanding conflicts and risks during economic operations and uphold the security of the national economy; and lay stress on analyzing causes and making suggestions at the levels of institution, mechanism, and system and promote the deepening of the reform and systemic innovation.

Along with the transformation of government functions, the establishment of a standard capital market, and improvement of corporate governance structure in State-owned enterprises, the relationship between government auditing and auditing by accounting firms, and between government auditing and internal auditing, should be more adaptable to the internal requirements of the socialist market economy. The provisions of existing audit laws and systems show that the relationship is mainly reflected in two aspects: (1) government audit institutions guide and supervise the internal audit work of entities being supervised in accordance with laws; and (2) audit institutions verify the audit reports issued by private audit firms when carrying out audit or special audit investigations, and transfer the violations of the laws and regulations or of practicing standards discovered through verification to the competent authorities for investigation. Meanwhile, audit institutions can also utilize the outcomes of internal audit and purchase private audit services.

3. CULTURAL FOUNDATION OF THE AUDITING SYSTEM OF SOCIALISM WITH CHINESE CHARACTERISTICS

Culture is the lifeblood of a nation and the spiritual foundation of its people. From the perspective of the relationship between cultures and systems, culture is the deepest factor affecting the institutional arrangements of a society. Although it doesn't have such an immediate impact like a legal, political, and economic system, it imposes a long-term and far-reaching influence on them through the power of morality and justice in imperceptible ways. Meanwhile, it also creates the atmosphere and condition for the practical execution of systems. Only when rooted in the historic traditions and cultural reality of a state can an institutional arrangement have strong vitality. In the context of historical and cultural differences, the auditing system varies from one country to another, representing their respective characteristics. The essence of China's excellent traditional culture and socialist core values jointly create the cultural foundations of the auditing system of socialism with Chinese characteristics.

(1) Excellent Chinese Traditional Culture Constitutes the Cultural Source of the Auditing System of Socialism with Chinese Characteristics

Generally speaking, culture refers to the summation of material and ideological wealth created in the process of social practice. In a narrow sense, it specifically refers to ideological wealth, which means the ideology, concepts, behavior, customs, and habits formed in a certain period within a specified group (a nation, a company, or a family) and all extension activities generated by the overall awareness of this group. Culture reflects the faith, value orientation, civilized norms, thinking mode, and lifestyle peculiar to a nation.

Chinese culture has a long history, with extensive and rich connotation. Chinese culture is a combination of morality in national history as well as various cultural thoughts and spiritual ideologies, and also the outcome of evolution and the development of Chinese civilization. Deeply rooted in China, it contains the cultural essence of all Chinese ethnic groups with vivid Chinese characteristics. As the accumulation of the deepest spiritual pursuit of the Chinese nation, Chinese traditional culture not only contains the fundamental spiritual gene but also represents the unique spiritual identification of the Chinese nation, with the values of the times—stressing kindheartedness, paying special attention to the welfare of all, being honest and keeping one's word, upholding justice, advocating concord, and pursuing great harmony.

It contains the values of "benevolence, righteousness, ceremony, wisdom, and integrity" and in-depth spiritual pursuit of striving constantly for self-improvement. It is the major bedrock of building the common spiritual home of the Chinese nation and also the profound foundation of developing socialism with Chinese characteristics. The specific contents are as follows: The broad view of national reunification and all nations living together peacefully; the social ideal of great harmony in which all are equal, talent and virtue are treasured; good neighborly relations established by being true to one's word; in governance, a stress on morality being the main guide and punishment only as a supplement; a moral outlook of benevolence and consideration of others; an educational philosophy of self-cultivation, self-discipline, and virtuous influence; a stress on social ethics, righteousness, and harmony; harmony between humankind and nature; and so forth.

Traditional Chinese culture is the spiritual heritage accumulated by the Chinese nation through long-term social practice, and also the spiritual reflection of a thinking mode peculiar to the Chinese nation. It runs through every aspect of the values, thinking, social customs and habits, morality, and politeness of Chinese people. The excellent Chinese traditional culture and its spirit have a profound effect on the concept, tenet, and objective of the auditing system and value pursuit of auditors. The auditing system of socialism with Chinese characteristics was established and developed on this basis and this is the reason why it fits more into China's conditions and better embodies the values of the Chinese nation and its longer vitality.

First, government auditing naturally gives top priority to safeguarding national security and the fundamental interests of the masses, which exactly embodies the spiritual pursuit of patriotism and people orientation in traditional culture, and highlights the "people-oriented" core values of traditional Chinese culture. As the old saying goes, the political aspiration that "I wish to be the first to worry about the nation's woes and the last to share in its prosperity," the patriotic feeling of "whatever my status is, I will never lay aside my concern for the nation" and " I will do whatever is needed to serve my country even at the cost of my own life, regardless of fortune or misfortune to myself," awe-inspiring righteousness of "never corrupted by wealth or status, depart from principle due to poverty or humble position, or bow down to power or force," the devotional spirit of "everyone will one day die; when my day comes, may my loyalty be inscribed in the pages of history" and "I will work heart and soul for my country to the day I draw my last breath," and so forth. All of these vividly embody the spirit of patriotism. Government auditing involves performing the supervisory responsibilities entrusted by the Constitution and relevant laws. The primary objective is to maintain the people's fundamental interests and national security. Specifically, starting from the most direct and most practical issues of interests most concerned by the people, audit institutions should strengthen the audit and audit investigation on special funds that relate to economic and social development and involve the immediate interests of people, so as to ensure that all funds are utilized in a reasonable and effective manner; efforts should be made to further safeguard and improve people's livelihood and enhance national governance. This fully embodies the spirit of patriotism and human care spirit central to traditional Chinese culture.

Second, the cultural thought of honest government and the pursuit of values in the history of China have a significant effect on the current auditing system that lays stress on combating corruption and building clean government. The ancient culture of honest government and effective systems and methods of punishment for corrupt officials attached great importance to improvement of the auditing system. For example, such "fair" images as Di Renjie (630–700), Bao Zheng (999–1062), and Hai Rui (1514–1587), who pleaded on behalf of the people, handled matters impartially with uprightness, removed bullies, and protected the law-abiding, are important cultural forces to encourage auditors to positively devote themselves to fighting against corruption. The time-honored traditional culture of combating corruption and building clean government has provided valuable resources and references for government auditing to strengthen its supervision and restriction on the exercise of power. Affected by such historic anticorruption culture, with the attitude of being highly responsible to both history and the laws, brave in shouldering responsibility and selfless and fearless, audit institutions at various levels adhere to investigating and revealing problems like abuse of power for personal gain, dereliction of duty, bribery and corruption, and insider trading, analyzing the features and rules of corruption, and striving to promote the establishment and improvement of anticorruption mechanisms in which officials are unable to and dare not engage in corrupt practices.

Third, the fine moral traditions of Chinese traditional cultures have produced positive influences on the ideology of auditors. Confucian culture is the most influential, most basic, and most fundamental part of tradition. The core is "the Four Principles and Eight Virtues," namely, "propriety, justice, honesty, and honor" and "loyalty, filial piety, benevolence, love, integrity, righteousness, harmony, and peace." If a State does not establish the "Four Principles," it will eventually perish; if a State does not follow the "Eight Virtues," public morals will decline. Traditional Chinese culture highlighted "righteousness" and "justice" rather than "benefit" and "desire," advocating justice, honesty, benevolence, loyalty, practice, tolerance, unbiasedness, steadfastness, and avoidance of evil, which constitute the basic features of the Chinese national spirit with patriotism at the core. In regard to self-cultivation, Chinese traditional culture fully emphasized self-restraint, introspection, and discipline; advocated integrity; and praised moral courage. The standard of self-restraint, internal examination, and self-discipline is the code of ethics of propriety, justice, honesty, and honor.

Terminology 4: Self-Restraint, Internal Examination, and Self-Discipline

The *Zhongyong* (*Doctrine of the Mean*) provides this comment on self-restraint: "On this account, the superior man does not wait until he sees things, to be cautious, nor till he hears things, to be apprehensive. There is nothing more visible than what is secret, and nothing more manifest than what is minute. Therefore, the superior man is watchful over himself, when he is alone."

Confucius says, "When internal examination discovers nothing wrong, what is there to be anxious about, what is there to fear?"

With regard to self-discipline, Confucius says, "When a ruler's personal conduct is correct, he will be obeyed without having to issue orders. If his personal conduct is not correct, he may issue orders, but they will not be followed."

While inheriting the fine moral traditions of Chinese traditional culture, audit institutions have summarized and abstracted the core values of auditors—"responsibility, loyalty, integrity, legality, independence, and devotion"—in combination with the essential features of the audit profession. In audit professional education and training, audit institutions always maintain that improvement of the moral integrity of auditors is a very important compulsory course. Auditors also continue to improve their self-cultivation in audit practice and seek continuous advancement in terms of the cultivation of morality and personality. In particular, auditors take the initiative to identify the prominent issues, analyze the ideological roots, and specify the corrective measures during the educational practice of the Party's mass line and the "Three Stricts and Three Honests" special education. China's cultural traditions stress introspection, self-discipline, and self-restraint. That is to say, "When we see men of worth, we should think of equaling them; when we see men of a contrary character, we should turn inwards and examine ourselves," and "I daily examine myself on three points," so as to discover any violation of general rules and ethics and correct it promptly.

(2) Socialist Core Value System Determines the Value Orientation of the Auditing System of Socialism with Chinese Characteristics

The core of culture lies in the values it reflects. The socialist core value system consists of Marxist thought, socialist common ideals with Chinese characteristics, national spirit centered on patriotism, the spirit of the times centered on reform and innovation, the socialist concept of honor and disgrace, and other important contents. Adherence to promoting the socialist core value system consolidates the common ideological foundation of the whole Party and people to unite and struggle and also determines the development orientation of socialism with Chinese characteristics.[13] Four specific contents of the socialist core value system affect each other and form a whole to jointly determine the value orientation of the auditing system of socialism with Chinese characteristics.

First, Marxist thought determines that the auditing system of socialism with Chinese characteristics must be established and improved in line with China's actuality. Marxism profoundly reveals the law of human social development. It embodies the value concept of "the masses are the creator of history" and serves as the scientific theory of guiding people to promote social progress and create a better life. To uphold the guiding position of Marxism, Party members and cadres should thoroughly learn the Marxist classics, and systematically grasp the position, viewpoint, and methodology of Marxism; unswervingly adhere to the basic principles of Marxism and closely integrate them into Chinese practice, historical characteristics, and aspirations of people, and guide new practice by further developing Marxism. In modern China, Marxist guiding thought is the guiding principle of establishment and improvement of the national governance system. Adherence to Marxist thought determines that the auditing system of socialism with Chinese characteristics must proceed on the basis of Chinese practice, historical characteristics and people's aspirations, and the objective of serving people wholeheartedly, serve the policy of reform and opening up, and improve the national governance system and governance capacity.

Second, socialist common ideals with Chinese characteristics have unified ideological recognition for the development of audit cause. As the fundamental system reflecting China's progress in modern times, socialism with Chinese characteristics epitomizes the fundamental interests and common aspirations of the overwhelming majority of people. To uphold the common ideal of socialism with Chinese characteristics, we should profoundly understand

---

[13] On October 18, 2011, the *Decision of the CPC Central Committee on Major Issues Pertaining to Deepening Reform of the Cultural System and Promoting the Great Development and Flourishing of Socialist Culture* was adopted at the Sixth Plenary Session of the 17th CPC Central Committee.

the historical inevitability and superiority of the CPC's leadership and China's socialist system, and that the path of socialism with Chinese characteristics is not only crucial to the realization of socialist modernization and the rejuvenation of China, but also the only way leading to a better life for the people. In this context, we should integrate our personal ideals into the common ideal, and rally people under the great banner of socialism with Chinese characteristics. Where there is no common ideal, there is no joint action. The development course and achievements of China's audit cause over the past 30 years are the outcome of audits for generations through positive exploration and joint struggles. It demonstrates that audit offices at all levels, as well as individual auditors, regard adherence to and development of the audit cause of socialism with Chinese characteristics as their common ideal and conviction as well as value orientation. Since the establishment, audit institutions have held high the great banner of socialism with Chinese characteristics, followed the path of socialism with Chinese characteristics more unswervingly, and contributed to adherence to and development of socialism with Chinese characteristics, always emphasizing that audit cause is an integral part of it. A common ideal guides audit offices at all levels, as well as individual auditors, to continuously promote the audit cause by their wisdom and efforts.

Third, national spirit and the spirit of the times provide the inexhaustible drive for the development of the audit cause. The national spirit centered on patriotism and the spirit of the times centered on reform and innovation are important contents of the socialist core value system. Patriotism is the most profound ideological tradition under which the Chinese people have struggled in a united way; reform and innovation are the most distinctive historical characteristics of contemporary China, which can best encourage the Chinese people to forge ahead. Accordingly, we should vigorously carry forward patriotism, collectivism and socialism, enhance the spirit of China's national dignity self-confidence and sense of pride, and encourage people to turn patriotic enthusiasm into actual action for the rejuvenation of the Chinese nation, taking the construction and defense of the socialist motherland as the greatest honor, and regarding damage to the national interest and national honor as the greatest shame. We should vigorously carry forward the spirit of the times centered on reform and innovation, inspire people to always maintain the spirit of keeping up with progress and forging ahead in a pioneering spirit, continuously emancipate the mind, never become conceited and never slacken the effort, and promote the sustained development of audit cause. The national spirit centered on patriotism and the spirit of the times centered on reform and innovation are the strongest motivations for promoting the audit cause of socialism with Chinese characteristics. Over the past 30 years or so, the fusion of the two elements has created a strong sense of responsibility and a historic mission for auditors. In this view, audit offices at all levels as well as individual auditors' fear of difficulties maintain their loyalty to the Party, people, and audit cause; convert patriotic enthusiasm into good audit practice; and always hold an enterprising spirit to promote the continuous development of audit cause.

Fourth, the socialist concept of honor and disgrace has affected the ideological concept of audit institutions and individual auditors. Socialist society refers to a society with coordinated development in material, political, spiritual, and ecological civilization. The socialist concept of honor and disgrace embodies the fundamental requirements of socialist morality and provides a basic moral rule and value standard for building a harmonious socialist society. This is mainly represented by the "eight honors and eight shames" outlook adapted to the socialist market economy, in line with socialist legal standards, the traditional virtue of the Chinese nation, and the developing trend of human civilization. It has solved basic morality issues about what should be done and what should not be done, and identified the value orientation and code of conduct of contemporary Chinese society. The socialist concept of honor and disgrace has a profound effect on the ideological concept of auditors and all work of audit institutions. From an ideological perspective, we should strictly enforce basic professional ethics, that is, rule of law, being law-abiding, upright, frank, objective, impartial, and diligent and keeping secrets, and "responsibility, loyalty, integrity, legality, independence, devotion," the core values of auditors, which are the reflection and embodiment of the socialist concept of honor and disgrace in auditing. Audit offices at all levels as well as individual auditors not only set an example in this regard but also become the major force to maintain the concepts by rigorous and detailed audit work, investigating falsehood and deception, loss and wastage, abuse of power, violations of laws and regulations, and other such unacceptable behavior.

(3) The Socialist Core Value Is the Ideological Force Propelling the Development of the Auditing of Socialism with Chinese Characteristics

Socialist core values are the soul of modern Chinese culture and the concentrated expression of the socialist core values system, reflecting its fundamental nature and basic characteristics, rich connotations, and practical requirements. The 18th CPC National Congress advocated "prosperity," "democracy," "civility," "harmony," "freedom," "equality," "justice," "rule of law," "patriotism," "dedication," "integrity," and "friendship" as the ultimate goals of socialist practice. "Prosperity," "democracy," "civility," and "harmony" are values at the national level; "freedom," "equality," "justice," and "rule of law" are social values; "patriotism," "dedication," "integrity," and "friendship" are values to be embraced by the individual. Together, they form the basic contents of socialist core values. In December 2013, the General Office of the CPC Central Committee distributed the *Opinions on Cultivating and Practicing the Core Values of Socialism*, setting out the requirements for the development of socialism with Chinese characteristics, inheriting the excellent Chinese traditional cultures and the outstanding achievements of human civilization, and reflecting the common value of the whole Party and society.

To promote the modernization of the national governance system and governance capacity, it is important to foster and carry forward the socialist core values, and to effectively integrate social consciousness. To comprehensively deepen the reforms in an all-round way, improve the socialist system with Chinese characteristics, and promote the modernization of the national governance system and governance capacity, we must first solve issues concerning the values. Only by accelerating the construction of a value system fully reflecting Chinese characteristics, national and historical characteristics, energetically fostering and carrying forward the socialist core values across the whole society, improving and integrating the ideological cultures and values of the whole society can we better improve the socialist system with Chinese characteristics and follow the path of socialism with Chinese characteristics unswervingly. It is an imperceptible process to foster and practice the socialist core values, whereas we must strive to foster and practice the socialist core values at every level and in all fields, and facilitate the socialist core values to continuously transform into social mass consciousness and people's conscious actions.

Socialist core values deeply influence and run through every aspect of the theory, system and practice of auditing. It unites the powerful force of promoting modernization of national governance, ensures the right direction for the auditing system of socialism with Chinese characteristics, and specifies the orientation and objective of auditing in exerting its role of guarantee and supervision. The auditing system is an important part of national governance, and its core value is to bring into play the "immune system" function in promoting and improving the sound operation of economic society and facilitating modernization of national governance and governing capacity. The basic contents of socialist core values, that is, democracy, rule of law, patriotism, and integrity, impose an immediate and significant influence on the core values of the auditing system, and promote the formation of audit concepts and values, that is, legality, performance, responsibility, honesty, and

Terminology 5: Socialist Core Values

"Prosperity, democracy, civility, and harmony" are the objectives of building a socialist modernized country and also an expression of the basic concept of socialist core values objectives. It stands at the supreme level and plays a leading role in the value concepts at other levels. *Prosperity* refers to a status of modern socialist country, under which the nation prospers and people are strong and powerful. It is the beautiful wish of the Chinese nation and also the material base of national prosperity and people's well-being. *Democracy* represents the best aspect of human society. The type of democracy we pursue is people's democracy whose nature and core are to ensure people remain as the masters of the country. It is the core of socialism and also a political guarantee of creating a better and happier life for people. *Civility* is a vital sign of social progress and also an important feature of a modern socialist country. It is a desirable state for the cultural construction of a modern socialist country, a summarization of national, scientific, and mass socialist cultures oriented toward modernization, the world, and the future, and also an important support for realizing China's rejuvenation. *Harmony*, the basic concept of Chinese traditional cultures, serves as a typical presentation of the living situation in which all people enjoy their right to education, employment, health care, aged care, and housing. It is the value appeal of a modern socialist country in social construction and also a vital guarantee for the harmonious, stable, sustained, and sound development of economic society.

"Freedom, equality, justice, and rule of law," the vivid presentation of wonderful society, embody the basic concepts of socialist core values at the social level. It reflects the essential attribute of socialism with Chinese characteristics and also the unswerving core value concept that has long been upheld by the Party. *Freedom*, specifically freedom in terms of personal will, existence, and development, represents the most beautiful expectation of human society and also a key social value pursued by Marxism. *Equality* means all citizens are equal before the law. Its value orientation is to achieve substantive equality continuously. It requires that human rights should be respected and guaranteed, and all members of a society should have the right to equal participation and development. *Justice*, namely, social equality and justice, is the fundamental value concept of a state and its society on the premise that human emancipation and the right of equality and freedom are enjoyed by all members of society. *Rule of law* is the basic mode of State governance. Building a socialist country under the rule of law is the basic requirement of socialist democracy with Chinese characteristics. It upholds and safeguards the fundamental interests of citizens through construction of a legislative system, becoming an institutional guarantee in realizing freedom, equality, fairness, and justice.

"Patriotism, dedication, integrity, and friendship," as the basic code of ethics for citizens, represent the basic concept of socialist core values from the perspective of personal behavior. Covering every sector of social moral life, it is the basic code of ethics citizens must abide by, and also the basic standard for appraising the moral behavior of citizens. *Patriotism* means the deep emotion of personal dependence on one's motherland, and also serves as the standard of conduct to regulate relations between individuals and their motherland. Closely related to socialism, it requires people to identify themselves with China's rejuvenation, promote national reunification, safeguard national unity and conscientiously serve the motherland. *Dedication* means a value evaluation on the code of professional conduct that requires citizens to be devoted to their duties, work unselfishly for the public interest, and serve society, fully reflecting the socialist professional spirit. *Integrity*, namely, honesty and trustworthiness, means the moral tradition of human society inherited over many centuries, and is also the major content of socialist morality construction. It emphasizes doing work faithfully, keeping promises and being honest with others. *Friendship* stresses that citizens should respect, care, and help each other and strive to form a new socialist interpersonal relationship.

Sources: China Steering Committee of Compiling and Reviewing Cadre Training Materials, *Construction of Socialist Harmonious Society.* Beijing: People's Publishing House and Party Building Books Publishing House, 2015, pp.165–166; Theoretical System of Socialism with Chinese Characteristics Research Center of the Ministry of Education, "Deeply Understanding the Connotation and Significance of Socialist Core Values." *People's Daily,* May 22, 2013.

openness. For example, the auditing system of socialism with Chinese characteristics was established when the rule of law was restored, and improved continuously during the process of strengthening legal construction; audit institutions at all levels continue to consolidate the concept of efficiency, positively carry out the performance audit, promoting and enhancing the performance of government and public resources; the concept of responsibility directly promotes the establishment and improvement of the accountability audit system, whereas the accountability audit is an important statutory duty of audit institutions. Since one of important objectives of auditing is to promote clean government, the concept of integrity enables audit institutions to be the major force tackling corruption. Influenced by the concept of openness, audit institutions publish important audit findings for the general public on a regular basis to make public the major violations and cases of corruption.

(4) Core Values of Auditors Are the Dynamic Force for the Improvement of the Auditing System of Socialism with Chinese Characteristics

Core values of auditors are the specific embodiment of Chinese traditional culture and socialist core values related to auditing. audit institutions always uphold and practice the socialist core values during team building and the entire process of auditing, whereas they have summarized and abstracted the core values of auditors—responsibility, loyalty, integrity, legality, independence, and devotion in combination with the main features of the audit profession.[14] Core values of auditors contain the essence of Chinese traditional culture and reflect the requirements of the fine moral traditions long inherent in such culture: "responsibility" stems from "filial piety" and "love"; "loyalty" stems from "loyalty" and "integrity"; "integrity" stems from "integrity" and "honor"; "legality" stems from "propriety"; "independence" stems from "righteousness"; and "dedication" stems from "due diligence." Traditional Confucian culture advocates "correct mind, self-cultivation, family management, national governance, and universal peace in succession," whereas the core values of auditors are to uphold their profession and shoulder responsibilities.

Influenced by Chinese traditional culture and guided by socialist core values, government auditing has further formed its value orientation, ethics, and professional habits around the objectives and missions. Audit institutions and individual auditors vigorously promote and positively practice the core values of auditors, carry forward audit spirit, adhere to the principle of respecting laws, seeking truth, making suggestions, and being selfless, fearless, responsible, and cautious, and innovating boldly, strictly getting rid of "Yong Lan San" (mediocrity, laziness, and desultory behavior) and "Jiao Jiao Mu" (delicacy, pretension, and the lack of energy),[15] and boosting the spirit. Audit institutions and individual auditors should engage in audit activities in an objective and realistic manner, instead of handling affairs according to their preference or prejudice, or the opinions of others. They must retain an objective and impartial attitude, never yielding to external

---

[14] In December 2008, the National Audit Work Conference proposed "audit culture philosophy education centering on "responsibility, loyalty, integrity, legality, independence, devotion'"; in July 2009, the State Audit Work Forum proposed to "strive to create the audit culture of 'responsibility, loyalty, integrity, legality, independence, devotion'"; in 2011, the National Audit Work Conference proposed "audit core values of 'responsibility, loyalty, integrity, legality, independence, devotion.'" Through years of debate and practice, the core values of auditors has been widely recognized by the vast number of auditors and all walks of life, becoming the core and soul of audit culture.

[15] "Yong Lan San" and "Jiao Jiao Mu": in English, *Yong* refers to mediocrity and inaction; "*Lan* refers to laziness without diligence; *San* refers to no restriction and desultoriness; *Jiao* (the first one) refers to delicacy and weak will; *Jiao* (the second one) refers to pretension and arrogance; and *Mu* refers to lack of energy and gloom.

Terminology 6: Modern Core Values for Auditors

Responsibility means, with the spirit and attitude of being highly responsible to the State and its people, history, and law, effectively performing the duties specified by the Constitution and relevant laws, devoting oneself to the audit cause, finishing tasks in accordance with orders and requirements, giving full play to the functions of auditing as an "immune system," acting as the guardian of public finances, earnestly safeguarding public interests and national security, promoting national governance, guaranteeing a sound operation of economy and society, and being accountable for any errors during auditing.

Loyalty means adhering to steadfast allegiance to the Party, the State, and its people, laws, and causes, firmly fostering the awareness of Party members, civil servants, and auditors, and always upholding truth and justice.

Integrity means adhering to vigilance, self-reflection, and self-discipline, strictly regulating thinking and behavior, seeking no personal gain, and working and living honestly.

Legality means advocating and respecting laws, consciously regulating one's words and deeds, auditing in accordance with legal provisions and requirements, and defending the dignity of the law by legal means within the legal mandate.

Independence means adhering to principles and being selfless and daring, standing up to the influence and disturbance of extraneous factors, and working impartially and objectively. Auditors must not participate in any activity prejudicial to audit independence and the management activity of an audited unit.

Dedication means working diligently and scrupulously without complaint or regret, and devoting oneself to development of the audit cause.

pressures. They must adopt standard and scientific audit technologies and methods, comply with the laws, regulations, policies, and provisions as well as industrial standards or conventions, obtain conclusions based on clear evidence, including proven facts and data, in order to establish the professional image of all auditors as being reasonable, evidence-oriented, fair, and objective; and they must work in a precise, meticulous manner, and conscientiously meet the work style requirements of being realistic and pragmatic, seeking high standards, developing and innovating unceasingly, auditing under strict management, and always being rigorous and cautious. The above value orientation, ethics, and professional habits not only demonstrate the profound connotations of Chinese traditional culture, but also retain the particularity of core socialist value system.

To sum up, the auditing system of socialism with Chinese characteristics has been established and improved on the basis of solid theoretical foundation, powerful system foundation, and profound cultural foundation. The system of theories of socialism with Chinese characteristics offers an ideological foundation and theoretical support for the formation and development of the auditing system of socialism with Chinese characteristics. The political and economic system of socialism with Chinese characteristics determines the institutional framework, basic functional localization, and active mechanism of the auditing system. Socialist core values and excellent Chinese traditional cultures inherited for thousands of years have determined the value orientation of auditing system development. In order to improve the auditing system of socialism with Chinese characteristics in the new historical period, we must adhere to the guidance of theories of socialism with Chinese characteristics, with the political and economic systems of socialism with Chinese characteristics as the base, and Chinese culture and socialist core values as the ideological support. Only in this way can we ensure that the auditing system of socialism with Chinese characteristics complies with China's national conditions and maintain its powerful vitality, so as to provide a guarantee for fully exerting the role of auditing in national governance.

CHAPTER THREE

Basic Framework of the Auditing System of Socialism with Chinese Characteristics

W ITH ABUNDANT CONTENT, THE AUDITING SYSTEM of socialism with Chinese characteristics consists of specific systems that interact and are interrelated. Its basic framework covers audit laws and regulations, audit organization system, audit duties and powers, auditor management system, and operational mechanism.

1. AUDIT LAW AND REGULATIONS

Audit laws and regulations provide the foundation and important support for the establishment and improvement of the auditing system of socialism with Chinese characteristics. They not only maintain the independence of government auditing, validity of audit results, and the authority and solemnity of auditing, but also provide reference and standards for the overall auditing work. Only with sound laws and regulations can we establish an independent auditing system and guarantee its smooth work. We can hardly exercise audit supervisory power independently without the support of a sound legal system of laws and regulations.

The legal system of auditing of socialism with Chinese characteristics covers: the Constitution, Audit Law and other relevant laws, Regulations Rules for the Implementation of the Audit Law and other relevant administrative regulations, local audit regulations, audit rules, and so forth, reflecting both the intrinsic logic of the legal system and the basic requirements for legality of auditing powers and auditing according to law.

(1) The Constitution of the People's Republic of China

The Constitution fundamentally guarantees lasting stability and security, unity of all ethnic groups within the country, economic development and social progress, thus serving as the overriding charter for governance.[1] It defines the fundamental system of the State and the regime, the basic political and economic organization, citizens' basic rights and obligations, and so forth.[2] The Constitution has supreme legal authority in the socialist system of laws with Chinese characteristics. All laws, administrative regulations, and local regulations must be formulated in accordance with its basic principles and requirements without conflict.

In the 1982 version, the People's Republic of China (PRC) Constitution specified China's implementation of an auditing system, laying the foundation for long-term development of the socialist audit cause with Chinese characteristics. First, it defined the system to be adopted, specifying that the State Council and local people's governments at and above county level should set up audit institutions with the China National Audit Office (CNAO) responsible for national audit work under the direction of the Premier of the State Council. Local audit institutions at all levels were to be under the dual leadership by the executive heads of people's governments at the corresponding levels and audit institutions at the next higher level. This provision shows that audit institutions are constitutional institutions and the auditing system is an integral part of the national political system. Second, the Constitution specifies the basic principles of China's supervision through auditing. Audit institutions are required to persevere in the principles of independently exercising their power of supervision through auditing in accordance with the law, subject to no interference by any other administrative organs, or any public organization or individuals. Third, it specifies the basic duties and mandates of the audit institutions. Audit institutions supervise through auditing the

---

[1] Information Office of the State Council, the White Paper on *Socialist System of Laws with Chinese Characteristics*, October 2011.
[2] Xu Chongde, *Constitution.* Beijing: People's University of China Press, 1999, p. 10.

revenues and expenditures of all departments at the corresponding level and of people's governments at lower levels, and the revenues and expenditures of all financial and monetary organizations, enterprises, and institutions of the State. Fourth, it determines the legal status of the auditor-general and the matters concerning appointment and removal. The Auditor General is a member of the State Council. The President of the People's Republic of China appoints and removes the Auditor General in pursuance of the decisions of the National People's Congress and its Standing Committee, upon the nomination by the Premier. The Auditor General is held accountable for the work of the CNAO. The Constitution stipulates the auditing system and thus ensures the constitutional status of the auditing system of socialism with Chinese characteristics.

Background Information 1: The Clauses of the *Constitution of the People's Republic of China* on Supervision through Auditing

Article 62 The National People's Congress exercises the following functions and powers:

....

(5) to decide on the choice of the Premier of the State Council upon nomination by the President of the People's Republic of China, and on the choice of the Vice-Premiers, State Councilors, Ministers in charge of ministries or commissions, the Auditor-General and the Secretary-General of the State Council upon nomination by the Premier;

....

Article 63 The National People's Congress has the power to remove from office the following persons:

....

(2) Premier, Vice-Premiers, State Councilors, Ministers in charge of ministries or commissions, the Auditor-General and the Secretary-General of the State Council;

....

Article 67 The Standing Committee of the National People's Congress exercises the following functions and powers:

....

To decide on the choice of Ministers in charge of ministries or commissions, the Auditor-General or the Secretary-General of the State Council upon nomination by the Premier of the State Council when the National People's Congress is not in session;

(continued)

....

Article 80 The President of the People's Republic of China, in pursuance of the decisions of the National People's Congress and its Standing Committee, promulgates statutes, appoints or removes the Premier, Vice-Premiers, State Councilors, Ministers in charge of ministries or commissions, the Auditor-General and the Secretary-General of the State Council; confers State medals and titles of honor; issues orders of special pardons; proclaims entry of the emergency state; and announces a state of war; and releases mobilization orders.

Article 86 The State Council is composed of the following personnel: Premier; Vice-Premiers; State Councilors; Ministers in charge of ministries; Ministers in charge of commissions; the Auditor-General; and the Secretary-General.

The Premier assumes overall responsibility for the work of the State Council. The ministers assume overall responsibility for the work of the ministries and commissions.

The organization of the State Council is prescribed by law.

....

Article 91 The State Council establishes an auditing body to supervise the revenues and expenditures of all departments under the State Council and of the local governments at all levels, and the revenues and expenditures of all financial and monetary organizations, enterprises and institutions of the State.

Under the direction of the Premier of the State Council and in accordance with the provisions of law, the auditing body independently exercises its power of supervision through auditing, without interference by any other administrative organ or any public organization or individual.

....

Article 109 Auditing bodies are established by local people's governments at and above county level. Local auditing bodies at all levels, independently, and in accordance with provisions of law, exercise their power of supervision through auditing and are responsible to the people's government at the corresponding level and to the auditing body at the next higher level.

(2) The Audit Law and Other Relevant Laws

Laws constitute the main part of the socialist legal system with Chinese characteristics and the foundation for the rule of law, and are used to deal with matters of fundamental and overall importance to national development and those affecting the country's stability and long-term development. No administrative or local regulations and rules can contravene the Constitution.[3] The laws on

---

[3] Information Office of the State Council, the White Paper on *Socialist System of Laws with Chinese Characteristics*, October 2011.

auditing formulated by the National People's Congress and its Standing Committee in accordance with the Constitution are the normative documents on supervision through auditing applicable nationwide with general binding force. The Audit Law and other laws relating to audit stipulate the basic contents of the auditing system of socialism with Chinese characteristics.

Formulated by the Standing Committee of the National People's Congress in accordance with the Constitution, the Audit Law is a special one regulating the auditing system and serves as the fundamental law on auditing. The Audit Law, as the law to implement the provisions of the Constitution, embodies provisions on supervision through auditing and stipulates the basic contents of the auditing system, that is, basic principles of supervision through auditing, audit institutions and auditors, audit institutions' duties and responsibilities, audit institutions' mandate, audit procedures, legal liabilities, and so forth, in a relatively comprehensive manner. The Audit Law is not only an organic law for audit institutions but also a procedural law on audit work, with large content concerning the substantive laws. The *Audit Law of the People's Republic of China* promulgated in 1994 involved two breakthroughs: first, it changed the phenomenon that China's audit institutions could not supervise the finances of the same level, and transformed the single mode of "lower-level audited by higher-level" for public finance audit to the combined mode of "same-level audit" and "lower-level audited by higher-level," greatly strengthening the authority of supervision through auditing; second, it expressly stipulates the system under which audit institutions should submit reports of audit result to the corresponding government and audit work reports to the NPC Standing Committee at the corresponding level entrusted by the government commission. Accordingly, supervision through auditing, as a channel for governments to strengthen budget control and for the NPC to improve its budget supervision, is more effective, and the legal status of audit institutions has been improved fundamentally. Summarizing practical experience and adopting international practice, the *Audit Law of the People's Republic of China* newly revised in 2006 further improves the mechanism and responsibilities for supervision through auditing, enriches the modes of supervision through auditing and standardizes the behavior of supervision through auditing.[4]

Other laws also stipulate the audit work accordingly, and they also relate to the audit laws and regulations of socialism with Chinese characteristics. There are two such categories: One covers laws on finance and economics, that is, the *Accounting Law of the PRC*, the *Law of the PRC on the Administration of Tax Collection*, the *Budget Law of the PRC*, the *Law of the PRC on Commercial Banks*, the *Securities Law of the PRC*, the *Government Procurement Law of the PRC*, the *Law of the PRC on*

---

[4] Refer to the relevant contents of Chapter I hereof for details about promulgation and revision of the Audit Law.

the Management of State-Owned Assets of Enterprises, the *Social Insurance Law of the PRC*, and so forth. These laws expressly stipulate the supervision of audit institutions in relevant fields, and also serve as an important basis for audit institutions to conduct audit evaluation, determine the nature of audit findings and mete out disposal and penalties for the violations by those audited bodies. The other category involves laws regulating the activities of government administrative organs, such as the *Law of the PRC on Administrative Penalty*, the *Administrative Reconsideration Law of the PRC*, the *Administrative Procedure Law of the PRC*, the *State Compensation Law of the PRC*, and so forth. China's audit institutions are government administrative organs and their supervision through auditing activities involve administrative behavior, hence they must strictly abide by the provisions of these laws that constitute the major part of audit laws and regulations.

(3) Regulations for the Implementation of the Audit Law and Other Relevant Administrative Regulations

Administrative regulations constitute an integral part of legal system of socialism with Chinese characteristics. The State Council formulates administrative regulations in accordance with the Constitution and laws. As the elaboration of laws, the administrative regulations embody the relevant systems stipulated by the laws in a detailed manner. The effect of administrative regulations is lower than that of laws but higher than that of local regulations and rules. The administrative regulations on auditing formulated by the State Council in accordance with the Constitution, Audit Law, and relevant laws are normative documents of auditing applicable nationwide with general binding force. The effective administrative regulations on auditing mainly include: the *Regulations for the Implementation of the Audit Law of the PRC*, the *Opinions of the State Council on Strengthening Audit Work*, the *Regulations concerning Accountability Audit for Leading Cadres of the Party and Government and Leaders of State-Owned Enterprises*, the *Interim Measures for supervision through auditing on the Central Budget Implementation*,[5] and so forth. Among them, the *Opinions of the State Council on Strengthening Audit Work* issued by the State Council in October 2014, in seven parts and consisting of 22 articles, focuses on solving bottlenecks restricting the development of audit and performance of audit functions, and provides the institutional guarantee for improvement of auditing: first, we must exert the guarantee role of audit in promoting implementation of national major decisions

---

[5] Refer to the relevant contents of Chapter I hereof for details of the *Regulations for the Implementation of the Audit Law of the PRC*, the *Regulations concerning Accountability Audit for Leading Cadres of the Party and Government and Leaders of State-Owned Enterprises* and the *Interim Measures for Audit Supervision on the Central Budget Implementation*.

and arrangements; second, we must strengthen the supervisory role of audit in promoting administration by law, and the building of clean government and the performance of duties; third, we must conduct comprehensive auditing to cover all public funds, State-owned assets, State-owned resources, and the performance of leading cadres' accountabilities; fourth, we must improve the mechanism for supervision through auditing. Any departments, organizations, or individuals related to the management, allocation, and utilization of public funds, State-owned assets, and State-owned resources should be subject to supervision through auditing, and cooperate with audit institutions without setting obstacles. The relevant departments and units must provide data, electronic information and necessary technical documentation of financial accounting, business and management required by auditors in a legal, timely, and comprehensive manner. The restrictive regulations that have been formulated should be revised or abolished accordingly. Fifth, it explicitly stresses implementation of corrective actions against the audit findings and strictly investigate and hold the responsible persons to account. Sixth, it is necessary to strengthen the institutional guarantee for audit work. Specific measures have been proposed for this, such as, strengthening audit team building, accelerating IT application in auditing, ensuring the resources and funds essential to the performance of audit functions, strengthening the leadership of audit institutions at the higher level over those beneath, improving the leadership mechanism of audit work, and so forth.

Many of other administrative regulations, administrative measures, decisions, orders, and relevant normative documents formulated and released by the State Council are also applicable to auditing, and pertain to the audit laws and regulations of socialism with Chinese characteristics. For instance, the *Regulations on Punishment for Illegal Fiscal Acts* and the *Provisions on the Transfer of Suspected Criminal Cases by Administrative Organs for Law Enforcement* provide an important basis for audit institutions to impose sanctions, and to transfer suspected crimes, and so forth; the *Notice on Issues Concerning Audit through Computer Information System* distributed by the General Affairs Office of the State Council is the important basis for audit institutions to conduct auditing through information system.

(4) Local Audit Regulations

Local audit regulations also constitute an integral part of legal system of socialism with Chinese characteristics. As long as there is no conflict with the Constitution, laws, and administrative regulations, people's congresses and their standing committees of the provinces, autonomous regions, municipalities, and larger cities may formulate local regulations according to their own situation and actual demands. Local regulations play an extension and improvement role to the national legislation. However, they are valid and effective only in the corresponding administrative region, with effect lower than that of the Constitution, laws, and administrative regulations. In recent years, some local people's congresses and their standing committees positively exercised their local legislative power and formulated many local audit laws by adhering to the local actuality of socioeconomic development. These local audit regulations play an important role in safeguarding the effective implementation of the Constitution, audit laws, and administrative regulations within the corresponding administrative regions, and promoting the development of the audit cause.

(5) Audit Rules

These include departmental rules and local government rules. Within their statutory functions, duties and limits of power, the component departments and directly subordinate institutions of the State Council are entitled to formulate and release departmental rules on adjusting the administrative relations within their jurisdiction in pursuance of laws, administrative regulations and decisions of the State Council. The CNAO, as a component department of the State Council, takes charge of audit work nationwide under the direction of the premier, and has the right to formulate departmental audit rules concerning government auditing. The audit rules in effect mainly cover the *Rules for Implementation of the Regulations concerning Accountability Audit for Leading Cadres of the Party and Government and Leaders of State-Owned Enterprises*, the *National Auditing Standards of the PRC*, the *Regulations on Safekeeping Material and Assets by Audit Offices* and so forth. Specifically, the *Rules for Implementation of the Regulations concerning Accountability Audit for Leading Cadres of the Party and Government and Leaders of State-Owned Enterprises*, of eight chapters with 60 articles, is jointly formulated by the Central Commission for Discipline Inspection, the Organization Department of the CPC Central Committee, the State Commission Office for Public Sector Reform, the Ministry of Supervision, the Ministry of Human Resources and Social Security, the National Audit Office of China and the State-Owned Assets Supervision and Administration Commission of the State Council, elaborating and improving such contents as the auditees of accountability audit, audit contents, audit evaluation, audit report, the application of audit results, organizational leadership and the execution of audit. The *National Auditing Standards of the PRC*, formulated by the CNAO, has binding force on both audit institutions and individual auditors, and works to set behavioral standards for audit institutions and individual auditors to perform their statutory audit functions, the professional criteria to execute audit business, the benchmark to evaluate the audit quality, and also the basic code of conduct that should be observed by audit institutions and auditors in auditing.

The people's governments of provinces, autonomous regions, municipalities, and large cities may formulate local government rules according to local situations and actual demands, but the rules must not contravene the Constitution, laws, and administrative regulations as well as other local regulations. They are only valid and effective within the corresponding administrative region, with an effect lower than that of the Constitution, laws, administrative regulations, and local regulations. In recent years, when leading local audit work, people's government of many provinces, autonomous regions, municipalities, and people's governments of large cities have proceeded from the local actuality of socioeconomic development, and formulated many local government audit rules within their statutory functions, duties, and limits of power in accordance with audit laws, administrative regulations, and local audit regulations. These play an important role in promoting the development of local audit cause.

In addition, the audit rules of the Central Military Commission for the Chinese People's Liberation Army also constitute an integral part of audit laws and regulations of socialism with Chinese characteristics. In January 1987, the Central Military Commission issued the *Rules of the Chinese People's Liberation Army on Audit Work (Trial)*. After the promulgation and implementation of the Audit Law, the Central Military Commission formulated and promulgated many special rules on People's Liberation Army (PLA) audit work in pursuance of the Audit Law. In April 1995, the Central Military Commission issued the *Audit Rules of the Chinese People's Liberation Army*. All headquarters and the Audit Office of the PLA promulgated relevant professional audit rules and audit norms.

Apart from the preceding regulations directly used to regulate or closely related to the audit work, other regulations concerning fiscal and financial revenues and expenditures and economic activities are widely applicable to audit work. These regulations work as the important basis for audit institutions and individual auditors to conduct audit evaluation, determine the nature of audit findings and mete out disposal for the violations, and also constitute an integral part of audit laws and regulations of socialism with Chinese characteristics.

The audit laws and regulations mentioned above are the centralized embodiment of the institutionalization and legalization of audit experience, and are continuously being improved along with China's promotion of democracy and rule of law. Hence, we should keep a historical, developmental, and interrelated viewpoint against the background of building a socialist country under the rule of law as a basic strategy, and always persevere in the spirit of rule of law, the requirements of law, and the basic principle of auditing according to law. To be specific, first, we should keep promoting the legitimacy of audit duties and mandate. We should strictly conduct auditing within the legal boundaries, perform duties properly and carry out work diligently and legally, avoiding neglect of duty and exercising power beyond the boundary of mandate. Second, we should adhere to ensuring the legitimacy of audit procedures. We should strictly implement the statutory audit procedures and continuously improve relevant regulations and operational procedures in line with the needs of audit practice, while achieving the goal of "having laws to abide by and having rules to follow" in audit work. Third, we should insist on promoting the legitimacy of audit methods. Proceeding from audit on the principle of authenticity, compliance, and performance of fiscal and financial revenues and expenditures, we should strictly standardize evidence collection, inquiry approval, and working paper preparation, as well as review of audit assignment; strictly regulate matters concerning issuance of audit reports, delivery of audit decisions, transfer of clues in cases, announcement of audit results, rectification of audit findings, and so forth. Fourth, we should stick to ensuring the legitimacy of audit standards. The statutory audit subject matters must be audited thoroughly and reported truthfully, and disposal and penalty should be imposed strictly in accordance with the statutory standards. Fifth, we should keep on working to ensure the legitimacy of the audit work. Any units and individuals that use and manage public funds, State-owned assets, and State-owned resources, as well as leading cadres with accountabilities must accept, coordinate, and support the audit according to law, providing a guarantee for audit institutions to perform their duties legally.

Background Information 2: Proposal and Development of Basic Strategy of the Rule of Law

After the founding of the People's Republic of China, the *Constitution of the People's Republic of China* was formulated at the First Plenary Session of the 1st Communist Party of China (CPC) National Congress in 1954. Thereafter, a number of basic laws and important regulations such as the *Organic Law of the National People's Congress of the PRC* and the *Organic Law of the State Council of the PRC* specified the socialist political, legal, and judicial systems and the basic principles of socialist legal system. However, a "left-leaning" tendency starting in the late 1950s, and the chaotic "cultural revolution" thereafter, seriously affected and damaged the construction of China's democracy.

Since the Third Plenary Session of the 11th CPC Central Committee, China ushered in a new era of socialist democracy construction and a new historic course of the rule of law. In 1978, the Third Plenary Session of the 11th CPC Central Committee clarified the unswerving policy of strengthening socialist democracy, stressing the need to institutionalize and legalize socialist democracy, maintain such systems and laws unchanged through the changes of leaders, their outlook and attention, and ensure that there are laws to abide by, the laws are observed and strictly enforced, and lawbreakers are prosecuted. In 1997, the 15th CPC National Congress determined rule of law as a fundamental principle by which the Party would lead the people in running the country, and building a State under "the socialist rule of law" as an important objective in creating a modern socialist country. In 1999, the *Amendment to the Constitution of the PRC* adopted at the Second Session of the 9th National People's Congress officially incorporated "rule of law" into the Constitution. In 2007, the 17th CPC National Congress made the decision of comprehensively implementing the rule of law as a fundamental principle, and speeding up the building of a socialist country under the rule of law. By 2010, China had formed a legal system of socialism with Chinese characteristics. At the Fourth Plenary Session of the 18th CPC Central Committee, the CPC made the special study and deployment for the major issues concerning the rule of law in its history, and issued the *Decision of the CPC Central Committee on Some Major Issues concerning Comprehensively Promoting the Rule of Law*, proposing the overall goal of building a legal system of socialism with Chinese characteristics and building a socialist country under the rule of law, and further specifying the development direction, overall objective, road map, and primary task of the rule of law.

Source: China Steering Committee of Compiling and Reviewing Cadre Training Materials, *Uphold and Develop Socialism with Chinese Characteristics*. Beijing: People's Publishing House and Party Building Books Publishing House, 2015, pp.149–150 (revised slightly).

▦ 2. AUDIT ORGANIZATION SYSTEM

From the perspective of management science, a organization system means the establishment of State organs, enterprises, and institutions, and division of administration duties and corresponding systems. The audit organization system, as an important content of the government auditing system, mainly stipulates matters in regard to the affiliation relationship among audit institutions, the relationship between upper- and lower-level audit institutions, the audit institutionalization framework, and so forth. The audit organization system of socialism with Chinese characteristics mainly involves the following aspects: audit institutions are government departments established in accordance with the Constitution, local audit institutions under the dual leadership, audit institutions established by the corresponding people's congress and under their supervision, the audit institutionalization framework consisting of four levels of audit institutions, and so forth.

(1) Establishment of Audit Institutions

In accordance with the Constitution and Audit Law, the State Council and local people's governments at and above county level set up audit institutions that are the statutory component of the governments at the same levels. Audit institutions carry out the audit under the direct leadership of the executive heads of the people's governments at corresponding levels, and report their work to the people's governments at that level. The work funds are guaranteed by the law. The heads of audit institutions should be members of the people's governments at the corresponding level. To maintain audit independence, the *Opinions of the State Council on Strengthening Audit Work* proposed that the principal heads of local governments at all levels should lead the corresponding audit institutions according to law, support the audit work, regularly hear audit work reports, promptly study and solve any prominent problems found in audit work, and regard audit results as an important basis of relevant decision making; should ensure audit institutions conduct audits, investigate problems, and make public the audit results according to law, subject to no interference by any other administrative organ, public organization, or individual; regularly supervise and check the execution of audit laws and regulations; and according to law, investigate any auditee entity that refuses to accept supervision through auditing, obstructs, interferes with, and refuses to cooperate or threatens, intimidates, and retaliates against the assigned auditors.

In terms of the relationship between audit institutions and people's congresses, audit institutions, as government administrative organs, are set up and supervised by the corresponding level of people's congress. Specifically, this relationship is mainly reflected as follows: First, the principal heads of audit institutions are determined by the corresponding people's congresses or their standing committees. To be specific, the Auditor General of the National

Audit Office is determined by the National People's Congress or its Standing Committee, and the principal heads of local audit institutions at all levels are determined by the standing committees of the people's congresses at the corresponding levels. Second, audit institutions should be responsible to the People's Congresses and their Standing Committees at the same level. The State Council and local people's government at and above the county level should submit an annual audit work report on budget execution and other financial revenues and expenditures, and a report on the rectification of problems disclosed in the audit work report to the relevant standing committee of the people's congress. When necessary, the latter may make a resolution upon audit work report. Third, audit institutions should be subject to supervision by the relevant people's congresses and their standing committees. People's congresses are entitled to remove from office the principal heads of audit institutions at the corresponding level through legal procedures.

(2) Relationship between Upper- and Lower-Level Audit Institutions

In accordance with the Constitution and Audit Law, the CNAO is responsible for national audit work and local audit institutions are under the leadership of those at the next higher level. Local audit institutions are held accountable and report their work to the people's government at the corresponding level and audit institutions at the next higher level, and are under the dual leadership of the executive heads of people's governments at the corresponding levels and audit institutions at the next higher level. The audit work shall be mainly subject to the leadership of the audit institutions at next higher levels. The Fourth Plenary Session of the 18th CPC Central Committee further strengthened the leadership of higher-level audit institutions over lower-level ones, and explored the unified management of audit institutions below province level in human, financial, and material resource terms. This creates a closer relationship between higher- and lower-level audit institutions, and is more conducive to exerting the concerted power of supervision through auditing.

The audit work of local audit institutions is mainly subject to the leadership of higher-level ones, shown as follows: First, the CNAO is responsible for national audit work, and local audit institutions at all levels should abide by and implement the audit guidelines, policies, national audit standards, and other rules and regulations on audit work. Second, higher-level audit institutions are responsible for formulating plans of audit assignments at the corresponding level and also the audit plans to be uniformly executed by the lower-level audit institutions, which in turn design their audit plans according to the requirements of the higher-level audit institutions and the people's government at the corresponding level, and report their work to the former. Third, lower-level audit institutions should submit a comprehensive report on the execution of audit plans to the higher-level audit institutions; if a lower-level audit institution participates in an audit project under the unified organization of a higher-level institutions, it should submit a report on project implementation. Fourth, higher-level audit institutions may authorize lower-level audit institutions to audit certain subject matters within their audit jurisdiction; higher-level audit institutions may directly audit the major subject matters within the audit jurisdiction of lower-level audit institutions; where a dispute arises on jurisdiction between audit institutions, the matter shall be determined by an audit institution's superior to the disputing parties. Fifth, lower-level audit institutions should submit audit result reports on the corresponding government level's budget performance and other financial revenue and expenditures to higher-level audit institutions; local audit institutions at all levels should submit special reports or report relevant information to higher-level audit institutions, if they find any major problems in an audit. Lower-level audit institutions must report to higher-level audit institutions while delivering audit results and clues to major cases to the government at the same level. Sixth, lower-level audit institutions should report the results of audit investigations to higher-level audit institutions after special audit investigation among relevant localities, departments, and units with regard to budget administration or management and use of State-owned assets and matters relating to State budgetary revenues and expenditures. Seventh, audit institutions at higher levels are entitled to supervise the audit law enforcement and quality of audit work by lower audit institutions, requiring the latter to modify or cancel audit decisions violating relevant State provisions, or directly change or revoke the decisions when necessary. Eighth, the higher-level audit institutions should deal with the administrative reconsideration proposed by audited entities against lower-level audit institutions, and make a decision according to law.

(3) Audit Institutionalization Framework

Chinese audit institutions have been gradually established since 1983 in accordance with the provisions of the Constitution issued in 1982 on the establishment of audit institutions by the State Council and local people's governments at and above county level. Through more than 30 years of development, China has formed a multilevel audit institutionalization framework covering central and local levels. The CNAO is not only a component ministry of the State Council but also the supreme audit institutions of China. Accordingly, the CNAO should execute laws, administrative regulations, and the decisions and orders of the State Council, and take charge of national audit work under the premier's leadership. As a component department of the State Council, the CNAO is endowed with statutory audit functions and directly engages in audit activities within its jurisdictional scope. Local audit institutions include audit offices established by the people's governments of provinces, autonomous regions, municipalities directly under the Central Government, municipalities with district division, autonomous prefectures, counties, autonomous counties, municipalities without district division, and municipal districts. Currently, there are 31 audit offices (bureaus) of provinces, autonomous regions, and municipalities, over 430 audit bureaus at the prefecture and city levels, and over 3,000 audit bureaus at the county and district levels.

Meanwhile, audit institutions may, as required by the work, establish satellite audit offices within the scope of their jurisdiction, upon the approval of the people's government at the corresponding level. In view of the fact that China has a vast territory and numerous auditees, and the geographical distribution of auditees within the jurisdiction of audit institutions is wide ranging, audit institutions set up satellite offices in some areas where the auditees are relatively concentrated and some government departments which have many affiliated units. At present, the CNAO has set up 18 regional offices in some central cities and 20 audit offices stationed in all departments of the State Council in departmental or transdepartmental forms with the approval of the State Council. Some local audit institutions have also set up their satellite offices in light of the local actual situation and work requirements to conduct audit work with the authorization of audit institutions.

The Chinese People's Liberation Army has set up audit institutions and takes charge of auditing under the leadership of the Central Military Commission. In July 1985, the Central Military Commission approved the establishment of the Audit Bureau of the People's Liberation Army, which was renamed the Audit Office of the People's Liberation Army and made subordinate to the PLA General Logistics Department in 1992. Currently, all headquarters, military regions, various categories of military, and armed police units have set up audit bureaus, while army groups, provincial military regions, armed police forces, and some units at the army and divisional level have set up audit divisions. In November 2014, the Audit Office of the People's Liberation Army was incorporated under the Central Military Commission.

The Chinese organization system has its unique features and remains distinctive in the world. This is commensurate with China's unique conditions of national governance at present. In the future, China will gradually explore and improve an audit organization system in line with the needs of national governance and give play to the role of government auditing as the bedrock and important guarantee of national governance.

3. DUTIES AND POWERS OF AUDIT INSTITUTIONS

To ensure that auditing can play an active role in all fields and levels of socio-economic development, the Constitution, Audit Law, and other relevant laws and regulations also grant corresponding powers to audit institutions while stipulating the duties and responsibilities of audit. The decision adopted at the Third and Fourth Plenary Sessions of the 18th CPC Central Committee proposed requirements for improving the auditing system. The *Opinions of the State Council on Strengthening Audit Work* required that "auditing should cover the implementation of policies and measures for stabilizing growth, promoting reform, adjusting the structure, benefiting people's livelihood, and preventing risks, as well as public funds, State-owned assets, State-owned resources, and the accountability of leading officials, to achieve full coverage of supervision through auditing." These decisions and requirements further enriched audit responsibility and mandate.

Background Information 3: Some Contents of the *Opinions of the State Council on Strengthening Audit Work*

2. Exerting the guarantee role of audit in promoting the implementation of national major decision-making and arrangements

(3) The implementation of policies and measures should be promoted. We should continuously organize the real-time audit on the implementation of national major policies and measures and macro control deployments. We should strive to supervise and inspect the specific deployment, execution progress and actual results and other aspects of all regions and departments in implementing policies and measures for stabilizing growth,

promoting reform, adjusting the structure, benefiting people's livelihood, and preventing risks. In particular, priority is given to major projects, the guarantee of major funds and the advancement of streamlined administration and decentralization, so as to promptly discover and rectify behavior related to disobeying orders and defying prohibitions, reflect good practice and experience, and new circumstances and new issues, and promote the implementation and improvement of policies and measures.

(4) The safe and efficient utilization of public funds should be promoted. We should sufficiently supervise the use of public funds and take strict precautions against violations of laws and regulations, such as corruption and waste, to ensure the safety of public funds. A stress on performance should run through the whole audit process. We should strengthen budget implementation and other audits of financial revenues and expenditures, pay close attention to the use of stock and incremental funds, reduce capital waste, revitalize the capital stock, and promote the reasonable configuration and efficient use of financial funds to ensure its better use for key purposes. By adhering to the spirit of the Central Eight Provisions and the "Three Provisions" of the State Council, we should strengthen auditing of the three public expenses, conference expenses, and the expenditures on construction of government buildings; promote strict economization and standardized management; and advance the cause of thrifty government.

(5) National economic security should be maintained. We should strengthen auditing of risks and hazards in economic operations, pay close attention to weaknesses and potential risks concerning budgetary issues, financial matters, and problems related to people's livelihoods, State-owned assets, energy, resources, and the environment, and focus on social instability caused by economic problems, especially local government debt, regional financial instability, and so forth. We must identify trends and problems and actively put forward suggestions on solving problems and mitigating risks.

(6) The people's livelihood and ecological civilization construction should be improved. Priority is given to strengthening supervision through auditing of major funds and projects for people's livelihood, such as those related to "agriculture, rural areas and farmers," social security, education, culture, medical care, poverty alleviation, disaster relief, and affordable housing. We should strengthen auditing over the use of land, minerals, and other

(continued)

natural resources, pollution control over air, water, and solid waste, and environmental protection; explore audits on natural resources and capital when responsible officials leave office; thoroughly analyze the situation about fiscal input, project progress, and development; and promote the precise implementation of policies that benefit the people and protect resources and the environment.

(7) Reform must be deepened. We must coordinate and cooperate in implementation of reform measures, and conduct systematic, integrated, and coordinated reform. We should correctly grasp the new situation of reform and development, identify outdated provisions that restrict development and hinder reform in a timely manner, and promote relevant improvements.

3. Strengthening the supervisory role of auditing

(8) Administration by law and compliance with the law should be promoted. We should increase the intensity of auditing over the situation of administration by law, pay close attention to failures and breaches in law enforcement, promote the construction of law-based government and safeguard the sanctity of the law. We should make strong efforts to reflect the issues that seriously prejudice the people's interests and hinder fair competition, so as to maintain market economic order, social fairness, and justice.

(9) The construction of a clean government should be promoted. Major violations of laws and rules found in an audit should be investigated thoroughly. The focus should be on the allocation of financial funds, major investment decisions and project approvals, significant procurements and bidding, loan issuance and securities trading, transfer of State-owned assets and equities, and trading of land and mineral resources. Furthermore, auditing should concentrate on tackling corruption; highlight issues related to the abuse of power for personal gain, dereliction of duty, bribery, insider trading, and other issues; and promote the construction of clean government.

(10) Performance of duties should be promoted. We should deepen accountability audit of leading officials, focus on supervision of officials' compliance with laws and disciplines, and promote the initiative and effective acts and duty performance of heads at all levels. We should expose misconduct, tardiness, and random acts of officials in accordance with laws and disciplines, and promote establishment of a sound and comprehensive accountability mechanism.

(1) Duties of Audit Institutions

From the perspective of requirements by national laws and regulations, audit duties are the tasks audit institutions should perform. From the perspective of audits, audit duties are also the functions and powers of audit institutions, namely, the scope of governance[6] powers of audit institutions. Reflecting distinct legality, the duties of audit institutions are expressly stipulated by laws and administrative regulations.

The *Constitution of the People's Republic of China* implemented in 1982 stipulates the basic duties of Chinese audit institutions, that is, to supervise through auditing the revenues and expenditures of all departments at the corresponding level and of people's governments at a lower level, and the revenues and expenditures of all financial and monetary organizations, enterprises, and institutions of the State. Through the Constitution, the audit laws, and regulations, as well as relevant rules formulated at different periods, the duties of audit institutions have been further clarified along with the deepening of reform and opening up, to meet the needs of developing and improving the socialist market economic system and transforming government functions.

Currently, Chinese audit institutions perform four major duties: First is supervision through auditing over the authenticity, compliance and performance of statutory subject matters; second is special audit investigation of specific subject matters relating to the national financial revenues and expenditures; third is professional guidance and supervision over the internal audit work of units that are subject to supervision through auditing by audit institutions in accordance with law; and fourth is verification of audit reports issued by public audit institutions over units that are subject to supervision through auditing by audit institutions in accordance with law.

1) Supervision through Auditing Over the Statutory Subject Matters

In accordance with the Audit Law and its Regulations for the Implementation as well as the relevant provisions, the following subject matters should be subject to supervision through auditing:

(a) The corresponding level's budget implementation and final accounts of all departments (including units directly under them) at the corresponding level.
(b) Budget implementation and final accounts of governments at the lower level.
(c) Financial revenues and expenditures of the Central Bank.

---

[6] Li Jinhua (chief editor), *Audit Theory Research*. Beijinga: Modern Economic Publishing House, 2005, pp. 229–230.

(d) Financial revenues and expenditures of State institutions and others using the government funds.

(e) Assets, liabilities, profits, and losses of enterprises and financial institutions with State-owned capital controlling their shares or playing a leading role. State-owned enterprises and State-owned financial institutions refer to solely State-owned enterprises and financial institutions. The enterprises and financial institutions with State-owned capital controlling their shares or playing a leading role mainly involve two categories: one refers to the enterprises and financial institutions whose State-owned capital accounts for over 50 percent of total capital (capital stock); the other covers enterprises and financial institutions whose State-owned capital accounts for not more than 50 percent of their total capital (capital stock) but the State-owned investment subjects have the actual right of control.

(f) Budget implementation and final accounts of construction projects fully or mainly financed by government investment. The construction projects subject to the supervision by audit institutions include: construction projects with government investment, namely, those fully financed by government funds such as budgetary investment funds, special construction funds, and funds raised through issuance of government debt; the construction projects dominated by government investment, namely, those mainly financed by the government investment. Among them, the construction projects dominated by government investment include those in which government funds occupy over 50 percent of total project investment, and construction projects in which government funds account for 50 percent or less of total project investment but the actual controlling right of construction and operation is held by the government.

(g) Financial revenues and expenditures of social security funds managed by government departments or by relevant units upon entrustment, public donations, and other relevant funds and capital. The social security funds subject to supervision through auditing include social insurance, public assistance, social welfare fund, and other special funds for social security undertakings. The public donations subject to supervision through auditing include various forms, that is, money, negotiable securities, and in-kind offers donated by domestic and foreign organizations or individuals of their own accord and without consideration. All other funds and capitals managed by government departments or by relevant units upon entrustment, that is, housing provident funds and lottery commonweal funds, are also subject to the supervision through auditing and should accept the supervision through auditing accordingly.

(h) Financial revenues and expenditures of projects with aid or loans provided by international organizations or governments of other countries.

The audited projects with aid or loans provided by international organizations or governments of other countries include: loans provided for the Chinese Government and its institutions; loans provided by international organizations or governments of other countries and their institutions for Chinese enterprises, institutions, and other organizations on the strength of guarantee offered by the Chinese Government and its institutions; aid or grants provided by international organizations or governments of other countries and their institutions; aid or grants provided by international organizations or governments of other countries and their institutions to entities managing relevant funds and capital upon the entrustment of the Chinese Government; and other aids and loans provided by international organizations or governments of other countries and their institutions.

Special Column 1: Auditing of Foreign Funds Application[7]

Auditing of foreign funds application refers to the activity whereby government audit institutions supervise the authenticity, compliance, and performance of economic activities to which the Chinese Government applies foreign funds and the corresponding fiscal and financial revenues and expenditures. In August 1984, when this activity began, the Department of Foreign Funds Application Audit of the CNAO performed a pilot audit of university development projects using World Bank loans. Since 1985, the CNAO has conducted audit notarization for many projects using loans from this source. The audit reports have been recognized by the World Bank and other organizations, and the audit quality of projects has enjoyed a high reputation in the international community. The CNAO also organized a special audit of railway projects receiving World Bank loans to strictly investigate major violations of laws and regulations, paying attention to imperfection at the systems, mechanisms, and institutions, in order to promote and strengthen management of railway projects. To seek experience and promote the auditing of Chinese-foreign joint venture and cooperative enterprises, the CNAO audited 200 Chinese-foreign joint ventures in 1992 alone.

In 1999, the CNAO established the principle of "integrating internal and external auditing, producing factual disclosure" to comprehensively strengthen the audit of projects using loans from international financial organizations, as well as foreign aid projects, and intensified its efforts in

(continued)

---

[7] Sorted out according to relevant data of the CNAO.

punishment and disclosure, playing a role in promoting the active, ratio-nal, and effective utilization of foreign funds. Great attention was paid to debt safety along with the good performance of audit notarization. In 2009, the CNAO organized an audit of the management of sovereign foreign debts of 32 provincial financial departments, and put forward sug-gestions on putting such debts and reserve funds for repayment of loans under budgetary control, and on reserving funds for repayment in the treasury storage. In 2010, the CNAO organized and conducted auditing of national foreign debt management, that is, the foreign debt risk control mechanism, scale, and structure. Auditing revealed the overall situation of China's foreign debt and promoted improvements in its management. From 2010 to 2011, the CNAO organized auditing of the construction, operation, and performance of projects involving government debt, cov-ering transportation, energy, and environmental protection. Priority was given to the effects of these projects in regard to water treatment, waste disposal, and so forth.

Audit standardization of foreign funds application has been strength-ened continuously. The *Specifications on Auditing Projects Using Loans and Aid from International Financial Organizations and Specialized Agen-cies of the United Nations* formulated in 1986 was the CNAO's earliest operational manual. Thereafter, according to the latest policies and regulations at home and abroad and the needs of audit work, the CNAO successively formulated regulations or guides, that is, the *Specifica-tions on Auditing Projects Using World Bank Loan*, the *Audit Manual for Projects Using Loans from International Financial Organizations*, the *Guide and Example for Compilation of Foreign-Related Financial Reports and Audit Reports*, the *Audit Practices of Chinese-Foreign Joint Ventures*, and the *Audit Guide for Projects Using Loans from the World Bank and Asian Development Bank*, of which the latter was designated by the World Bank as training materials for audit institutions of other countries.

(i) Situation regarding the performance of heads of the Party, government, and State-owned enterprises. This accountability audit requires that audit institutions supervise and inspect the performance of heads of State organs, State-owned financial institutions, enterprises, and institutions during their terms of office within their statutory limits of powers. It covers all main leading officials of the Party and government from township to provincial departmental levels, including local Party committees, governments, judicial and procuratorial organs, as well as heads and administrative heads of the Party committees (including Party groups and Party working committees) of such units as Party and government departments, public institutions, and mass organizations at all levels of the Central and local governments, including executive deputy heads presiding over the work for more than one year. Where a leading offical at the higher level holds a concurrent post of head of a department or unit but doesn't assume any accountability, the auditee shall be the deputy head actually responsible for the routine work. For the audit of heads of State-owned enterprises the auditees should be the legal representatives of the enterprises (including financial enterprises) and of those in which the State-owned assets occupy a holding or dominant position. As required by the Party Committee and the government as well as the management and supervision departments of officials, audit institutions may conduct an accountability audit of the Chairmen, General Managers, Party Committee Secretaries, and other main leaders who do not serve as legal representatives but exercise the corresponding duties in actual fact. Audit institutions may, according to the requirements of the local Party committee and government, conduct an accountability audit on heads of village Party organizations and villagers' committees, community Party organizations, and community residents' committees.

(j) Implementation of national major policies and measures and macro control deployments. In accordance with the requirements of the *Opinions of the State Council on Strengthening Audit Work*, audit institutions should continuously organize a real-time audit on the implementation of national major policies and measures and macro control deployments. Every effort should be made to supervise and inspect the specific deployments, execution progress, and actual results and other aspects of all regions and departments in implementing policies and measures for stabilizing growth, promoting reform, structural adjustment, benefiting people's livelihood, and preventing risk. In particular, priority is given to the implementation of major projects, guarantee of major funds, and advancement of streamlined administration and institutional decentralization, so as to promptly discover and rectify any such behavior as disobeying orders and defying prohibitions, reflect good practice and experience and new circumstances and new issues, and promote the implementation and improvement of all policies and measures.

(k) Computer information system of auditees. In accordance with the *Notice of the General Affairs Office of the State Council on Issues Concerning Audit Work by Computer Information System*, audit institutions are entitled to check the information system with which auditees manage their financial and government revenues and expenditures through a computer information system. If audit institutions have any question about the authenticity of electronic data, they may test the relevant computer information system.

(l) Performance of accountabilities of leading officials regarding natural resources and assets. In pursuance of the *Decision of the CPC Central Committee on Some Major Issues concerning Comprehensively Deepening Reform* adopted at the Third Plenary Session of the 18th

(continued)

CPC Central Committee, it is necessary to explore ways to compile a natural resource balance sheet, conduct natural resource audits when leading officials leave their offices, and establish a lifelong accountability system for ecological and environmental damage.

(m) Other subject matters that are subject to auditing by audit institutions as stipulated by laws and administrative regulations. For instance, in accordance with the Government Procurement Law, audit institutions are entitled to supervise through auditing over government procurement behaviors; government procurement supervision administration departments and all parties concerned should accept the supervision of audit institutions in related activities.

Besides, upon the approval of the people's government at the same level, an audit institution may conduct supervision through auditing over entities and projects to which financial funds are appropriated in terms of authenticity, compliance, and performance of their acceptance and utilization.

Background Information 3: Some Contents of the *Notice of the General Affairs Office of the State Council on Issues Concerning Audit Work by Computer Information System*

1. Audit institutions are entitled to check the information system with which auditees manage their financial and government revenues and expenditures through computer (hereinafter known as the computer information system). Audited entities should, in accordance with the requirements of audit institutions, provide electronic data, necessary computer technical documentation, and other materials relating to the financial and government revenues and expenditures. When audit institutions audit the computer information system, the audited entity should cooperate by providing the necessary working conditions.

   If an audited entity refuses or delays provision of electronic data information relating to audit projects, or refuses or hinders examination, the audit institution concerned may handle such behavior in accordance with Article 49 of the *Regulations for the Implementation of the Audit Law of the PRC*.

2. The audited entity's computer information system should be equipped with a data interface in conformity with national standards or industry standards; where any computer information system in service has no such proper data interface, the audited entity should convert the data required by audit institutions into a readable format.

   Where an audited entity's computer information system is discovered as not conforming with the laws, regulations, and the provisions and standards of competent departments of the government, the audit institution may order it to make correction within a specified time limit or replace it. In case of a failure to make correction or replacement, the audit institution should circulate a notice of criticism and suggest the competent department to deal with the audited entity accordingly. If, through auditing, an audit institution finds an auditee's is intentionally using a computer information system with fraudulent features, the audit institution should investigate the responsibility of the unit and persons concerned according to law.

3. In accordance with the regulations on the storage life of vouchers, account books, account statements and other accounting data in paper forms, as well as the materials relating to economic activities, auditees should save the electronic data processed through their computer information system, and should not execute any operation of overlapping, deletion, or destruction within the specified time limit.

4. If audit institutions have any questions about the authenticity of electronic data of the auditee, they may test the computer information system. Auditors should, upon the request to test the computer information system, put forward a test plan to supervise the audited entity's operator to carry out the test according to the plan.

   Audit institutions should explore network remote auditing actively yet prudently.

5. Auditors should implement audit standards strictly and any damage to the audited entity's computer information system during the audit is prohibited. Auditors should be obliged to keep confidential State secrets and business secrets they might acquire during the audit, and should not use any of such confidential information for any purpose unrelated to the audit. Where an auditor discloses State secrets and the audited entity's business secrets to which he/she has gained access, the audit institution concerned should impose an administrative penalty accordingly; where a crime is involved, the case should be transferred to the judicial authorities for investigation in accordance with law.

(continued)

All regions and relevant departments should attach great importance to audit through a computer information system and give their full support and coordinate with audit institutions in their work. Audit institutions should strengthen training on business and technology, and cultivate the professionals who are skilled in auditing through computer information system, to ensure smooth audit work.

2) Special Audit Investigation in Terms of Specific Matters Relating to State Financial Revenues and Expenditures

Special audit investigations are defined as: In accordance with audit laws and regulations, and relevant provisions of the State, audit institutions carry out special audit investigations among relevant local authorities, departments, and units with regard to budget administration or special matters relating to State financial revenues and expenditures. In accordance with the provisions of the national audit standards, audit institutions can carry out special audit investigations on specific matters relating to budget administration or the management and use of State-owned assets in the following circumstances: issues involving macro, universal, policy-based, or institutional mechanisms; cross-trade, cross-region, and cross-unit matters; matters involving large amounts of nonfinancial data.

The special audit investigation aims to analyze the reasons for universal and emerging problems from the perspective of policy, system, management, and so on, and to put forward suggestions on improving macro policy, perfecting legal system and strengthening comprehensive management, so as to maintain national security, promote democracy and rule of law, and to safeguard the sound operation of economic society.

3) Guidance and Supervision Over the Internal Audit Work of Units That Are Subject to Supervision through Auditing by Audit Institutions in Accordance with Law

In accordance with the provisions of the Audit Law, units that are subject to supervision through auditing should place their internal audit work under the professional guidance and supervision of audit institutions. In practice, audit institutions at all levels generally guide and supervise the internal audit work through the relevant self-discipline organization (namely the China Institute of Internal Auditors). Over many years, under the guidance and supervision of the CNAO, the Institute has successively issued the *Internal Auditing Standards*,

Audit Profession Ethics of Internal Auditors, specific auditing standards and practical guides to internal audit, and made revisions at the appropriate time, forming a relatively complete standard system of internal audit and basically providing a systemic foundation for internal audit. Meanwhile, under the support, guidance, and supervision of audit institutions, the institutes of internal audit at all levels have made great efforts to summarize their experience in internal audit, to conduct relevant theoretical discussion, train internal auditors, transform internal audit results, and to learn and absorb domestic and foreign experiences, playing an important role in promoting the sound development of internal audit.

4) Verifying the Audit Reports Issued by Public Audit Institutions for Units That Are Subject to Supervision through Auditing by Audit Institutions in Accordance with Law

One of important responsibilities of audit institutions endowed by the Audit Law is to verify the audit reports issued by public audit institutions for units that are subject to supervision through auditing by audit institutions in accordance with law. The said verification scope mainly covers whether public audit institutions violate laws and regulations and professional ethics, whether their audit procedures comply with the requirements of profession ethics, whether the audit evidence is sufficient and appropriate, and whether the issued audit reports are true and legally correct.

Audit institutions generally verify the audit reports issued by public audit institutions for audited entities or investigated units in combination with the audit or special audit investigation. Where the verification results reveal misrepresentation and other circumstances of audit reports issued by public audit institutions in violation of the laws, regulations, or professional ethics, the audit institutions should transfer the cases to the competent authority for investigation of responsibility of related public audit institutions and individuals, and also make an announcement according to the provided procedures.

(2) Audit Jurisdiction System

To comprehensively perform audit responsibilities, it was found necessary to establish an audit jurisdiction system to scientifically define the scope of responsibilities of audit institutions, and reasonably divide the jurisdictional scope among audit institutions, including the division of responsibility between the CNAO and local audit institutions, and among local audit institutions at all levels and audit institutions in different places.

1) General Principles of Audit Jurisdiction

With regard to audit projects beyond the scope of the accountability audit, related audit institutions should determine their audit jurisdictional scope according to the affiliating relationship of audited entity's fiscal and financial affairs or the relationship of supervision and management of State-owned assets. This is the general principle for determination of the audit jurisdictional scope corresponding to the system featuring "the corresponding level of budget and government" and decentralized administration of State-owned assets. Audit institutions should first determine the audit jurisdictional scope according to the affiliating relationship of the auditee's fiscal and financial affairs; where audit institutions cannot determine this because the affiliating relationship is unclear or unavailable for some reason, they should make a determination on the basis of the relationship of supervision and management of State-owned assets. Besides, the financial institutions, enterprises, institutions, and construction projects invested in by two or more State-owned investment entities should be subject to supervision through auditing by the audit institution that has the jurisdictional right over the principal investment subject.

2) Accountability Audit Jurisdiction System

Unlike other forms of auditing, the auditees of accountability audit are the principal heads of the Party and government and leaders of State-owned enterprises. Such accountability audit should be determined on the basis of administrative authority over cadres, rather than the affiliating relationship of auditees' fiscal and financial affairs or the relationship of supervision and management of State-owned assets. That is to say, the accountability audit of heads of the Party and government and leaders of State-owned enterprises handled by the cadre management departments of Party committees and governments at all levels should be organized and conducted by the audit institution at the same level as the department. Where the administrative authority over cadres is inconsistent with the affiliating relationship of the auditee's fiscal and financial affairs and the relationship of supervision and management of State-owned assets, the organizational department with administrative authority over cadres and the audit institution at the same level should jointly determine the audit institution to exercise the audit. In addition, the principal heads of audit institutions should also be subject to the accountability audit. In detail, through negotiation between the Party committee at the corresponding level and the audit institutions at a higher level, the latter becomes responsible for accountability audit of principal heads of local audit institutions, on the principle of "lower-level audited by higher-level"; after the premier's approval, the accountability audit of the Auditor General of the National Audit Office should be organized and conducted specifically according to the premier's requirements.

3) Authorized Audit, Direct Auditing System, and Settlement Mechanism of Disputes Over Audit Jurisdiction

For central audit institutions, the CNAO may, within its audit jurisdiction, authorize lower-level audit institutions to audit projects other than those of central budget implementation and final accounts of departments of the Central Government (including organizational units), the budget implementation situation and final accounts of lower-level governments and financial revenues and expenditures of the Central Bank; for local audit institutions, the higher-level audit institutions may, within their audit jurisdiction, authorize the lower-level to audit those projects other than the corresponding level's budget implementation situation and final accounts of all departments at the corresponding level (including organizational units), and the budget implementation situation and financial accounts of the lower-level audit institutions. Higher-level audit institutions may directly audit the major projects within the audit jurisdiction of the lower-level audit institutions. Where a dispute arises on audit jurisdiction between audit institutions, the matter has to be determined by an audit institution superior to both parties in dispute.

(3) Powers of Audit Institutions

The powers of auditing have compulsory force reflecting State will, and no interference by any other administrative organs, public organizations, enterprises, institutions, and individuals is allowed. The powers of auditing have distinct legality legitimating the contents, conditions, and procedures of its work exercise. The powers of audit institutions should be commensurate with the incumbent audit responsibilities, and well matched with the status of audit institutions within the national governance system.

To ensure audit institutions effectively perform their responsibilities, the Audit Law and its Regulations for Implementation, as well as other laws and regulations, endow Chinese audit institutions with corresponding powers. Compared with most foreign audit institutions, Chinese audit institutions not only have general authority (i.e., the right to request the submission of materials, right to examine the auditee's relevant data and assets, right to investigate and obtain evidence from relevant units or individuals in regard to audit projects, right to request the auditees and relevant departments to take corresponding measures, right to seek assistance of relevant departments, and the right to notify or publish auditing results), they also have the right to adopt administrative compulsory measures and to make decisions on processing and punishment.

1) Right to Request the Submission of Materials

As the most basic right of audit institutions, the right to request the submission of materials is the prerequisite of performing audit supervisory responsibilities. Audit institutions are entitled to request the audited entity to provide data relating to its financial and fiscal revenues and expenditures, including data of financial accounting, business, and management. Both paper versions and electronic data should be provided. Audited entities should provide various data required by audit institutions within the specified time limit according to their requirements, and any refusal, delay, or misrepresentation is prohibited; if there is any such behavior, the auditee assumes corresponding legal liability. Meanwhile, the principals of audited entities are liable for the authenticity and completeness of the data they provide, and make written commitments in this regard. Audit institutions should keep strictly confidential the data acquired in their work.

2) Right to Examine

The right to examine is an important right of audit institutions and the core audit power.[8] Audit institutions have the right to examine the data and assets relating to the affairs of the target of an audit, as well as their fiscal and financial revenues and expenditures. Materials to be examined include: vouchers, account books, financial account reports and other materials relating to fiscal and financial revenues and expenditures, the electronic data system through which the audited entity manages its fiscal and financial revenues and expenditures, and the relevant paper and electronic materials. The assets to be examined include all economic resources that can be measured in currency and owned or controlled by the audited entity, that is, all types of assets, creditor's rights, and other rights. When an audit institution exercises its right to examine according to law, nobody can either refuse or escape examination by transferring, concealing, falsifying, and damaging the data relating to financial and fiscal revenues and expenditures or by transferring and concealing the assets acquired in violation of national provisions; those committing such an offense assume corresponding legal liability.

---

[8] Guo Zhenqian, *Auditing in China.* Beijing: China Audit Publishing House, 1997, p. 37.

3) Right to Investigate and Obtain Evidence

Audit institutions have the right to carry out investigations of issues relating to audit projects involving the units or individuals concerned and obtain relevant testimonial materials, so as to ascertain the facts. The units and individuals concerned are required to support and assist the audit institutions in their work by providing truthful information and relevant testimonial materials. Besides, audit institutions have the right to inquire into the accounts and deposits of auditees lodged with financial institutions. When audit institutions inquire into the accounts and deposits of auditees in financial institutions, the latter must cooperate and provide all requested materials. To exercise such power, audit institutions must abide by strict procedures and undertake an obligation of confidentiality.

4) Right to Adopt Administrative Compulsory Measures

During their work, audit institutions are entitled to directly take certain coercive measures against audited entities or notify relevant departments to do so under specific circumstances. Currently, Chinese audit institutions have the following rights to adopt administrative compulsory measures: the right to deal with violations, the right to handle the safekeeping of materials and assets, the right to notify or require relevant departments to take coercive measures such as suspending appropriation or use of funds, and the right to apply for the freezing of deposits. Among them, removing violations or safekeeping materials and assets serve as a coercive measure audit institutions can directly take. The coercive approach audit institutions adopt against offenders directly or through relevant departments, can effectively combat illegal acts, safeguard national interests, and ensure a smooth audit. As the coercive measures may have an immediate influence on the rights of the auditee, audit institutions must exercise such power in line with the specific conditions and by following strict procedures, without prejudicing legal business activity or productive and operational activities.

5) Right to Seek Assistance

Audit institutions have the right to seek the assistance of relevant departments during the performance of their supervision through auditing responsibilities, when they cannot perform their duties and obtain appropriate and sufficient audit evidence due to limitations, or fail to prevent violations from damaging national interests. According to the needs of audit work, they may request the assistance of the departments of public security, supervision, finance, taxation, customs, price control, the industry and commerce administration as well as financial institutions. Relevant departments should render positive assistance and support, and strictly protect the secrecy of the audit situation.

6) Right to Transfer and Recommend

With regard to any problems found, audit institutions have the right to transfer them to relevant departments for further disposal, or report them to the audited entity and relevant departments, recommending corresponding measures. With its wide coverage, the right of Chinese audit institutions to transfer and recommend is specific to the violations of an auditee and of its responsible persons and relevant departments. Evidence of violations of the laws and rules identified may be transferred to the organs of discipline inspection and supervision, justice, procuratorate, public security, and so forth, for further investigation; and the opinions on correction and improvement may be put forward in regard to the systemic, mechanical, and institutional problems uncovered.

7) Right to Dispose and Punish

Audit institutions have the right to dispose of and punish any acts violating State regulations on fiscal and financial revenues and expenditures. Specifically, audit disposal refers to the corrective action legally taken by audit institutions against any such violations. Audit punishment refers to the sanction measures enforced in such cases involving the Audit Law and its Rules for Implementations. Audit institutions mainly are allowed to take the following disposal measures: ordering auditees to turn over within a time limit the part of the revenues due, or ordering the return of State-owned assets used illegally or income gained unlawfully, or ordering reprocessing in accordance with the national unified accounting system. Audit punishments include: warning, circulated criticism, fines, confiscation of illegal gains, and other punishment permitted by law.

8) Right to Notify or Publish Auditing Results

Audit institutions have the right to report to relevant government departments or make public the results of an audit and special audit investigation. In doing so, however, they must keep confidential State secrets and the business secrets of the auditees in accordance with law, abide by relevant stipulations of the State Council, handle specified confidentiality formalities and apply for approval from their auditing principals. Without authorization, the internal and satellite organs of audit institutions and individuals must not make public the results of audit and audit investigation. With regard to audit projects in which different levels of audit institutions participate at different times under unified organization, the results of audit and audit investigation should, in principle, be announced in a unified way by the organ in charge of the project. Additionally, as the announcement of audit results of a listed company involves the interests of a great number of non-State shareholders and public investors, and may also affect the capital market to some extent, audit institutions should notify the listed company of contents to be announced five days in advance.

The above provisions on audit duties and powers specify the scope and approach for audit institutions to their work. However, audit institutions may not always be able to bring all targets within their jurisdiction under supervision in a short term due to the restrictions in organizational deficiencies, personnel quality shortcomings, conflicting demands, and so on. Therefore, audit institutions should make overall plans and highlight specific foci. Audit practice over years shows that reform priority and central tasks vary in different periods during the construction of socialism with Chinese characteristics, as does the focus of government service in different areas. Hence, audit must be flexible and adaptable. In this view, it is necessary to firmly grasp the needs of reform and opening up and scientific development, rule of law and the fight against corruption, and determine the audit focus within the statutory duty scope of auditing. As was mentioned in Chapter I, the process of the establishment and development of the auditing system of socialism with Chinese characteristics is a process in which supervision through auditing is conducted on the principle of focusing on the central tasks, serving overall interests, and relating to the primary tasks of all places and governments at all levels, so as to effectively exert the audit role. This process reflects the positioning and function of supervision through auditing during the construction of socialism with Chinese characteristics. Accordingly, auditing must keep pace with the times and seek continuous development and improvement.

4. AUDITOR MANAGEMENT SYSTEM

Auditors directly exercise the right of audit supervision and directly carry out audit supervision activities. Chinese audit institutions are government administrative organs, and auditors are national public servants who perform their official duties according to law. Auditors should meet the overall requirements for public servants, perform their obligations, and enjoy their rights accordingly. The management of auditors, including their employment, appointment and removal, appraisal, reward and punishment, salary, benefit and insurance, resignation, dismissal, and retirement, shall be conducted in conformity with the Civil Servant Law and other national provisions. In view of the special nature of audit work, the State has formulated some special provisions and requirements for auditors in terms of recruitment, appointment and removal, professional technical qualification, occupational education, appraisal and evaluation, professional requirements, and so forth.

(1) Professional Requirements for Auditors

Audit supervision is a profession with strong principles and high specialization, which requires auditors to perform in conformity with relevant professional requirements.

First, is complying with laws and regulations and national audit standards. The basic professional requirement for public servants is to behave in an exemplary fashion in complying with the Constitution, and laws and regulations. Besides, auditors must strictly follow the national audit standards in view of the special features of their work. As the code of conduct for auditors in fulfillment of their statutory audit responsibilities, the national audit standards are a minimum requirement for audit work, the basic criteria to measure its quality and also the basis to determine and discharge the responsibilities of auditors. Auditors should strictly abide by the national audit standards in their work, and explain the reasons for any failure of compliance and assume liability for the consequences incurred thereof. To ensure auditors following the national audit standards and requirements for audit independence, audit institutions also lay down strict discipline separately.

Second, it is a requisite condition for auditors to abide by professional audit ethics scrupulously. Auditors shall follow the fundamental ethical requirements embodied in the key words of adherence to the rule of law, integrity, objectivity and fairness, diligence and sense of duty, and protecting professional secrets. Adherence to the rule of law means that auditors have a duty to carry out the supervision through auditing in accordance with the statutory mandate, powers, and procedures in order to maintain irreproachable professional conduct. Integrity (honesty and candidness) requires auditors to observe the principles and not to yield to external pressures; apply absolute honesty in reporting the facts and audit findings; abide by the standards of cleanness and self-discipline, and abstain from the use of their official position for private benefits; and protect national interests and public interests in the course of the work. Objectivity and fairness require that auditors shall strive to be objective and impartial in all work conducted, particularly in the audit conclusions, which shall, therefore, be based exclusively on appropriate and sufficient evidence, and audit evaluations and recommendations for dealing with the issues disclosed through auditing, which shall be made with a truth-seeking attitude. Diligence and sense of duty means that auditors shall perform their audit functions in an earnest and obligated manner, with devotion and respect, diligently and efficiently, conscientiously and painstakingly, in order to ensure the high quality of audit work. Protecting professional secrets requires that auditors shall not divulge State secrets or business secrets that they have known in the conduct of audit. Auditors shall not provide or disclose information in terms of materials obtained in the auditing process, audit records and other relevant information about the audit to third parties, except for the purposes of carrying out audit mandate or upon approval of competent authorities. Any auditor who violates the professional audit ethics shall get criticism and reeducation and administrative penalty; where the case involves a crime, the criminal responsibilities shall be investigated according to law.

Third, professional competence is required. Audit work is highly professional, so auditors must possess the necessary professional competence, including professional knowledge, skills, and experience nescessary to perform the audit. Auditors must be eager to learn and strive to maintain and enhance their professional competence. Meanwhile, audit institutions should take practical and effective measures for auditors to maintain and improve the professional competence. For specific projects, audit institutions shall assign the appropriate staff to the audit team to ensure that the team as a whole possess professional competence required by the audit project concerned. Where the information technology used by the audited entity may significantly affect the realization of the audit objective, the overall professional competence of the audit team shall include its competence in the field of information technology.

In the conduct of audit, auditors shall maintain an appropriate exercise of professional judgment and due professional care, keep an alert and skeptical attitude to any possible material irregularities in the audited entity, evaluate with reasonable care the audit evidence obtained to determine whether it is appropriate and sufficient, and draw audit conclusions in a convincing manner. In addition, the auditors shall communicate with the audited entity and listen to views and arguments of the audited entity, be objective and fair in reaching audit conclusions, respect and protect the legitimate interests of the audited entity, perform the audit in a civilized manner and avoid any conduct that might discredit auditors' professional image, and maintain a sound professional relationship with the audited entity.

(2) System for Employment, Appointment, and Dismissal of Auditors

Means of employment of auditors include recruitment, transfer, and engagement, of which recruitment means merit-based enrollment through national civil servants examination within the authorized personnel. The necessary expertise and skills for audit work can be added to the scope of recruitment examination for auditors. Public servants who are recruited through examination should hold a bachelor's degree or above. Persons who have audit professional qualification or relevant practicing qualification are preferred for employment under equal conditions. The probationary period of newly recruited auditors is one year. Qualified auditors who pass the probation will be employed; otherwise, the employment will be canceled. Transfer means transferring a person engaging in public affairs in the State-owned enterprises, undertakings, and civil societies to audit institution, in accordance with the regulations on administration of public servants. Audit institutions should rigorously investigate the transferred candidates and grant an approval according to the administration jurisdiction. When necessary, they can require the candidates to take the examination. Public servants transferred to various levels of audit institutions holding office at or below the level of deputy, especially those engaging in audit practice, must possess the conditions and qualifications as set forth in laws and regulations; besides, they shall generally have a bachelor's degree or above, audit expertise and relevant technical skills, and working experience of over five years in fields finance and economics, law, computer knowledge, engineering, management, and so forth. Engagement means employing public servants to hold the highly professional posts, that is, engineering audit, audit of resources and environment, and IT audit, upon the approval of competent departments of public servants at or above the provincial level. A written engagement contract should be concluded on the principle of equality, voluntariness, and consensus. The conclusion, alteration, or rescission of an engagement contract should be filed with the competent department of public servants at the same level on record.

The election and appointment system apply to auditors, of which the former is applicable to executive heads of audit institutions at all levels and the latter to others. In accordance with the Constitution, the Auditor General of the National Audit Office is nominated by the premier of the State Council, approved by the National People's Congress or its Standing Committee, then appointed and removed by the president. The Auditor General holds his term for five years and can be reappointed. In accordance with the Organic Law of the State Council and relevant stipulations of the State Council, the CNAO has several Deputy Auditors General, one director of the Joint Meeting for Central Accountability Audit and one Auditor-in-Chief to assist the Auditor General and be accountable to the Auditor General. The appointment and dismissal of Deputy Auditors General is determined by the State Council. As specified by the people's congress at various levels and the organic laws of local people's government, the executive heads of local audit institutions at all levels are nominated by the executive heads of the people's government at the corresponding level, appointed and removed from office upon the decision of the standing committee of the people's congress at that level, and filed with the people's government at a higher level for reference. The appointment and dismissal of deputy heads of local audit institutions are determined by the local governments at all levels. Deputy heads shall assist and be responsible to the executive heads of audit institutions. Meanwhile, in accordance with the provisions of the Audit Law, the appointment and dismissal of heads and deputy heads of local audit institutions at all levels should be subject to the prior opinions of higher-level audit institutions. Heads of audit institutions must not be dismissed or replaced at random unless they are found guilty of illegal acts or negligent of duties or are considered no longer qualified for the post.

(3) Professional Qualification System of Auditors

The audit professional qualification system is implemented to guarantee the high-quality professionalization of audit teams. Professional qualification is composed of three grades: junior auditor, auditor, and senior auditor. The State organizes the junior, intermediate, and senior qualification examinations of national audit profession in a unified manner. In accordance with the relevant national stipulations, the persons who pass the junior and intermediate qualification examinations can obtain the corresponding qualifications of junior auditor and auditor; the persons who pass the senior qualification examination and assessment can obtain the qualifications of senior auditor. Lead auditors in audit projects should generally have the professional and technical qualifications at or above intermediate grade.

(4) Professional Education System for Auditors

In order to ensure that auditors have sufficient professional competence, audit institutions implement a professional education system. Audit institutions shall formulate a professional education plan for auditors, organize various activities, and appraise the participation and performance. Professional education mainly covers the following aspects: audit expertise and relevant specialized knowledge, relevant laws and regulations, national audit standards and relevant professional norms, professional competence, business management knowledge and technique, and so forth. Audit institutions shall regularly organize education and training programs for auditors, such as professional training, audit business management training, comprehensive management training, and refreshment and updating training of knowledge and skills. The programs of professional education can be conducted in various ways, such as traditional off-job training and face-to-face teaching, online training, case study, and laboratory simulation. Auditors can also learn experience and improve their work capacity by means of field practice on secondment and study visit in grassroots areas with harsh conditions, enterprises, institutions, and construction units of major projects. Audit institutions also set up designated training agencies to strengthen the professional education on offer. For example, the CNAO establishes its Audit Academy and can provide training and teaching services for auditors nationwide.

(5) Performance Evaluation System for Auditors

In order to stimulate the enthusiasm of auditors, guide and encourage them to consciously improve their quality and achieve excellent performance, audit institutions implement a performance evaluation system. The scope of evaluation covers morality, capacity, diligence, performance, and honesty, of which the performance is the key area. Routine evaluation and regular evaluation can be conducted, while the latter generally refers to annual appraisal and is based on routine evaluation. The results fall into four classes: excellent, competent, basically competent, and incompetent, serving as the important basis for post adjustment, class and salaries of auditors, awards and punishment, and so on. Audit institutions shall reward the individual auditors or groups who have achieved outstanding work performance, significant accomplishment and contribution, or other outstanding practice. Meanwhile, in the conduct of selecting and appointing of officials, audit institutions have maintained the mechanism of treating morality as the core, style of work as the basis, capacity as the focus, and performance as the orientation, and accomplished the dynamic linkage with the performance evaluation system for auditors.

5. AUDIT OPERATION MECHANISM

Mechanism refers to the process and function in which elements of a system interact with each other. As an integral part of the government auditing system, the audit operation mechanism mainly functions to address issues of how audit institutions and auditors work and how the audit work plays its role. In the context of auditing system of socialism with Chinese characteristics, audit institutions have developed a set of unique and effective audit operation mechanisms adapting to China's national conditions through continuous exploration and innovation in practice. Compared with that of most foreign countries, China's audit operation mechanisms feature a distinct administrative nature and cover the whole process of audit practice, mainly including audit work plan, audit project implementation, audit results reporting and publishing, audit quality control, rectification of problems disclosed in the audit, settlement of audit disputes, coordination, and cooperation with related parties, and so forth.

(1) Audit Work Plan

1) System of Strategic Plan on Audit Work

Audit institutions implement the system of stategic planning on audit work to ensure sustainable and sound development of audit cause. The strategic plan serves as a guide of audit institutions for the development of audit work, mainly involving significant matters such as guiding principles, overall objectives, and main tasks of audit work in the near future. To further consolidate and improve the audit work, the CNAO and local audit institutions at all levels, from the perspective of strategic development, have formulated the strategic development plan of audit work based on their rich experience. The strategic development plan generally is made on a rolling basis of five-year period. These plans for different periods feather both the consolidation and improvements both in time and contents.

(a) System of Plan of Audit Assignments In order to ensure a well-scheduled conduct of audit work, audit institutions implement the system and prepare the annual plan of audit assignments, which serves as the overall arrangement of all the audit assginments in advance. Audit institutions should prepare the annual plan of audit assignments according to the statutory responsibilities and jurisdictional scope, focusing on central tasks of the government, with full consideration given to the requirements of the people's congress, administrative heads of governments at the corresponding level, and relevant leading authorities for audit work, as well as matters entrusted by relevant

departments. To produce a well-developed plan, audit institutions should focus on the integration and coordination of audit assignment, establish the database of auditees by industry and field based on the basic information about the auditees, classify and determine audit emphases and frequency, and so on. The development of both the medium- and long-term strategic plan and annual plans should highlight the focus of annual audit and ensure the realization of full-coverage audit in a certain period.

To adapt to the status of the Chinese auditing system, the annual plan of audit assignments follows the administration of unifield leadership and hierarchical responsibility. Audit institutions should submit the annual plan to the executive head of the local government at the same level for approval and then to the audit instituion at the next higher level. Meanwhile, audit institutions at higher levels should integrate audit resources at all levels to comprehensively conduct the audit of key funds and key projects relating to the overall situation or industry, instruct audit institutions at lower levels to prepare annual plans of audit assignments, and offer the recommendations on key fields or the project arrangements, so as to integrate audit resources and bring to the overall efficiency.

(b) System of Audit Plan   Audit insitutions carry out the system of audit plan to facilitate the accomplishment of annual plan. The business department of an audit institution should prepare an audit plan if, according to the annual plan of audit assignments, audit institutions shall organize a number of teams to jointly execute one audit assignment in a unified way or conduct the audit of the same type separately. The audit plan for key projects should be submitted to the people's government at the corresponding level for approval. The plan assigns the detailed tasks of unified audit to specific teams, puts forward the unified objectives, scope, contents, and emphasis of audit, and stipulates the matters concerning organizational mode, division of labor, coordination, summarization, and disposal. This will help audit teams to accomplish the audit tasks with the guidance of the audit plan, meet unified quality requirements, and realize audit objectives expected; in the meantime, it can ensure the effective coordination among all audit teams with concerted steps to highlight audit priorities and further utilize the audit results for the smooth completion of the plan.

(2) Execution of Audit Assignments

1) System of Audit Notification

The system of audit notification is implemented to safeguard the lawful rights and interests of auditees and ensure the smooth conduct of audit. Audit institutions should send a letter of audit notification to the auditee three days prior to the audit. In case of some circumstances that audit institutions have to handle an emergent matter or the auditee is suspected of serious violations of laws and regulations, audit institutions can directly carry out the audit on the presence of the audit notification upon the prior approval of the people's government at the corresponding level. With regard to the accountability audit, audit institutions shall send the letter of audit notification to the leading official to be audited as well as his/her present or former working unit. The letter of audit notification is a legal instrument to idenfity the rights and obligations between audit institutions and auditees, and the basis for the audit teams to fulfill their tasks. Upon arrival at an auditee, the audit team shall generally organize related personnel of the former to hold an entrance meeting in which the audit team will read out the letter of audit notification, with the discipline of audit work, and raise the requirements for cooperation. During the audit, the audit team should announce the title of the audit assignment, the provisions of audit discipline, whistleblower hotline, and the contact information of the audit team. Besides, audit institutions should inform the relevant enterprises and financial institutions where State-owned assets occupy a holding or leading position within 7 days of the completion of the annual plan of audit assignments in which these enterprises and financial institutions are listed as the auditees.

2) System of Audit Program

The system of audit program is implemented by audit institutions to strengthen the administration of audit assignments and improve the efficiency. Audit program refers to a detailed arrangements of audit work made by audit team to smoothly achieve audit objectives and complete the tasks. On the stage of audit execution, the audit team should prepare an audit program based on its preliminary understanding of the auditees. The audit program should be approved in accordance with the relevant provisions. The program for general audit assignments should be approved by the leader of the audit team and filed with the business department of the audit institutions for reference, and that for key audit assignments should be submitted to the heads of audit institutions for approval. The audit team can adjust the audit program when necessary, and these adjustments are generally approved by the leader of the audit team. However, any adjustment in regard to key matters including audit objective, the leader of the audit team, audit focus, the completion time for field audit, and others should be submitted to the head of the audit, institutions for approval.

3) System of Audit Evidence

Audit institutions follow a system of audit evidence to ensure that the audit conclusion is made based on clear facts and solid evidence. Audit evidence refers to all the information and facts that auditors have collected and used to serve as a reasonable basis for audit conclusions, including the evidence obtained when auditors tried to get an adequate understanding of the audited entity and examined specific subject matters. Obtaining audit evidence is the core of audit work and also the foundation for audit institutions and auditors to reach correct audit conclusions. Auditors should obtain audit evidence in accordance with their statutory mandate and procedures and in line with the criteria, facts, consequences, and causes to identify the irregularities. The audit evidence acquired by auditors should always be appropriate and sufficient.

4) System of Audit Documentation

In order to truly and completely reflect the process and results of an audit, audit institutions implement the system of audit documentation. This is an important means of reflecting the original auditing process, inspect the results and quality of the audit, and define audit responsibilities. Auditors shall document in an authentic and complete manner the process of audit implementation, conclusions they have drawn, and important management issues relating to audit assignments. There are three types of audit documentation: the records of inquiries, working papers and records of important management matters, of which the working papers should be examined by the leader of audit team. Audit documentation aims to support auditors in preparation of audit program and audit reports, certify auditor's compliance with relevant laws and regulations and national audit standards, and facilitate the guidance, supervision, and inspection of auditors' work.

5) System of Audit Field Management

Audit field management refers to a series of activities, that is, planning, organization, coordination, and control of audit execution and relevant matters, carried out by audit team during a period from entering at the auditee to begin the audit to the time of submitting audit results. Audit institutions implement the accountability system of the leader of the audit team under which the leader is ultimately responsible for all aspects of field audit, including audit execution, discipline, confidentiality, and safety, as well as the quality of audit program and audit report. With regard to such matters as the preparation and adjustment of the audit program, discussion on key audit matters, review of working papers and audit evidence drafting audit report, and analysis of the feedback by the auditees, the audit team should convene a meeting for collective discussion in a timely manner. The leader should promptly report to the audit institution assigning the audit team in any of the following circumstances: discovering clues of serious violations of laws and regulations; receiving important whistleblows and reports; asking for the assistance or coordination of relevant authorities; any serious circumstances relating to discipline, confidentiality, safety, possible damage to audit independence, and impact to the audit. During the audit, auditors should strictly abide by eight provisions of audit discipline and other regulations against corruption, as well as national laws and regulations on confidentiality, and strengthen the administration of field audit resources. It is required that auditors should jointly bear the meal and lodging expenses with the audited units. The expenditure breakdown, attendance record, and expense reimbursement situation for fieldwork funds should be announced within the corresponding unit.

(3) Audit Results Reporting and Publication

1) System of Audit Report

Audit institutions implement the system of audit report in order to truly and completely reflect audit results. An audit report is a legal instrument providing auditor's opinions and conclusions issued by an audit institution after completing necessary procedures, reflecting the audit results in a comprehensive manner. Issuing audit reports to the auditees is the basic channel and method of communicating audit results.

In pursuance of National Auditing Standards, audit teams shall submit audit reports after implementation of audits and, in the name of the audit institution, after going through the stipulated approval process, solicit feedback for the audit reports from audited entities, investigated entities, and the responsible persons who might be held to account. The auditees should provide a written opinion within 10 days from the receipt of the audit report from the audit team; if no written opinions are given within 10 days, it is deemed that the auditees do not challenge the audit reports. For ensuring audit quality, the report must be examined and approved after the control review by the business department of the audit institution and assurance review by the competent assurance review units. Audit reports in principle should be approved by business meeting of audit institutions; in rare circumstances, as authorized by the heads of audit institutions, they may be examined and approved by other members of the audit institutions' top management. Audit reports should be delivered to the auditees after they are officially signed by the heads of audit institutions.

For the accountability audit, both an audit report and audit result report should be issued. After an accountability audit report is examined and approved in line with the specified procedures, the audit team should seek the opinions of the leading officials audited and their units. The opinions of the Party committee at the corresponding level, related leaders of the government, and leading group of accountability audit, as well as relevant members of the Joint Meeting of Accountability Audit at the corresponding level should also be solicited upon necessity. After examining and approving the audit team's report in line with specified procedures, audit institutions should issue their accountability audit report signed by their heads to the audited leading officials and their units. Meanwhile, audit institutions should summarize the report of accountability audit results to be submitted to the management and supervision departments, mainly, reflecting the performance of the accountability of the audited leading officials, major problems found through auditing, responsibility identified, methods of audit disposal, and recommendations. Audit institutions should report the concluding documents of the accountability audit including the audit result report to leading officials of the Party committee and government at the corresponding level, and submit to the organization department that authorized the accountability audit, with a copy to relevant members of the leading group (Joint Meeting). If other authorities are involved, they can also be informed when necessary.

When carrying out real-time audits, audit teams shall notify, in the name of the audit institution, the audited entities of problems found during real-time audits, and request the entities to make corrections accordingly. After the completion of periodic real-time audits, the audit institution shall issue an audit report. The report shall include problems found yet not corrected by the audited entity, as well as significant problems that have been corrected and the status of correction.

2) System of Audit Disposal and Punishment and Audit Transfer

To strengthen the correction of problems found through auditing, audit institutions implement the system of audit disposal and punishment and audit transfer.

Audit institutions shall, within their mandates, make penalty decisions on activities that breached State regulations on government or financial revenues and expenditures, and issue letters of audit decisions on the basis of the audit report to make the disposal and punishment. Audit institutions should, prior to making a penalty decision on imposing a large-sum fine, notify the audited/

investigated unit and the persons concerned of their right to request a hearing. If the conditions for the hearing are met, the audit institution should hold it in accordance with the provisions of relevant laws and regulations.

Audit institutions shall, in accordance with relevant laws and regulations, notify the entities under audit or investigation and those responsible in a timely manner, and listen to their explanation and argument, where the facts, reasons, basis, or decisions for punishment in the approved letters of audit decisions are not consistent with, and more severe than, that listed in the draft audit reports for comment.

Audit institutions shall issue a letter of audit case transfer on the basis of audit report and transfer to the relevant authorities, where audits or special-purpose investigative audits identify issues that, according to relevant laws and regulations, shall be transferred to competent authorities or entities for correction, penalty, or to hold relevant persons to account, or any conflicts of stipulations concerning financial revenues and expenditures of higher authorities followed by the audited units with the laws and adminisrative regulations. Duty crimes, in which relevant entities or individuals are suspected of embezzlement, bribery, and dereliction of duty, or where staff members of State organs take advantage of their powers to commit other major crimes, should be transferred to procuratorial agencies for further investigation; other economic crime cases should be transferred to public security authorities for further investigation; the cases where an economic crime is not suspected, but the persons concerned need to be investigated for liability due to their violations of Party and government discipline, should be transferred to the disciplinary inspection organs or relevant management departments for further investigation; other issues that should be disposed of by competent departments (units), supervision authorities, or governments at various levels should be transferred to them as applicable. Relevant authorities shall carefully verify the clues of alleged violations of laws and discipline transferred by audit institutions, and return the results in time. Audit institutions shall follow up the investigation of matters transferred and make the results public at an appropriate time.

3) System of Audit Newsletter, Specific Report, and Comprehensive Report

To make full use of audit results, audit institutions implement the system of audit newsletter, specific report, and comprehensive report. Audit institutions at various levels can report audit results to the people's government at the corresponding level, higher-level audit institutions, and relevant supervision and management departments in the forms of audit newsletter, specific report, and comprehensive report.

Audit institutions may report the suspected major violations of law, major problems with regard to the policies for and implementation of national government and financial revenues and expenditures, major problems that pose a threat to national security, and significant matters impacting people's interests, to the government at the corresponding level or the audit institution at the next higher level in the form of specific reports or audit newsletters. If some problems uncovered in an audit needs to be resolved through discussion between the corresponding department and the government at a lower level, audit institutions in practice can notify the audit results in the form of a transfer letter.

Audit institutions may consolidate audit processes and results, and prepare comprehensive audit reports, when audit projects are organized by the same audit institution, and submit to the government at the corresponding level and the audit institutions at the next higher level, or circulate to related authorities.

4) System of "Two Reports"

The term *two reports* refers to an abbreviation of the audit result report and audit work report. Audit institutions implement the system of two reports in accordance with the Audit Law and other laws and regulations.

The audit result report refers to the report on the audit of budget implementation as well as other government revenues and expenditures at the corresponding level for the previous year, submitted annually by an audit institution to the executive heads of people's government at the corresponding level and audit institutions at the next higher level on the audit results and other fiscal revenues and expenditures for the previous year. The CNAO, under the leadership of the Premier of the State Council, exercises supervision over the implementation of the central budget as well as other government revenues and expenditures, and submits audit reports thereon to the premier. Local audit institutions at various levels shall, under the respective leadership of the executive heads of the people's government at the corresponding level and audit institutions at the next higher level, conduct audit on the budget implemented at the corresponding level as well as other government revenues and expenditures, and submit reports on the audit results to the people's governments at the corresponding level and audit institutions at the next higher level.

The audit work report refers to the report on the audit of budget implementation as well as other government revenues and expenditures for the previous year, submitted annually by the people's governments at and above county level to the standing committees of people's congresses at corresponding levels. The State Council and the local people's governments at and above county level should annually present the audit work report prepared by audit institutions on budget implementation as well as other government revenues and expenditures to the standing committees of the people's congresses at the corresponding level. The audit work report should give priority to the audit results regarding budget implementation. When necessary, the standing committees of the people's congress shall adopt resolution on the audit work report. The State Council and local people's governments at and above county level shall report to the standing committee of the people's congrss at the corresponding levels the results of rectification and solution of the problems mentioned in the audit work report. In practice, an audit institutions shall, on behalf of the government at the corresponding level, prepare the draft audit work reports, which, after examination and approval by the head of government at the corresponding level, with authorization of the government at the corresponding level, shall be presented to the standing committee of the people's congress at the corresponding level.

5) System of Announcement of Audit Results

Audit institutions implement the system of announcing audit results in accordance with the law. In the announcement of audit or investigation results, audit institutions shall not publicize any information involving state secrets or business secrets, issues under investigation and prosecution, and other information that shall not be publicized according to laws and regulations. Information involving business secrets may be released by audit institutions, upon the approval of the obligees or which audit institutions consider that non-disclosure may significantly impair public interests. With regard to the audit assignments/engagements that are organized by one audit institution and carried out by several audit institutions at various levels, the overall publication of audit and investigation results shall, in principle, be the responsibility of the organizing audit institution.

6) System of Disclosure of Government Information

In accordance with the *Regulation of the People's Republic of China on the Disclosure of Government Information* as well as other laws and regulations, audit institutions should establish the system of disclosure of government information. Government information refers to what is generated or acquired by audit institutions during the fulfillment of their duties, recorded and stored in a certain form. Disclosure can be taken in two forms: initiative disclosure and disclosure upon application. Such information should be disclosed on its own initiative: the mandate and institutional setting of audit institutions, audit laws and regulations and other normative documents, audit plan of strategic development and annual arangements, the minutes of important meetings and audit business, and others. Citizens, legal entities, or other organizations may, in view of their special needs in regard to production, life, and scientific research, apply to audit institutions for relevant government information. The government information provided upon application should be the existing information held by audit institutions, without any need to further summarize, process, analyze, or reproduce. Any government information related to State secrets, internal management, and others that should not be disclosed in accordance with the laws and regulations, shall not be made public. For government information involving business secrets and personal privacy, or probably resulting in the impact to the lawful rights and interests of a third party after disclosure, a written opinion of such third party should be obtained before the disclosure upon application; when necessary, it can be submitted to the relevant authorities for examination and approval. Audit institutions should reply within 15 days of receiving the application; the time required for seeking the third party's opinions should not be included. Any expense for providing government information upon application, other than the costs for retrieval, reproduction, mailing, and so on according to relevant regulations, shall not be charged. Such information should not be provided by other organizations and individuals in the form of paid services. Where an applicant argues that the audit institution fails to perform its obligation of information disclosure, he/she may report it to the administrative organ at the next higher level, supervision department, or the competent authorities of information disclosure. Where an applicant argues that the audit institution's specific administrative behavior during information disclosure infringes his/her lawful rights and interests, he/she may apply for administrative reconsideration or submit the matter to administrative litigation in accordance with the law. The audit institution concerned should promptly correct the relevant problems concerning information disclosure found through administrative reconsideration and lawsuit.

(4) Audit Quality Control

The mechanism of audit quality control is influenced by many factors, such as the size of the audit institution and the geographical distribution, nature, and complexity of the audit business. Despite no specific clauses in regard to the system of audit quality control, the National Auditing Standards do make explicit provisions on the following aspects: objectives and elements of audit quality control, respective responsibilities of member of an audit team (lead auditor), the leader of the audit team, the business department to which the audit team belongs, assurance review units and relevant heads of the audit institution in the quality control of audit assignments and their due accountabilities, archiving and management of audit documentation, quality examination and annual appraisal of the audit business, selection of excellent audit projects, evaluation on the system of audit quality control, and so forth. These regulations embody the concepts of audit quality control over the whole process with everyone involved.

1) Hierarchical Audit Quality Control

Articles 175 through 186 of the *National Auditing Standards of the PRC* elaborate the duties in regard to audit quality control and their due accountabilities stemming from any failure in the performance of their duties for the following people: members of audit team, lead auditor, team leader, business department of audit institution, assurance review units, Auditor-in-Chief, and relevant heads of audit institution. These regulations ensure relevant personnel participating in the implementation and management of the audit project perfectly understand their respective duties and responsibilities, as well as the realization of the quality control objective.

2) Mechanism of "Control Review–Assurance Review–Approval" for Audit Report

With regard to audit reports and audit decisions, the audit institutions implement a mechanism involving control review by the business department, assurance review by the corresponding units, and final approval, in order to secure the quality and reliability of audit results. After finishing the field audit, the audit team should submit audit reports and other relevant documents to the business department for control review. The business department is mainly responsible for reviewing the accomplishment of audit assignment by the audit team, the quality of audit evidence and documentation, as well as conclusive audit documents such as audit reports. Business units of audit institutions shall submit reviewed and amended audit reports, letters of audit decisions, and other audit materials, together with review opinions in written form, for assurance review. Based on the audit program, departments responsible for assurance review shall focus on the process and results of audit implementation, and review the accomplishment of audit assignment by the audit team, the quality of audit evidence and documentation as well as conclusive audit documents such as audit reports, and the compliance of audit procedure, and then issues the opinion. Audit reports and letters of audit decisions shall, in principle, be examined and approved by audit business meetings of audit institutions. In rare circumstances, as authorized by the heads of audit institutions, they may be examined and approved by other members of the audit institutions' top management.

3) System of Registration and Reporting of Intervention in Audit Work

Audit institutions implement the system of registration and report of intervention. During the whole process of the audit work covering drafting audit program, determining and verifying audit matters, preparing and reviewing audit conclusive documents and audit information, transfering cases evidence, and announcing of audit results, whenever any person exerts an influence on auditors beyond the normal working procedures, explicitly or implicitly asks them not to thoroughly investigate the related matters, fails to report or falsely announce the problems found, tries to through auditing so as to mitigate or even exempt from audit disposal and punishment, or query about audit work, auditors should register and report the audit project that the intervention is related, the nature of the intervention and its method, the name, unit, and title of each intervening person, and the handling and results of intervention, within one business day of the occurrence. Such documents should be included in the archives of the audit project.

4) System of Audit Quality Check

The implementation of audit quality check system meets the needs of China's audit institutions to conduct hierarchical supervision under the dual leadership system. Since 1997, the CNAO has organized quality checks of audit projects on its business departments, field offices, and local audit institutions. In 2000, the CNAO issued the *Provisional Regulations on Audit Quality Checks for Audit Assignments*. Some local audit institutions also promulgated their specific measures for audit quality checks successively in consideration of local actuality. The current Auditing Standards explicitly stipulate that audit institutions shall exercise an audit quality check system for the audit assignments of the audit departments, field offices or audit institutions at the lower levels. In practice, the units of audit institutions in charge of legal affairs are generally responsible for organizing audit quality checks or annual spot-check.

5) System of Excellent Audit Project Selection

Article 195 of the *National Auditing Standards of the PRC* defines the system of excellent outstanding audit project selection, and stipulates that audit institutions may organize at a regular basis the appraisal and screening for the excellent audit projects, and commend the selected excellent audit projects. Since 2002, the CNAO has organized the appraisal and screening for national excellent audit projects annually, covering its audit departments, field offices and local audit institutions of the CNAO.[9] From 2002 to 2014, a total of 255 projects undertaken by the CNAO and local audit institutions received recognition (see details in Table 3-1). Meanwhile, local audit institutions at various

TABLE 3-1 Schedule of Outstanding Audit Projects Selected by the CNAO in 2002–2014

Year	Number of the CNAO's Projects		Number of Projects of Local Audit Institutions	
	Outstanding	Awarded	Outstanding	Awarded
2002	5	14	\	\
2003	5	12	\	\
2004	5	12	\	\
2005	8	15	\	\
2006	8	18	10	20
2007	8	18	10	22
2008	8	20	10	23
2009	8	21	15	33
2010	9	22	15	33
2011	9	22	15	34
2012	10	20	15	30
2013	11	21	15	30
2014	10	20	15	30
Total	104	235	120	255

Note: This table is prepared in accordance with the CNAO's decisions on awarding the annual excellent audit projects (or the Circular of the General Office of the CNAO on annual excellent audit projects)over the years.

[9] Compiled by Editorial Committee of Auditing Cadres Professional Education Training Materials under the CNAO: *Interpretation of National Audit Standards*, p.171, Beijing: China Modern Economic Publishing House, 2012, p.171 August.

levels also followed this practice of the CNAO and arranged the appraisal and screening for the excellent audit projects. The demonstration and guidance of excellent audit project contributes to the improvement of audit quality and standardization of audit institutions at various levels.

(5) Rectification of Problems Disclosed by the Audit

For a long time, China's audit institutions have energetically promoted the rectification of problems revealed in audit, striving to enhance the audit effect and exert its role effectively. In accordance with the Audit Law, Regulation on the Disclosure of Government Information, National Auditing Standards, and other relevant stipulations, audit institutions are responsible for carrying out an audit and announcing the results, while the audited entities are responsible for the rectification of problems found and announcing the results. Besides, the governments at various levels of are obligated to supervise the rectification, and competent authorities of the State are responsible for the supervision and necessary assistance. Audit results and corresponding rectification shall be regarded as an important basis for appraisal, award, and punishment.

1) System of Rectification by Auditees

Auditees subject to audit have a responsibility and obligation to rectify any problems found, report the results of rectification to audit institutions and announce their results according to laws. Auditees should duly rectify and carefully study the problems revealed and audit recommendations, report the results of rectification to the government or competent authorities at the same level while notifying audit institutions in written form, and make a public announcement. The head of an auditee, as the first responsible persons for rectification, is obligated to effectively carry out the rectification, and will be subjected to censure due to the ineffective rectification. In case of ineffective rectification and repeated violations after frequent auditing, relevant personnel will be strictly held to account.

2) System of Government Supervision Over Rectification

All levels of governments shall conduct special study on the rectification of problems found in the audit of budget implementation and other financial revenues and expenditures every year, and incorporate the rectification of uncovered problems into the scope of supervision, so as to strengthen the supervision and inspection of the rectification.

3) System of Supervising and Assisting Rectification by Relevant Authorities

Competent departments of the State have the responsibility and obligation to urge auditees to rectify and assist in implementing relevant audit recommendations and opinions, and inform audit institutions of the implementation. Competent authorities of auditees are obligated to urgently correct problems found through auditing, study these typical, universal, and tendentious problems reflected in the audit in a timely manner and seek improvement. With regard to the suggestions of audit institutions on punishing an auditee as well as imposing sanctions on a person in charge with competent accountability and others with competent accountability, the relevant authorities and units should make a timely decision according to law and inform audit institutions of results in writing.

4) System of Follow-up of Rectification by Audit Institutions

Audit Institutions have the responsibility and obligation to inspect and supervise the rectification based on audit results, and should establish an effective system of inspection and follow-up. During the audit, audit team should timely urge the audited entity to correct any problems found and promptly improve its management to eradicate problems from source. After the issuance of audit reports and audit decisions, audit institutions shall inspect or inquire about the rectifications made by audited entities or other related entities within the prescribed time. Audit institutions shall, according to laws, adopt necessary measures for failure to make corrections or incomplete rectifications. Specifically, where an audited entity fails to execute an audit decision, audit institution should order it to do so within a specified period; if there is no response, the audit institution may apply to the people's court for compulsory execution, and suggest the competent authorities and units to impose the sanctions to the person in charge with competent accountability and others with competent accountability. After inspection, and follow-up, audit institution shall consolidate audit rectifications, and submit reports to the government at the corresponding level on the rectification of problems identified in the audit work reports. On this basis, the State Council and local people's governments at and above county level shall report the correction and disposal results of problems mentioned in the audit work report to the Standing Committee of the local people's congress. Moreover, audit institutions also have the right to make public the inspection results of rectification.

Background 5: Some Contents on Rectification in the Opinions of the State Council on Strengthening Audit Work

V. Pay close attention to the rectifications of problems revealed through auditing

(14) Improve the accountability mechanism for rectification. As the principal persons responsible for rectification, the heads of the audited entities shall focus on the rectification of problems identified, and supervise the rectification personally when it comes to major issues. Problems identified shall be fixed in time, and audit recommendations carefully studied. Audit institutions shall be informed of the results of rectification in written form, which, in the meantime, shall also be reported to governments of the same level or competent departments and announced to the public.

(15) Strengthen the supervision and inspection of rectification. Governments of all levels shall specifically study the auditing of major policies and arrangements of the country and the execution of relevant policies and measures, as well as the rectification of problems identified through auditing the execution of their own budget and other revenues and expenditures, which shall be inspected and supervised. For the problems revealed through auditing, the departments in charge of the audited entities shall supervise the rectification in time. Audit institutions shall establish a tracking mechanism to monitor the rectification, and request the assistance of relevant authorities in carrying out the rectification if necessary.

(16) Strengthen accountability for rectification. All regions and departments shall regard audit findings and rectification results as important references for performance evaluations, rewards and punishment. Major problems revealed through auditing shall be handled in accordance with laws and disciplines, and relevant persons shall be held accountable. Problems that signal unfavorable trends identified through auditing shall be studied without delay, and provisions and regulations shall be improved. The heads of audited entities that fail to make thorough rectifications shall be interviewed, whereas those who fail every audit and rectification shall be called to account strictly.

(6) Settlement of Audit Disputes

The exercise of audit mandate by audit institutions should be supervised by auditees. Audit institutions should assume corresponding legal liability if they violate the law or exercises its audit mandate improperly. To prevent audit institutions and auditors from abusing their audit supervisory power and fully safeguard the lawful rights and interests of auditees, an efficient and convenient mechanism for settlement of audit disputes has been established.

1) System of Applying for Government Ruling

In pursuance of the auditing regulation, where an audited entity refuses to accept audit decision on financial revenues and expenditures made by an audit institution through supervision in accordance with the provisions of Article 16 and Article 17 of the *Audit Law of the PRC as well as* Article 15 of the *Regulations for the Implementation of the Audit Law of the PRC*, it can, within 60 days from the date of receiving the audit decision, apply to the people's government at the corresponding level to which the audit institution belongs for making a ruling, which should be final ruling to both the auditee and audit institution, and the auditee shall not apply for any administrative reconsideration or instituting any administrative litigation. The ruling shall be handled by the legislative affairs office of the people's government.

2) System of Applying for Administrative Reconsideration or Instituting Any Administrative Litigation

If, except for the above-mentioned circumstance for applying for government ruling, an audited unit refuses to accept the audit decision made by an audit institution on the financial revenues and expenditures, it can apply for administrative reconsideration or institute an administrative litigation to the people's court. It should apply for administrative reconsideration within 60 days from the date of receiving the audit decision; where an audited unit directly institutes an administrative litigation, it should do so within three months from the date of receiving the audit decision; where it is dissatisfied with the reconsideration decision and institutes an administrative litigation again, this should be done within 15 days from the date of receiving the decision of administrative reconsideration.

3) System of Complaint, Review, and Reexamination

The corresponding mechanism for settlement of audit disputes is also available in the event that, during accountability audit, a leading official subject to audit is dissatisfied with the result. The leading official may, within 30 days from the date of receiving the report, lodge a complaint with the audit institution issuing the audit report, which, in turn, shall make a reexamination decision within 30 days from the date of receiving the complaint. Where the audited leading official still disagrees with the reexamination decision, he/she may, within 30 days from the date of receiving the decision, apply for review to the audit institution at the next higher level, which in turn has 60 days to make the corresponding decision. The review decision of the audit institution at the next higher level and the reexamination decision of the CNAO shall be the final.

(7) Coordination and Cooperation with Parties Concerned

Under the leadership of the Party committee and government at the corresponding level, audit institutions attach great importance to the coordination and cooperation with all parties including competent departments of the people's congress, disciplinary inspection organs, judicial authorities, and media in the course of audit work, and have established a flexible and efficient mechanism of coordination and cooperation with parties concerned with good effect. This is of great significance in making the work more effective, enhancing the audit supervision, facilitating auditees to strengthen rectification, and fully exerting the role of audit supervision.

1) Coordination and Cooperation at the Stage of Audit Planning, Implementation, and Utilization of Audit Results

At the stage of audit project initiation, audit institution shall determine audit projects based on the central tasks of the government, and with full consideration of the requirements of the people's congress, administrative heads of governments at the corresponding level and relevant leading bodies for audit work, and the matters entrusted by relevant departments or required to be audited. During the field audit, especially in the process of evidence collection, audit institutions often need to seek assistance from the organs of public security, supervision, finance, taxation, customs, price control, industry and commerce administration, and other units as well as financial institutions, when they encounter difficulties in performing the audit due to the restrictions in their law enforcement approaches, mandates and audit scope. For the application of audit results and rectification, audit institutions also need the coordination and cooperation of relevant competent authorities of government, judicial authorities, and media, to ensure the realization of audit objectives.

2) Coordination and Cooperation in the Accountability Audit

To strengthen leadership over the accountability audit, the Party committees and governments at various levels have established the system of Accountability

Audit Joint Meeting. The Joint Meeting, consisting of the departments of disciplinary inspection, organization, audit, supervision, human resources and social security, and State-owned assets supervision and administration, takes charge of studying and making the policies and systems relating to accountability audit, supervising and announcing the progress of the audit, and coordinating to solve the relevant problems in the work.[10]

3) Coordination and Cooperation in Investigating the Major Irregularities

To enhance the exposure and punishment of major economic crimes and irregularities, audit institution at various levels have established a system of close liaison, coordination and cooperation in collaboration with the departments of disciplinary inspection, supervision, public security and procecutor, strengthened the transfer and disposal of matters found through auditing and beyond the scope of the audit mandate, and made satisfactory achievements. Generally, the clues in cases transferred through auditing feature large amounts, high social attention, strong nature of investigation, and so forth, serving as a favorable foundation for case investigation and handling, thus become an important source to the organs of disciplinary inspection, supervision, inspection, and judiciary at various levels. Since 2000, the CNAO has, in collaboration with the Ministry of Public Security, Supreme People's Procuratorate, the Central Commission for Discipline Inspection, the Ministry of Supervision, etc, successively issued the notices on establishing the system of case transfer and strengthening coordination and cooperation. The Ministry of Public Security and the Supreme People's Procuratorate have also assigned their respective liaison officers to the CNAO, for daily coordination. In recent years, audit institutions have also coordinated and cooperated with the inspection of the Central of CPC, such as being briefed of audit supervision before inspection, strengthening the consultation on evidence uncovered, promoting the information sharing of audit and inspection, and establishing a mechanism of feedback for case investigation and handling, and so forth.

---

[10] Refer to the Provisional Regulations on the Economic Responsibility Audit of Party and Government Cadres and Leaders of State Owned Enterprises.

CHAPTER FOUR

Features, Effects, and Experience of the Auditing System of Socialism with Chinese Characteristics

T HE AUDITING SYSTEM OF SOCIALISM WITH CHINESE CHARACTERIS-
TICS (hereinafter referred to as "the auditing system") was established
on the Chinese audit history, which can be extended back to thousands
of years ago, and enriched and improved in recent times by constantly summing up experience during the process of establishing and improving the
socialist market economic system in line with China's national conditions.
Audit practice proves the auditing system of socialism is an important fundamental institutional arrangement for China's national governance, becoming
its bedrock and important guarantee. Summarizing 30 years of experience in
auditing system building is of great significance to further development and
improvement.

1. FEATURES OF THE AUDITING SYSTEM OF SOCIALISM WITH CHINESE CHARACTERISTICS

Most countries (regions) in the world have established their own distinct national auditing systems, which varied from each other due to the differences in governance goals, needs and modes (see Appendix B). Compared with others, the socialistic auditing system has distinctive Chinese characteristics.

(1) Features of the Auditing System

1) Audit Institutions Belong to Administrative Institutions

Audit institutions of the vast majority of countries are constitutional institutions, but differ in setting. Audit institutions of some countries are independent of the legislative, judicial and administrative organs, but are responsible to the legislative bodies. For example, Germany established the Federal Court of Auditors according to its fundamental law; as a constitutional institution, it is one of the supreme federal agencies independent of the legislative, judicial, and administrative organs. Audit institutions of the United States, Australia and some other countries are also independent of their administrative organs, and are responsible to the parliaments or lawmaking bodies such as the U.S. Congress. Others, still, are independent of both legislative and administrative organs, and have certain right of judicial decision. For example, the French Napoleonic Code formally promulgated in 1807 stipulated that the national court of auditors be a Supreme Court with powers including that of final decision. Some countries' auditing institutions exercise the power of both auditing and supervision. For example, the Constitution of the Republic of Korea provides that the Board of Audit and Inspection is led by the President and is responsible for government supervision. Audit institutions in some countries come under government departments. For example, the China National Audit Office led by the Premier of the State Council, independently exercises the right of audit supervision, and submits its reports to the National People's Congress upon entrustment by the Government. Local audit institutions at all levels, respectively under the leadership of the executive heads of people's governments at the corresponding levels and the audit institutions at the next higher level, are responsible for auditing work within their administrative areas.

Thus, audit institutions of China, acting as specialized supervisory bodies, are government departments, belonging to administrative institutions. This system currently has the following advantages:

First, it helps to improve the pertinence of audit supervision. Audit institutions under the direct leadership of the executive heads of the people's governments at corresponding levels; can treat audit work more consciously as an important part of overall economic and social development; strengthen auditing in implementation of major guidelines and policies, and the macro control measures of the Party Central Committee; enhance audit supervision over key areas, key sectors, and key funds; ensure smooth policy implementation; ensure in-place implementation of policies and measures; promote democracy and the rule of law; safeguard national security and national interests; and promote comprehensive, coordinated, and sustainable economic and social development.

Second, it helps to improve the timeliness of audit supervision. Thanks to the leadership of Party committees and governments at all levels, as well as the support and coordination of relevant departments, it facilitates timely reporting of audit results, the application of audit results, and government supervision over the correction of any audit problems uncovered. It also helps improve the timeliness of audit supervision and the audit supervisory effect.

2) Local Audit Institutions Are Responsible to the Governments at Corresponding Levels and Audit Institutions at the Next Higher Level

Countries differ in the relationship between audit institutions at higher and lower levels. For instance, India, Portugal and a few other countries only have one-level audit institutions, which are the national level. There is no local audit institutions and local audit work is carried out by the dispatched agencies. Countries that do have audit institutions at different levels may also have differences in terms of the relationship between supreme audit institutions and local ones. For example, in some countries like the United States, United Kingdom, and Japan, supreme audit institutions and local ones are completely equal, without any relationship of administrative subordination. The Board of Audit and Inspection of South Korea and other independent supervision organs have the relationship of guidance and cooperation; the Court of Auditors of France can accept an appeal against a local audit court and make a final judgment; the supreme audit institution of the Philippines conducts vertical management of local audit institutions.

China's local audit institutions implement the dual leadership system. Higher-level audit institutions lead lower ones in audit work, which determine the unity and multilevel features of the country's audit institutions. On the one hand, it adapts to the national conditions of China as a unitary state and the State system of administrative control. The State Council, as the highest administrative organ, conducts unified leadership of local administrative organs at all levels. Local people's governments manage the administrative work within their jurisdiction, leading subordinate departments and lower-level people's governments. Audit institutions established by local people's governments are led by executive heads of people's governments at the corresponding level, and also the audit institutions at the next higher level. On the other hand, the system meets the requirements for transformation of government functions under socialist market economy conditions. The relationship between the Central Government and local governments has undergone a process of transformation from administrative power decentralization to establishment and improvement of a reasonable overall decentralization system.[1] Under the socialistic market economy, the principle of giving full play to the initiative and enthusiasm of local governments under the unified leadership of the Central Government should be followed. Higher-level audit institutions control the overall audit work, thus being able to better grasp audit trends right down to grassroots level. This helps to strengthen the unified leadership of audit business and improve the quality and level of all audit work. Meanwhile, audit institutions established by local people's governments are mainly responsible for audit supervision of these governments in regard to the conditions of their financial revenue and expenditure, while the people's governments at that levels focus on management of audit institutions in personnel and financial affairs and daily work, which helps to fully mobilize the government's initiative and enthusiasm to strengthen management of audit institutions and ensure their smooth operation.

Since the establishment of the system, higher-level audit institutions have taken a lot of effective measures to strengthen leadership and guidance of lower-level organs, particularly in terms of their ideology, business management and audit practice. First, the system of briefing on important subjects was established to ensure lower-level audit institutions receive timely information on the political and economic situation, the guiding ideology of audit, organization, and implementation conditions of major audit projects, important laws and regulations, and important audit results. This helps lower-level audit institutions keep abreast of State policies and overall audit work and strengthen their macro awareness and overall awareness. Second, higher-level audit

---

[1] Yu Keping, *China's Political Reform towards Good Governance, 1978–2008*. Beijing: Social Sciences Academic Press, 2008, p. 94.

institutions strengthen plan guidance, providing guidance to subordinate units in regard to their annual work, define the audit priorities for the coming year, and guide the lower-level audit institutions to determine their own work plans and priorities and carry out the audit work focusing on the local economic environment. Third, higher-level audit institutions strengthen the coordination and guidance in normalization of audit laws, regularly organize quality inspections of audit projects and a rating system for excellent audit projects, and help lower-level audit institutions to conduct audit according to law and improve the overall audit quality.

Fourth, higher-level audit institutions integrate audit resources, properly arrange and organize lower-level audit institutions to get involved in unified audit projects or special audit investigation projects, focus on idea guidance, reflection of common problems from the macro perspective, and timely sum up and promote good auditing experiences and practices.

Fifth, higher-level audit institutions strengthen audit business authorization management, delegate some mandate to lower-level audit institutions, and conduct industry authorization audits and random examination and reviews of authorized audit projects in terms of plan implementation, quality, and results.

Sixth, higher-level audit institutions strengthen business training, guidance, and exchanges, and play a role of demonstration and normalization by holding professional audit training classes and themed symposia, the formulation of special audit guidelines, the promotion of typical audit cases, and so on.

Seventh, higher-level audit institutions strengthen the building of the leadership and teams of officials of lower-level audit institutions, make efforts to improve the measures for dual management of officials of local audit institutions, and implement the system of two-way communication between personnel at different levels.

Eighth, higher-level audit institutions have been accelerating informatization, helping lower-level audit institutions solve practical difficulties and problems in this process, organizing the communication of major typical cases concerning the application of computer audit techniques, and helping improve the practical technology skills of auditors.

Ninth, through the information-sharing mechanism, lower-level audit institutions can timely submit comprehensive business reports to higher-level audit institutions, and report any major event at any time and annual audit work according to the requirements.

In recent years, China's audit institutions at various levels have tightened their relationship. Article 18 of the Opinions of the State Council on Strengthening Audit Work stipulates that higher-level audit institutions strengthen the leadership of lower-level audit institutions, establish and improve the systems of work reporting, and so on. The Decision of the CPC Central Committee on Some Major Issues Concerning Comprehensively Promoting the Rule of Law adopted at the Fourth Plenary Session of the 18th CPC Central Committee stipulates that higher-level audit institutions must enhance the leadership of lower-level audit institutions and explore the unified management of audit institutions below the provincial level in human, financial, and material resources.

3) Reporting to the Standing Committee of the National People's Congress upon Entrustment by the Government

Regardless of the relationship between audit institutions and legislative bodies, audit institutions of most countries submit audit reports to the latter. See Table 4-1 for details. For example, the German Federal Court of Auditors does not accept parliamentary leadership, but offers audit results to Parliament and makes suggestions to improve the management and use of public funds; the French Court of Auditors is not responsible to Parliament, either, but it does submit audit findings and suggestions.

China's audit institutions do not directly report to the National People's Congress, but annually submit audit work reports to the Standing Committee of the NPC at the corresponding level upon government entrustment. The Audit Law of the People's Republic of China stipulates that the State Council and local people's governments annually submit audit work reports about budget implementation and other financial revenue and expenditure conditions to the National People's Congress (NPC) and its Standing Committee, focusing on budgetary implementation. The *National Audit Standards of the People's Republic of China* (PRC) stipulates that, in accordance with laws and regulations, the audit institution, on behalf of the government at the corresponding level, should draft the audit work report on budget implementation and other financial revenue and expenditure conditions, which, after being approved by the chief executives of the government at the corresponding level, is submitted to the Standing Committee of the NPC at the corresponding level upon entrustment by the people's government at that level. This shows that an audit institution's submitting audit reports on behalf of the government to the NPC is a way for all governments to be responsible to the people's congresses at the corresponding level and their Standing Committees and to accept their supervision. This way focuses on reflecting existing problems and relevant handling and rectification conditions, and budget implementation situation is further highlighted to help the NPC Standing Committee fulfill the responsibilities of

TABLE 4-1 Main Features of Supreme Audit Institution Mode[a]

Supreme Audit Institution Mode	Responsibility System of Auditor General	Collegiate System of the President of Audit or the Committee of President	Responsibility System of the President of the Audit Court
Heads	Auditor General	President/committee of President	President/Chief President
Organization structure	All the powers, authorities, responsibilities are given to the Auditor General; internal implementation of the hierarchical structure.	Independent members of the Court of Auditors or the Committee have certain freedom in the selection of work methods; decisions are made by the collegial mechanism or the committee composed of all members, or by both.	Independent members of the Court of Auditors are also the judges with the right of punishment and disposition.
Accountability mechanisms	All expenditures are approved by the parliament; annual reports are compiled by government sectors and other public institutions; supreme audit institution is responsible for auditing the accounts; the Auditor General reports to the parliament or the committee of the parliament in charge.	All expenditures are approved by parliament; annual reports are compiled by government sectors and other public institutions; supreme audit institution is responsible for auditing the accounts; the committee of collegial system reports to parliament or the committee of the parliament in charge.	All expenditures are approved by parliament; accounting personnel are responsible for handling expenditure affairs and compiling the financial statements; state accounts are checked by the Ministry of Finance; personal accounts are audited by supreme audit institution, which has the right to revoke or impose penalties on government officials; state accounts are audited and reported to the parliament by supreme audit institution.

(continued)

TABLE 4-1 (Continued)

Supreme Audit Institution Mode	Responsibility System of Auditor General	Collegiate System of the President of Audit or the Committee of President	Responsibility System of the President of the Audit Court
Relationship with the parliament	Closely related to the parliamentary committee in charge; may execute accountability.	Closely related to the parliamentary committee; may execute accountability over government or public institutions according to the audit report.	Independent or largely independent of parliament.
Audit type	Separate fiscal audit, forensic audit and benefit/performance audit, supervision impact assessment.	Legitimacy audit/compliance audit, performance audit, supervision impact assessment.	Legitimacy audit/compliance audit with the right of penalty, optional performance audit, supervision impact assessment.
Reporting system	All the audit reports should be submitted to parliament or the parliamentary committee in charge.	All the audit reports should be reported to the parliament or the parliamentary committee in charge.	Submit the annual audit report about the implementation of State budgets to parliament or the head of the state.

[a] Refer to *How to Improve the Role and Influence of Audit Report—Guide for Supreme Audit institutions*, compiled by the first divisional committee of INTOSAI Capacity Building Committee, and translated by Division of International Cooperation, National Audit Office, *Foreign Audit Information*, 2012, No. 3 (totally 63). (See http://cbc.courdescomptes.ma/ for the original text.)

final account approval and supervision over the implementation of government budget. Meanwhile, before the end of each year, an audit institution shall sum up the rectification work related to problems mentioned in the audit report and submit this to the people's government at the corresponding level. On this basis, the State Council and local people's governments above county level report on the rectification and disposal results of problems mentioned in the audit work report to the Standing Committee of the local people's congress. This approach reflects that audit institutions are responsible to the people's congresses and their Standing Committees at the corresponding level. This approach helps the Standing Committee enhance guidance and supervision of audit work, and also ensures the enforcement and authority of audit.

(2) Features of Auditing Duties and Authorities

1) Supervision Scope of Government Auditing Reflects Chinese Characteristics

Despite differences, the government auditing of different countries also have something in common in terms of their supervisory scope; similarities in government functions and the professional and technical features of audit dictate that there are some common audit duties. The vast majority of countries have established audit institutions mainly to ensure the safe, full, and effective use of public funds and State-owned assets. Audit of the management and use of public funds and State-owned assets is a fundamental duty. For example, audit institutions of such countries as Canada, France, Sweden, Britain, Russia, and South Korea audit government departments, public institutions, social insurance institutions, State-owned enterprises, joint venture enterprises partially owned by the State, and other enterprises enjoying national financial subsidies or tax preferences, as well as units involved in the management, allocation, and use of public funds.[2] However, due to differences in national conditions and national governance mode, the audit institutions concerned do not possess the same supervisory scope. For example, the U.S. Governmental Accountability Office has eight main responsibilities: reviewing the duty performance of the federal government; conducting follow-up audit of the implementation of major diplomatic, military, and economic policies; conducting prospective policy analysis of major risks in terms of politics, economy, society, and national security, and offering opinions and legislative proposals; evaluating whether some regulations are formulated by the federal government departments in

---

[2] Chen Taihui et al., *Audit Law*, 1st ed. Haikou: Hainan Publishing House, April 2000, pp. 105–106.

accordance with legal procedures prior to their submission for legislative approval; legally judging the liabilities federal officials should assume in use of financial funds, and the complaints made by stakeholders involved in bidding/tendering for government procurement projects; auditing and investigating fraudulent behavior; conducting information system security audits; and delivering audit opinions on the financial statements of the federal government and its agencies, annual financial reports, and management of State-owned assets.[3] The Accounts Chamber of Russian Federation audits the preparation and implementation of federal budget plans, financial statements, annual financial reports, disclosure of government debts, State-owned assets management, the behavior of financial institutions, and other major issues affecting national security and people's livelihood; it also undertakes responsibilities for combating corruption and crime, conducting strategic audits, and dynamically supervising the implementation of major strategies and policies. The German Federal Court of Auditors audits the implementation of federal budget plans, financial statements, and annual financial reports, and also has the right to participate in the preparation and discussion of federal budgets. The Office of Comptroller and Auditor General of India is responsible for preparing and auditing the financial reports and other final annual reports of the federal government, the states, territories and government agencies.[4]

Like other countries, China has its own distinctive political and economic systems. The Constitution and various laws endow audit institutions with appropriate supervisory authority mainly embodied in the following aspects: First, audit institutions supervise the management and use of State-owned assets. Adapting to the national conditions of the basic economic system of keeping public ownership as the mainstay and allowing diverse forms of ownership to develop side by side, and governments being the owners of State-owned assets, audit institutions conduct audit supervision of State-owned enterprises and State-owned financial institutions, as well as enterprises and financial institutions in which State-owned capital plays a controlling or dominant role. Second, they supervise the management and use of State-owned resources. Both the Constitution and laws stipulate that urban land, minerals, rivers, forests, waters, and other elements belong to the State. Audit institutions are responsible for supervising the management and use of land, minerals, forests, rivers, waters, grasslands, beaches, mountains, wastelands, animals, cultural relics, and other State-owned resources. Third, audit institutions supervise handling of public funds. Audit institutions are responsible for the supervision

---

[3] Scientific Research Institute of the China National Audit Office, *Introduction to Foreign Audit Supervision System*. Beijing: China Modern Economic Publishing House, 2013, pp. 11–13.
[4] Ibid.

of public financial funds, government funds, government debt funds, State capital budget funds, as well as various kinds of funds managed by government departments or by relevant units upon entrustment, including social insurance funds, socially donated funds, international assistance and loan funds, housing provident funds, and lottery commonweal funds. Fourth, adapting to the principle that the Party manages officials, audit institutions conduct audit supervision of party and government leaders and State-owned enterprise leaders in fulfillment of their economic responsibilities, and conduct supervision and restriction in regard to exercise of public power. Fifth, audit institutions are responsible for revealing hidden economic risks, paying close attention to potential risks, weaknesses, and possible social instability factors concerning finance; people's livelihood; State-owned assets, energy, resources, and environmental conservation, especially the situation of local government debt and regional financial stability; and safeguard national security. In addition, they have the right to review the audit reports issued by social audit institutions for audit supervision objects in accordance with law and to guide and supervise the internal audit work of latter according to the law.

Although China's audit supervision scope is relatively wide, the audit institutions never participate in or intervene in decision-making and management processes. The audit institutions of Germany and India, for example, participate in budgeting and deliberation, while their Chinese counterparts are mainly responsible for auditing the authenticity, legitimacy, and effectiveness of financial management, budget execution, and final settlement; they submit relevant audit reports and maintain the audit role of independent external supervision.

2) Economic Accountability Audit of Leading Officials

Rule by law is an important symbol of modernization of the national governance system and governance capacity. Administering officials according to law, and administering power according to law, are important aspects of rule by law. For thousands of years, China's government auditing has always involved official inspection and assessment, serving as an important way to restrict and supervise the exercise of power. The economic accountability audit is one with Chinese characteristics. It means the inspection and evaluation of State organs and State-owned enterprise leaders in fulfillment of their economic responsibilities by audit institutions upon entrustment of the management departments of officials. The economic accountability audit derived from the needs of power supervision and restriction in the period of continuously deepening political and economic system reform with constant improvement. In May 1999, the General Office of the Communist Party of China (CPC) Central Committee and the General Office of the State Council issued the Interim Provisions on Economic Accountability

Audit of Leading Officials below the County Level during the Term of Office and the Interim Provisions on the Economic Accountability Audit of State-Owned Enterprises and State Holding Enterprise Leaders during their Term of Office (hereinafter referred to as the "two Interim Provisions"), marking the formal establishment of the economic accountability audit as a supervisory system. In February 2006, this was written into the Audit Law of the PRC with the gradual legislation of the economic accountability audit. In October 2010, the General Office of the CPC Central Committee and the General Office of the State Council promulgated the Provisional Regulations on the Economic Accountability Audit of Party and Government Officials and Leaders of State-Owned Enterprises as the system was continuously improved. In July 2014, seven central ministries and commissions jointly issued the Rules for the Implementation of Regulations Concerning Economic Accountability Audit for Leading Officials of the Party and Government and Leaders of State-Owned Enterprises, which was another milestone in development of the system. The overall effect is to improve the management supervision system of officials, and it also provides an important basis for implementing the supervision and accountability mechanism ensuring a match between powers and responsibilities, and power supervision, providing compensation for infringement and investigating law-breaking liabilities. It has become an important system for supervising the Party and State officials.

The economic accountability audit as an important aspect of "restricting and supervising powers with powers according to the law" is also an important link of "putting power in a cage" and an important part of the socialistic auditing system with Chinese characteristics. Along with the continuous development and improvement of the system, comprehensive supervision of "economic" powers at all levels and categories of leading officials is realized. On the one hand, the audit of leading officials from the Party and government organs and State-owned enterprises with key "powers" focuses on checking whether they are effectively performing their duties, correctly exercising power, or are engaged in behavior that violates laws and rules within their areas and units, to effectively prevent power from being abused, remedy decision-making mistakes, and investigate anomalous behavior. On the other hand, an objective, fair, realistic audit and evaluation of leading officials in work performance and responsibility fulfillment through professional and technical means facilitates the assessment, appointment and dismissal, and rewards and punishment system for leading officials. In accordance with the provisions, an audit institution submits the concluding documents of the economic accountability audit to the main responsible comrades of the Party committee and government at the corresponding level, as well as the organization department that authorized the audit, with a copy to relevant member units of the economic accountability audit-leading group. During the application of audit findings, discipline inspection and supervision departments accept the cases involving alleged violation of the laws and discipline transferred by audit institutions, and will investigate them. In accordance with the audit findings and relevant provisions, the organization department will deal with the audited-leading officials and other relevant personnel, and place a copy of the audit findings into their personal files, which will serve as an important basis for the subsequent activities of assessment, appointment and dismissal, and rewards and punishment. The situation of economic responsibility fulfillment and rectification in regard to audit findings constitute an important part of the democratic life meeting and for the leadership to present their work reports to officials. Within their level of responsibility, the human resources and social security departments will handle the related matters concerning assessment, appointment and dismissal, and rewards and punishment of audited leading officials and relevant personnel. State-owned assets supervision management departments must regard audit findings as an important basis for the evaluation of an enterprise's operating performance and the assessment, appointment and dismissal, rewards and punishment of audited leaders, and urge full implementation of the audit decisions and rectification requirements.

Background 1: Part of the Rules for the Implementation of Regulations Concerning Economic Accountability Audit for Leading Officials of the Party and Government and Leaders of State-Owned Enterprises, about the Application of Audit Findings

The Rules for Implementation stipulate the main duties of relevant departments in application of economic accountability audit findings.

The main duties of discipline inspection and supervision departments are as follows: (1) accepting cases transferred by audit institutions according to discipline and the laws; (2) investigating any behavior violating laws and disciplines discovered through economic accountability audits according to requirements; (3) study in a timely way the typical, universal, and tendentious problems reflected in audit findings; and (4) informing audit institutions in an appropriate way of the application of any audit findings.

Main duties of organization departments are as follows: (1) including the economic accountability audit into the management supervision system of officials in accordance with the relevant work requirements; (2) dealing with audited leading officials and other relevant personnel in accordance with the audit findings and relevant provisions; (3) placing copies of the economic accountability audit findings into the files of the audited leading officials, which will serve as an important basis

(continued)

for assessment, appointment and dismissal, rewards and punishment; (4) regarding the situation of economic responsibility fulfillment and rectification highlighted by the audit findings as an important part of the democratic life meeting and the leadership work report meeting; (5) studying typical, universal, and tendentious problems reflected in the audit findings, and regarding them as a basis for taking relevant measures and improving the relevant system provisions; and (6) informing audit institutions of the application of audit findings in an appropriate, timely manner.

Main duties of human resources and social security departments are as follows: (1) in accordance with relevant provisions, handling the related matters concerning assessment, appointment and dismissal, rewards and punishment of audited leading officials and relevant personnel within the bounds of their authority; (2) timely study of typical, universal, and tendentious problems reflected in audit findings, and regarding them as a basis for taking relevant measures and improving system provisions; and (3) informing audit institutions of the application of audit findings in an appropriate, timely manner.

Main duties of State-owned assets supervision management departments are as follows: (1) in accordance with relevant requirements for management of leaders of State-owned enterprises, including the economic accountability audit into the system for management and supervision of leaders of State-owned enterprises; (2) regarding audit findings as an important basis for the evaluation of enterprises' operating performance and the assessment, appointment and dismissal, and rewards and punishment of audited leaders; (3) during the management and supervision of state-owned enterprises, the reform of State-owned enterprises and the disposal of State-owned assets, effectively applying audit findings; (4) urging relevant enterprises to implement the audit decisions and rectification requirements; (5) timely studying typical, universal, and tendentious problems reflected in audit findings, and regarding them as a basis for taking relevant measures and improving system provisions; and (6) informing audit institutions of application of audit findings in an appropriate, timely manner.

Main duties of relevant competent authorities are as follows: (1) disposing and punishing any violations of laws and rules transferred by audit institutions, within the stipulated bounds of their authority; (2) urging relevant departments and units to implement the audit decisions and rectification requirements, and effectively applying audit findings during management and supervision of related industries and units; (3) timely studying typical, universal, and tendentious problems reflected in audit findings, and regarding them as a basis for taking relevant measures and improving relevant system provisions; and (4) informing audit institutions of application of audit findings in an appropriate, timely manner.

3) Follow-up Audit of Implementation of Policies and Measures

Policies are the guidelines formulated by a State for achieving the routes and tasks in a certain historical period, and also an important way to strengthen the macro control and management. Promoting the implementation of major policies is an effective way for audit to serve national governance, and also one important feature of China's government auditing. In this regard, government auditing has natural advantages, playing a unique role: on the one hand, government auditing, not being hindered by any sectoral interests, is independent, objective and impartial, and can fully promote policy implementation; on the other hand, government auditing with the mission of "establishing legal systems and common rules and scrutinizing its policies" enjoys closer familiarity with the policies and laws, and thus can fully promote policy implementation through its good professional advantages. For this reason, the CPC Central Committee and the State Council require audit institutions to fully play a role of "catalyst" to deepen reforms and as supervisor of policy implementation, ensuring smooth policy implementation and improving the execution of power. The Opinions of the State Council on Strengthening Audit Work explicitly stipulates that promoting the implementation of policies and measures is an important duty of audit institutions, which shall constantly organize follow-up audits over implementation of major national policies and measures, and macro control deployments, and focus on supervising and checking various regions and departments in the planning, progress, and actual effect of implementing the policies and measures for stabilizing growth, promoting reform, adjusting the structure, benefiting people's livelihood, and preventing risks, so as to promote further implementation of policies and measures.

In recent years, the audit institutions of China have focused on supervising and checking the implementation of policies and measures of the Party and the State, made efforts in supervising and checking the implementation of policies and measures concerning finance, banking, industry, land, taxation, and environmental protection, respectively, on the basis of auditing true and legitimate benefits of financial revenue and expenditure, and have revealed and investigated in a timely way behavior violating policy requirements, disobeying orders and ignoring prohibitions, to ensure smooth policy implementation; they have deeply analyzed the situation and effects of realizing policy objectives, revealing and reflecting the problems including imperfection, misconnection, and mismatch of policies and measures, and failure to realize objectives, in order to make policies and measures more realistic, reasonable, and effective; they also have played the advantage of audit which is independent, objective, and involving all aspects of economic and social development, paid close attention to economic and social development, revealed and reflected new situations and new problems, and provided a reference and basis for the timely adjustment and improvement of policies and measures, thus having achieved good results.

Related Background 2: Part of the Opinions of China National Audit Office on Further Playing the Role of Audit on Promoting the Implementation of Policies for Stabilizing Growth

2. Major Tasks

(d) Promoting acceleration of major construction projects. According to the national special plans and regional development strategies, review the major national engineering projects related to the information grid and oil gas networks, eco-environment protection, clean energy, food and water conservancy, transportation, health and pension services, and security of energy and mineral resources, as well as major construction projects of urban infrastructure and affordable housing, from the perspectives of timeliness of planning and investment approval, progress, fund guarantee, completion acceptance, project operation and other aspects, to help all parties better fulfill responsibilities, improve the approval efficiency and quality, and play the guiding role of government investment in stimulating economic growth and promoting structural adjustment.

(e) Promoting overall use of financial funds. Continue to strengthen the audit of financial stock funds of all levels, pay special attention to the problems such as missed investment, missed use, low benefit, incomplete scope of liquidation and revitalizing financial stock funds, slow progress, and evasion of problems through expenditure misrepresentation and sudden arrangement, and promote acceleration of liquidating and revitalizing assets; strengthen the audit of special funds for people's livelihood improvement, structural adjustment, and others; reveal the problems including multiple management, multiple distribution, cross-repeating, complex allocation, and lagging of issuing orders; promote the integration and optimization of the same category of special funds; and improve the measures and systems for management of special funds.

(f) Promoting implementation of major policies. In fiscal policies, there is a need to pay special attention to whether all regions optimize the structure of fiscal expenditure and guarantee the timely availability of funds for projects under construction. In tax policies, it is necessary to pay special attention to whether all regions implement preferential tax policies, intensify the rectification and standardization of the import and export charging mechanisms, and further reduce the burdens shouldered by the real economy, especially the small and micro enterprises. In monetary policies, special attention should be paid as to whether all regions give full play to the financial support role of the real economy and help support major project financing. In policies concerning industry and people's livelihood, it is necessary to pay special attention to whether all regions intensify their support to industries in regard to pensions, health, insurance, science and technology, information technology, and new energy; take effective measures to promote industrial restructuring and upgrading; or have unveiled specific measures to support the development of e-commerce, logistics, energy conservation and environmental protection, culture, sports, and other growth sectors so as to foster new economic growth points.

(g) Further streamlining administration and delegating power to lower levels. It is necessary to supervise and check the progress and effects of all sectors and regions in canceling items requiring administrative examination and approval or delegating the examination and approval power to the lower-level organs, or comprehensively abandoning administrative approval and deepening the reform of the commercial system, as well as stepping up efforts in clearing up and standardizing intermediary services regarding administrative examination and approval; pay special attention to whether the transformation of government functions is in place after decentralization of administrative examination and approval powers as part of the effort to achieve enterprise deregulation and facilitate entrepreneurship; put forward suggestions for correcting prominent problems, and promoting the amendment and improvement of related supporting systems and rules to create conditions for public entrepreneurship and innovation.

(h) Prevention of potential economic risks. It is vital to pay close attention to the uncertainties that may occur during the reform process, as well as the risks and problems that may arise during economic structural adjustment; pay special attention to government debt risks and track the potential risks of and find solutions for stock debts; pay attention to changes in the quality of financial institution assets, and track and reflect the conditions for financial innovation, Internet finance, and informal finance, as well as the changes in cross-border capital flows.

4) Authority in Regard to Audit Disposal and Punishment and Taking Coercive Measures

In the process of fulfilling audit supervision duties, audit institutions of all countries are generally given the authority of inspection, investigation, reporting, and recommendation. In addition to these aspects, the Court of Auditors of France also has certain jurisdictional authority such as punishment. However, this authority applies only to individuals; that is, it is an authority of judgment over the case in which financial fund losses result from an individual civil servant's dereliction of duty and the missing funds need to be recovered from him/her. Authority of disposal and punishment of the Board of Audit and Inspection of South Korea means it is entitled to ask relevant departments to punish or discipline responsible officials. The audit institutions of China have broader authority of audit disposal and punishment and taking coercive measures.

They are entitled to directly dispose of and punish any behavior related to fiscal revenue and expenditure and financial revenue and expenditure violating State provisions; this means taking corrective measures and directly conducting audit disposal in both regards. Meanwhile, for any behavior related to financial revenue and expenditure that violates State provisions, the Audit Law and its enforcement regulations, audit institutions can directly conduct audit punishment. If any target of an audit is found to violate State provisions regarding financial revenue and expenditure, the Audit Law and its enforcement regulations, refuses or delays to provide materials related to audit, provides materials that prove to be untrue and incomplete, refuses or in other ways obstructs inspection, or refuses to rectify a situation after being ordered to do so, the audit institution, on the basis of audit disposal, is entitled to directly conduct audit punishment of the audited businesses or relevant responsible personnel.

Authority of audit disposal and punishment is an important authority of China's audit institutions. They directly deal with and punish behavior in regard to fiscal revenue and expenditure and financial revenue and expenditure violating State provisions, which conform to the national conditions of China. Currently, phenomena of violating laws and rules are relatively common in the field of finance and economics. As State administrative organs, the audit institutions enjoy the right to disposal and punishment, which is vital. On the one hand, this is conducive to timely correction and punishment of all kinds of violations of the laws and rules related to fiscal revenue and expenditure and financial revenue and expenditure; on the other hand, it is also conducive to supervising and correcting the not-in-place management and law enforcement of the relevant competent economic authorities, reducing administrative law enforcement costs and raising administrative law enforcement efficiency. It is also conducive to enhancing the deterrence of audit supervision, and promoting smooth audit and bringing into full play the audit supervisory function.

During audit, in specific circumstances, audit institutions are entitled to directly take certain coercive measures against offenders or notify relevant departments to do so, which is also an important feature of China's audit authority. Among them, removing or safekeeping materials and assets is a coercive measure that may be directly undertaken by audit institutions. Audit institutions may notify or require relevant departments to take coercive measures such as suspending appropriation or use of funds, and freezing deposits. The approach that audit institutions directly take coercive measures against offenders, or notify relevant departments to do so, can effectively combat the relevant illegal acts, safeguard national interests, and ensure a smooth audit.

(3) Features of the Auditor Management System

1) High Professional Requirements

Audit institutions of China are government departments, and auditors are national public servants. Management of auditors, therefore, follows the provisions and requirements for management of all Chinese civil servants and highlights the professional characteristics of audit. Auditors must have strong professional knowledge, professional skills, and work experience enabling them to engage in audit business. Audit institutions of many countries hire related professionals to provide the technical services of audit or outsource a lot of audit work. Slightly different from audit institutions of other countries, however, audit institutions of China, apart from hiring few external professionals in the fields of investment audit and enterprise audit, carry out the vast majority of the work through in-house auditors, thus raising very high requirements for specialization. In terms of professional knowledge, along with the continuous expansion of the government auditing scope, audit institutions need not only persons with knowledge of audit and accounting work, but also a considerable number of personnel with certain professional knowledge in the fields of law, computers, architectural engineering, environmental engineering, economic management, and the like. In order to ensure that auditors have necessary professional competence, the State sets higher requirements for the professionalism of auditors and implements a relatively strict professional access system. In accordance with State provisions, in addition to passing the national civil service examination, newly recruited auditors will participate in an additional examination to test their professional knowledge and skills. Besides the conditions and qualifications stipulated by relevant laws and provisions, any personnel employed by an audit institution by work transfer must have a bachelor's degree or above, professional acknowledge of audit and relevant skills, as well as more than five years of audit-related work experience. Audit institutions of China actively promote the vocational education system, constantly strengthen education and training, and create favorable conditions for auditors to improve their professional standards, maintain and improve their professional competence. In addition to the implementation of the audit professional qualification system, audit institutions also take measures to encourage personnel to participate in all kinds of on-the-job learning, academic and degree education of related disciplines and obtain relevant professional qualifications.

2) Strict Disciplinary Requirements

A good blacksmith needs to toughen himself for the hard work involved. Audit institutions are the specialized supervision departments of the State. Auditors directly exercise the right of audit supervision and directly carry out audit supervision activities. In order to guarantee that audit institutions and auditors independently exercise the right of audit supervision strictly in accordance with the law and ensure they serve the people, the State has put forward strict rules of professional conduct, codes of ethics and disciplinary requirements for auditors. Auditors not only need to strictly comply with laws, regulations, and national audit standards and adhere to audit professional ethics, but also need to abide by the disciplines of politics, organization, confidentiality, incorrupt construction, finance and economics, and so on. Any auditor violating disciplines shall be dealt with and punished by means of criticism and education, persuasion and admonition, circulating a notice of criticism, and organizational or disciplinary disposal according to the seriousness of the offending behavior; anyone suspected of a crime shall be transferred to the judicial organ for investigation. Meanwhile, in order to achieve stricter governance of audit teams and ensure audit independence and an incorruptible approach to audit work, some audit institutions impose pressures on themselves and consciously seek to improve their disciplinary requirements. For example, in accordance with the requirements of the State Council, the China National Audit Office issued the strict audit disciplinary code known as the "Eight Restrictions" in 2000, stipulating that auditors shall not have any economic ties with the person or organization being audited. In 2008, this was revised and improved according to changes in the situation. Driven by the China National Audit Office, some local audit institutions have also formulated audit disciplines in accordance with local conditions and implement the requirements of the Eight Restrictions.

Related Background 3: Main Contents of the Notice of the National Audit Office Issuing the "Eight Not Allowed" Audit Work Discipline (Revised in 2015)

1. Auditors are not allowed to ask the person/organization being audited to reimburse or to subsidize their accommodation, meal fees, traffic, communication, medical treatment, and so on.

2. Auditors are not allowed to accept any gifts and cash from the audit target or get paid by giving lectures and other means without approval.

3. Auditors are not allowed to participate in activities arranged by the audit target, such as banquets, entertainment, and tourism.

4. Auditors are not allowed to seek profits by making use of the state secrets, business secrets, and inside information gotten in audit work.

5. Auditors are not allowed to intervene in the approval or distribution of the funds, assets, and resources managed by the audit targets according to law.

6. Auditors are not allowed to sell goods or to introduce business to the audit target.

7. Auditors are not allowed to intervene in the audit work upon the audit target's request.

8. Auditors are not allowed to impose any requirements unrelated to the audit on the audit target.

3) Comprehensive Examination and Evaluation

As an important method for strengthening management of the audit work, examination and evaluation can greatly guide and motivate auditors to improve their qualifications and performance. Different from audit institutions in some countries that lay emphasis on examination and evaluation of auditors' fulfillment of professional duties, audit institutions of China stress comprehensive examination and evaluation to give full play to the guiding and incentive function of such activities, and seek to build an examination and evaluation mechanism with ethnics as the core, responsibility as the foundation, capability as the key, performance as the orientation, and system as the guarantee. The scope of examination and evaluation covers political quality, ethical conduct, work style, ability, performance, and integrity, especially work performance. For instance, the focus of examination and evaluation for active audit staff lies in the individual's performance in organizing or completing audit projects with high quality, investigating violations of the laws and disciplines in strict accordance with the law, putting forward specific and practical audit recommendations, or promoting innovation of audit methods or technologies; as for those personnel engaged in integrated management services, the focus of examination and evaluation lies in their performance in strictly implementing policies, making scientific and overall arrangements, improving work efficiency, or providing high-quality services. In the fields of examination and evaluation, regular and fixed examinations are undertaken to avoid overgeneralization. Audit institutions stress application of examination and evaluation results as an important basis for the appointment and dismissal, and rewards and punishment of auditors.

(4) Features of the Audit Operating Mechanism

1) Integrating Audit Resources to Realize Interaction between Higher and Lower Levels

Concentrating efforts and integrating resources to do big things is an important aspect reflecting the superiority of socialism with Chinese characteristics. The premise of doing big things is to integrate resources effectively. The Chinese auditing system makes it possible for audit institutions to undertake big tasks. According to the Constitution and laws, the National Audit Office as a department of the central government is in charge of the nationwide audit work under the guidance of the Premier of the State Council. Local governments at the county level or above set up local audit institutions carrying out the local audit work under the leadership of local governments and audit institutions at a higher level. This guidance of lower by higher levels is the organizational foundation for effective resource integration. Under the system, audit institutions at the higher level can organize and lead the audit institutions at lower levels to jointly undertake large audit projects in a unified and synchronous way, through the "Five Unification" approach, namely, unified organization and leadership, unified audit scheme, unified standard, unified audit report, and unified audit announcement." They can thus integrate resources to form the audit resultant force, size up the situation, find and analyze problems, and put forward suggestions from the perspective of system, mechanism, and institution, so as to give full play to the important role of audit in improving national governance.

In many countries where the central audit institution doesn't lead or guide the local audit institutions, it's difficult to undertake large-scale audit projects at the multigovernment level, greatly restricting the macroscopic characteristics of audit results. In recent years, supreme audit institutions in some countries have tried to carry out the unified audit or synchronous audit with local audit institutions but have encountered some difficulties in practice and ended up with unsatisfactory audit results due to system deficiencies. Comparatively speaking, thanks to their system advantages, audit institutions of China are able to integrate audit resources and concentrate efforts to tackle major projects, which has frequently attracted much international attention. In 2011 through 2014, more than 40,000 auditors were organized successively for comprehensive audit of the debts of local governments, social security funds, governmental liabilities, land transfer revenues and expenditures, and cultivated land protection. These large national audit projects organized in a unified way revealed striking problems and hidden dangers in the economic and social aspects, while showing the resource integration capability of the audit institutions of China and the advantage of concentrating efforts on big aspects of the socialist political system.

Special Column 1: Audit on Land Transfer Revenues and Expenditures and Cultivated Land Protection in 2014

The audit covered 29 provinces, 200 municipalities, and 709 counties. From 2008 to 2013, these regions approved 2.0757 million hectares of land for construction, gained land transfer revenues of 13.34 trillion yuan, and spent 12.93 trillion yuan, providing an important foundation and support for social and economic development. By the end of 2013, these regions had not supplied or used 866,600 hectares of land for construction, with the accumulated land revenue surplus of 590.896 billion yuan. Major problems found during audit were as follows:

1. *Land transfer revenues and expenditures.* The main problems include that 366.423 billion yuan of land transfer revenue wasn't collected, with the inflated income of 146.778 billion yuan earned through the use of idle income and other methods; the illegal expense of 780.746 billion yuan was used for administrative expenses, external loans, the construction of office buildings and hotels, and so on. During the land requisition and demolishing phase, 1.741 billion yuan was

(continued)

underpaid and 1.057 billion yuan was squeezed or defrauded by local governments and units through false information. In addition, some local regions didn't have standard land revenue and expenditure accounts, with 835.875 billion yuan stranded in the financial special accounts or directly spent for finance expenses; some local regions deducted or refunded the land transfer income of 721.811 billion yuan to support economic development.

2. *Land for construction.* The main problems included 387,700 hectares of land that was approved in various illegal ways or beyond the plan or authority; 144,300 hectares of land transferred through illegal agreements or false bidding, auction and listing, or in the form of coarse land sales; 218,600 hectares of land occupied for renting purposes instead of being expropriated or used by changing the planning conditions. Some administrative staff bought land at low prices for affiliated persons or conducted matchmaking for illegal reselling, which resulted in the loss of State-owned equity.

3. *Land use and farmland protection.* A total of 88 of 236 new urban areas receiving a spot-check had broken the land or urban planning regulations and 122,100 hectares (8%) of land was not used in 152 areas for a long time; 1,135 of 1,742 local development zones were constructed (with a built area of 691,000 hectares) through illegal approval, and there were 553 illegally expanded areas covering 3.7915 million hectares. In regard to cultivated land protection, by the end of 2013, a total of 67 counties out of 709 subject to spot-checks had a basic farmland area quotient of 72,500 hectares less than that required (3% lower) and 1.4176 million hectares of planned basic cultivated land (4%) turned out to be uncultivated; among more than 10,000 spot-checked land remedial projects, inflated farmland and unqualified farmland accounted for 10 percent and 33 percent, respectively, and 10.946 billion yuan of remediation funds was misappropriated.

After the problems were disclosed during the audit, 25,500 hectares of idle land and idle funds of 264.3 billion yuan were activated, 24,000 cases of illegal land use were corrected, 2,500 people were punished, and 2,800 systems were established and improved. Through the audit, 158[5] cases of seriously violating laws and disciplines were transferred to the relevant departments.

2) Follow-up Audit on Major Matters

At present, some foreign audit institutions have also proposed to conduct a follow-up audit on the management and use of fiscal funds but have failed to implement it efficiently due to system problems such as federal and local power

---

[5] *Source:* The Report of the State Council on the Audit on the Central Budget Implementation and Other Fiscal Revenues and Expenditures in 2014.

boundaries. For instance, the Australian National Audit Office has regarded the follow-up audit of federal fiscal funds as one of its biggest challenges. Comparatively speaking, China's follow-up audit on major matters has distinctive features in terms of scale, level and scope. The fundamental reason is that the Chinese unitary state structure allows audit institutions to track the fund flow and process through multiple levels and areas, thus forming a complete supervisory chain for public funds, State-owned funds, and resources. However, audit institutions of China encounter some difficulties. One is the fact that China has various large-scale government-invested projects while natural disasters frequently occur requiring special funding to cope with them; the other is that the public decision-making process is not legalized and scientific enough, and national governance has high reality demands for the follow-up audit in terms of process control and information feedback. In the second half of 2005, the National Audit Office started the whole-process follow-up audit of fiscal revenues and expenditures of the Beijing Olympic Games and construction projects at Olympic venues, which led to BOCOG (Beijing Organizing Committee for the Olympic Games) and relevant departments to improve systems and measures and standardize management. Since 2008, audit institutions have further highlighted the perspective and constructive nature of audit, actively conducted whole-process follow-up audits on major construction projects related to the national economy and people's livelihood, special resources development, and environmental protection, major emerging public events and the implementation of national major policies and measures, including post-disaster reconstruction in Wenchuan, Yushu, and Zhouqu to repair earthquake damage; large-scale projects of public construction such as the Beijing-Shanghai high-speed railway; and the policy of "Expanding Domestic Needs, Keeping Steady Growth."

The follow-up audit has incorporated the external supervisory mechanism into the whole operation and management process of major events, realized the effective combination of single concurrent audit with ex post audit, static audit with dynamic audit, and partial audit with all-round audit. Compared with the traditional ex post audit, for major emerging events, the follow-up audit has advantages and features of timely involvement, the check point being advanced, whole-process monitoring, and profound contents that highlight prevention, which helps identify potential and tendentious problems in a timely way. This effectively prevents illegal and delinquent tendencies from becoming openly corrupt actions, helped the country avert economic losses, and also safeguarded the construction quality and overall process, promoted implementation of national major policies and measures, and greatly improved the effects of audit supervision.

Special Column 2: Audit of Post-Disaster Reconstruction after Wenchuan Earthquake[6]

On May 12, 2008, Wenchuan in Sichuan Province suffered a severe 8.0-magnitude earthquake.

In September 2008, the National Audit Office published the Opinions on the Audit Arrangements for Post-Disaster Reconstruction after the Wenchuan Earthquake, which defined the tasks of the National Audit Office and audit institutions of the three disaster-stricken provinces and 20 reconstruction-funding provinces (cities). The National Audit Office established an audit leading group of post-disaster reconstruction and set up coordinating groups in audit institutions at three levels in Sichuan Province, Shaanxi Province, and Gansu Province, related cities (prefectures) and severely affected counties (cities, zones), respectively. Adhering to the principle of "Overall Arrangement, Level-to-Level Responsibility, Overall Assurance and Separate Announcement," they set up the system of the "Five Regulars." The first aspect was regular coordination: the coordinating groups at different levels held coordinating meetings regularly to discuss problems and difficulties facing the audit. Second was regular creation of various schemes: according to the requirements for post-disaster construction and audit work at different stages, they worked out project audit plans on a regular basis and conducted follow-up audit step by step in a planned way. The third aspect was regular reporting: audit institutions at various levels reported to the National Audit Office every month and made summary reports every half-year, and the National Audit Office reported the audit findings to the State Council at the same half-yearly rate. The fourth aspect was regular notification: the National Audit Office compiled and distributed work reports and reported on the situation of local audits regularly. The fifth aspect was regular announcement: pursuant to the principle that "he who carries out the audit shall make the announcement," the National Audit Office and local audit institutions announced the audit situation of post-disaster reconstruction to the public.

As for this follow-up audit, audit institutions put forward the work objective of "Promotion and Assurance," that is, to promote smooth post-disaster reconstruction and to ensure no major problems occur, highlighting five key approaches: (1) advance scientific reconstruction by comprehensively checking the implementation and effects of post-disaster reconstruction plans and policies under the guidance of national planning; (2) advance incorrupt reconstruction by severely investigating and dealing with illegal and delinquent behavior and economic crimes, with the reconstruction fund as the main focus; (3) promote standard

---

[6] Summarized from the relevant announcements and reports on audit results by the CNAO.

reconstruction by tracking and checking various links in the entire project construction and management process, with the construction project as the main focus; (4) promote efficient reconstruction by tracking and checking progress and the capital usage effects; and (5) promote transparent reconstruction by disclosing the follow-up audit process and results in a timely and active way, with public disclosure as the main focus.

In the follow-up audit, audit institutions stuck to focusing on prevention and actively innovated various audit modes, and worked hard to achieve the "Three Combinations." First, this meant combining the whole-process follow-up audit of major projects with the special audit investigation of major events, understanding the general situation and features of a certain problem and deeply analyzing classic cases, and establishing causes to promote solutions; second, combine follow-up audit with regular audits to expand audit coverage, including the follow-up audit of post-disaster reconstruction, the audit of local government budget implementation, the economic accountability audit of principal personnel of party committees and governments at different levels, and the audit of special funds; and third, combine the follow-up audit of audit institutions with the supervision of the functional departments and internal audit offices of party committees and governments at different levels, and also take other measures including joint inspection, timely reporting of the audit situation, and supervising rectification, to improve the supervisory efficiency of the audit work.

In the most recent three years, audit institutions at all levels conducted the follow-up audit on 27,902 post-disaster reconstruction projects with planned investment of 767.8 billion yuan in the 51 severely disaster-stricken areas and afflicted areas in Sichuan, Gansu, and Shaanxi provinces, accounting for 79 percent and 63 percent of the total planned investment and projects respectively; audit institutions at all levels handled a cumulative on-site audit workload of 742,400 persons/day, cumulatively sent out 4,377 audit notices, submitted 14,680 audit information bulletins and audit reports, and made public 107 issues of follow-up audit findings.

3) Stress on Revealing and Investigating Major Violations of Laws and Rules

Audit institutions of many countries have played an important role in revealing and investigating major violations of laws and rules. For instance, the Government Accountability Office (GAO) launched a special audit of then vice president Dick Cheney's alleged fraud, and revealed the truth of the collusion between government officials and businesses in the United States. The European Court of Auditors and the U.K. Audit Commission conducted a thorough investigation into members' acts of fiddling expenses and claiming subsidies illegally, and so on; the French media paid great attention to presidential spending compliance problems disclosed by the French Court of Audit. The South Korean Board of Audit and Inspection deeply probed fraud by senior officials.[7] According to Russian law, the Court of Auditors of the Russian Federation is responsible for evaluating the scientific level of anticorruption laws and policies, assessing the anti-corruption effects, revealing corrupt behaviors concerning the usage of national fiscal funds and the management of State-owned assets, supervising the performance of using anti-corruption special funds, and providing training for people engaged in combating corruption. It transferred 176 cases and instituted legal proceedings against 72 criminal cases in 2011 alone.[8]

Compared to those audit institutions mentioned above, the audit institutions of China pay more attention to finding and investigating clues regarding major cases and thus play an important role in the national action of combating corruption and upholding integrity. The National Auditing Standards of the People's Republic of China has clear and specific stipulations regarding audit institutions and auditors' investigation of major illegal behavior. According to the work requirements of comprehensive audit, highlighting key points and investigating major cases put forward by the State Council, audit institutions at all levels have regarded the investigation of serious illegal and delinquent behavior and economic criminal cases as a prime task, and reinforced investigation in practice, which has saved the country a great amount of potential economic losses, frightened the corrupt from into desisting and played an important role in combating corruption.

The way audit institutions focus on revealing and investigating illegal and delinquent behavior and major cases complies with the reality of Chinese social and economic development. For the capacity building of supreme audit institutions of countries at different levels, the INTOSAI Capacity Building Committee Chairman Ahmed El Midaoui has stressed the developed countries should focus on performance audit and effectively integrate it with the risk management and strategic audit; emerging market countries, meanwhile, should continuously consolidate their existing achievements in checking for errors and preventing drawbacks and deepen the work of the performance audit; the priority of audit of developing countries is to check errors and prevent drawbacks and steadily

---

[7] See introduction on websites of the U.S. Government Accountability Office (www.gao.gov), European Court of Auditors (www.eca.europa.eu), National Audit Office of UK (www.nao.gov .uk), Cour des Comptes of France (www.ccomptes.fr), and Board of Audit and Inspection of the Republic of Korea (www.bai.go.kr).

[8] Scientific Research Institute of the China National Audit Office, *Introduction to Foreign Audit Supervision System*. Beijing: Modern Economic Publishing House, 2013, p. 22.

advance the influence of the performance audit. At present, China is undergoing a transformation in social and economic development. Due to reasons such as unsound mechanisms and systems, there still exist illegal and delinquent behavior and economic crimes to some degree, which may be especially frequent in some fields and links. Therefore, currently an important task is to combat and curb economic crimes and strictly enforce economic discipline for better national governance. That audit institutions emphasize the investigation of illegal and delinquent behavior and major cases is in line with the current needs of national governance.

Related Background 4: Provisions of *National Auditing Standards of the PRC* on Major Illegal Behaviors

Article 112. While engaged in an audit, auditors shall be professionally prudent and pay full attention to possible major illegal behavior.

Article 113. The major illegal behavior mentioned hereof refers to the behavior of audit targets and relevant personnel that involve a big amount of money, violate the laws and regulations, and cause huge national economic losses or major harmful social influence.

Article 114. For major illegal behavior alleged against audit targets and relevant personnel, auditors shall assess the motivation, nature, consequence, and illegal composition of the actions.

Article 115. When investigating audit targets and information related to their actions, auditors can focus on the following matters related to the major illegal behavior:

1. The situation of the major illegal behavior prevailing in the industry to which the audited units belong.
2. Relevant laws and regulations and the implementation.
3. The facts or clues of major illegal behavior linked to audit targets, which supervision departments have discovered and confirmed.
4. The possible motivation and reasons for major illegal behavior.
5. Relevant internal controls and their implementation.
6. Other items.

Article 116. Auditors can estimate possible major illegal behavior by focusing on the following circumstances:

1. Exceptions to specific economic activities.
2. Abnormal changes reflected in financial and nonfinancial data.
3. Clues provided by relevant departments and public tip-offs.

(continued)

4. Those reflected and reported by the public and media.

5. Others.

Article 117. Auditors can estimate the nature of possible major illegal behavior and determine the inspection emphasis based on the actual situation, work experience, and abnormal phenomena found in the audit. When inspecting possible major illegal behavior, they should focus on high-risk areas and links.

Article 118. When finding clues of major illegal behavior, audit teams or audit institutions may take corresponding measures as follows:

1. Add experienced and competent personnel to the audit work.

2. Prevent relevant units and personal from knowing the inspection time, matters under review, scope, and methods in advance.

3. Expand the inspection scope to cover any possible field related to major illegal behavior.

4. Obtain necessary external evidence.

5. Take preservation measures according to the law.

6. Ask relevant organs for assistance and coordinated cooperation.

7. Report to the government and relevant departments.

8. Other necessary corresponding measures.

4) Focus on the Role of Trial Mechanism in the Audit Quality Control

Audit institutions of all countries pay much attention to audit quality control and have established related systems based on audit quality control factors. They generally conduct control over auditors and the audit process to avoid risks and realize their objectives. For instance, the U.S. Audit Office established an audit quality control system that shows the leadership of audit institutions paying close attention to high-quality audit. The system provides a reasonable guarantee for policy implementation and compliance with ethical rules, applicable laws, and regulations.

The National Auditing Standards of the PRC contain clear and specific provisions on audit quality control and responsibility, which reflect the concepts of whole-staff participation and whole-process control. Remarkably different from the audit institutions in other countries, those of China lay special emphasis on the execution of the quality control mechanism of "Review by the Business Department–Trial by the Trial Agency–Final Judgment" for the conclusive audit documents and highlight the role of trial in the quality control mechanism while controlling auditors and the overall audit process. As mentioned in Special Column 3, after finishing audit tasks, the audit team must submit the materials including the audit reports to the audit business department for review. This, in turn, will submit the reviewed and possibly modified reports together with the written audit opinions to the trial agency. Based on the audit implementation scheme, the trial agency focuses on the audit process and results, checks the work performance of the audit team, the quality of evidence and audit records, as well as conclusive audit documents such as final audit report, and the situation of audit compliance, and then issue a trial opinion. If it finds the audit evidence in regard to major matters is insufficient, the trial department can ask the audit team to provide supplementary evidence; if it finds that the statement of facts in the audit report or the written audit decision is not clear or that laws and regulations have been applied inappropriately, or that standards applied, or the audit evaluation, or the nature of the decision and punishment opinions are inappropriate and need to be corrected, the trial department can amend the audit report and the written audit decision directly. In addition, regarding the problems of the audit project that cannot be solved, the trial department can ask the audit team to research and make improvements in the future. Clearly, it's an important link of audit project quality control that the trial departments checks and controls audit implementation as well as documents covering the audit findings seriously. Strict audit law regulations and operational procedures, as well as the special mechanism of "Review-Trial-Approval," provides a strong guarantee for the quality control of Chinese audit institutions.

5) Publish the Auditing Findings to the Public

Different from the audit institutions in some countries that disclose the audit reports to the public, audit institutions of China don't make such a disclosure on specific projects, but publish the audit findings, and the results of investigating and inspecting audit reports of social audit institutions in the form of an announcement. The announcement of audit findings comes into being based on the audit report and the special audit investigation report and excludes any information related to national and business secrets, information under investigation or other information that cannot be disclosed according to the laws and regulations. Audit institutions can either publish the findings of one single audit or single audit investigation project, or publish the results after integrating similar information comprehensively, such as the rectification situation of audit targets or investigated units and the investigation conditions of some case clues found in the audit. According to the statistics, since the system of announcing audit findings was established, nationwide audit institutions have published over 60,000 such documents.

Special Column 3: Results Regarding the Audit by the CNAO on 2,448 Mining Rights Cases

[Time: February 6, 2015]

Pursuant to provisions of the *Audit Law of the People's Republic of China*, from 2013 to 2014, the National Audit Office (CNAO) conducted an audit on some of the exploration rights and mining rights (hereinafter collectively referred to as mining rights) in 14 provinces (autonomous regions and municipalities), namely: Shanxi, Inner Mongolia, Hebei, Henan, Heilongjiang, Anhui, Hunan, Yunnan, Jiangxi, Shaanxi, Gansu, Hubei, Hainan and Chongqing, focusing on examination of 2,448 mining rights (see Annex 1) transfer related transactions and collection of mining rights related funds since 2004. In general, in recent years, the relevant localities have implemented the relevant policies and regulations regarding mineral resources, continued to strengthen the management of mining rights transfer transactions and the collection of relevant funds, promoting integration of mineral resources and market building, and resource development and utilization efficiency has improved. However, in some regions mining rights management is not stringent, and operations are not up to norm. The audit found the presence of illegal and irregular matters in 806 cases of mining rights transfer and transactions (see Annex 2), some mineral and taxation authorities under-levied, and used mineral resource revenues irregularly. The specific situations are as follows:

I. **Local Minerals Authorities Irregularly Examined and Approved Mining Rights Registration, involving 716 Minerals Rights Cases (see Annex 3). There are three main situations:**

1. Approval and issuance of prospecting permits or mining permits ultra vires or by adopting a "turning big items into small ones, breaking up the whole into parts" approach to circumvent the approval authority constraints. In accordance with state regulations, permits for exploration rights for minerals such as gold, lead and zinc with a prospecting investment of more than 5 million yuan, mining rights for mineral deposits above large-scale and exploration rights for coal prospecting blocks covering an area greater than 30 square kilometers, shall be issued by the Ministry of Land and Resources, but the audit found that 75 cases of mining rights failed to be submitted to the Ministry of Land and Resources for approval and issuance of permits in accordance with provisions, instead were examined and issued permits by minerals authorities at the provincial and lower levels; among which, the largest

planned prospecting investment was 6.5572 million yuan, and the largest coal prospecting block covered an area of 303.99 square kilometers.

2. Irregular approval of establishing new, continuing or changing registration of mining rights that failed to meet statutory conditions or submitted incomplete information and other formalities. Among these, irregular approval of establishing new mining rights mainly included the following four situations: failure to obtain environmental impact assessment examination and approval, mining rights establishment proposal yet to be approved, failure of the mining rights applicant to possess the stipulated funds or legal person qualifications, and overlap with prospecting (mining) extents of other mining rights, involving 170, 27, 25 and 7 mining rights cases respectively; irregular approval of continuing mining rights mainly included the following two situations: continuation of exploration rights during the same prospecting phase while failing to reduce the prospecting area in accordance with stipulations, and approval to continue while failing to pay the required charges, involving 100 and 60 cases respectively.

3. Irregular transfer of mining rights by agreement in the name of attracting investment, resolving historical issues, developing tourism and supporting enterprise development, etc. The Ministry of Land and Resources had clearly stipulated that, beginning in August 2003, transfer of mining rights of mineral properties proven using state investment shall be carried out through tender, auction or listing; in January 2006, it further clarified the scope of the mining rights transfer through tender, auction and listing, but the audit found 252 cases of mining rights with issues of irregular transfer through agreement.

II. **Local Minerals Authorities, Geological Exploration Units or State-owned Mining Enterprises Irregularly Selling, Transferring or Acquiring Mining Rights and Related Equity through Fixed Pricing, involving 90 Mining Rights Cases (see Annex 4). There are two main situations:**

1. In the sale, transfer, or acquisition of mining rights, the price was directly fixed without assessment, or via a reverse process of first fixing the price then undergoing assessment, involving 85 cases of mining rights and equity in relevant companies. The above practices violated stipulations that in the sale or transfer of mining rights resulting from state funded exploration, and when mining enterprise restructuring, changes in state-owned property rights and the acquisition of non state-owned assets involve mining rights, qualified assessment agencies shall be entrusted to assess the

(continued)

mining right, and the verified and approved assessment value be used as reference for determining the sale, transfer or purchase price.

2. Irregular manipulation of the transfer or sale price of mining rights and equity of relevant companies, involving five mining rights cases. The main ploys included inflating resource reserves, evading assessment of reserves of associated resources, adjusting assessment parameters, etc.; some cases actually failed to pay transfer fees according to the contract price.

III. Local Minerals Authorities and Tax Authorities Under-levied 20.009 Billion Yuan of Mineral Resource Related Funds (see Annex 5).

Local minerals authorities under-levied 18.998 billion yuan of mining rights charges, under-levied 521 million yuan of mining rights overdue fees and fees for the use of funds, under-levied 411 million yuan of mineral resource compensation fees, under-levied 41.9588 million yuan of mining rights usage fees; local tax authorities under-levied 36.87 million yuan of resource tax.

IV. Local Minerals and Finance Authorities Used 10.639 Billion Yuan of Mineral Resource Related Funds in Violation of Their Prescribed Purpose (see Annex 6).

Local finance and minerals authorities used beyond their prescribed purpose: 6.089 billion yuan for other engineering projects, 3.683 billion yuan for balancing budget revenues and expenditures, 207 million yuan to make up for administrative expenses, and 660 million yuan for irregular lending.

With respect to the above issues, the CNAO in accordance with the law has submitted audit reports and issued audit decisions. Leads to cases of alleged illegalities and irregularities found in the audit have in accordance with the law been transferred to relevant departments for further investigation.

As of the end of 2014, through recovery or confiscation of illegal income, returning funds according to their original channels and other measures, a total of 69.68 billion yuan of irregular or illegal problematic funds have been rectified, more than 40 systems related to the management of mining rights and price and tax have been formulated or improved. Next, the CNAO will continue to follow the rectification situation. Specific rectification results will be announced to the public by the governments of the relevant provinces (autonomous regions and municipalities). Leads to cases of alleged violation of discipline and law will be announced pending further investigation by relevant departments in accordance with the law.

Annexes 1–6 (omitted).

2. PRACTICAL EFFECTS OF AUDITING SYSTEM OF SOCIALISM WITH CHINESE CHARACTERISTICS

Through more than 30 years of efforts, the framework of the auditing system of socialism with Chinese characteristics has been basically established. With the constant improvement of laws and regulations as well as system contents and functions, audit supervision has been playing a more and more important role in safeguarding economic and financial order, improving efficiency of public fund usage, promoting sound economic and social development, and advancing modernization of the national governance system and governance capacity. The system's efficiency is embodied in the operation and implementation. From the perspective of specific work efficiency in the past 30 years or more, audit institutions at all levels have jointly improved revenues and reduced losses of over 2 trillion yuan, transferred more than 30,000 cases of major violations of laws and rules as well as of crimes, and submitted more than 3.8 million pieces of various audit information and reports.

(1) Improve Economic Benefits

In the past three decades, audit institutions have always regarded strengthening the audit work on the base of the true and legitimate benefits of financial revenue and expenditure as a vital task. In the audit of public finance, audit institutions have focused on the authenticity of fiscal revenues and expenditures, disclosed and investigated problems such as fraudulent applications and claims on budget funds, misappropriation of public funds, and inflating financial and fiscal revenues and expenditures, thus improving revenue and lowering expenditure; in the audit of major special funds and major investment projects, audit institutions have paid attention not only to disclosing wastage in activities such as construction, fund use, and public consumption, but also to the situation of public fund usage efficiency and social and ecological benefits, thus improving usage efficiency of public funds. In the audit of State-owned financial institutions, audit institutions have focused on the authenticity of assets, liabilities as well as profits and losses, especially nonperforming assets, disclosed and investigated violations of laws and rules including illegal operations, falsification, and loan fraud through external and internal collusion, thus safeguarding the authenticity and reliability of financial information; in the audit of State-owned enterprises, audit institutions have focused on the authenticity of the management and profits of State-owned assets, disclosed and investigated behavior such as nonstandard financial accounting, unsubstantiated profits and losses, as well as disorderly asset management; restored the veracity of economic activities; and prevented loss of State-owned assets. Audit institutions have effectively safeguarded the economic and financial order, provided correct information and a reliable basis for government decision making, directly increased fiscal revenues and reduced losses, and improved economic returns. According to statistics, through correction of problems found in audits since 1983, the national audit institutions have directly increased fiscal revenues and reduced expenditures of more than 1.8 trillion yuan, of which more than 260 billion yuan was directly contributed by the National Audit Office of China. Through correction of the problems found in audits since only 2008, the national audit institutions have directly increased fiscal revenues and reduced expenditures of more than 20 billion yuan (not including the amount involved in major cases uncovered since 2008). In audit performance, the National Audit Office of China has estimated that in recent years the audit fund expenditure of every one yuan yields an audit result worth more than 100 yuan, with an average audit outcome of more than 40 million yuan per auditor per year. See Tables 4-2, 4-3, and 4-4.

TABLE 4-2 Fiscal Revenue Growth Promoted by Audit Institutions Since the Establishment

Unit: 10,000 yuan

Year	Nationwide Audit Institutions	National Audit Office
From 1983 to 1984	17,701	
1985	178,878	46,183
1986	283,172	17,881
1987	251,920	16,338
1988	306,709	17,035
1989	1,542,655	103,697
1990	752,117	62,284
1991	538,291	120,850
1992	498,417	99,733
1993	514,646	98,467
1994	775,849	220,330
1995	1,094,656	407,921
1996	1,915,079	712,486

Unit: 10,000 yuan		
Year	Nationwide Audit Institutions	National Audit Office
1997	1,778,304	521,003
1998	2,125,238	692,892
1999	2,547,085	873,010
2000	2,685,633	991,502
2001	2,365,996	388,168
2002	3,174,287	862,712
2003	2,491,195	384,066
2004	3,852,137	933,321
2005	4,189,483	477,977
2006	4,917,528	428,424
2007	6,147,973	413,712
2008	8,325,350	594,482
2009	8,020,911	737,442
2010	8,663,639	160,709
2011	14,838,134	946,165
2012	24,420,842	2,508,502
2013	38,155,445	8,610,540
2014	33,104,514	3,950,808
Total	180,473,784	26,398,640

Note: Data drawn from the Compilation of National Audit Statistics.

TABLE 4-3 Supreme Audit Institutions' Input-Output Ratios of China, the United States, and United Kingdom from 2010 to 2013

Year Supreme Audit Institutions	2010	2011	2012	2013
National Audit Office of China	1:82	1:96	1:116	1:252
U.S. Government Accountability Office	1:100	1:82	1:105	1:102
National Audit Office of the United Kingdom	1:11	1:16	1:24	1:16

Note: The statistics come from the official websites of the National Audit Office of China, the U.S. Government Accountability Office, and the National Audit Office of the United Kingdom of which the input-output ratio of 1:24 of the National Audit Office of the United Kingdom in 2012 is calculated according to the annual report.

TABLE 4-4 Main Performance of the National Audit Office of China from 2010 to 2014

Year Performance Indicators	2010	2011	2012	2013	2014
Audit outcome measurable by currency (100 million yuan)	649.5	866.8	1,282.0	2,752.1	3,090.17
Audit outcome per capita (10,000 yuan)	2,139	2,835	4,029	8,665	9,274
Input-output ratio	1:82	1:96	1:116	1:252	1:256
Special audit reports, comprehensive report and audit briefing (piece)	3,260	2,010	2,728	2,158	1,286
Audit report and special audit investigation report (piece)	521	535	810	719	342
Audit announcement (piece)	35	42	30	32	23
Completed notarial audit project of foreign assistance loan (piece)	102	99	94	78	51
Auditees' rectification measures taken according to audit recommendations (piece)	347	942	2,251	1,828	2,026
Case evidence and matters transferred to judicial offices and discipline inspection organs	131	177	351	408	423

Note: The table is based on the performance report of the National Audit Office of China. According to the report, the audit performance includes the audit result measurable monetarily and the audit result nonmeasurable monetarily. Rectification measures taken to address problems found through auditing could help increase fiscal revenues and reduce expenditures as well as save losses in the rectification, which are measurable monetarily; the audit result that embodies the constructive nature of audit at the mechanism and system level is also an important audit result, though it cannot be simply measured monetarily.

When directly improving the economic benefits from their work, the audit institutions have also focused on promoting reform and deepening the audit of public finance management, budget enforcement and budget drafting continuously. In addition, they have made efforts toward strengthening audit on transfer payment by departments with capital allocation rights and on the special funds such as treasury stock funds, paid constant attention to the problems concerning the system and structure of budgetary revenue and expenditure, clearing and consolidation of special transfer payments, activation of stock funds and public finance management performance, and improved the performance of public fund use.

Special Column 4: 2014 Audit Situation of Financial Stock Funds[9]

The audit results show the finance departments at all levels had a large sum of unused balance due to untimely amendments to related provisions and insufficient overall management. By the end of 2014, spot checks of 22 central government departments revealed they had stock funds of 149.508 billion yuan, and 18 provincial financial departments had stock funds of 1.19 trillion yuan. By the end of February 2015, the central departments referred to above were required by the Ministry of Finance to make overall arrangement for activating stock funds of 9.786 billion yuan; the 18 provinces mentioned above were required to liquidate and turn over special carryover funds of more than 18 million yuan under the overall arrangement of the central government. The main factors affecting the circulation of stock funds include:

1. Most revenue for special purposes in the budget cannot be arranged in an overall way according to the management measures currently in effect. In 2014, the revenue included in the public budget management scope, but assigned for special purposes, reached 625.725 billion yuan (accounting for 9.7 percent); for instance, the revenue of 3.969 billion yuan from the vehicle purchase tax was still carried over at the end of the year as the scope of expenditure was expanded continuously, although such revenue was carried over in successive years; the government fund budget of 72.01 billion yuan was carried over at the end of the year (equal to 17.53 percent of revenues in that year).

2. The expenditure budget involving statutory matters showed rigid growth, with large sums of idle funds. For instance, central government expenditure on science and technology carried over in the Ministry of Finance accounts totaled 42.6 billion yuan by the end of 2014; more than half of this had been carried over for more than five years; nearly half of stock funds of the central government departments were funds set aside especially for education and science and technology. Meanwhile, the approach of "rigid uniformity" for involved matters also resulted in interregional imbalance.

3. Some reform measures or work arrangements lagged behind, affecting the effective use of project funds. By the end of 2014, the unused balance of venture capital investment funds raised by 14 provinces since 2009 reached 39.756 billion yuan (accounting for

(continued)

[9] *Source:* The Report of the State Council on the Audit on the Central Budget Implementation and Other Fiscal Revenues and Expenditures in 2014.

84 percent), including four provinces that never used any such funds; among 82 unfinished projects of integrated heavy metal pollution prevention and control in 17 provinces during the 12th Five-Year Program, 21 were suspended or never even began, and 19 fell far behind plan requirements. Among the special funds for 11 provinces allocated by the central government, the amount of 338 million yuan (accounting for 11 percent) was carried over for more than two years.

4. Financial special accounts weren't cleared thoroughly, resulting in the large amounts of leftover funds. The scope of liquidation of local financial stock funds didn't include the financial special accounts. The stock funds of provincial financial special accounts of 18 provinces had reached 214.569 billion yuan by the end of February 2015, over 60 billion yuan of which had been carried over for more than two years. In a spot check focusing on 175 special accounts of nine provinces opened at 141 bank branches, it was found 35 should be cancelled; the scale of special account funds amounted to 35 percent of balance of treasury deposits at the same term, and four provinces also misrepresented expenditure to transfer the treasury funds of 66.708 billion yuan to the financial special accounts.

(2) Ensure Smooth Policy Implementation

To realize the Chinese Dream of the great rejuvenation of the Chinese nation calls for all regions and all departments to faithfully implement policies and measures of the CPC Central Committee and the State Council, and efforts need to be made to unite all parties concerned for the purpose. It is true that "the worth of any plan lies in its implementation." As an important part of the national supervision system, government auditing has the advantages of comprehensiveness, professionalism and independence. Auditing can realize a comprehensive and accurate statement of the basic situation, reflect practical problems in an objective and true manner, and supervise implementation of central decisions and macro control policies.

For over 30 years, audit institutions of China have laid stress on key auditing points and strengthened supervision to ensure the smooth implementation of national major decisions, policies, and measures in accordance with the work arrangements of the Party and the government at each term. For example, audit institutions examined enterprises with great profits or losses, the clearing of fixed investment projects in progress, the clean-up and reorganization of companies, and the controlling of consumption funds, with a focus on "two increases and two reductions" and "improvement and rectification"; conducted all-round auditing on the city ledger of the grain industry, income tax collection, and so on by focusing on the reform of the grain distribution system and the system of sharing income tax; organized auditing on the funds for "agriculture, rural areas and farmers," land, education, public health, social security, disaster relief, environmental protection, and so on by focusing on the implementation of the Western Development strategy, the construction of a new socialist countryside and the building of a harmonious socialist society, and the like; organized and conducted auditing on the effects of the international financial crisis on the country's commercial banks and the real economy, implementation of policies for benefiting small and medium-sized enterprises (SMEs), the structure of new loans being made by key commercial banks and the like with a focus on the international financial crisis, expansion of domestic demand and guarantee of continued growth; implemented the whole-process real-time audit of earthquake relief work and post-disaster reconstruction after the Wenchuan, Yushu, and Zhouqu earthquakes; and the hosting of major public events such as the Beijing Olympic Games, Shanghai World Expo, and the Asian Games, with a focus on the organization and implementation of major public matters and key public works, as well as the real-time audit on such projects as the Beijing-Shanghai High-Speed Railway, second line of the West-East natural gas transmission project, the Three Gorges Project, south-to-north water diversion project, Xiluodu Hydropower Station, and the central government funds for development of Xinjiang; conducted auditing on the funds for social security, government-subsidized housing projects, layout adjustment of rural primary and middle schools, "agriculture, rural areas and farmers," education, medical care, and cultures, with a focus on securing people's livelihood; and organized auditing on the management of land and mineral resources, the implementation of measures for energy conservation, emission reduction and environmental protection, and the prevention and control of water pollution. Through these audit activities and construction of the necessary auditing systems, the audit institutions have been able to investigate behavior involving the disobeying of orders and the defying of prohibitions, timely reflected new circumstances and new problems arising during the execution of policies, proposed countermeasures, and promoted the implementation and improvement of policies and measures.

Special Column 5: Audit of Fixed Assets Investment[10]

Auditing of investment in fixed assets is a nationally effective supervisory measure, and also an important part of national audit supervision. Audit institutions set up special offices for investment in fixed assets early on. From 1983 to 1993, they carried out the investment audit from single financial audit on infrastructure to auditing of projects that had been halted or suspended, key projects prior to the beginning of construction, the engineering budgets and the final accounts, and so on, which promoted the implementation of State polices on reducing the investment scale and adjustment of the investment structure. From 1994 to 2003, the investment audit focused on key national construction projects, national bonds and special funds for key industries. In particular, priority was given to the construction funds for seven industries, that is, the State-owned grain reservoir, water conservation, highways, railways, rural power network reconstruction, airports, and urban infrastructure, that require more input of funds from the sale of treasury bonds and concern the national economy and people's livelihood. Auditing was extended, and more than 2,600 national debt construction projects were investigated. This effectively guaranteed the implementation of a series of national key decisions and deployments for expanding domestic demands.

In 2004, the investment audit entered a stage of comprehensive development. First, auditing on industry investment is deepened continuously. The National Audit Office of China successively organized an audit on 529 key water conservancy projects, 554 danger-removing and reinforcement projects of defective reservoirs, 247 grain and oil storage projects, 76 airport projects, 39 first-class highway projects, 25 key railway projects, 18 key power projects, West-East Power Transmission Project and others, and highlighted the issues of institutions, mechanisms, and systems widespread among all industries. Second, the real-time audit of major projects was conducted comprehensively. Audit institutions timely organized the real-time audit of national major investment projects like the Three Gorges Project; the Beijing-Shanghai High-Speed Railway; south-to-north water diversion project; West-East natural gas transmission project; project of supporting Xinjiang and Tibet, Xiluodu, and Xiangjiaba Hydropower Stations; major public events including the Beijing Olympic Games, Shanghai World Expo, and the Guangzhou Asian Games; as well as the reconstruction projects

---

[10] Sorted out according to relevant data of the CNAO.

after disasters such as the Wenchuan disaster, Qinghai Yushu disaster, Yunnan Yiliang earthquake, and Gansu Zhouqu Debris Flow Disaster, which effectively promoted the smooth accomplishment of national major projects and events.

To regulate the investment audit, the National Audit Office of China successively formulated the Provisional Regulations on Audit Processing of Construction Projects, Auditing Standards of National Construction Projects, Administrative Measures for Auditing of Government Investment Projects, Regulations on Auditing of Government Investment Projects, and so on, which made provisions on the auditing scope and contents of government investment projects as well as the auditing deadline for final accounts of completed projects. Moreover, these provisions propose specific requirements for quality control of investment auditing and strengthening management of external professionals.

Since the 18th National Congress of the Communist Party of China, the Central Party Committee and the State Council have issued a series of policies and measures as well as various policies to insist upon interval regulation, highlight orientation and accurate regulation, and make overall arrangements for stabilizing growth, promoting reform, adjusting the structure and benefiting people's livelihood. The Opinions of the State Council on Strengthening Audit Work was issued in October 2014, which emphasized "exerting the guarantee role of audit in promoting the implementation of national major decisions and deployments," and "continuously organizing the real-time audit on the implementation of national key policies and measures as well as macro control deployments." These provisions strengthen the real-time audit of policy implementation in the name of the State Council and have become an important part of China's audit supervision system. Since 2014, audit institutions have successively organized and conducted the real-time audit of implementation of national major policies and measures as well as macro control deployment, strengthened the supervision and inspection of specific deployments, progress in execution and actual results and other aspects involving all regions and all departments in implementing the polices and measures for stabilizing growth, promoting reform, adjusting the structure, benefiting people's livelihood, and preventing risks. In particular, the priority has been given to implementation of major projects, guarantee of major funds and advancement of streamlining administration and instituting decentralization. This not only ensures policies are thoroughly implemented and improved continuously, but also exerts the guarantee role of audit in promoting the implementation of national major decisions and deployments. Through only one year of practice, audit institutions in China have explored new ways for the real-time audit of national economic policies and macro control measures during this process, and thus guaranteed the smooth implementation of national major decisions.

Special Column 6: Real-Time Audit on the Implementation of Policies for Stabilizing Growth Since 2014

To further promote the implementation of policies for stabilizing growth, promoting reform, adjusting structure and benefiting people's livelihood, the State Council decided the National Audit Office of China should organize audit institutions nationwide to carry out real-time audits from the middle of August 2014. Through this, they were not only able to master the overall situation and reveal prominent problems, but also offer audit opinions and recommendations. Hence, the General Office of the State Council specially issued the *Work Plan for Real-Time Audit on the Implementation of the Measures for Stabilizing Growth, Promoting Reform, Adjusting the Structure and Benefiting People's Livelihood*, covering a real-time audit on the implementation of 63 policies and measures in 19 aspects.

The Report of the State Council on the Audit on the Central Budget Implementation and Other Fiscal Revenues and Expenditures in 2014 reflected the existing audit situation: the audit conducted in the first quarter of the year revealed some problems still exist of untimely advancement and unsound execution.

1. Some major investment projects suffered from a long approval cycle, untimely commencement and slow construction progress. Through a spot check of 600 projects, with applied or planned investment totaling more than 910 billion yuan, it was found that 43 projects were not approved for over half-a-year due to late application to the central competent authorities, with four years and seven months as the maximum, involving energy, communications, water conservancy, energy-saving and environmental protection, as well as independent innovation; in addition, 557 approved projects didn't commence construction on schedule, with 56 approved in 2013 or even earlier. In regard to enhancement of construction, 46 percent of major water conservancy projects where Central Government investment reached 38.237 billion yuan had only completed 68 percent of the work under the investment plan and four of them had a completion rate as low as 20 percent; among eight bases under the Phase 2 planning for a national oil products reserve, three had extended their construction periods, with the longest extension being three years; there were also six rail projects which overran by 2.931 billion yuan (accounting for 25 percent) and five water conservancy projects involving 2.23 billion yuan (21 percent).

2. Some departments and local offices did less than they should have done in streamlining administration and delegating more power to lower governments. By the end of March 2015, 12 administrative approval items under the administration of General Administration of Quality Supervision, Inspection and Quarantine, State Forestry Administration, Ministry of Finance, Civil Aviation Authority, etc. had not been cancelled or consolidated according to requirements. 133 occupational qualification licensing items set individually by 15 provinces hadn't been canceled. Some units directly entrusted or designated affiliated units in disguised form to handle the administrative approval items. In 2014, the illegal charges reached 724 million yuan, of which 277 million yuan for evaluation, authentication, and so on was collected by 11 central departments and the departments of environmental protection and housing and urban-rural development in four provinces, 447 million yuan was defined and collected illegally by 16 affiliated units of government departments.

3. Some departments were insufficiently coordinated in regard to implementing specific measures for commercial system reform. The national uniform measures for "Three (Tax Registration Certificate, Industrial and Commercial Business License and Organization Code Certificate) in One" hadn't been issued by the end of March 2015. Different approaches were adopted everywhere including "uniform issuance of three certificates," "one certificate with three numbers," and "one certificate, one code," resulting in difficulty in handling cross-regional business. The relevant system of business approval has not been revised and perfected. For example, 14 laws involving 18 of 152 business registration items adjusted for post-approval haven't been revised; after the execution of measures for the change from paid contribution to subscription of registered capital, and from annual inspection to annual reporting, and so on, more than 50 sets of provisions on the submission of capital verification or annual inspection certificates hadn't been cleared up in a timely way.

4. Relevant departments didn't thoroughly implement convenient measures for import and export customs clearance services. In regard to service charges, a spot check of 80 import and export enterprises revealed there were still 81 service charges being imposed in the import and export links. In some cases, there were 20 different charges and the amount of some charges accounted for 12 percent of the goods value. A spot check of 59 enterprises handling the procedures for tax exemption on the import of key components and raw materials of major technical equipment revealed approval involved six different departments and the

(continued)

approval cycle was about five months; during the period of approval, these enterprises provided guarantees for 2,090 separate transactions according to the amount of tax exemption, which therefore resulted in the drop of tax deductible by approximately 25 percent. In regard to customs inspection, mutual recognition of inspection and quarantine results couldn't be achieved comprehensively between the customs authority and quality inspection department, or between port and original production point. Separate processing is still necessary.

(3) Safeguard National Security

National security is the primary task of national governance. In recent years, government auditing has focused on risk-oriented system construction to safeguard the national interests and ensure economic development. In addition to uncovering violations and noncompliance issues, government auditing attached much importance to revealing risks; reflecting outstanding contradictions; revealing weak links and potential risks existing during economic and social operations; proposing reform measures and countermeasures to prevent and mitigate risks; detecting trends and tendencies so as to prevent localized problems from becoming global ones; and paying close attention to national financial security, financial security, the security of State-owned assets, security of people's livelihood, security of resources and the environment, and information security, so as to practically maintain the national interests and national security. The priority of auditing system building was changed from compliance audit to risk disclosure. The concept, procedures, and related operational mechanisms were adjusted and improved gradually.

Over the past 30 years or so, audit institutions have always taken safeguarding national security as a major task of audit work. Adhering to the principle of focusing on the central tasks and serving the overall interests, audit institutions organized special audits covering the assets, liabilities, profits, and losses of financial institutions, overseas investment, government debts, and financial derivatives business of central enterprises, in order to highlight and timely reflect some trends and tendencies in the fields of finance, people's livelihood, State-owned assets, resources, and energy, as well as information, grain, environment and social stability, revealing outstanding contradictions and potential risks in all aspects of national governance, preventing risk in a timely way, and making suggestions. Through auditing, they not only provided reliable information for safeguarding State economic security, but also enhanced the establishment and perfection of a series of measures and methods involving national governance. In particular, audit institutions have attached much importance to revealing all risks and problems that might emerge in the course of economic structural adjustment since 2008, especially exacerbation of contradictions between economic slowdown and relative capacity surplus, outstanding problems in economic development needs and environmental and resource restrictions, and the increase of fiscal and financial potential risks. First, audit institutions paid close attention to the reality of assets, liabilities, profits, and losses of financial institutions and State-owned enterprises; normalization of business management and outstanding risks facing innovative development; and conducted real-time inspection on investment of credit funds, development of Internet finance, and cross-border capital flows. They also seriously investigated violations of laws and rules, such as transfer of benefits, illegal fund-raising, and online gambling and fraud, and defended the bottom line of preventing systemic and regional financial risks. Second, audit institutions paid continuous attention to risks posed by government debt, conducted real-time inspection on the defusing of stock debts; focused on the borrowing, management, and use of new debt; and prevented waste and the formation of new risks.

Special Column 7: Conducting an Overall Audit on National Government Debts

In accordance with the *Audit Law of the People's Republic of China and the Notice of General Office of the State Council on Doing Well in Audit of National Government Debt*, with the great support and positive coordination of all departments under the State Council, local Party Committees and governments at all levels as well as relevant units, the National Audit Office of China organized 54,400 auditors to conduct an overall audit on debt levels of the central government, 31 provinces (autonomous regions and municipalities) and five municipalities with independent planning status, 391 cities (prefectures, autonomous prefectures, leagues and districts), 2,778 counties (county-level cities, districts, and banners) and 33,091 townships, checking all involved personnel, accounts, and objects in person, from August to September 2013. The audit covered debts for whose repayment governments were responsible, debts where governments had a liability to guarantee should

(continued)

repayment become difficult, and the debts where governments might undertake certain bailout duties when repayment was a problem. The audit involved 62,215 government sectors and institutions, 7,170 financing platform companies, 68,621 budget subsidy public institutions, 2,235 public utility institutions, and 14,219 other institutions, involving 730,065 projects and 2,454,635 separate debts. For each debt, the auditors undertook verification and evidence collection and solicited the opinions of relevant authorities, institutions, and local governments at all levels, respectively.

As the audit results show, by the end of June 2013, the debts for which governments at all levels nationwide had a repayment responsibility reached 20,698.865 billion yuan; debts for which governments guaranteed repayment reached 2,925.649 billion yuan; and the debts where governments might undertake a certain bailout duty totaled 6,650.456 billion yuan. The above audit completely revealed the overall situation of local government debt, objectively reflected the positive role of debt capital, disclosed prominent problems and potential risks of debt management, offered constructive audit opinions, and fully played the role of auditing in safeguarding national security and promoting and improving national governance.

(4) Promote Administration According to Law

An important objective of modern national governance is to strengthen the supervision and restriction on the exercise of power and establish honest, efficient, responsible, and transparent government. To adapt to this requirement, government auditing started from supervising and checking fiscal and financial revenue and expenditure, focused on responsibility performance and responsibility investigation, and urged governments to clarify and implement responsibilities and safeguard normative and orderly national governance based on a constructive and critical approach.

As an institutional arrangement specified in the form of the Constitution, government auditing promoted and normalized the allocation and exercise of power, and paid close attention to such exercise and the performance of responsibility. Checking by audit institutions fully covers public funds, State-owned assets, State-owned resources, and leading officials' performance of their accountability. Through supervising and inspecting the truthfulness and compliance of accounting information, and standardization and efficiency of budget execution, they ensured that the exercise of power in regard to fiscal and financial revenue and expenditure, as well as relevant economic activities as the major carrier, were supervised and restricted, and financial and economic order was safeguarded. The accountability audit was conducted on main leading officials at all levels of local Party committees and governments, judicial organs, procuratorial agencies, Party and government departments, public institutions, and mass organizations at all levels of the Central and local governments, as well as legal representatives of State-owned and State-holding companies. Through the audit, they normalized the allocation and exercise of power, ensured a match between powers and responsibilities, and power supervision, and guided leading officials to abide by laws and rules and conduct due diligence.

Since the establishment of the accountability auditing system, audit institutions of China totally audited nearly 450,000 leading officials. Through the audit, a large number of leading officials who correctly fulfilled their economic duties and achieved outstanding work performance were affirmed, praised, and promoted. Some leading officials who were falsely accused were able to be exonerated after the audit. A number of leading officials were dismissed, demoted, removed, or punished in other ways since they failed to correctly exercise power. With reference to the audit results, relevant departments dismissed, demoted, or removed more than 18,000 persons. More than 8,500 audited leading officials and other personnel involved in illegal matters were transferred to disciplinary inspection organs and judicial organs to be further dealt with. Through accountability auditing, we firmly grasped two key points—the exercise of power and performance of responsibility—strengthened the supervision and management over leading officials and the construction of ruling power of the Party, promoted the establishment and perfection of responsibility investigation and accountability mechanism, boosted the supervision and control of the exercise of power, and played a positive role in strengthening anticorruption construction, promoting the development of the economics and social sciences, and improving national governance.

(5) Promote Anti-corruption

The essence of corruption involves the use of public power to promote personal interests, and poses a serious threat to national governance. Government auditing takes preventing and revealing corruption as an important approach of the "immune system" function in national governance, and takes a leading role in the fight against all forms of corrupt activities. Three aspects are taken into account: First, most of the corruption and fraudulent activities closely relate to funds, assets, and resources. The audit work always focuses on the nation's wealth, and can easily detect encroachment; second, government auditing is independent, and no administrative organ, social group, or individual may interfere with it; hence it can work to reveal problems objectively and fairly; third, government auditing covers all financial funds and institutions, and can uncover evidence in a timely and effective manner. Over the past 30 years or so, more than 30,000 cases of violating laws and rules and criminal cases have been transferred to disciplinary inspection organs and judicial organs for real time. From 2011 to 2014, the number of major cases transferred by audit institutions nationwide reached over 1,600, 2,300, 2,600, and 7,600, respectively.

At the early stage of Chinese reform and opening up, the newly established audit institutions positively participated in the crackdown on economic crimes in order to meet the requirements for high discipline in finance and economics. For example, in September 1983, an investigation team consisting of the National Audit Office of China, Ministry of Finance, and the National Government Offices Administration discovered that the latter's office in the Inner Mongolia Autonomous Region had concealed profit of over 16.67 million yuan, which rose to 31.94 million yuan on further investigation; from October to November 1983, under the unified leadership of the Central Commission for Discipline Inspection, the National Audit Office of China, Ministry of Finance, and Government Offices Administration of the State Council formed two working groups to investigate and clear up issues related to the distribution of physical goods and allowances to staff members of the Ministry of Geology and Mineral Resources and Ministry of Coal Industry and the illegal acquirement of cash through fraudulent activities, and so on. By focusing on improving the economic environment and reorganizing the economic order, audit institutions made more efforts to uncover and investigate violations of laws and rules. For example, the National Audit Office of China audited Kang Hua Development Corp., China International Trust and Investment Corp., Everbright Industrial Co., China Industrial and Commercial Economic Development Corp., and China Rural Trust and Investment Corp. in October 1988. It uncovered the illegal operations of the "Five Companies" and totally confiscated 51.33 million yuan of illegal gains, plus penalties and supplementary taxes, and transferred the relevant responsible persons to the disciplinary inspection organs and judicial organs for processing; in 1993, through audit of the Changtu grain system of Liaoning Province, the National Audit Office of China uncovered serious problems, such as confused management of materials and articles of the grain system, uncontrolled labor expenses, interception of incomes, overstatement of losses, and so on. Upon the investigation of relevant departments, Gui Bingquan, former director of Changtu Grain Bureau; Zhao Fu, former director of Daxing Grain Depot of Changtu County; and Hu Yuzhang, former director of Daxing Business Office of Changtu Agricultural Bank were sentenced to death for bribery, corruption, dereliction of duty, or combined punishments. Xu Lianzhong, former Vice Chairman of the Chinese People's Political Consultative Conference of Changtu County was sentenced to life imprisonment.

After 1998, according to the instruction of the State Council concerning "integrating point with face, highlighting major cases" and "injuring all of a man's fingers is not as effective as chopping one off," audit institutions strictly enforced laws, seriously investigated major violations of laws and regulations as well as economic cases, and promoted the in-depth advancement of the struggle against corruption. For example, through the audit of Tianjin Jixian County Office of the State Administration of Taxation in March 1999, the National Audit Office of China discovered problems such as falsifying VAT invoices, and interception and embezzlement of national taxes, resulting in the tax loss of 17.48 million yuan. Besides, the county had privately set up a "unit-owned exchequer" to release bonuses and buy cars without authorization, and so on. In 2001, the National Audit Office of China discovered through the audit of national debt construction projects that Lu Wanli, former director of the Department of Communications of Guizhou Province (then a deputy to the National People's Congress and General Manager of Guizhou Expressway Group Co., Ltd.) had colluded with private owners to falsify and conduct covert deals in the tendering and bidding of highway construction and material procurement, resulting in cumulative fiscal losses of more than 98 million yuan. In that case, Lu Wanli was sentenced to death for bribery along with confiscation of all his properties, and deprivation of his political rights; in May 2004, the National Audit Office of China discovered through accountability auditing on leaders of the former State Power Company that Lin Kongxing, then vice chairman of China Electricity Council, had abused his position for personal gain as the director of the Central China Electric Power Administration and general manager of the Central China Electric Power Group. His daughter and son-in-law made covert deals in contracting for electric power projects and supplying goods to electric power units, producing unlawful proceeds of 83 million yuan. Lin Kongxing was sentenced to fixed-term imprisonment of 13 years for bribery, plus confiscation of personal property worth 500,000 yuan, and was deprived of his political rights for five years.

In recent years, audit institutions have focused on deeply analyzing the features and rules of corruption cases under the new situation, paid close attention to major fields and key links including allocation of financial funds, decision making of major investment projects and project approval, procurement and tendering and bidding of major materials supply, loan disbursement and security exchange, State-owned assets and equity transfers, and transactions of land and minerals. Audit institutions didn't ignore any doubtful points in any project or funding arrangement. They thoroughly investigated each case to reveal any problems including abuse of power for personal gain, dereliction of duty, bribery and corruption, insider trading, damage of resources, environmental damage, and damage of the public interest, and fully led the determined fight against corruption. For example, the National Audit Office of China conducted the central budget implementation audit in 2008, where it was found that Li Peiying, former president of Capital Airport Holding Co., took advantage of his office to illegally invest abroad and call loans, plus accepting bribes and other corrupt actions. Li Peiying was sentenced to death and suffered confiscation of all his personal property and loss of political rights. In 2009, the National Audit Office of China discovered through financial audit that the National Development Bank had illegally loaned 300 million yuan to Zhengzhou Economic and Technological Development Zone, whose management committee then lent 16.25 million yuan to a company as a "financing award." After the case was transferred to the CPC Central Disciplinary Committee and Ministry of Supervision, it was finally discovered that Wang Yi, former Vice President of the National Development Bank, and other persons had accepted a bribe of over 10 million yuan. Wang Yi was sentenced to death with a two-year reprieve, suffered confiscation of all personal property, and deprived of his political rights for life; in 2010, the National Audit Office of China discovered during an audit of CITIC Securities Co. Ltd., that Wang Jianzhong, former Vice President of Beijing Shoufang Investment Consultation Co., Ltd., taking advantage of his influence, had recommended the former's stock to the public to manipulate the security market through buying in advance, front-running trades, and other means regarding the stock account under his control, thus gaining unlawful income. Wang Jianzhong was sentenced to having 125 million yuan of such unlawful proceeds seized, along with an equal amount of penalties, as well as lifelong disbarment from the securities market. Meanwhile, the qualification of Beijing Shoufang Investment Consultation Co. Ltd. to engage in the securities investment consultation business was revoked; in 2011, the National Audit Office of China discovered through audits of the financial revenues and expenditures of rail transportation companies that He

Hongda, a former member of the Leading Party Group of the Ministry of Railways and Director of its Political Department, had overstepped his authority during his time as Director of the Harbin Railway Bureau, arbitrarily arranging for it to issue favorable industry review opinions for the equity financing of an associated listed company. Due to being suspected of accepting bribes, He Hongda was sentenced to fixed-term imprisonment of 14 years; from 2009 to 2011, the National Audit Office of China discovered in a real-time audit on the Beijing-Shanghai High-Speed Railway that a number of companies had offered bribes running into hundreds of millions of yuan to an enterprise controlled by Ding Yuxin (alternate name: Ding Shumiao), a private business owner, so as to win the bid for various related projects. The Central Commission for Discipline Inspection undertook an all-round investigation, while relevant units of the National Audit Office of China rendered positive cooperation to the investigation. They uncovered major violations by Liu Zhijun, former Minister of Railways and over 10 leading officials at the bureau level, along with Ding Yuxin and a number of private business owners. On July 8, 2013, the Beijing Municipal No. 2 Intermediate People's Court sentenced Liu Zhijun to death with a two-year reprieve, confiscation of all personal property, and deprivation for life of his political rights.

In investigating major violations of laws and rules, audit institutions also focused on analyzing system vulnerabilities and systemic problems reflected by the cases, which provided clear targets for relevant departments to carry out a precise crackdown, addressing both symptoms and root causes and being able to fight against corruption at source. Audit institutions also prepared and implemented the investigation result announcement system of audit case transfer, and enhanced the social environment for the anticorruption struggle. (See Table 4-5.)

(6) Safeguard the Interests of the People

Whether livelihood problems can be properly addressed not only is a vital expression of national governance, but also determines the political direction to a considerable extent, and is related to its basic soundness and credibility. Government auditing is designed to guard public funds and maintain the fundamental interests of the people. Government auditing strengthens audit supervision in implementation of people's livelihood projects, funds, policies and measures, and safeguards the fundamental interests of the people by boosting the auditing of funds for people's livelihood, the resource environment and other aspects. The audit reveals and reflects the situation about "agriculture, rural areas and farmers," urban low-income people as well as

TABLE 4-5 Clues of Major Violations of Laws and Rules from Audit Reports of the Central Budget Implementation and Other Fiscal Revenues and Expenditures in 2008–2014 Discovered and Transferred by the National Audit Office of China

Year	Number of Cases Submitted to the State Council or Transferred to Relevant Departments	Involved Persons	Case Features
2008	119	221	The main characteristic is that offenders encroached on and transferred State-owned assets to seek illegal benefits, but the forms, means, and methods were concealed and diversified, mainly reflected in the following aspects: (1) seeking benefits for small groups or individuals by abuse of power and illegal decision making; (2) transfer and encroachment of State-owned assets by collusion; (3) fraud involving bank loans by means of fictitious transactions, false guarantees, violation of laws, and even internal and external collaboration; and (4) manipulating stock prices and seeking personal gains by the agency of professional advantages or insider information.
2009	104	473	First, the links and fields where the cases take place are relatively concentrated, mainly involving approval, decision making, granting of credit, and tendering and bidding; second, the cases mostly involved "group crime" and "interrelated crime" in which offenders seek gains through internal and external collaboration; third, the violations of policy-type financial institutions and public institutions with weak management are increasingly apparent; and fourth, the criminal skills are higher, professional, and intelligent.
2010	139	—	First, taking advantage of power for "rent-setting" and "rent seeking," or fostering agents to misappropriate financial funds or State-owned assets; second, taking advantage of public resources to access a number of non-public units, or implement violations in multiple areas; third, concealing illegal activities under a legal cover, such as false capital contributions, false projects, illusory contracts, and dummy vouchers, etc.

2011	112	300	First, most of cases involve seeking personal gain by public rights, impairing public resources and damaging the people's interests, with the tendencies of affecting people's livelihood; second, the cases become the new mode of corruption crimes in some fields by means of power-for-money deals through "intermediary services" and third-party arrangements; and third, lawbreakers take advantage of the fast development of new businesses and new technologies, and relevant lagging regulatory mechanism and construction of legal system.
2012	175	630	With strong involvement in stakeholders and long chain of interests, the cases are mostly "group crimes" and "interrelated": (1) abuse of power for rent setting and rent seeking; (2) infringement and money making by means of insider or associated trading; (3) Internet-based implementation; and (4) impairment of the public interest.
2013	314	1,100	The cases take place mainly in the departments and units that have concentrated administrative power or right of approval and hold important State-owned assets and resources: First, community corruption is serious; second, the mode of crimes is more obscure; and third, the earnings of power-for-money deal are long term.
2014	801	5,000	First, the cases mostly involve public funds, State-owned assets and the fields with relatively concentrated State-owned resources; second, the cases largely relate to public officers' abuse of their power and internal and external collaboration; third, offenders seek personal gains by use of various "soft strength"; and fourth, the cases involve covert operations in the name of social welfare undertakings and implementation of policies.

Note: The table is compiled on the basis of the summary of audit reports of the Central Budget Implementation and Other Fiscal Revenues and Expenditures in 2008–2014, wherein the number of involved persons in 2010 was not mentioned, and the number of involved persons from 2011 to 2014 was over 300, 630, 1,100, and 5,000, respectively.

the management of the projects and funds for the people's livelihood, such as education, medical care, housing, and social security. It also reflects the implementation of policies and measures for development and utilization of resources and eco-environment protection, rectifies issues seriously impairing and damaging the interests of the people, and promotes thorough implementation of policies and measures for benefiting the people and environmental protection.

Over the past 30 years or so, audit institutions have always taken safeguarding the people's interests as the fundamental objective and dedicated to promoting the harmonious and sustainable development of economy and society. Priority is given to strengthening audit supervision of major funds and projects for people's livelihood. The focus is to highlight and inspect the implementation of policies for benefiting and enriching the people, timely revealing and rectifying behavior that seriously damages the immediate interests of the people as well as social problems possibly occurring in terms of land acquisition, relocation of residents, and restructuring of enterprises. For example, in regard to agriculture, audit institutions focused on the special transfer payment funds for supporting agriculture, funds for the four subsidies for grain farmers, comprehensive agricultural development funds, construction funds for agricultural infrastructure, development funds for modern agricultural production, and so on, and focused on revealing and investigating major violations occurring during the management and use of funds starting from the implementation of policies and measures of the central government for supporting rural development as well as allocation, disbursement, management, and use of funds based on safeguarding the immediate interests of the people. The social security fund audit closely focused on the overall situation of the Party and government, and the concerns of the people, again highlighting matters involving people's livelihood, such as national social security funds, social insurance funds, disaster relief funds, housing provident funds, urban minimum subsistence allowance, new pension for rural residents, new medical security for rural residents, urban government-subsidized housing, and so on. The audit investigated and rectified the violations of laws and regulations that impaired the people's interests and prejudiced the safety and benefit of social security funds, revealed the prominent problems during the management and execution of social security policies, and reflected institutional defects, mechanism barriers, and management vulnerabilities affecting sound development of the social security system. Besides, through the audit, audit institutions have been able to promote and improve a social security system that is more fair and sustainable and fitted to benefit from its advantageous functions.

Special Column 8: Audit Situation of Social Security[11]

In 1998, the National Audit Office of China established the Social Security Audit Division. Before this, on many occasions, it had organized various professional audit institutionizations to conduct larger-scale special audits on social security. Audits on the pension insurance fund and the unemployment insurance fund for national enterprise employees were conducted in 1992 and 1996, for example. In 1996, the National Audit Office of China also organized a special audit on the welfare lottery and its use of funds gathered. In 1998, it organized the audits on the management and use of relief funds and relief materials for areas in the Yangtze River basin suffering devastating floods, as well as on housing funds for some areas. After audit institutions of social security were set up nationwide, the National Audit Office of China organized a unified audit and investigation of the basic pension insurance fund for enterprise employees in four consecutive years, and also organized audits on the basic living allowance and reemployment fund for laid-off workers, the basic medical insurance fund, and the relief fund for the Dayao earthquake.

After the 16th CPC National Congress, it proposed that, in accordance with the requirements of building a harmonious society, audit institutions should focus on the social insurance audit comprehensively, and mainly check the effectiveness, operational process, and authenticity, safety, and standardization situation of social security funds. Social insurance audit changes the nature of the work from the compliance audit to effectiveness audit, the scope from financial services to social security business, and the focus from simple investigation of violations of rules and disciplines to inspection and management of loopholes and system defects. The National Audit Office of China successively organized the audits and investigations of the social insurance fund, housing provident fund, relief fund, rural social endowment insurance fund, and the funeral industry; on the basis of authenticity and legitimacy, the focus was on checking and evaluating the execution of existing systems and mechanisms, the effects of implementation of policies and systems, and the efficiency of fund management and use.

In 2008, audit offices of all levels nationwide were organized to conduct an overall real-time audit of funds and supplies for relief work after the Wenchuan Earthquake. They audited a total of 18 central departments and units, 1,289 provincial departments and units of 31 provinces (autonomous regions and municipalities) and the Xinjiang Production and Construction Corps, 5,384 prefecture-level departments and units,

(continued)

---

[11] Sorted out according to relevant data of the CNAO.

and 24,618 county-level departments and units; the audit was extended to 3,845 towns and 9,526 villages in Sichuan, Gansu, Shaanxi, Chongqing, and Yunnan provinces (municipalities), and 76,709 affected households. This work promoted the legal and orderly collection of relief funds and materials, timely in-place appropriation, open and transparent distribution, strict and standard management, compliant and effective use, and safe and complete storage, thus making the Party and governments rest assured that all was well.

In 2009, the CNAO audited the gathering, management, and use of funds for subsistence allowances to urban residents, as well as the implementation of relevant policies, urged the Ministry of Civil Affairs to conduct special law enforcement supervision of social assistance policies and the management and use of special funds on a national scale, and urged various regions to establish and improve relevant systems and methods. In 2010, it organized a real-time audit on relief funds and materials for the Qinghai Yushu Earthquake and Gansu Zhouqu Debris Flow Disaster, and promptly urged the relevant units to appropriate and use relief funds and distribute aid materials according to the provisions, playing an important role in maintaining social stability, and resettling affected people, and so on.

In 2012, based on the State Council's instructions, the CNAO organized over 40,000 auditors nationwide and set up over 3,000 audit groups to carry out an overall audit of national social security funds. At the end of October 2012, corrected problems in violation of discipline and regulations by this process involved 31.57 billion yuan. The amount involved in recovering funds, clearance and standardization, implementing financial aid and recovering social security premiums, and modifying and improving relevant policies, reached 202.771 billion yuan. Based on an audit recommendation, various regions established and improved 1,173 relevant social security systems, established the individual account of basic endowment insurance for 6.2183 million insured people, bringing in 1.2907 million who met the requirements and removing 2.1133 million who did not.

Since 2012, the CNAO has organized over 10,000 auditors from special representative offices and audit institutions at all levels to conduct real-time audits on affordable housing projects of cities and towns nationwide on a yearly basis, focusing on the investment, construction, distribution, institutions management, and related policy implementation. This helped to promote standardized management and fair distribution.

(7) Promote the Deepening of Reform

Reform is the self-improvement and development of national governance to keep pace with the times, and the only true path for improving and developing the system of socialism with Chinese characteristics. By reforming and changing the aspects and links of the productive relationship that can no longer meet productivity demands, it can gradually improve the mechanisms of economic and social scientific development, and achieve more efficient allocation and use of resources, so as to achieve good national governance. Government auditing is characterized by strong independence, wide scope, familiarity with policies and regulations, and an ability to grasp the detailed situation. It can analyze problems from a macro and global viewpoint, closely combine regular and performance audits, reveal problems and loopholes in policies, systems, and management, and propose solutions at the system and mechanism level, thus effectively protecting the smooth progress of reforms, promoting the continuous deepening of various reforms and playing a positive role as a "catalyst" in deepened reform.

For over three decades, audit institutions have always paid equal attention to prevention and investigation and actively promoted reform according to the work deployments of the Party and all governments based on improvement of the market economic system at different stages. First, audit institutions have analyzed reasons from the perspectives of institution, mechanism and system, offered proposals, and promoted reform in the key areas of finance, banking, investment and financing, State-owned enterprises and social security, the gradual establishment of systems and mechanisms conducive to scientific development, and the continuous development and improvement of the socialist system with Chinese characteristics. Over the past decade, audit institutions nationwide have put forward over two million audit recommendations, and promoted the formulation and improvement of over 50,000 rules and regulations. The CNAO has made suggestions on budget refinement, the establishment of a complete, unified government budget system, improvement of the budget enforcement effect, deepened reform of the investment and financing system, improvement in online payment management, enhanced policy support to enterprise structural adjustment and railway development, and the improvement of the debt management mechanism, which have strongly promoted reforms in finance, banking, State-owned asset management, and so on. Second, audit institutions have seriously investigated problems and loopholes concerning system implementation and management, and strengthened management and prevention measures in this regard. Over the past decade, audit institutions nationwide have submitted more than 2.6 million reports, and urged audit targets to take more than 150,000 corrective measures, thus improving and strengthening management. Third, in recent years, audit offices have firmly investigated and dealt with failures to abide by the law, loose law enforcement, and failure to punish lawbreakers, made suggestions on formulating and amending laws and regulations, promoted the formulation of the Law on the State-Owned Assets of Enterprises and Regulations on the Implementation of the Tendering and Bidding Law, participated in the coordination of more than 700 laws and regulations, and vigorously promoted construction of democracy and the rule of law.

Related Background 5: Audit Promotes Improvement of the Government Budget System

A complete, unified government budget system is the foundation for strengthening fiscal management. In recent years, audit institutions have made efforts to promote all-inclusive budget management, and focused on revealing and reflecting existing problems in its integrity, and promoting incorporation of all government revenues and expenditures into the budget. The Audit Report for 2013 made in-depth analysis of the audit situation from the perspectives of budgeting, resource allocation, policy implementation, budget enforcement, and drafting of final accounts. In central public finance management, the report points out the presentation and disclosure of some budget items was not standard, the scope of the State-owned capital management budget was incomplete, and 34 percent of central transfer payments were not included in the spot-checked provincial budgets for the beginning of a new fiscal year; there were still many phenomena of "bundling" budgeting and commissioned budgeting; some investments were allocated to unqualified units or projects, the fund budget prepared on the principle of "expenditure is determined by revenue" was quite different from the actual expenditure, and the State-owned capital management budget could not fully reflect the policy requirements; some special funds were shared by different budgeting institutions, and some projects received repeated investment by different divisions of the same institution; plans for budget enforcement were not released according to procedures, the levels of budget were changed frequently, and some matters were not truthfully reported to the National People's Congress; the drafting of the final accounts was not complete or refined; in terms of financial foundation management, too many special local financial accounts were opened, and treasury cash management was not in place, etc. The report reveals that the delimitations of public finance budgets, governmental fund budgets and State-owned capital operational budgets were not clear after analysis of their functions and overlapping arrangement of funds was prominent. In central government budget management, the report found relevant budget systems did not reflect actual conditions, some expenditure ranges were unclear, standards were imperfect, budget constraints were not strong, and there were no specific standards for budget management of central budget units. Such problems affected the unity and integrity of the national budget system, and also restricted the government's budget management right and the NPC's supervision right. To this end, the report offered proposals on accelerating improvement of the unified, standardized system of government budget, strengthening the organic linkage between budgets, scientifically arranging expenses according to their functional orientation, strengthening the transfers from the government fund budget and State-owned fund management budget to the general public budget, and intensifying the clearing and consolidation of government funds and State-owned capital operating incomes, gradually establishing a government finance reporting system, and improving the criteria on quotas of basic expenditures and project expenditures.

In September 2014, the State Council promulgated the Decision of the State Council on Deepening the Reform of Budget Management Systems, which explicitly stipulated the necessity of improving the government budget system; clarifying the revenue and expenditure boundaries of the general public budget, government fund budget, State-owned capital management budget, and social insurance fund budget; establishing a government budget system with clear positioning and divisions, including government revenues and expenditures in budget management; strengthening overall management of the government fund budget, State-owned capital management budget and general public budget; establishing a mechanism for including overall use funds within the government fund budget into the general public budget; and intensifying the transfer of State-owned capital management budget funds to the general public budget. In November 2014, the Ministry of Finance issued the Notice on Improving the Government Budget System, explicitly stipulating the need to improve the government budget system; strengthen the integration of the government fund budget and general public budget, State-owned capital management budget and general public budget, and various funds of the latter; improve relevant laws and regulations for reforming of the tax and fee system, gradually canceling special items including the urban maintenance and construction tax, sewage charge, the costs for prospecting rights and mining rights, and compensation for mineral resources; and conduct an overall rearrangement.

Source: Report of the State Council on the Audit on the Central Budget Implementation and Other Fiscal Revenues and Expenditures in 2013, Legally Performing Audit Supervision Duties and Effectively Promoting the Anticorruption and Integrity Construction and Reform Deepening—Interpretation of the Report of the State Council on the Audit on the Central Budget Implementation and Other Fiscal Revenues and Expenditures in 2013.

(8) Promote Openness and Transparency

With a view to making Party affairs and government affairs more open and promoting democratic management and democratic supervision, audit institutions have gradually established the system of audit results announcement and information disclosure. In 2003, the CNAO announced the audit results of special funds for the severe acute respiratory syndrome (SARS), marking the formal implementation of the announcement system. Over the past decade, audit institutions at all levels have together published more than 60,000 social announcements on audit results. The audit results announcement system raises higher requirements for quality work by audit institutions, further mobilizes society to form a joint force of supervision, and plays a very important role in promoting the government information disclosure. (See Table 4-6.)

In recent years, audit institutions, while announcing audit results, have vigorously promoted the openness of budgets, three public expenses, and situation of rectification after the audit, and have achieved good social repercussions. Disclosing the audit plan, procedure, and results according to law not only serves as an important channel for the public to understand the duty performance of government departments and participate in national governance, but

TABLE 4-6   Audit Results Announcements in 2003–2014

Unit: piece

Year	Audit Institutions Nationwide	National Audit Office of China
2003	794	1
2004	518	7
2005	796	4
2006	1,465	5
2007	1,950	6
2008	2,936	12
2009	4,127	16
2010	7,668	23
2011	8,038	39
2012	9,948	37
2013	10,958	32
2014	10,891	23
Total	60,089	205

also makes the latter more open and transparent. In 2013, the CNAO allowed 10 central enterprises and three banks that had been audited to announce their rectification situation when the audit findings were announced. This approach is an effective attempt to promote identification and correction of problems.

3. EXPERIENCE OF BUILDING THE SOCIALIST SYSTEM WITH CHINESE CHARACTERISTICS

After about three decades of hard exploration, China has made great achievements and accumulated rich experience in building a socialist auditing system with Chinese characteristics, mainly including the following:

(1) Adhere to the leadership of the Communist Party of China, which provides a political guarantee for the establishment and development of the auditing system.
　　Adhering to the Party's leadership is the unique advantage of the socialist auditing system with Chinese characteristics. The auditing system is a basic political system of China, and also an important part of the supervision system of the Party and the State. The Communist Party of China has always attached great importance to audit work and institutional improvement. In 1933, the Provisional Central Government of the Chinese Soviet Republic set up the Central Auditing Commission in Ruijin, Jiangxi Province, and Chairman Mao Zedong approved the promulgation of the Audit Regulations of the Executive Committee of Central Government of Chinese Soviet Republic, which is the first audit law of the regime under the leadership of the CPC. Audit supervision played a positive role in helping China gain victory in the Chinese People's War against Japanese Aggression and the following War of Liberation, and promoting the rapid recovery and rapid development of national economy after the founding of the People's Republic of China and before the reform and opening up (1978). The PRC Constitution promulgated in 1982 established the socialist audit supervision system, and opened a new chapter of China's socialist audit cause.
　　Adhering to the Party's leadership is a fundamental guarantee for establishment and development of the auditing system. In the past 30 years or so, audit has played an irreplaceable role in maintaining the financial and economic order, and promoting the construction of clean government, the rule of law and the deepening of reform, and provided an important basis for the formulation of major economic decisions and major policies of the

CPC Central Committee and the State Council. Through such efforts, China has made great achievements in auditing system construction under the direct leadership of the Party, and significantly improved its international status and influence. For example, the system of Accountability Audit for Leading Officials of the Party and Government and Leaders of State-owned Enterprises has been increasingly improved through constant exploration under the direct leadership of the CPC Central Committee and Party committees at all levels. The accountability auditing system is not only a unique auditing system of supervising and restricting power with power, but also an important contribution to the global auditing system.

Adhering to the Party's leadership is the essence of building the socialist auditing system with Chinese characteristics. The PRC Constitution stipulates the leading status of the Party in the socialist cause. The audit is strongly political, policy oriented, global, and macro. For continuous development and improvement of the socialist auditing system with Chinese characteristics, we must adhere to the Party's leadership, and strengthen the Party's leadership over the audit work from the perspectives of politics, route, road, direction, ideology, and organization. Audit institutions at all levels must closely rely on the Party's leadership; always adhere to the theory of socialism with Chinese characteristics; always grasp the correct political direction; earnestly implement a series of decisions and deployments of the Party Central Committee on strengthening audit supervision; promote improvements in governance and promote economic, social, and scientific development; and make greater contributions to further enriching and developing the socialist auditing system with Chinese characteristics.

(2) Adhere to the laws of socialism with Chinese characteristics, which provide a legal basis for the establishment and development of the auditing system.

Law is an important weapon of national governance. The socialist legal system with Chinese characteristics is the legal foundation in keeping with the nature of socialism with Chinese characteristics, the legal embodiment of innovative practices and the guarantee for the prosperity of socialism with Chinese characteristics. The nature of a country's legal system is determined by the nature of its social system. The auditing system is an integral part of socialist legal system with Chinese characteristics. The right of audit supervision is conferred by the Constitution. The basis, procedures, and standards of audit are statutory, and audit is an important means to maintain and promote the rule of law. China's current auditing system was established according to the 1982 Constitution. Afterwards, the Audit Law and its implementing rules, the Regulations on Accountability Audit of Main Party and Government Leading Officials and State-owned Enterprise Leaders, and other important laws and regulations were promulgated, which provided a sufficient legal basis and legal guarantee for government auditing, and also provided basic rules for the continuous improvement of the socialist auditing system with Chinese characteristics.

Adhering to the laws of socialism with Chinese characteristics is an inevitable requirement for construction of China's auditing system. The Fourth Plenary Session of the 18th CPC National Congress makes clear the overall goal of promoting law-based governance is to build a socialist legal system with Chinese characteristics and a socialist country under the rule of law. As an important institutional arrangement to oversee and restrict power by power, government auditing necessarily requires auditing system construction should follow and serve the construction of the socialist legal system with Chinese characteristics, and latter must always serve as the start and end point of auditing system construction. Therefore, only by adhering to the laws of socialism with Chinese characteristics can we better develop and improve the socialist auditing system with Chinese characteristics.

(3) Insist on the exploration and innovation of audit practices, to test and check system construction.

A system is not a product of nature or imagination, but is established based on the rich production practice of individuals or groups. Constant exploration and innovation of audit practice will help test system construction, and ensure its scientific and valid nature, which is a basic experience of building a socialist auditing system with Chinese characteristics.

The establishment and improvement of the system for the accountability audit of Party and government officials and leaders in State-owned enterprises during their term of office has fully proved this point. Although the legal status of the accountability audit, as a socialist audit supervision system with Chinese characteristics, was finally determined with revision of the Audit Law in 2006, the practice can be traced back to the 1980s when the accountability audit of factory directors leaving their posts and the contract operation responsibility audit were already being conducted. In 1999, the General Office of the CPC Central Committee and the General Office of the State Council issued the Interim Provisions on Accountability Audit, providing a legal basis and environment for audit institutions to extensively conduct their work in this regard. In 2006, on the basis of summarizing the audit practice of the previous 20 years, the accountability audit was written into the Audit Law and established as an important part of the overall system. In order to improve practice and further promote audit normalization, in 2010, the General Office of the CPC Central Committee and the General Office of the State Council issued the Regulations Concerning Accountability Audit for Leading Officials of the Party and Government and Leaders of State-Owned Enterprises, compiled according to experiences in practice and problems encountered along the way. In 2014, seven central departments jointly issued the Rules for the Implementation of Regulations Concerning Accountability Audit for Leading Officials of the Party and Government and Leaders of State-owned Enterprises, which further refined and enriched the system.

Since its establishment, audit institutions have always based their work on China's national conditions and actual situation of audit, and creatively carried out various tasks, having changed from simple account checking to audit of the capital, business, material, and information flows, from single audit of fiscal and financial revenue and expenditure to accountability audit, from a single-point discrete audit to multipoint linkage audit, from simple partial audit to all-round audit, from simple static audit to the combination of static and dynamic audit, from the simple ex post audit to the combination of concurrent audit and ex post audit, from simple micro audit to the combination of micro and macro audit, and from the initial hand-checking of accounts to audit through big data, cloud computing, and other advanced technologies. These practices and explorations promote the formation of a relatively complete audit supervisory network and a good mechanism for sustainable development and progress of audit work, and further enrich and promote the development of the socialist auditing system with Chinese characteristics.

In the past three decades, the system has been improved through continuous exploration and innovation, tested by practice and ultimately proved to be scientific and effective. Under new historical conditions, we must always base the work on practice, pay attention to new governance needs and new audit practices, and continuously enrich, test, develop, and improve the socialist auditing system with Chinese characteristics through exploration and innovation.

(4) **Strengthen study of audit theories, to guide and support system development.**

The auditing theory system of socialism with Chinese characteristics is the theoretical generalization and upgrading of socialist audit practice as well as the theoretical representation of the socialist auditing system with Chinese characteristics. Enriching and developing it is inseparable from guidance by scientific auditing theories and continuous creation of needed scientific audit theories.

In the initial stages of reform and opening up, and periods of economic system exploration, audit institutions in China explored audit practice while organizing much theoretical research, and basically established a series of viewpoints on audit definition, audit procedure, audit institution-alization, leadership system, audit function, relationship between audit subject and audit object, relations among government auditing, internal audit and social audit, how audit serves macro management, how to strengthen legalization, institutionalization and standardization of audit work, and audit development, and so on. Such research plays an important role in unifying the thoughts and the proper identification and clarification of some basic issues of audit, and also provides an important theoretical basis and reference for the drafting and formulation of professional auditing systems and norms.

At the time when efforts are being made to establish and improve the socialist market economic system, research into audit theory has been continuously deepened along with audit practice. In the process of exploration and innovation, audit institutions have summarized the audit laws, continuously organized in-depth research on the various professional audits, audit methods and techniques, audit management and other issues; carried out in-depth discussions of basic theoretical problems mainly focused on the establishment and improvement of the socialist market economic system and practice of the scientific outlook on development, and so on; and basically established an auditing theory system of socialism with Chinese characteristics. During this period, we have gained further understanding of the nature of audit, changed the definition of audit from "independent economic supervision" to "tool of the democratic rule of law," and from "the product of democratic rule of law, and the means of promoting democratic rule of law" to "an endogenous 'immune system' in the national governance system," basically gaining an understanding of the relationship between audit and accountability, between audit and democratic rule of law, and between audit and national governance, and further established a series of viewpoints on audit functions and objectives, basic audit features, and so on. These interrelated concepts, ideas, and viewpoints run through all aspects of the auditing of socialism with Chinese characteristics. Theoretical research and an understanding of auditing of socialism with Chinese characteristics not only serve as important guidelines for innovation in the operational mechanism, but also provide an important theoretical basis and support for formulation and amendment of the Audit Law and its implementing rules, as well as the compilation, revision and improvement of national auditing standards.

It can be said that the auditing theory system of socialism with Chinese characteristics was formed with the development and improvement of the overall system. Continuous deepening of theoretical research on audit, and constant improvement of the auditing theory system of socialism with Chinese characteristics are essential for further systemic development.

Related Background 6: Auditing Theory System of Socialism with Chinese Characteristics[12]

The auditing theory system of socialism with Chinese characteristics systematically makes clear a number of important issues on audit including the definition, object, reason, process, means, and trend of audit work. Specific contents are as follows:

- The nature of socialist auditing is the core issue for the system of auditing theory of socialism with Chinese characteristics, and is the premise of answering the questions on audit functions, objectives, features, exercise, and infrastructure construction. Government auditing is a fundamental institutional arrangement of using power to restrict power in accordance with the law. In essence, government auditing is one of the endogenous supervision and control systems of national governance. National governance needs determine the generation of government auditing, national governance objectives determine the direction of government auditing, and the national governance mode determines the system and form of government auditing.

- Functional positioning of auditing of socialism with Chinese characteristics. From the perspective of institutional property, legal status, functions, and roles, government auditing is the bedrock and important safeguard in promoting national governance modernization. It has the functions of preventing, revealing, and resisting risks. The prevention function of government auditing means that, through its deterrence role and the advantages of independence, objectivity,

---

[12] For relevant argumentations, refer to Liu Jiayi (chief editor), *Study on the Auditing Theory of Socialism with Chinese Characteristics*, Rev. ed. Beijing: The Commercial Press, China Modern Economic Publishing House, May 2015, Edition 1.

impartiality, innovativeness, and the coverage of all aspects of the economy and society, the government auditing can prevent risks to economic and social operation and can strengthen the governance system's "immunity." Through supervising and inspecting the implementation of governance policies and measures, government auditing offices can objectively reflect the real situation and reveal problems, and promote better governance. The resistance function of audit means that, by improving and standardizing the system, government auditing offices can resist and inhibit the various "diseases" in the economic and social operation and guard against all kinds of risks, thereby contributing to improved national governance. Prevention, revelation, and resistance are the three ways in which government auditing performs its "immune system" function. They are interconnected and constitute an organic whole in the practice of audit work, and jointly safeguard the healthy development of the national economy and society. Among them, revelation is the foundation, resistance is the key, and prevention is the purpose.

■ Objectives and tasks of socialist auditing with Chinese characteristics. Based on different levels, they can be divided into fundamental, realistic and immediate objectives. The first is to safeguard fundamental public interest; the realistic objective is to promote rule of law, safeguard people's livelihood, and promote reform and development. It should well serve as the "defender" of national interests, the "security officer" of economic development, the guardian of public funds, the "supervisor" of the exercise of power, the "sharp sword" of anticorruption, and the "catalyst" of deepened reform. The direct objective is to monitor and evaluate the reality, legality and effectiveness of the fiscal and financial revenue and expenditure of audited units. According to China's current situation, the key task is to safeguard national security, especially economic security. Audit institutions should pay attention to the State's fiscal security, financial security, State-owned assets security, livelihood security, resource and ecological security, and information security; reveal existing risks; and propose countermeasures to prevent and resolve risks.

■ Features of the socialist auditing with Chinese characteristics. All of the work should be based on openness, initiative, service and understanding the overall situation, and insisting on criticism, supervision, micro investigation and disclosure, adaptability and independence, which are five major features of the current government auditing. Government auditing organs are required to investigate and expose major violations of laws and regulations and seek clues in suspected cases of economic crime; discover, analyze, and research problems in systems, mechanisms, institutions, and policy; offer audit opinions and suggestions; promote the implementation and improvement of

(continued)

policies, laws, and systems; and further advance macro, constructive, initiative, and timely audit.

■ Exercise of socialist auditing with Chinese characteristics. Audit institutions must always adhere to the principle of "conducting audit according to law, serving the overall situation, focusing on the central task, highlighting the key points and being realistic and pragmatic"; audit institutions must closely embrace the needs of economic and social development, make clear the objectives of the fiscal, financial, business, accountability, resource, and environment and foreign audits, and improve the pertinence of audit work; audit institutions must follow audit procedures and standards, and safeguard audit quality; audit institutions must innovate their operational ways and methods, integrate audit resources, achieve scientific management, and improve the efficiency and effect of audit work; and audit institutions must closely coordinate and cooperate with other parties involved to maximize the audit role.

The auditing theory system of socialism with Chinese characteristics is open, and will be constantly enriched and improved with practice to play its role in guiding the development of the socialist audit cause with Chinese characteristics.

(5) Adhere to the principle of "based on national conditions and absorbing foreign experience" for the development of the socialist auditing system with Chinese characteristics.

Audit institutions have always attached great importance to learning the advanced foreign experience. In May 1982 and May 1984, China joined the INTOSAI and Asian Organization of Supreme Audit Institutions (ASOSAI). As an important member of the two organizations, the CNAO has, over the years, always regarded them as important platforms for learning and exchange, and has actively participated in the projects of experience sharing and cooperation, drawing on the good practices and experience of other countries. In the early stages of reform and opening up, Chinese audit institutions organized special research projects on foreign auditing systems, and audit institutions of the United States, Australia, Canada, and other countries sent their experts to help train Chinese auditors and made many suggestions on the arrangement and development of China's auditing system. For over 30 years, audit institutions of China, while "going global," have also invited foreign experts to China to give lectures and impart experiences. Each year, China has also dispatched many special training and investigation teams to other countries for international discussion and exchange, learning, training and investigation, and timelier, in-depth understanding and mastery of advanced audit experience and practices.

Understanding and mastering foreign experience and practices does not mean copying; it does mean analyzing and absorbing according to China's national conditions, enriching and improving the audit supervision system to meet national conditions and also become more scientific and effective. For over 30 years, historic achievements made in the development of the socialist auditing system with Chinese characteristics fully prove the nation has successfully opened up a road of socialist auditing with Chinese characteristics. The largest feature lies in the focus on learning and the constant approach of basing on national conditions and absorbing ideas, instead of blind action and blind copying of foreign experiences. This is mainly embodied as follows: First, the audit leadership system with Chinese characteristics in line with national conditions is selected, and, like other countries, China safeguards the independence of audit in terms of law, institutional setting and personnel, and so on; second, China draws on foreign experience in announcing audit reports, gradually promoting audit results announcements according to the actual conditions of China's economic and social development and audit development, which promotes democratic rule of law; third, based on the actual conditions of reform and opening, establishment and improvement of the socialist market economy system, and transformation of government functions in the primary stage of socialism, audit institutions regard uncovering and investigating major violations of laws and rules as an important task, thus ensuring the audit plays a key role in combating corruption in a more direct way; fourth, audit institutions of China learn and apply advanced foreign performance audit techniques and methods, combine the audit of the true and legitimate benefits of financial revenue and expenditure with the performance audit, carry out comprehensive audit works, and seek to improve efficiency and effect; fifth, after absorbing and drawing on useful contents of foreign audit standards, China formulated and revised the National Audit Standards of the PRC in line with national conditions and also able to better regulate and guide audit behavior.

Whether an auditing system of a country is scientific and effective mainly depends on its compliance with national conditions. Broadly speaking, China's fundamental national condition is that it is still on the primary stage of socialism and will remain so for a long period. This is the overall context within which the Chinese people led by the Party carry out institutional design and innovation, and is also a foothold for the development and improvement of the socialist auditing system with Chinese characteristics. Its establishment and improvement fully considers the specific conditions and characteristics of national economic and social development, and deeply accords with the conditions of Chinese traditional culture and history. Whether an auditing system can remain vital mainly depends on its adaptability. The socialist auditing system with Chinese characteristics established and developed according to national conditions always involves self-improvement through the absorbing of foreign experiences in auditing system construction, so it can always remain advanced, meet the requirements of the time and maintain its vitality and advantages. To further develop and improve the socialist auditing system with Chinese characteristics, we must make sure the system continue to be based on national conditions, and absorbing and drawing on foreign experiences, while following the road of a socialist auditing system with Chinese characteristics.

(6) Adhere to comprehensively promoting the infrastructure construction, to consolidate the foundations for development and improvement of the auditing system.

Vigorously carrying out audit work and establishing and improving the relevant auditing systems, audit institutions have always attached great importance to infrastructure construction in terms of personnel, auditing techniques and methods, auditing theory, and auditing culture. The National Audit Work Outline (1999–2003) unveiled in 1998 stressed the necessity of strengthening team building, legal construction, and promotion and application of modern audit means, methods and techniques, seriously carrying out and making achievements in the construction of talents, methods and technologies, to fundamentally promote the audit cause.[13] In accordance with requirements, audit institutions nationwide have taken measures to strengthen infrastructure construction and achieve coordinated development of the audit business and the construction of talents, methods and technologies. In 2008, the CNAO proposed to comprehensively strengthen audit infrastructure construction in team building, legalization,[14] informatization, theory, and culture, so as to consolidate the foundations for sustainable scientific development of the audit cause.

[13] Li Jinhua (chief editor), *The History of Audit in China*, Vol. 3. Beijing: China Modern Economic Publishing House, 2004, p. 273.
[14] From the Audit 2008–2012 Audit Work Development Plan of China National Audit Office, the "legal system of audit" was changed into "legalization of audit."

One of the important reasons for the sustained and rapid development of the socialist audit cause with Chinese characteristics over the past three decades has been adherence to comprehensively promoting infrastructure construction and consolidating the foundations for long-term development of the audit cause and the improvement of the auditing system.

Audit institutions attach great importance to audit team construction, adhere to strict management, continuously deepen reform of the official and personnel system, and have formulated a series of effective measures for leadership construction, selection and appointment of officials, specialized construction, educational training, supervision and management. In 2008, the CNAO especially formulated the Audit Professional Team Construction Plan (2008–2012) and the Auditors' Education and Training Plan (2008–2012), which specific arrangements for audit talent team building. Through unremitting efforts, a team comprising more than 90,000 high-quality auditors reliable in politics, skilled in business, strong in practical ability, and dedicated, has been set up. This is a decisive force and constitutes important capital in promoting continuous development and progress in the socialist auditing system with Chinese characteristics.

China continuously strengthens audit legalization and has put forward specific arrangements and requirements for the development and improvement of the auditing system. Audit institutions attach great importance to legal construction, emphasize improvement of audit laws, regulations and rules, and make efforts to improve auditing standards and guidelines, regarding law-based audit as a fundamental principle of the work. The National Audit Work Plan (2008–2012) made by the CNAO presented explicit requirements for audit legalization. Through 30 years of efforts, a multi-layered but inherently coordinated system of socialist audit laws with Chinese characteristics on the basis of the Constitution, with the Audit Law and the Rules for the Implementation of the Audit Law as the core, supported by local audit laws and regulations, has been basically established. This shows audit has become legalized, institutionalized and standardized, which is of great significance to ensure audit according to law and help auditors and audit institutions comprehensively perform their supervisory duties. While improving the system of audit laws and regulations, audit institutions at all levels also carry out law popularization activities, help auditors improve the awareness, ability and initiative to work in strict accordance with the laws, rules and regulations, as well as auditing standards and guidelines, make provisions on civilized audit, strengthen audit quality control and standardize audit practices, thus ensuring the effective implementation of the laws and regulations, and improving the standardization level of audit. Promoting audit legalization provides a basis and guarantee for audit institutions to comprehensively perform their responsibilities and fully play their supervisory role.

Adapting to the overall development trend of information technology, particularly digital and network technology, audit institutions vigorously promote audit information construction, which strongly supports the improvement and effective implementation of the auditing system technically. As early as 1987, the CNAO set up a Computer Office responsible for studying and guiding the work of audit information construction including computerized audit. In 2002, the CNAO officially launched the "Golden Auditing Project." In 2008, it issued the Information Technology Development Plan (2008–2012), making further deployments for audit informatization. In the 21st Century, based on the "Golden Auditing Project," audit institutions have gradually established an audit information system with application systems (including audit implementation, management and exchange systems) as the core, with information resources (including the audit management database and audit business database), with computer equipment and a network environment as the basic infrastructure, with security systems (including the system of cascade protection and grade protection, the national audit antivirus system, and the information system operation monitoring system) as the safety guarantee, with audit information laws and regulations, business norms and technical specifications as the legal basis, and with a high-quality audit team familiar with information technology as the manpower guarantee. This audit information system strongly supports audit institutions in innovating their operational mechanisms, fully performing their audit responsibilities and giving full play to the role of audit supervision.

By strengthening theoretical construction, audit institutions have regulated and improved the level of practice, and guided and supported the development and improvement of the auditing system. The CNAO and local audit institutions at all levels attach great importance to research on audit theories, conducted useful exploration of socialist audit theories with Chinese characteristics, and made a number of achievements with important influence. In 2009, the CNAO began to implement the key scientific research project system. By 2014, 67 key scientific research projects had been completed, and the research results contributed much to the improvement of audit practice and system improvement. In 2010, the CNAO issued the Opinions on Further Strengthening Research on Audit Theory to sum up audit experience under the guidance of the theory of socialism with Chinese characteristics, actively explore the law of audit development, vigorously promote theoretical innovation, and make auditing theory research more pertinent, forward-looking, constructive, and effective, and better play the role as an audit "think tank" in theoretical and practical guidance and decision making. In accordance with the requirements, the CNAO and local audit institutions at all levels strengthened their investment in theoretical research and construction of scientific research institutions; improved the research operational system; achieved fruitful results in terms of basic audit theories, application theories, and techniques; enriched and improved socialist audit theories with Chinese characteristics; and provided ideological guidance and intellectual support for the development and improvement of the auditing system.

Audit culture is a powerful spiritual force to promote the development of the socialist audit cause with Chinese characteristics. Audit institutions attach great importance to audit culture construction, organize special audit groups to study it, including core values and concepts of audit, audit spirit, and audit cultural construction, in order to refine the core values of auditors. In December 2008, the audit culture of "responsibility, loyalty, integrity, legality, independence, devotion" was proposed at the National Audit Work Conference. In July 2009, the Government Auditing Work Forum proposed creating the audit culture of "responsibility, loyalty, integrity, legality, independence, devotion."[15] In 2011, the National Audit Work Conference proposed to vigorously carry forward these core values. In January 2012, the Party Group of the CNAO issued the Opinions of the Party Group of the National Audit Office of China on Strengthening Audit Culture Construction, making provisions and arrangements regarding the significance, guiding ideology, overall goals, main principles, major tasks, safeguard measures, and practical way of strengthening audit culture construction.[16] By strengthening audit culture construction and guiding auditors to practice the core values of "responsibility, loyalty, integrity, legality, independence, devotion," audit institutions have improved team cohesion, creativity and combat effectiveness, built a common ideological and moral foundation and spiritual home, and provided a solid foundation and internal support for scientific development of the audit cause and the development and improvement of the auditing system.

---

[15] Liu Jiayi, Vigorously Strengthening the Building of Audit Team and Promoting Scientific Development of Audit Cause, document of the Government Auditing Work Forum in 2009.
[16] The Opinions of the Party Group of China National Audit Office on Strengthening Audit Culture Construction, January 2012.

CHAPTER FIVE

Future Development of the Auditing System of Socialism with Chinese Characteristics

O IMPROVE THE AUDITING SYSTEM CONTINUOUSLY in practice, on the basis of profound understanding its laws of development, we should draw lessons on the history of audit development and make adjustments in line with changing external environment and requirements of the times. Currently, government auditing finds itself in a new situation and with a new mission amid advancing the strategic layout of the "Four Comprehensives." In this regard, we must firmly stress promoting "reform, development, rule of law and anticorruption," and speed up development to ensure the system keeps pace with the times, develops into a complete, scientific, standardized, and effective system, matures in the course of strengthening audit, and gives full play to its role of bedrock and important guarantee for the modernization of national governance.

 ## 1. GENERAL GOAL AND REQUIREMENT FOR FURTHER IMPROVEMENT OF THE AUDITING SYSTEM OF SOCIALISM WITH CHINESE CHARACTERISTICS

(1) General Goal

The decision of the Fourth Plenary Session of the 18th CPC Central Committee explicitly requires improvement of the auditing system and protecting the right to exercise audit independently. According to the requirement, considering the duties, tasks and professional characteristics of audit work, we need to strengthen reform and innovation, improve the audit management system which ensures audit execution independently according to law, and establish an auditors' management system with auditing professional features, so as to constitute the socialist auditing system with Chinese characteristics, which is corresponding to the modernization of the national governance system and governance capacity. Under the system, we could give full play to the important role of auditing in safeguarding the people's fundamental interests, ensuring the implementation of national major decision-making deployment and national economic security, and promoting the deepening of reform, the rule of law, the construction of a clean government, and crackdown on corruption.

(2) General Requirement

First, we should always adhere to the leadership of the Communist Party of China (CPC). The CPC provides the core guidance to the cause of socialism with Chinese characteristics. Adherence to CPC leadership is the fundamental precondition for us to achieve overall victory as the most essential feature of socialism with Chinese characteristics. To improve the auditing system, this is a basic requirement for maintaining the perpetual nature of the auditing system of socialism with Chinese characteristics and also a political guarantee for sound development of the audit cause. Adherence to CPC leadership means to earnestly implement a series of deployments of the CPC Central Committee on strengthening audit, and to always follow the correct political direction. This will enable Party committees and governments at all levels to strengthen their leadership over audit, put forward the objectives, tasks and emphases of auditing surrounding their primary tasks, listen to important audit reports, and support audit institutions to work independently according to law. On the principle of Party administers officials, we should strengthen leading officials and audit team building, improve the cultivation and management mechanism of audit officials,and allocate audit forces reasonably. While exploring and improving the auditing system in practice, audit institutions at all levels must always act in consistency with the Party Central Committee in both thinking and action, support and implement all decisions and deployments of the Party and the State, work under the leadership of the Party committees and governments at various levels, and strictly follow Party discipline, making due contributions to strengthening Party building and implementation of its policies in the new period.

Second, we should firmly adhere to the strategic layout of the "Four Comprehensives." Since the 18th CPC National Congress, the Party Central

Committee with General Secretary Xi Jinping as the core has been working under the strategic thought and layout of the "Four Comprehensives" (comprehensively building a moderately prosperous society, comprehensively deepening reform, comprehensively implementing rule of law, and comprehensively strengthening Party self-discipline) based on the fundamental realities of China and the requirements for adhering to and developing socialism with Chinese characteristics. This specifies the strategic objectives and measures for audit work under the new situation, providing theoretical guidance and practical guidelines for realizing the "two centenary goals" and the China Dream for the great rejuvenation of the Chinese nation. Defining the strategic policies, key fields and primary objectives of our work under the new situation, the strategic layout of "Four Comprehensives" is a general plan for ruling and administering the country, and also a "road map" for modernizing national governance. Characterized by strong professionalism, independence and a macro nature, government auditing, as an important part of national governance, involves all aspects of economic and social development, playing a key role in revealing risks, promoting reform, supervising implementation and punishing corruption by firmly stressing the principle of "jurisdictional control, personnel administration and wealth management," becoming an important tool of promoting the implementation of "Four Comprehensives." By closely focusing on "reform, development, rule of law and anticorruption," government auditing institutions should enhance and innovate their supervision methods, effectively fulfill their supervisory responsibilities, speed up full coverage of audit supervision, keep improving the auditing system, and ensure its role as the bedrock and important guarantee for modernizing national governance.

Terminology 1: Specific Connotations of "Four Comprehensives"

Comprehensively building a moderately prosperous society, comprehensively deepening reform, comprehensively implementing rule of law, and comprehensively strengthening Party self-discipline constitute an organic whole, where each element is endowed with its dedicated scientific connotation and great strategic significance.

"Comprehensively building a moderately prosperous society" is an important step in the "Three-Step Development" strategy proposed by the CPC Central Committee. Based on the goal of comprehensively building a moderately prosperous society set forth at the 16th and

(continued)

17th CPC National Congresses, to adapt to changes in the internal and external situation, the 18th CPC National Congress proposed new requirements "to attain the goal of completing the building of a moderately prosperous society in all aspects by 2020"; that is, the economy should maintain sustained and sound development; people's democracy should be expanded; the country's cultural soft power should be improved significantly; living standards should be see a significant rise; major progress should be made in building a resource-conserving and environmentally friendly society. Meanwhile, it is emphasized that the moderately prosperous society we will comprehensively build is a well-off society in an all-round way to the benefit of one billion-plus people, featuring comprehensive development in economic, political, cultural, social, and ecological civilization, and laying a solid foundation for realizing the grand goal of socialist modernization and great rejuvenation of the Chinese nation.

"Comprehensively deepening the reform" is an important deployment set forth at the Third Plenary Session of the 18th CPC Central Committee. The *Decision of the CPC Central Committee on Some Major Issues Concerning Comprehensively Deepening Reform* adopted at the Third Plenary Session of the 18th CPC Central Committee in November 2013 made an all-round deployment in this regard. The Third Plenary Session of the 18th CPC Central Committee stressed that the policy of reform and opening up is a critical choice determining the destiny of contemporary China, and also an important instrument for the undertakings of the CPC and the Chinese people to catch up in great strides. The overall goal of deepening the reform comprehensively is to improve and develop socialism with Chinese characteristics, and to promote the modernization of the national governance system and capacity.

"Comprehensively implementing the rule of law" is an important deployment set forth at the Fourth Plenary Session of the 18th CPC Central Committee. The *Decision of the CPC Central Committee on Some Major Issues Concerning Comprehensively Promoting the Rule of Law* adopted in October 2014 made overall planning and comprehensive deployment for comprehensively promoting the rule of law and building a socialist country under the rule of law. It stressed the rule of law was an essential requirement and important guarantee for adhering to and developing socialism with Chinese characteristics and also an imperative requirement for realizing the modernization of the national governance system and its capacity.

"Comprehensively strengthening Party discipline building" is a strategic deployment proposed by General Secretary Xi Jinping in his address at the Summary Meeting of the Party's Mass Line Educational Practice Activities. At the opening of his speech, General Secretary

Xi Jinping put forward this significant strategy of "comprehensively strengthening the Party discipline building." In the context of the Party building, he also proposed the mission requirements for "adhering to the Party discipline building under the new situation" in eight aspects, that is, implementing the responsibilities for the Party discipline building, adhering to the combination of construction of Party ideology and governance of Party discipline, strictly enforcing interparty political life, persevering in strict management of officials, thoroughly improving the style of work, managing Party discipline strictly, exerting the people's supervisory role and thoroughly grasping the laws of the Party discipline building.

Third, we should adapt to new situation of economic and social development. China has entered a new era whereby it is comprehensively realizing the great rejuvenation of the nation. Accordingly, it is faced with new situations and new tasks in improving national governance and socioeconomic development, responding to the concern of the era, realizing the people's well-being and building a modern China. On the one hand, the ideological concept, ways of living and thinking of the people have greatly changed by globalization and informationization. Information technology (IT) applications, that is, Internet and big data, has provided an effective approach for upgrading public administration services and helping the government improve decision making, and has helped us to solve pressing problems (such as environmental pollution) concerning national governance. Meanwhile, the development of the Internet and IT also adds complexity to national governance, bringing unprecedented new challenges to national governance and socioeconomic development. However, China's socioeconomic development is also challenged by new tasks. The following audit tasks are much tougher than before: performing the duties of audit according to law, promoting the implementation of the Central Government's macroeconomic policies and measures, and improving the quality and benefits of economic development; promoting innovation in an all-round manner, transforming modes and adjusting the structure; safeguarding people's fundamental interests, and promoting social harmony and stability; ensuring national security, preventing and reducing risks; promoting environmental protection, conservation, and utilization of resources and energy and ecological civilization construction; improving systems and mechanisms, comprehensively deepening the reform and promoting the rule of law. Hence, against such a background, a key issue unavoidable for the further development and improvement of the auditing system of socialism with Chinese characteristics is how audit institutions can adapt themselves to the information-based development trend, change their ideas, clarify their concepts, and improve their methods to realize the transformation from a single-point disconnected audit to multipoint coordinated audit, from simple partial audit to all-round audit, from simple static audit to the combination of static and dynamic audit, from the simple ex-post audit to the combination of concurrent audit and ex- post audit, and from simple micro audit to the combination of micro and macro audit, so as to realize the leapfrog advancement in the capacity, grading and level of auditing, and give full play to the role of audit in promoting the modernization of national governance and sound development of national economy.

Fourth, we should fully play the role of audit for national governance. As an integral part of national political system, government auditing is generated and developed to meet the objective needs of national governance. Historically, national governance demands determine the generation of government audit, national governance objectives determine government audit direction, and the national governance mode determines audit system and mode used. Functionally, as an institutional arrangement for supervising and restricting powers according to law, government auditing pertains to the scope of supervision and control, serving the decision-making organs and playing a role of monitoring and restraining the executive organs. It is widely recognized in the world that government auditing plays an important role in promoting and improving national governance. In 2013, the XXI INCOSAI (International Conference of Supreme Audit Institutions) held in Beijing, endorsed the *Beijing Declaration*, specifying the common objective for supreme audit institutions of all countries, namely, to promote good national governance and global governance; besides, it also proposed a way to reach this goal. Development and improvement of the auditing system of socialism with Chinese characteristics aim to better play the role of government auditing in improving national governance and promoting the modernization of the national governance system and capacity. To this end, all tentative plans and considerations about improving the auditing system must proceed from the starting point and supreme goal: that is, to facilitate audit institutions to better realize the full coverage of auditing in terms of public funds, State-owned assets and State-owned resources, and serve as the "defender" of national interests, the "security officer" of economic development, the guardian of public funds, the "supervisor" of the exercise of power, the "sharp sword" of anti-corruption, and the "catalyst" of deepened reform.

Terminology 2: Modernization of the National Governance System and Capacity

The national governance system and capacity are the concentrated reflection of systems and the system implementation capacity of a country. The term refers to the institutional systems for governing the country under the leadership of the Party, including the systems, mechanisms, laws, and regulations in regard to economy, politics, culture, society, and ecological civilization, as well as Party building. National governance capacity refers to the capacity of managing social affairs through national systems, including reform, development and stability, domestic and foreign affairs, national defense, and governance of the Party, the State, and the military. The two elements are organic and complementary. Without them, governance capacity cannot be enhanced; without enhanced governance capacity, efficiency of the national governance system cannot be achieved.

To modernize the national governance system and capacity, we must keep pace with the times, reform the systems and mechanisms, laws and regulations inapplicable to current requirements for practice and development, and continuously create new ones to make the systems more reasonable and efficient, thus achieving governance over all matters of the Party, the country and the society that is institutionalized, standardized and routine. We should work hard to strengthen our governance capacity, enhanced our awareness to the importance of work in accordance with the system and the law, and strive to be good at using of the system and laws in governing the country, so as to turn the advantage in system into the national management efficiency, and raise the level of the ruling party's government in a reasonable, democratic and law based level.

Quoted from the article entitled "Unifying Our Ideas according to the Decision of the Third Plenary Session of the 18th CPC Central Committee," published by General Secretary Xi Jinping in *Seeking Truth*, No. 1, 2014.

It is vital to safeguard the independent exercise of audit supervisory power in accordance with the law. Fundamentally, auditing is a monitoring behavior subject to two basic principles, namely, "according to law" and "independence." The decision of the Fourth Plenary Session of the 18th CPC Central Committee explicitly requires improvement of the system and protecting the right to exercise audit supervision independently. Audit institutions must first effectively strengthen the cognition of the rule of law and the capacity of compliance with the law, conduct audit within the legal mandate, and ensure the legality of audit subjects and audit procedures, as well as identification and treatment of audit findings.

Strengthening the independence and authority of audit is the key to ensure that audit institutions can comprehensively perform their duties and effectively play their role. Judged from the development and improvement of auditing systems at all times and in all countries, the primary task is to strengthen and safeguard the independence and authority of audit institutions. As early as 1977, *The Lima Declaration* adopted by the International Organization of Supreme Audit Institutions (INTOSAI) specified that independence was the basic principle of auditing; in 2007, the XIX INCOSAI adopted the *Declaration on the Independence of Supreme Audit Institutions* (also called the *Mexico Declaration*), stressed eight principles for safeguarding audit independence, namely, the eight pillars, as shown in Figure 5-1; by the end of 2014, the resolution on *Enhancing the Efficiency, Accountability, Benefit and Transparency of Public Administration by Boosting Supreme Audit Institutions* adopted at the 69th General Assembly of the United Nations reiterated the significance of supreme audit institutions being independent, and encouraged member states to implement the declaration on independence in compliance with their respective institutional structure. For further development and improvement of auditing system of socialism with Chinese characteristics, we must regard it as a basic requirement to effectively safeguard the audit institutions' independence in exercising their supervisory power according to law.

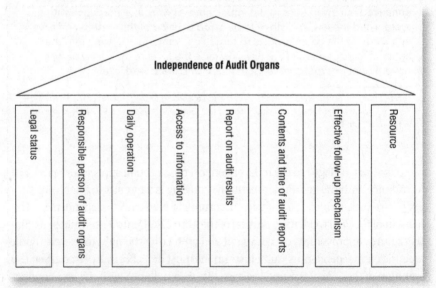

FIGURE 5-1 Eight pillars of audit independence indentified by the *Mexico Declaration* of the International Organization of Supreme Audit Institutions

2. PRINCIPLES INDISPENSABLE FOR DEVELOPMENT AND FURTHER IMPROVEMENT OF THE AUDITING SYSTEM OF SOCIALISM WITH CHINESE CHARACTERISTICS

First, be problem oriented. Problems involve some form of conflict. Where there is a conflict, there must be a problem.[1] Problems are the echo of the times and also the source of reforms. General Secretary Xi Jinping has pointed out, "Existing problems have forced us to reform, and reforms are deepened once problems are tackled and solved."[2] Along with the development of times and changes of situation, problems not adaptable to the situations and development requirements are coming out, which requests reforming auditing system and improving audit operation mechanism. The process of development and improvement of the auditing system is, in nature, a process in which we continuously find and solve problems. Hence, to improve the auditing system, we must adhere to the principle of problem orientation, bravely face problems and identify problems, whereby we can do everything with a definite purpose in mind. As noted by General Secretary Xi Jinping: "Only by solving the specific problems of the times based on the era can we promote social progress."[3] We should make best use of legal frameworks and legal methods to exercise the role of legal system in guidance and normalization, unite our common understanding of institutional reform, conquer the institutional problems and promote the improvement of auditing system legally and in order. With regard to the audit problems, we should thoroughly analyze the institutional reasons, grant authorization in accordance with legal procedures, conduct pilots in appropriate regions, make bold innovation, and actively seek countermeasures and methods for solving problems; meanwhile, we should, as quickly as possible, consolidate the relatively mature reform experience and effective reform measures proved in practice, and upgrade them into audit laws and regulations to supplement the *Audit Law of the PRC* and its Rules of Implementation, and local audit regulations.

Second, there is the experience accumulated in the construction of auditing system of socialism with Chinese characteristics. Through 30 years

---

[1] Mao Zedong, "Oppose Stereotyped Party Writing," speech at Yan'an officials' Meeting, February 8, 1942.
[2] Speech at Non-Party Personages Workshop held in Zhongnanhai on September 17, 2013.
[3] Xi Jinping, Problem is Slogan of Age, Previous Post. Hangzhou: Zhejiang People's Publishing House, 2007.

of development, we have accumulated major valuable experience in the following aspects: (1) adhering to the CPC's leadership, which provides a political guarantee for the establishment and development of auditing system; (2) adhering to the socialist laws with Chinese characteristics, which provides a legal basis for the establishment and development of the auditing system; (3) adhering to studying of audit theories that offer a guide and support for development and improvement of the auditing system; (4) adhering to the exploration and innovation of audit practice which provides trials and examination for audit system development and improvement; (5) adhering to the principle of "based on national conditions and absorbing foreign experiences" that can improve the auditing system of socialism with Chinese characteristics; and (6) adhering to comprehensively promoting the infrastructure construction to consolidate the foundations for development and improvement of the auditing system. Such experience crystallizes the hard exploration and wisdom of auditors over the years, and has been proved effective and correct in the achievements of the auditing system of socialism with Chinese characteristics over the past 30 years or so. Hence, it is very precious. We must persevere in such basic experience and methods enabling us to avoid detours and to be more efficient in developing and improving the auditing system of socialism with Chinese characteristics.

Third, we should stick to top planning, overall advancement, key breakthrough and staged implementation. Comrade Mao Zedong pointed out in his book *On Practice* that we should discover truth through practice, and then prove and develop the truth in practice. Improvement of the auditing system is systematic, and we should give full consideration to the complexity and difficulty of reforms and make it possible to achieve the goal of top planning, integrated design, classified advancement, overall advancement, priority to the easy, key breakthrough, and staged implementation. According to the requirements of "improving the system and protecting the right to exercise audit oversight independently" proposed at the Fourth Plenary Session of the 18th CPC Central Committee, we should decompose the task of improving the institutional systems, organize staged implementation, explore laws through innovation of audit practice, and draw on the essence to improve good working methods and experience and apply them to new audit practice. We should promote all reforms in a reasonable and orderly way and ensure that all measures for system building and reforms support and link with each other organically, with top priority given to reforms in key fields related to the overall situation. We should seek new breakthroughs at key links in the chain of success, and solve problems concerning lack of adaptability of various systems and mechanisms so as to develop the auditing system continuously and keep pace with the times.

3. KEY TO DEVELOPMENT AND FURTHER IMPROVEMENT OF THE AUDITING SYSTEM OF SOCIALISM WITH CHINESE CHARACTERISTICS

It is a primary responsibility and mission to develop and improve the auditing system of socialism with Chinese characteristics and make it more effective in protecting the right to exercise audit independently, more adaptable to China's time-honored history and culture of auditing, and more conducive to fully exerting the audit role in promoting modernization of national governance system and governance capacity around the strategic layout and requirements of comprehensively building a moderately prosperous society, comprehensively deepening the reform, comprehensively implementing the rule of law, and comprehensively strengthening the Party discipline building. In the process, we should reflect China's basic conditions and draw lessons from and adopt the advanced experience of other countries. The development and improvement of auditing system of socialism with Chinese characteristics involve six aspects: audit system, audit duties and authority, audit operation mechanism, audit professionalization, supervision over audit institutions, and audit law system.

Terminology 3: Contents of the *Decision of the CPC Central Committee on Some Major Issues Concerning Comprehensively Promoting the Rule of Law* adopted at the Fourth Plenary Session of the 18th CPC Central Committee on Strengthening the Audit Supervision and Improving the Auditing System

The restrictions and supervision on the use of administrative power should be strengthened. We should improve the systems of inner-party supervision, NPC supervision, democratic supervision, administrative supervision, judicial supervision, audit supervision, social supervision, and public opinion supervision, so as to establish the scientific and effective restriction and supervision system of power operation and make it more effective.

We should improve the auditing system to protect the right to oversight independently. Auditing should fully cover public funds, State-owned assets, State-owned resources and the leading officials' performance of accountability. Higher-level audit institutions must enhance their leadership over lower-level audit institutions. Audit institutions should explore unified management below province level in staffing financial and material resources. Audit professionalization should be enhanced.

(1) About the Auditing Arrangement

The audit arrangement lies at the core of an audit system. Improvement involves four aspects:

1. About the establishment of audit institutions. As mentioned earlier, different countries establish different supreme audit institutions according to respective national conditions and basic political and economic systems, though most of SAIs are established under Constitution of respective countries. Some institutions under the leadership of legislative bodies, remain independent of the legislative, judicial and administrative organs, or report to the legislative bodies; some have certain rights of judicial decision; and some countries adopt the integrated mode of audit and supervision, such as South Korea. No matter what type of establishment is involved, audit institutions of all countries play an important role in national economic and social development. Along with development and changes in the political, economic, and social environment of China, audit institutions are getting increasingly high expectations. Reform helps to eliminate institutional obstacles prejudicial to the audit role. In the current academic community, there are three viewpoints on the future development of China's audit institutions' establishment.

   First, the existing audit system should remain unchanged. It is considered that the existing establishment of audit institutions and arrangement of audit system are well adapted to China's political and economic development at the present stage, and effective, as has been proved by the practice of over the past 30 years or so, playing an important role in supporting and safeguarding audit institutions to fully exert their audit efficiency. So no change is necessary.

   Second, the existing audit system should be reformed. It is argued that, by borrowing ideas from many other countries, especially those with a developed market economy, audit institutions should be elevated to constitutional institutions independent of the administrative establishment, and take charge of external audit supervision over the management and use of resources of the government and reporting their work to the people's congress. Two advantages are identified: First, audit institutions are independent of the governmental establishment, strengthening audit independence; second, such a system strengthens the external audit supervision of the NPC over government financial budget management, improves the arrangement of China's financial budget auditing system and contributes to legalized and rational management of financial budgets.

Third, an integrated establishment system of audit and supervision should be implemented. It is argued that, by drawing on Chinese historic experience and the practices of South Korea and other countries, China can separate audit institutions from the administrative establishment, and establish the Supervisory Ministry of Auditing as a constitutional institution. The advantages include: (1) it is consistent with the positioning specified by the Fourth Plenary Session of the 18th CPC Central Committee that, audit supervision is an integral part of the national restriction and supervision system of power operation, in parallel with inner-party supervision, NPC supervision, democratic supervision, administrative supervision, judicial supervision, social supervision, and public opinion supervision; (2) it caters for the realistic development trends of full audit supervision coverage and an increasingly wide-ranging role in recent years; (3) it accords with the cultures that China has implemented the system of combining supervision and examination in its history of audit; (4) it is in line with the system design of national governance system whereby auditing, as a fundamental institutional arrangement of national governance system, pertains to the supervision and control system independent of the decision-making and execution systems; (5) the enhancement in the establishment hierarchy of audit institutions can further strengthen the independence and authority of auditing, and eliminate institutional obstacles unfavorable to fully exerting the role of audit institutions.

Despite different strengths, all above modes must proceed from the strategic layout of the "Four Comprehensives" strategic layout, concentrate on protecting the right to exercise independent oversight, and maximize the audit role.

2. Strengthening the leadership of higher-level audit institutions over lower-level ones. This is an important measure for promoting the coordinated development of audit cause. To enhance the overall force and independence of audit supervision and the overall arrangement of national audit work, the following measures can be taken: (1) Officials' management should be strengthened. Appointment and dismissal of heads of lower-level audit institutions must be approved by higher-level ones in advance. (2) The leadership of higher-level audit institutions in organization and business should be intensified. Higher-level audit institutions should enhance their overall arrangement and management of audit project plans, reasonably allocate resources, and properly conduct major project audits relating to the overall situation. Lower-level audit institutions should submit their annual audit project plans to the higher level for filing. (3) The administration mode should be innovated and reporting system of major matters

should be improved. Audit institutions must report major matters and audit results to the audit institution at next higher level. The mechanisms of audit institutions management, business inspection and evaluation should be improved, and the systems of work report, leaders' report on their work, and so on should be implemented.

3. Exploring unified management of audit institutions below province level in human, financial and material resources. Currently, there are more than 90,000 auditors nationwide, including more than 70,000 based in over 2,000 counties and cities. Generally speaking, unified management of audit institutions below province level in human, financial and material resources helps to safeguard audit independence, strengthen leadership of provincial audit institutions over local audit work, coordinate audit staff and resources within the province, and intensify the responsibilities of audit institutions for improvement of the regional governance. Meanwhile, the implementation of policies and measures of the Central Committee and the use of various special funds generally involve the grassroots that feature a long chain, multiple levels, and demands for supervision and timely follow-up. From this perspective, the unified management of audit institutions below the province level in human, financial, and material resources can form a complete network of audit supervision, bring everything under supervision and effectively ensure smooth policy implementation; additionally, it facilitates higher-level audit institutions to grasp the overall situation, timely detect and reflect on the risks and hazards through all the linkages, and safeguard national economic security.

In exploration, we should insist on overall design, implementation of pilots, and make progress step by step after summing up experience. Measures include: First, the leading officials' management system of local audit institutions should be improved. The principals of audit institutions at the prefectural and county levels should be managed by the provincial Party committee (Organization Department of the CPC). Local Party committees, governments and higher-level audit institutions should strengthen their management over the qualifications of leading officials of lower-level audit institutions. The responsible persons of audit institutions should, in principle, have work experience in terms of economy, law, and management. Second, audit staffing should be configured reasonably. Coordinated by provincial audit institutions, the personnel departments of provincial institutions should take charge of unified management of staffing of local audit institutions. Local auditors should be subject to unified recruitment. Efforts should be made to strengthen the management of provincial audit institutions in terms of officials, business activities, and finances, to enrich the business force at the prefecture and county levels, and to set up affiliated agencies of audit institutions. Third, the management system of funds and assets can be improved. The funds and assets of audit institutions below the province level should be subject to unified management of relevant provincial departments. The standard of all funds for local audit institutions should be confirmed locally in the context of the actual situation, and within the existing framework of laws and regulations. It should not be inferior to the existing standard. The work concerning appraisal of properties and funds and transfer of assets must always be well done according to provisions. Fourth, the unified management mechanism of audit project plans should be established. Audit project plans of local audit institutions must be subject to unified management of provincial audit institutions, which, in turn, should concentrate on local main tasks, organize local audit forces in a unified way, and properly conduct auditing on major projects relating to the overall situation, according to local actualities in economic and social development. Except the audit projects under the unified organization of higher authority, audit institutions at the prefecture and county levels, in combination with local main tasks, should put forward the annual audit plan at the corresponding level, and carry it out after submission to the local government for examination and then to the provincial audit institutions for approval. In view of actual needs, higher-level audit institutions may organize lower-level audit institutions to conduct non local cross auditing. Fifth, the system of audit result reporting and announcement can be improved. After listening to the opinions of administrative heads of the corresponding government and submitting to higher-level audit institutions for approval, audit institutions at the prefecture and county levels should report the corresponding level's budget performance and other financial revenue and expenditure situations to the standing committee of relevant people's congress according to specified procedures. Sixth, the audit law enforcement responsibility system must be improved. Higher-level audit institutions need to strengthen supervision on the audit quality of units below them. The quality control mechanism of audit business needs improving improved to define the duties and authority. Where major problems of audit quality are found, the investigation system of law enforcement fault liability must be strictly implemented on the principle of integration of powers and responsibilities. Seventh, efforts should be made to promote overall audit informatization and establish a provincial audit data system by focusing on the development and improvement of a national unified audit information system. Relevant electronic data collected by local audit institutions is subject to centralized management according to the standards, methods and requirements of the China National Audit Office (CNAO). Provincial audit institutions must strengthen unified planning of local audit informatization and intensify their support to the informatization construction of grassroots audit institutions.

4. Other measures for enhancing the independence of audit institutions, include: first, improvement of the registration system of audit intervention behavior, and stronger implementation of the provisions of "not subject to interference by any other administrative organs, social groups, or individuals,"[4] further safeguarding the independent exercise of audit supervisory power in accordance with the law. Second, in order to independently conduct audit supervision in accordance with the law, audit institutions at all levels must not engage in various kinds of discussion and coordination and other work unrelated to the statutory duties of auditing; auditing beyond the scope of corresponding duties and authority, and their own capacities and in violation of legal procedures; and participating in appraisal and evaluation activities, that is, evaluation and scoring of the audit by the target entity. Third, we should further define and guarantee any essential data and information to which audit institutions have access during the performance of their duties; meanwhile, relevant departments, financial institutions, and State-owned enterprises and institutions, in the light of audit needs, should legally provide audit institutions with the electronic data and necessary technical documents of their units related to the fulfillment of duties, to ensure smooth auditing in accordance with the law. Fourth, we should further strengthen the application of audit results, integrate audit supervision with the principles of managing officials by the Party, disciplinary inspection, investigation, and accountability, regard the audit results and rectification situations as the important basis for appraisal, appointment and dismissal, award and punishment of leading officials, and incorporate the leading officials' accountability audit results and rectification of problems found into the important contents of assessing leading officials and the inspection and appraisal for accountability in building the CPC work style and clean government, which will serve as an important basis for appraisal of members of the leading team of the CNAO in terms of anti-corruption performance, annual performance, and employment performance. Fifth, the correction of problems found through auditing must be strengthened.

[4] Article 5 of the Audit Law of the People's Republic of China.

Relevant departments and units should strengthen supervision and inspection, carry out a regulatory talk with main leaders of audited entities with ineffective rectification and repeated violations after frequent auditing, and strictly investigate and hold offenders to account. The standing committees of the people's congresses at all levels should combine the work concerning the correction of prominent problems uncovered through auditing, examination and supervision of governments, and departmental budgets and final accounts, and establish a reporting mechanism for listening to and deliberating on the rectification situation. Sixth, the audit results announcement should be enhanced. Audit institutions must announce audit results in accordance with laws and regulations, while audited units should make public their rectification results.

(2) About the Scope of Audit Duty and Authority

The newly revised Budget Law of the PRC imposes new requirements for audit work. The Third and Fourth Plenary Sessions of the 18th CPC Central Committee also made deployments for improving the auditing system. The Opinions of the State Council on Strengthening Audit Work defines the guiding ideology, overall objectives and primary missions in the new period. Accordingly, we need to further improve the duties and authorities of audit institutions in several aspects.

1) Improving the Working Mechanism Commensurate with Full Coverage of Auditing

This was explicitly required by the Fourth Plenary Session of the 18th CPC Central Committee and the *Opinions of the State Council on Strengthening Audit Work* (issued by the State Council [2014] No. 48). Accordingly, audit institutions must bring all public funding, State assets, and State-owned resources under examination to achieve full audit coverage and give full play to the role of auditing in a more comprehensive and effective manner. Judging from current audit work, we need to clarify several basic viewpoints in researching and promoting full audit coverage.

First is the meaning of full coverage. Full coverage mentioned herein refers to auditing of departments and units related to the management, allocation, and application of public funds, State-owned assets and State-owned resources, as well as principal leading officials of the Party and government and leaders of State-owned enterprises. For effective full coverage, with step-by-step emphases, the frequency of auditing should be as follows: one audit for key departments and units every year, at least one audit for other audit targets in a cycle, at least one audit within the term of office of leading officials, and a whole-process follow-up audit of implementation of major State policies and measures, key investment projects, special funds and investment projects.

1. Full coverage should be in depth, with step-by-step emphasis. Auditing should focus on each project, but should not cover all units and only pursue quantity.
2. Full coverage should be with emphasis. Auditing should focus on the central work of the Party and the government on the basis of the overall situation to determine key areas and matters of greatest concern.
3. Full coverage should be step by step. Auditing should progress in a planned way and according to concrete conditions.
4. Full coverage should be effective. Auditing should not reveal problems purely from book accounts, but should "widely" cover audited objects, "precisely" reflect situations, "deeply" investigate problems, "thoroughly" analyze causes, and "effectively" take measures and make suggestions, so as to fully exert the constructive role of auditing.

Second is the content of full coverage, which involves four categories of audit targets:

1. Full coverage of auditing on public funds. Audit institutions shall audit all revenues and expenditures, funds under control of government departments or other units upon the commission of the government, and the relevant economic activities. Audit institutions mainly inspect compliance with State laws and regulations during the fund-raising, management, distribution, and use of public funds; the implementation of major State policies and measures and macro control deployment; the authenticity, legality, and performance of management and use of public funds and wastage; and so forth; the situation about investment with public funds and project progress, and development of causes; and the situation about the financial revenues and expenditures, budget implementation and final accounts drafting of departments and units that manage and use public funds, as well as the performance of duties in order to promote safe and efficient utilization of public funds.
2. Full audit coverage of State-owned assets. Audit institutions should audit the internal and external State-owned assets controlled, used, and operated by administrative institutions, State-owned enterprises and those in which State-owned capital plays a controlling or dominant

role (including financial enterprises). Audit institutions should mainly inspect the situation about the compliance with State laws and regulations and the implementation of major State policies and measures and macro control deployment during the management, use, and operation of State-owned assets, their authenticity and integrity, and increase in value; the management of quality and operational risks of such assets; and the duty performance of the relevant asset management departments, so as to safeguard the safety of State-owned assets and improve the operating performance accordingly.

3. Full coverage of auditing on State-owned resources. Audit institutions should audit State-owned natural resources such as urban land, minerals, rivers, forests, grasslands, waters, and so on; State-owned intangible resources like franchise and pollutant discharge rights; and other resources owned by the State as specified in laws and regulations. Audit institutions should mainly inspect compliance with State laws and regulations during the fund-raising, management, distribution, and use of public funds; the implementation of major State policies and measures and macro-control deployment; the development and utilization of State-owned resources and ecological environmental protection; the collection, management, distribution, and use of funds; the construction and operational effectiveness of resources and environmental protection projects; and the duty performance of resource managerial departments, so as to promote the intensive and economic use of resources and ecological civilization construction.

4. Full coverage of auditing on the leading officials' performance of accountability. Audit institutions should conduct an accountability audit of performance by leading officials of the Party and government from local Party committees, governments, judicial organs, and procuratorial agencies, as well as principal leading officials and administrative principal leading officials of the committees of the Party and government departments, public institutions, and mass organizations at all levels of the Central and local governments, as well as legal representatives of State-owned enterprises. Audit institutions must inspect the situation about leading officials' implementation of economic guidelines and policies and decision-making deployment of the Party and the State, and their compliance with relevant laws and regulations as well as financial disciplines, the situation about the formulation, implementation, and effect of development strategies, policies, and measures of the corresponding regions, departments, and units; the implementation and effect of systems on major decisions and internal control; and the situation about personal observance to relevant provisions

on honest government and incorruption, and so forth, to ensure leading officials comply with laws, disciplines, regulations and fulfill their responsibilities.

Third is the way of realization of full audit coverage of auditing. To achieve this goal, audit institutions need first to break through the narrow concepts of industry auditing, project auditing, and regional auditing to effectively establish a scientific concept of government auditing. In the contents and scope of auditing, we should integrate auditing of finance, banking, accountability, resources and environment, and people's livelihood, and internal and external audits. The integration of audit resources must cover audit plans, annual plans, project programs, and relevant organization and implementation; frontline operation and backstage data analysis; and business operation and fundamental research. To improve their role, audit institutions need to strengthen their ability to investigate problems and promote development, analyzing causes and promoting reforms, urging rectification and advancing responsibility performance, combating corruption and boosting construction of an honest government, and promoting fairness and justice and advancing democracy and rule of law. The purpose is to maximize efficiency of audit supervision through transformation of audit concepts and improvement of working mechanisms. The ways of realization of full coverage vary among the four categories of audit targets.

1. Auditing of public funds should focus on "money." An audit institutions should determine the targets of an audit plan according to such factors as the significance, size and management and allocation authority of public funds. Focusing on the operation of public funds and implementation of major policies, audit institutions combine the audits of budget execution and draft final accounts and special fund reports, and follow-up auditing of major investment projects, mainly supervise key departments and units concerned, and intensify the auditing of key links relating to management, allocation and use of funds, so as to achieve full coverage of the key departments and units horizontally, and on the allocation, management, and use of funds vertically.

2. Auditing of State-owned assets should focus on "units." An audit institutions determines the key targets of an audit plan according to such factors as the size of State-owned assets, management status and strategic position of management subject. Auditing should concentrate on the assets, liabilities, profits, and losses of State-owned enterprises (including financial enterprises) and incorporate the situation about management and use of

State-owned assets into the contents of annual budget execution auditing or other special audits of administrative institutions.

3. Auditing of State-owned resources should focus on the "elements" involved. An audit institution should determine key targets of an audit plan according to such factors as the scarcity, strategy and distribution of State-owned resources. Auditing must be intensified in regions with abundant resources and suffering serious damage. Key State-owned resources are subject to special audit. Audit institutions must regard the situation about the exploitation and development of State-owned resources, as well as ecological environmental protection as an important part of leading officials' accountability audit, and audit off-term officials regarding natural resources and assets.

4. An accountability audit should focus on "people." While preparing an audit plan, the audit institutions should determine key targets and the audit cycle according to such factors as the post nature of leading officials, importance of their performance of accountability, and the size of funds, assets, and resources under their management. During auditing, audit institutions should adhere to combined auditing during term of office and at the end of the term, and integrate the accountability audit with audits of finance, banking, enterprises, resources and environment, and foreign affairs, to realize the unified arrangement and coordinated implementation of projects.

Naturally, to achieve full coverage of auditing, we need also to research the unified integration of audit resources, innovate techniques and methods of auditing, and enhance audit capacity and efficiency. We will mainly elaborate this point in the section on the audit mechanism.

Special Column 1: Situation of Relevant Audits on Resources and Environment Protection[5]

Some audit projects arranged by the CNAO in its early days covered the audit of resources and environment protection funds. In 1985, the CNAO audited environmental assistance funds for Taiyuan, Lanzhou, Changsha, and Guilin in collaboration with the Ministry of Finance and the former State Bureau of Environmental Protection; in 1993, the CNAO audited the sewage charges of 13 cities including Harbin; in 1996, the CNAO audited the transfer price for State-owned land use. Focusing on the collection, management, and use of funds, these audits also involved resource management and environmental protection, accumulating much experience in further exploring and improving the audit of resources and environment.

(continued)

_____

[5] Sorted out according to relevant data of the CNAO.

In 1998, the CNAO set up the Department of Agriculture, Resources, and Environmental Protection Audit, to define the functions of resources and environmental auditing. In 2001, for the first time it audited projects for returning cultivated land to forest. The audit revealed the problems and difficulties existing in the work of returning cultivated land to forest, and various opinions were presented. In July 2003, the CNAO set up a leading group for coordinating environmental audits, and established the coordination mechanism featuring "unity, division of labor, establishing complementary advantages and efficient operation" for audits of environment and relevant specialties. In July 2008, the *CNAO Program for the Development of Audit Work 2008–2012* explicitly proposed to establish the mode of resource and environmental auditing in the context of China's national conditions. In September 2009, the CNAO issued the *Opinions on Strengthening Resource and Environmental Auditing*.

Since 2003, the CNAO has successively undertaken a number of resource and environmental audit projects for water pollution control in key watersheds, natural forest conservation program, water pollution control in the Bohai Sea, environmental protection of the Qinghai-Tibet railway, revenue from land sales, land arrangement, energy conservation and emission reduction, exploitation, utilization and protection of mineral resources, and so forth. Through auditing, the CNAO investigated a number of cases concerning violations of laws and regulations, strictly enforced discipline inspection in finance and economics, and promoted standardized management of special funds and implementation of environmental protection policies.

The CNAO actively participated in international exchanges on environmental auditing. In October 2000, it was elected as chair of the Environmental Auditing Committee of the Asian Organization of Supreme Audit Institutions (ASOSAI), and also undertook the routine work of the Committee's Secretariat. From 2006 to 2007, it conducted a cooperative audit of wind-blown sand prevention and control in partnership with the South Korean Board of Audit and Inspection. This was the first cooperative audit project of environment among Asian audit institutions.

2) Establishing and Improving the Real-Time Auditing System on the Implementation of National Major Policies and Measures and Macro Control Deployments

This requirement is specified by the *Opinions of the State Council on Strengthening Audit Work*. National major policies and measures and macro control deployments involve major reform measures, planning of the national economy and social development, annual plans and work tasks in the economic and social fields formulated and implemented by the CPC Central Committee and the State Council, as well as various policy arrangements for regulation and control over the national economic operations. On the one hand, real-time audit reveals the problems existing in implementation of major national policies and measures and macro control deployments, and facilitates timely investigation of distorted policy implementation, disobeying orders and defying prohibitions, and to supervise and ensure the smooth implementation of policies; on the other hand, real-time audit reflects the new progress of reform and development. It helps to identify outdated provisions that restrict development and hinder reform in a timely manner and can offer up suggestions on improvement. This not only safeguards the implementation of all policies and measures in a more reasonable and effective manner, but also provides a reference point for macroeconomic policies and measures, and their adjustment and improvement.

In audit practice, we should comprehensively audit the implementation of national major policies and measures and macro control deployments while focusing on the central economic tasks of the CPC Central Committee and the State Council. Meanwhile, we should highlight the audit focus in different periods and regions according to the requirements of socioeconomic development in different periods and in line with the cardinal direction of national macro control. First, we should inspect overall implementation, including the situation about formulation of specific measures for implementation, task decomposition, work progress, and improvement of the systemic guarantees by all relevant departments and regions according to the scope of their duties and assignments. Second, we should inspect policy implementation, including: whether the formulation and revision of various plans are being completed on schedule; whether all reform measures are implemented; main difficulties and problems encountered during the implementation of key construction projects under the national program and construction progress compliance; whether various financial funds and credit funds directly relating to policy implementation are in place and being used in an efficient and timely way; whether the national industrial policy is executed exactly, and whether such elements as financial funds, credit funds and land are being properly invested in line with national industrial policy and macro control deployment; and whether various government measures for streamlining administration and instituting decentralization are being followed exactly, and so forth. Third, we should analyze any institutional bottlenecks and unexpected situations are encountered along the way, including possible misconnections and mismatches with other regulations in effect, new situations and new problems during the implementation of relevant regulations and deployments, as well as hidden risks arising during economic operations. Fourth, for any problems found through real-time audit, we should deeply analyze all aspects and causes, identify the responsible contributor of each link, and propose opinions and suggestions on auditing aspects. During the audit implementation and real-time audit in the next step, we should supervise and urge the related units to strengthen their efforts to correct problems found in the audit and carry out a responsibility investigation. Fifth, attention should be paid to summarizing and reflecting the good experiences and practices of all regions and departments during the implementation of national major policies and measures and macro control deployments.

Remarkably different from traditional audit in terms of objective requirements, critical mission, audit content, organizational, techniques and methods, as well as audit achievements, the real-time audit on the implementation of policies and measures requires that audit institutions and individual auditors must handle the following aspects: not only grasp the overall situation and macro policy, but also understand the actuality of regions and units; not only focus on changes and upgrades of policies in a timely way, but also promote the implementation of specific measures and matters for the units and persons involved; not only audit-relevant plans, programs, deployments, and proposals, but also audit the funds flow, business flow, logistics flow, and information flow; not only maintain the sustainability of real-time audit, but also achieve the close collaboration and coordination as a unity; not only guaranteeing audit quality, typical cases, in-depth audit and accountability audit, but also promote deepening reform and improvement of the institutional system in a timely and efficient, coordinated way; not only adhering to the principles, but also proficiently promoting problem solving. Hence, the real-time auditing system on a one-year basis may be considered. By quarter, each audit cycle is composed of four working stages: We should conduct auditing while seeking opinions, preparing reports, supervising rectification and suggesting the improvement of institutions, mechanisms and systems, so as to effectively improve audit efficiency. Based on comprehensive auditing, audit institutions must be able to grasp the focus of work at each stage. For example, the work in the first quarter should give top priority to plans and deployments of the current year and the progress of completed matters at the end of the previous year; in the second and third quarters, the work should concentrate on the accomplishment of work tasks that have already reached the stipulated time nodes, the progress of national major construction projects and priority projects, allocation and use of financial funds and credit funds, as well as the continued implementation of various policies and measures; in the fourth quarter, the work should comprehensively reflect the accomplishment situation of year-round work tasks, implementation of various policies and measures and actual results achieved. Except for single real-time audit projects, audit institutions should pay attention to the implementation of national major policies and measures and macro control deployments when audit projects involve finance, banking, enterprises, resources and environmental protection, investment, people's livelihood, accountability, and so forth, and prepare a special report on uncovered problems and incorporate it into the real-time audit report.

3) Improving the Auditing System of Budget Implementation and Final Accounts Drafting

The new *Budget Law of the PRC* proposed a series of reform measures for the construction of budgets and final accounts system and the fiscal administration, and legally requires auditing of draft final accounts prepared by financial departments. In practice, the CNAO has been exploring the auditing of central final accounts (draft) since 2010, but the situation reflected and acquired through this activity was not very complete and mature. Therefore, we need to research how to further implement the combined audit of budget implementation and draft final accounts, comprehensively audit the overall situation and track government budgetary revenues and expenditures, and inspect the authenticity and legality of budget implementation. Moreover, in the draft final accounts, we should reveal and reflect the difference in budgets and final accounts, propose audit opinions in regard to authenticity, completeness and compliance; besides, we also need to research the mode of proposing draft audit opinions and audit reports.

The CNAO is currently exploring a method of central budget implementation audit by stages, that is, an audit mode in which all work and all links of approval, distribution, issuance, adjustment and apportionment, application of budgetary revenues and expenditures as well as preparation of draft final accounts is handled in successive stages. An audit cycle, from April to May the following year, refers to the period from the time of implementation of the central government budget plan adopted at the National People's Congress to when the Ministry of Finance submits the draft final accounts for the period to the State Council. During implementation, the combination of field audit, network-based audit and electronic data documentary audit is applicable. Field audit falls into three stages: the first stage of auditing is, in principle, conducted in April of that year, focusing on the situation of budgeting and approval by Central Government departments, and the allocation and distribution of transfer payment budgeting from the Central Government to local units; the second stage of auditing, commencing in July, gives priority to the increase and decrease of budgets, the allocation and distribution of special transfer payment funds of the Central Government under the organization of its various departments, and the allocation, payment, and use of transfer payment funds from the Central Government by all provinces; from November to the following May, the third stage of auditing mainly covers the overall situation of central government budget and budget implementation by all departments, the preparation of draft final accounts of the Central Government and departments, the transfer payment funds managed and used by provinces, and the overall evaluation on the central final accounts and the realization of relevant policies and objectives. As the first and third stages of field auditing overlap, we should pay equal attention to the budget implementation audits of two fiscal years, but with different priorities. For each of audited departments of the Central Government (or each province), the CNAO will issue an audit notice, hold an audit meeting, and release an audit report and an audit decision for every audit cycle. Such operations by stages have changed the work from post-supervision to a combination of real-time supervision and post-supervision, which not only enhances the integrity, the macro and constructive nature and the timeliness of central budget implementation but also encourages better performance of the duties of auditing the draft final accounts.

Special Column 2: Audit of the Draft of the Central Budget Implementation and Final Accounts

As the statements of the central final accounts (draft) provided by the Ministry of Finance show, in 2014, the general public budget revenues totaled 6,549.345 billion yuan and expenditures 7,499.345 billion yuan, with a deficit of 950 billion yuan; the governmental fund budget revenues totaled up to 503.959 billion yuan and expenditures 431.949 billion yuan, with surplus of 72.01 billion yuan carried over to the next year; the operational budget revenues of central State-owned capital totaled 156.31 billion yuan and expenditures 141.912 billion yuan, providing a 14.398 billion yuan surplus carried over to the next year.

The difference from the budget implementation situation was reported to the National People's Congress: the revenues of general public budgets and final accounts increased by 344 million yuan;

expenditures decreased by 1.325 billion yuan, mainly due to a tax rebate; all that was used to supplement budgets, consolidate and regulate funds. The revenues of governmental fund budgets and final accounts increased by 1.057 billion yuan; expenditures decreased by 0.005 billion yuan; additionally, the revenues turned over by local governments increased by 2.438 billion yuan; all was carried over to the next year. Major problems found during audit were as follows:

(a) Statement system of draft final accounts was unsound. First, the balance sheet was not included. When the capital was acquired through issuing government bonds, the general budget accounting didn't incorporate this as debt, but as debt revenues, so that the situation of government assets and liabilities was not reflected accurately. Second, the general public budget expenditures were not listed and classified according to their economic nature.

(b) Changes to the budget were greater than indicated. This included: expenditures by the Central Government were adjusted up by 72.447 billion yuan, while being adjusted down by 66.043 billion yuan; expenditures for tax rebates and transfer payments were adjusted up by 59.694 billion yuan, while being adjusted down by 87.987 billion yuan.

(c) Expenditures against excessively allocated capital of previous years were not disclosed. For instance, the excessively allocated capital of previous years directly paid to seven special projects like "subsidies for purchasing superior varieties of crops" reached 4.705 billion yuan, which was credited against the expenditures in 2014.

(d) The connection between the central final accounts (draft) and departmental draft final accounts was insufficient. For instance, spot checks of 22 central government departments revealed their revenues of final accounts in 2014 reached 565.719 billion yuan, but the central final accounts only reflected financial allocation revenues of 280.565 billion yuan (accounting for 49.6 percent), excluding the undertaking revenues, and so forth.

Data source: The Report of the State Council on the Audit on the Central Budget Implementation and Other Fiscal Revenues and Expenditures in 2014.

4) Establishing and Improving the Auditing System of State Capitals of State-Owned Enterprises

This is one of the measures of the Central Government for promoting and deepening State-owned enterprise reform. According to the requirement, audit institutions should supervise domestic and foreign enterprises and financial institutions that are wholly State-owned or in which State-owned capital plays a controlling or dominant role, other projects and units acquiring or using State-owned capital, as well as State-owned assets supervision and administration authorities. Audit supervision mainly involves their compliance with national laws and regulations, the implementation of national major policies and measures and macro control deployments, the establishment and execution of major decision-making systems, the establishment and execution of corporate governance structure and internal control system, the reality, legality, and effectiveness of financial revenues and expenditures, and the quality of audit reports issued by social intermediary agencies for relevant units, and so forth. The aim is to reveal major violations of laws and regulations, significant losses and waste, significant impact on reality, significant violations of industry policies, and poor performance of resources utilization and environmental protection, and duties. Audit seeks to reflect prominent conflicts and hidden risks, analyze problems and make suggestions at the institutional level, promote State-owned enterprise reform, and enhance the competitiveness and influence of the State economy.

Flexible and effective audit methods should be adopted for developing and improving the auditing system of State-owned enterprises and State capital. First, an annual audit should cover the assets, liabilities, profits and losses of State-owned enterprises, the operational budget implementation of State capital, and the duty performance of State-owned assets supervision and administration authorities. Second, the accountability of leaders of State-owned enterprises should be audited at least once during their term of office, and more audits should be conducted with regard to key fields and specific audit targets. Third, the special and significant investment projects of State-owned enterprises should be subject to real-time audit; special audits should be conducted with regard to significant acquisitions and mergers, transfer of State-owned assets, large-amount fund application, financial derivation business, and so forth. Fourth, a network-based auditing system should be created. For key State-owned enterprises, the real-time audit supervision system should conduct network-based auditing and enhance the audit efficiency and effect. Fifth, audit institutions should combine internal and external auditing, government auditing and internal auditing, audits of overseas operational institutions and resident non-operating institutions, and adopt reasonable and effective audit methods in conformity with domestic and foreign laws and regulations. Through the budget execution audit, audit of assets, liabilities, profits and losses, the accountability audit, special audit investigation, and so on, audit institutions can gradually establish the regular auditing system of overseas State-owned assets.

Meanwhile, in view of the conflict between the serious inadequacy of audit forces and repeated supervision, audit institutions can explore ways to integrate the same or similar duties of different departments and enrich government audit forces. Audit institutions can implement the dispatch auditing system for State-owned enterprises, and set up affiliated agencies in monitoring key State-owned assets, to take charge of regular audits, realize targeted and regular audit supervision on internal and external State-owned assets, and enhance supervisory efficiency.

5) Establishing the Auditing System of Off-Term Officials regarding Natural Resources and Assets

This is a new requirement proposed at the Third Plenary Session of the 18th CPC Central Committee. The auditing of off-term officials regarding natural resources and assets is a key point for improvement of the ecological civilization system, and also a specific part of improving leading officials' performance appraisal. Audit targets mainly involve major leading officials of local Party committees and governments at all levels. Such important fields as land, water, and forest resources; mine and geological environment control; air pollution prevention; and so forth are mainly audited. Auditing covers the duty performance regarding management of natural resources and assets and environmental protection during the term of office of audited leading officials, to urge them to uphold the correct view on achievements and promote intensive and economical use of natural resources and assets as well as ecological environmental safety.

The core of auditing of off-term officials regarding natural resources and assets is to define responsibilities, which is also difficulty of auditing. From the macro perspective, the objective of such auditing is to help leading officials better perform their responsibilities in the management of natural resources and assets and ecological environmental protection, improve the leading officials' performance appraisal system, and urge them to establish scientific values for their achievements. Key audits may be considered when a region suffers significant changes in natural resources and assets in kind and important questions about environmental protection are raised in the appointment of leading officials. In such a case, audit institutions should objectively analyze the cause of change and the problems like the decrease in quality and quantity of natural resources and assets, quality degradation, and environmental pollution due to human factors, and define the leading officials' responsibilities in a practical and realistic way. The application shows that audit results provide an important basis for assigning responsibilities, investigation, and accountability.

As there is no ready experience in this regard, and the systems and mechanisms for management and accounting of natural resources and assets are also unsound, audit institutions have to act as circumstances permit and gradually advance their work based on pilot programs. In practice, audit institutions should determine the contents and emphases of auditing according to the characteristics of endowment of natural resources and assets and environmental protection at all places, organize and conduct the target-oriented auditing, and adhere to the principle of summarizing while trial and publicity, so as to refine the practical experience into the solidified audit techniques and methods.

(3) About the Audit Operation Mechanism

A scientific and efficient audit operation mechanism is of vital importance to smoothly realize the expected goal of audit and fully exert its functions. The existing audit operation mechanism is effective, but it should be possible to further optimize and improve it in the following six aspects.

1) Improving the Audit Plan and Program Systems

First, the overall arrangement of audit plans should be strengthened. Audit institutions should create an audit target database by industry and sector to classify and determine audit emphasis and audit frequency based on awareness to the base number of entities involved. Second, for the medium- and long-term audit plan and annual plan, audit institutions should highlight the focus of the annual audit and ensure full coverage in a certain period. Third, audit institutions should integrate audit resources at all levels and various professional audits among audit institutions at all levels, and comprehensively audit key funds and key projects relating to the overall situation or industry, to make overall plans that mirror each other in content and interconnect in their implementation time, providing integrity and macro control in audit supervision. Meanwhile, audit institutions should strengthen the argumentation on audit work programs and plans, and fully listen to opinions and suggestions of all parties, to make them more adaptable to the needs of China's socioeconomic development, and to make the established objectives, measures, and arrangements more specific and measurable.

2) Improving the Organizational Way of Joint Auditing from Multidimensional and Multiple Angles

Under the new situation, the stronger relevance and coupling of socioeconomic development require accomplishing some complicated and arduous audit tasks in a unified way and by greater application of the organizational approach of joint auditing from multidimensional and multiple angles. Accordingly, audit institutions should strengthen their overall planning and integration in terms of audit forces, audit plans, project management, organization and implementation, application of results, and so on; flexibly apply effective methods like "lower-level audited by higher-level," "cross audit;" or a unified audit group; and flat management to realize the organic unity of multiple specialties, efficient coordination of multiple departments, effectively strengthening the integrity, wholeness, and macro nature of audit supervision.

3) Creating an Audit Work Pattern of Big Data

In line with the needs of informatization, audit institutions actively apply big data technology, establishing a national audit data system and digital audit platform, strengthen data analysis, enhance the capacity of information technology to identify problems, make an evaluation and judgment and conduct macro analysis, and form the unique "government auditing cloud." Improvements are needed in the national uniform audit information system to achieve system-wide participation and whole-industry coverage. Audit institutions should accelerate the informatization of all work to gradually realize internal full-process digitization in terms of audit plan formulation, resource allocation, organizational management, quality control and application of results, and external collection of all kinds of information data relating to the economy and society. Besides, audit institutions should create a national audit data system, and also accelerate building a national analogue audit laboratory. Second, it is necessary to positively apply big data technology for in-depth exploration, profound relevance and deep analysis. Audit institutions should further summarize and generalize the digital audit methods of "overall analysis, recognition of questionable points, precise verification and systematic research"; positively apply the emerging technologies like "cloud computing," data mining, analog simulation, and intelligent analysis to enhance audit efficiency; strengthen associative analysis on data among all fields; and enhance the capacity to judge and evaluate the macroeconomy and perceive economic risks. Third, we need to realize the intelligent management of data and improve the level of audit decision making and management. Audit institutions should energetically promote the digital audit command system, which should have the following functions: (1) the function of decision-making support to provide various data analysis results for audit decision making, and create a decision-making basis for reasonably allocating audit resources, improving audit efficiency, and enhancing the development and application of audit results; (2) the perceptive function to share data with a network-based audit system and audit management system; (3) the function of information transmission to transmit all useful information among audit institutions at all levels and among audit institutions and audit sites in a fast, accurate, safe, and reliable manner; (4) the function of information display to provide a dynamic display of the work status and progress of audit projects in the form of graphics, words, charts, audio and video, and so on and support access according to needs and authorization. The establishment of this system will lay a solid foundation for realizing audit modernization.

4) Improving the Audit Reporting System, the System of Government Information Disclosure, and the Rectification and Examination Mechanism

First, audit institutions should further advance the combination of audit results announcement and audited units' rectification disclosure in an open and transparent way, so as to facilitate the supervision of society and public opinion and improve audit effect. Second, the combination of audit results announcement and audit affairs disclosure should be further consolidated. Audit institutions should disclose audit results, audit recommendations, and the audit project implementation situation including objectives, scope, and methods of auditing, so as to further promote the openness and transparency. Third, the follow-up audit on rectification should be further strengthened. When necessary, audit institutions should specially audit the rectification situation of key audit projects and announce the results, so as to promote implementation of audit decisions, suggestions, and measures, and improve the audit effect.

5) Improving the Performance Report System of Audit institutions

Based on the CNAO's experience in performance measurement and reports in recent years, it should further improve the performance report system of China's audit institutions in the context of the actual situation and by drawing lessons from the experience and practice of counterparts in other countries. On the one hand, the CNAO should stipulate the contents, key performance indicators and the relevant methods of measurement essential to a performance report so as to increase the comparability of performance information among audit institutions. On the other hand, the CNAO can explore systematic and standardized methods during the audit performance appraisal. In particular, a third-party independent evaluation mechanism should be introduced, to increase the objectivity and reliability of performance information.

6) Improving the System of Purchasing Social Audit Services

By summarizing past practice in appointing intermediary agencies to assist in the audit business, we should gradually expand the scope of purchasing social audit services comprehensively, regulate the purchasing procedures for audit institutions, and specify the responsibilities and obligations of audit service suppliers and professionals. Meanwhile, we should develop and improve the supervision and evaluation mechanism for ensuring quality in purchasing audit services, and punish violations of professional ethics, such as providing audit services of poor quality and disclosing secrets.

(4) About the Audit Professionalization

The Fourth Plenary Session of the 18th CPC Central Committee and the *Opinions of the State Council on Strengthening Audit Work* explicitly proposed to advance the construction of audit professionalization. It stressed the need to strengthen the thought, ability, discipline, honesty and work style of audit teams by regarding morality as the core, capacity as the focus, style of work as the basis, and performance as the orientation, and strive to create an invincible army that is loyal, honest, responsible, and accountable. On the one hand, we should expand the channels of cultivation and exercise of auditors; improve the mechanisms of qualification, career advancement, education and training, performance appraisal, incentive and restriction, and occupational guarantee; and inspire and mobilize the inner dynamics and career passion of auditors. On the other hand, we should strengthen training and education, and improve the overall knowledge and comprehensive quality of audit teams through universal ability training; through professional skill training, we should focus on cultivating high-grade, precision, and advanced professionals, and urge a number of auditor experts and specialists to get involved.

Specifically speaking, to advance audit professionalization, we should improve the classified management system for auditors in conformity with the occupational features of audit, establish the competency and qualification management system, and improve the selection and appointment system and the vocational guarantee system, so as to improve the quality of auditors in a planned way.

1) Establishing a Classified Management System for Auditors

A management system of auditors in line with audit needs should be established in accordance with the provisions of the *Civil Servant Law of the PRC* and the characteristics of auditing. According to the needs of duty performance by audit institutions, we should clearly set out the requirements for professional and technical posts and integrated management posts, and implement a classified management of civil servants in these aspects. We should reasonably determine the professional and technical posts of auditing, and give priority to audit institutions at the prefecture and county levels. If conditions permit, the civil servants of professional and technical posts and comprehensive management posts of auditing may transfer mutually to meet work needs.

2) Establishing a Post Order of Professional and Technical Civil Servants of Auditing

We should establish a post order of professional and technical civil servants of auditing whereby the auditors' ability should match their responsibilities and authority. We should reasonably determine the classification of professional and technical civil servants of auditing at all levels. Generally, the posts of professional and technical civil servants of auditing shall not be higher than the specifications in corresponding units. We should establish a performance appraisal system and a job promotion mechanism for professional and technical civil servants of auditing.

3) Improving the Selection and Appointment Mechanism for Auditors

A classified recruitment system of the professional and technical civil servants of auditing and the comprehensive management civil servants should be adopted. In the recruitment course, the expertise and skills necessary for audit work can be regarded as an extended examination, to increase the proportion of professional auditors continuously. Personnel to be transferred should, in principle, have working experience or relevant professional qualifications in economy, law, and management. We can expand the recruitment channels for special talents and implement a system of appointment of posts with strong specialization. We should implement the audit professional qualification system, and set up the senior professional qualification of auditing. This is one of the requirements for appointment of the professional and technical civil servants of auditing and the comprehensive management civil servants with the requirements for competence. Audit group head, chief auditor, and other auditors for key business posts must meet all the job requirements for appointment.

4) Improving the Responsibility Investigation Mechanism for Auditing Posts

We should create a list of powers and responsibilities of auditing posts to implement the quality control responsibilities by grades and improve the responsibility investigation mechanism for the various posts. When an audit quality problem occurs, we should strictly hold the responsible person to account, lower or cancel his/her rank, and treat him/her in accordance with disciplines and regulations. Persons who conceal major problems, disclose key information, and intervene with audit activities must be punished severely in accordance with laws and discipline.

5) Improving the Occupational Guarantee Mechanism of Auditing

Deepening reform of the wage system for organs and institutions, we should carry out overall studies on the wages and benefits of auditors. For auditors under the national administration staffing program, we should implement the policy that the posts of civil servants are in parallel with their class, which, in turn, correspond to wages and benefits, in accordance with relevant policies and regulations. The working subsidy policy for human resources of audit institutions should be improved. We should develop and improve the protection mechanism for auditors' performance of their statutory duties, implement the system of registration and reporting for acts of intervention with audit work, establish the disposal mechanism for audit institutions and individual auditors, and properly handle matters arising out of audit duties in accordance with the law. We should improve the professional education and training system of auditing, and make the occupational development plan to continuously enhance the competence of auditors.

(5) About Supervision of Audit Institutions

Strengthening supervision over audit institutions is a specific requirement for democracy and the rule of law and good national governance, and also an important aspect for improvement of the socialist audit system with Chinese characteristics. Based on past supervision by Party committees, people's congresses, and governments over audit institutions, we should seek further improvements to meet the requirements for oversight over supervisors, and strengthen the restrictions and supervision on administrative power of audit institutions. This involves five aspects.

(1) Strengthening the Supervision of Higher-Level Audit institutions Over Lower-Level Audit institutions

First, implement the dual reporting system in which the audit institutions at or below the provincial level reports to the audit institution at the next higher level and the people's government at the corresponding level; second, implement the system of regular inspection by higher-level audit institutions over the behavior of the lower level, and correct any violations of national audit standards and inappropriate audit decisions made by lower-level audit institutions; third, implement the system in which lower-level audit institutions submit the normative documents to higher-level audit institutions for registration and examination before issuance; fourth, implement the system of business evaluation and award and punishment by higher-level audit institutions on those of a lower level; fifth, implement the system in which the appointment of responsible persons of lower-level audit institutions need to be approved by a higher level.

(2) Improving the Accountability Audit System for Main Leading Officials of Local Audit institutions[6]

First, principal leading officials of local audit institutions should accept at least one accountability audit during their term of office. Second, in conducting the accountability audit of principal leading officials of lower-level audit institutions, the higher-level institutions can conduct auditing directly or authorize other audits institutions to do so, to ensure the full coverage of auditing on the accountability of principal leading officials of local audit institutions. Third, accountability audit results of principal leading officials of audit institutions should be made public step by step.

(3) Creating a List of Powers and Responsibilities of Audit institutions

We should prepare a list of powers and responsibilities of audit institutions in accordance with laws and regulations to specify internal agencies, functions, powers, procedures, responsibilities and supervision ways, as well as the channels of complaint about violations by audit institutions and individual

---

[6] Article 6 of the Regulations Concerning Accountability Audit for Leading Cadres of the Party and Government and Leaders of State-Owned Enterprises stipulates, the leading cadres" accountability audits are determined according to the administrative authority over cadres. Through the negotiation between the Party committee at the corresponding level and the audit organ at the next higher level, the accountability audit of leading cadres of local audit organs is organized and conducted by the audit organ at the next higher level. The accountability audit of the Auditor General of the CNAO shall be submitted to the Premier of State Council and implemented upon approval.

auditors, and make them public by network to accept public supervision. The list of powers and responsibilities of audit institutions shall be updated timely in accordance with the provisions of laws and regulations.

(4) Improving the System of Special Auditors

We should promote the standardization and institutionalization of auditing by special auditors, and fully exert the functions of democratic supervision of democratic party and nonparty personage over audit institutions. We should screen and appoint special auditors from broader fields and scopes, make the most of the advantages and specialties of special auditors, regularly listen to their opinions and suggestions, and report the acceptance of opinions or suggestions to special auditors. We should prepare an annual plan for survey and consulting activities relating to some important audits in which special auditors participate, and conduct review and summarization at the end of the year.

(5)Exploring and Establishing an External Auditing System for Audit institutions

Like other public sectors and units, audit institutions should accept external auditing, and further explore and establish an external auditing system for audit institutions based on existing regulations and practice. The following aspects may be considered: (1) Audit institutions should regularly accept external auditing organized by the Party committees, people's congresses, governments and higher-level audit institutions. (2) The contents of external auditing on audit institutions mainly involve the accountability of responsible persons, the implementation of national relevant principles and policies by audit institutions, the situation about organizational management and business operations of audit institutions, and the situation about budget implementation and preparation of draft final accounts. (3) The external auditing of audit institutions is conducted by an audit institutions or relevant intermediary agency designed or employed by the organ which is responsible for organizing the external auditing on audit institutions.

(6) Strengthening the Supervision of Society and Public Opinion

Audit institutions should enhance openness and transparency, and the disclosure of the audit process and audit results, and accept the supervision of society and public opinion.

(6) About the Audit Law System

We should improve the legal system of administrative organizations and procedures, and enhance the legality of institutions, functions, powers, procedures, and responsibilities. Administrative organs must perform all statutory functions and duties and not do anything unauthorized by law, which is the basic requirement for the rule of law and administration by law specified at the Fourth Plenary Session of the 18th CPC Central Committee. To further develop and improve the auditing system of socialism with Chinese characteristics, we must improve the audit law system, and explicitly stipulate the audit institutions, audit duties and authorities, audit procedures and operation mechanisms, responsibilities and supervision of audit, and so forth, so as to provide a fundamental basis and legal environment for auditing according to law.

First, we must revise and improve the provisions of the Constitution, the Audit Law and other laws and regulations on audit supervision. Based on national governance needs and through full discussion, we must make a scientific and reasonable arrangement for the audit system, audit duties and authority, audit procedures and operational mechanisms, encouraging all places to formulate and improve local audit regulations and rules according to local actuality, ensure the clear positioning and explicit responsibilities of audit institutions over national governance, and exert the role of auditing in the national governance through sufficient approaches and effective mechanisms.

Second, we must further improve the institutional system of audit rules. As codes of conduct that must be obeyed by audit institutions and individual auditors, the national audit standards provide important restrictions and instructions for auditing. In accordance with the provisions of laws, regulations, and rules on audit supervision, we should draw lessons from internationally advanced audit experience and practice specific to actual problems in auditing; earnestly research, revise, and improve the national audit standards to embody the requirements of existing laws, regulations, and rules, and the concept of the auditing system of socialism with Chinese characteristics; and play the role in guiding and helping auditors to better perform their duties. Meanwhile, the audit guide should be updated, formulated, revised, and improved, so it can direct specific operations of auditors in specific audit fields and the application of specific audit techniques. We should improve the auditing of internal management systems, that is, audit business management, quality control, clean government building, appraisal and responsibility investigation, in combination with audit work, improve and implement the reporting system for major matters, and enhance the standardization of audit management. We should develop and implement the drafting system, examination system, collective deliberation system, disclosure and announcements system, and the like for normative auditing documents, and promote auditing system development in a routine and scientific way.

Information on Development of China's Auditing System

Period	Conditions of National Governance	Name of Auditing System	Form of Auditing System	Laws on Auditing System	Key Auditing Concepts or Practices
Zhou Dynasty	Rule the country in accordance with the *Rites of Zhou*, give top priority to the people's interests in major matters, select excellent talents, and advocate honesty and faithfulness, to promote Chinese civilization and build a State based on ceremonies. In the late Zhou Dynasty, chaos existed at the beginning of emperor's arbitrary listening and accounting.	Official Auditing System	Zaifu—performs governance, inspects monthly and yearly accounts by listening for differences, and interprets the authority and ranks of the king, ministers, and officials.	In the Eastern Zhou Period, dedicated laws on audit supervision and financial penalties, i.e., *Law of Verifying Properties of Government Departments* emerged.	Guan Zhong, a legalist chancellor and reformer of the State of Qi, proposed that "If a country is dedicated to developing agriculture, industry and commerce, it will get rich; If a country can establish a legal system and common rules, scrutinize its policies, establishing routine, and cultivate competent officials, it will achieve prolonged stability." Han Fei-tzu pointed out, "chaos originated from the king's arbitrary listening and accounting," and proposed "to address the existing problems and improve the system of 'Listening and Accounting.'"

| Han Dynasty | Inheriting the political pattern of centralization of authority and separation of the three powers of the Qin Dynasty, the Han Dynasty implemented the strategy of advocating Confucianism outwardly, but practicing legalism inwardly, and unity of rites and laws, ranking among top four kingdoms in the ancient times. In the late Han Dynasty, the post of Yushi Dafu (Censor-in-Chief) was abolished, resulting in the inferior powers of auditing officials. Fundamental social order and law declined gradually. | Censorate Auditing System | Censor—Independent of the government administrative systems and responsible for supervising all officials, rectifying from every aspect and achieving integration between supervision and auditing, "inspecting the local government authorities at various levels and carrying out on-site auditing during supervision." | Law of Administrative Reports System, Nine Articles of Supervisory Censor, Six Articles for Prefectural Governor, and so forth, constituted a relatively systematic legal system of audit. | The History of the Former Han: The emperor set the official rank of Jianmu (Supervisor) to supervise the misconduct of ministers, and the rectification situation of Sicha (Auditor). Cao Cao proposed that "Audit, as a well-planned action, should be precise and profound, without any mispresentation." |

(continued)

Period	Conditions of National Governance	Name of Auditing System	Form of Auditing System	Laws on Auditing System	Key Auditing Concepts or Practices
Tang Dynasty	The Tang Dynasty implemented the system of Three Councils and Six Boards, forming a political pattern in which "the imperial secretariat is responsible for appointment, and its affiliated agencies are responsible for refuting and suggesting; ministers are responsible for implementation"; the powers of decision-making, implementation, and supervision were separated and balanced mutually. In the late Tang Dynasty, most original auditing systems of Bibu abolished, greatly impairing the national finance.	Bibu (Court of Auditors) Auditing System	Bibu—A government audit supervision system that, independent of public finance and with certain jurisdiction, and featuring the "unity of special audit, concurrent audit and internal audit by different departments respectively," was used for audit supervision and formed together with the setup of censor and the three departments of the State Financial Commission.	The dedicated audit laws included the *Legislative Articles of Bibu* and the *Conventions of Bibu*, which specified the scope, contents, procedures, time, ways, result handling, and other aspects of auditing.	"The purpose of correction is to conduct auditing accurately through investigation, and report audit results to urge rectification; the core of checking is to check and supervise losses and hazards through reviewing"—this defined the value orientation of audit cultures and the professional ethical qualities of auditors.

Song Dynasty	Based on the Tang Dynasty's system, the Song Dynasty advocated political openness, and put mental pursuits above material arts, whereby the economy and culture flourished as never before. The name of audit institution originated from the Song Dynasty. In the late Song Dynasty, the independence of auditing was weakened.	Auditing system of the Court of Auditors	Court of Auditors—The Northern Song Dynasty inherited the Bibu auditing system; the Southern Song Dynasty set up the Court of Auditors, which "audited the account books of revenues and expenditures, all taxes and budgets for revenues and expenditures," and auditing covered the imperial family, army and government officials, and the like. Auditing functions were extended to decision-making consultation.	The *Penal Complex of Song* specified that, "It should remain unchanged throughout the Song Dynasty." The Court of Auditors based on emperor's orders, laws, legislative articles, conventions, and so on. In the reign of Emperor Yuanfeng, it was stipulated that "an official who discloses embezzlement of public funds would be rewarded by three percent of involved value."	"The decision-making and consultation function of audit was taken seriously and enhanced." This clarified the function of auditing in the aspect of decision-making consultation; "Any official who gains a salary must accept audit." This clarified the coverage of auditing. The Court of Auditors and such organs as Sanbugou Office, Dumokan Office, Mabujun Office, and Dupingyou Office were collectively referred to as the "Six Courts."

(continued)

Period	Conditions of National Governance	Name of Auditing System	Form of Auditing System	Laws on Auditing System	Key Auditing Concepts or Practices
Ming Dynasty	The Ming Dynasty abolished the Counsellor-in-Chief, Censorate, and Bibu, and the pattern of separation of three powers, and the Six Ministries were directly responsible to the emperor, resulting in the unprecedented reinforcement of absolute monarchy. The earlier period presented strong national power, but the mid and late period saw political corruption, social instability and emergence of secular culture. Kedao audit system substituted for the full-time and independent Bibu auditing system, resulting in the decline of auditing.	Kedao Audit Supervising System	Censorate, Jishizhong (an imperial attendant) of the Six Ministries in Feudal China exercised audit power concurrently. The Censorate was responsible for exposing misdeeds of government offices, appraise officials and managing the Supervisory Censors from the Court of Censors; Jishizhong of the Six Ministries was responsible for controlling, suggesting, supplementing, and appropriations, and audited the affairs of the Six Ministries and all offices. "Kedao audit" combining supervision and examination made achievements at the early stage, but showed numerous defects in the mid and late period.	Based on *Law of Ming Dynasty* and the *Yuzhi Dagao*(a special criminal law in Ming Dynasty), Kedao auditing system catered for the absolute monarchy of the Ming Dynasty, but the legalization of audit was thus on the decline as the full-time and independent audit institutions were canceled.	In the mid and late Ming Dynasty, the emperor ordered two different groups of the Kedaoguan (supervisory officials) to supervise and report work to each other, resulting in endless disputes. It was a worry that some arguments were excessive and inapplicable. As they often bore ill wills, more opinions would mean nothing but more chaos.

| Qing Dynasty | The Qing Dynasty inherited the system of the Ming Dynasty, but the autocratic imperial power was much reinforced. In the mid and late period, the Qing Dynasty gradually fell behind the world due to political rigidity, cultural despotism, and seclusion from the outside world as well as stagnant thinking. In the late Qing Dynasty, the Censorate existed merely in form. | The Censorate Auditing System | The Censorate (Incorporated into Jishizhong of the Six Ministries in the first year of emperor Yongzheng's reign). Inheriting the audit mode of combining supervision and examination of the Ming Dynasty, the Censorate was responsible for reporting misdeeds of the officials, performing governance duty, giving a thorough narration about governance, verifying all government affairs, checking records, supervising salt trading and transportation, and so forth. In the later period, the audit supervision became a mere formality. | Collection of Laws of Qing Dynasty enacted by Emperor Yongzheng recorded that the Censorate exercised the audit supervisory power, with strong authority; then in the late Qing Dynasty, the rule of man was increasingly strengthened. | In the late Qing Dynasty, five ministers including Dai Hongci (1853–1910) in the Memorial on Changing the National Government System for Preparation of Constitutionalism asserted that the Ministry of Civil Affair was responsible for checking the financial matters, and the Congress and Accounting Inspection Court were responsible for supervision. The Censorate almost had the independence as that of judicial judgment, so it could eliminate all malpractices. |

(continued)

Period	Conditions of National Governance	Name of Auditing System	Form of Auditing System	Laws on Auditing System	Key Auditing Concepts or Practices
The Early Days of the Republic of China and Nanjing KMT Government Period	Dr. Sun Yat-sen put forward the separation of five powers in administration, legislation, justice, examination and supervision, ushering in the era of a democratic republic. In the later period, the army and other governmental institutions refused to accept audit supervision, so that the Nanjing Nationalist KMT Government declined gradually.	Supervisory Ministry Auditing System	At the early stage, the Court of Auditors was established in parallel with the Executive Yuan (Ministry), the Supervisory Institute, the Supreme Court, and other offices, and then restructured it into a subsidiary body of the Supervisory Institute. Audit work vigorously supported the National Revolution and the War of Resistance against Japanese Aggression, but auditing hardly exerted its role after the privileged stratum came to power.	The *Constitution of the Republic of China* clearly stipulated the legal status of auditing and responsibilities of audit institutions. Correspondingly, four audit laws were promulgated successively.	The separation of five powers, auditing according to law and other thoughts were developed in China with far-reaching impact.

| New Democratic Revolution Period | Under the leadership of the Communist Party of China, the Chinese people underwent the Great Revolution, the Agrarian Revolutionary War, the National War of Resistance against Japanese Aggression and the Liberation War. The People's Republic of China was founded in 1949, marking the reincarnation of the Chinese nation in the world. | Audit Committee System | In 1924, Anyuan Railway and Mine Workers Club set up an independent Financial Review Board. In 1927, the CPC Central Leadership established the post of the Central Audit Commissioner after the 5th CPC National Congress. In 1934, the Central Executive Committee set up the Central Audit Committee in parallel with the Central People's Committee, Central Revolutionary Military Affair Committee, and other offices, whereby a highly authoritative and independent audit institution was created. Auditing played an active role in stabilizing and developing the financial economy of liberated areas, supporting the war of liberation, preventing corruption and extravagantness, and maintaining the spirit of being honest in performing official duties. | *In 1926, the Canton-Hong Kong Strike Committee released the Organization Law of Audit Bureau; in 1934, Comrade Mao Zedong signed and approved an order of the Central Executive Committee to promulgate the Audit Regulations of the Executive Committee of Central Government of Chinese Soviet Republic.* | Stressing the Political Property of Auditing—Mao Zedong, in the *Report on the Peasant Movement in Hunan*, regarded the works such as "clearing up accounts and inflicting penalties" with audit nature as the second important matter, namely, to fight the landlord politically; stressing the Policy Functions of Auditing; safeguarding the full implementation of Soviet's financial policies, and making clear the audit regulations and stressing the Authority of Audit Supervision. The Auditing Commission was in parallel with the Central People's Committee, Central Revolutionary Military Affair Committee, and other offices. |

(continued)

Period	Conditions of National Governance	Name of Auditing System	Form of Auditing System	Laws on Auditing System	Key Auditing Concepts or Practices
Before Reform and Opening Up	The CPC led the Chinese people in socialist revolution and construction, accomplished major of the Socialist Reform by reference to the Soviet Model, underwent the splendor of building socialism, and suffered the setbacks such as "Great Leap Forward" and "the cultural revolution."	The independent auditing system was not established.	Around 1952, the national financial supervision institutions were established in succession, while audit institutions at all levels were canceled and merged successively. Afterwards, China didn't establish any independent professional audit institution, but the supervisory work of audit nature existed in the form of campaign-style auditing, i.e. financial examination and supervision, "Three-anti Campaign," "Five-anti Campaign" and "Four Cleans-up" to a varying extent. Campaign-style auditing played a certain role in curbing corruption and extravagantness, however, adverse effects such as the chaos of unrealistic comparison, rising quotas at each level and alienation from reality also appeared.	In 1950, the draft *Interim Audit Regulations of the People's Republic of China (Draft)* were not officially issued as China drew lessons from the Soviet Union. Since then, the campaign-style audit activities sprang up, and gradually deviated from the legal track.	Stressing the Role of "Reckoning"—In 1959, Comrade Mao Zedong proposed, "Reckoning would promote unity; reckoning would help to prevent cadre corruption and extravagantness, and maintain honesty; reckoning would teach cadres the operation management methods; reckoning would teach 500 million peasants to manage their communes, and supervise all levels of cadres of the communes to behave right only, so as to realize the supervision by masses and the true democratic centralism."

Since Reform and Opening Up	China has made remarkable achievements in social and economic development. With economic prosperity, political stability and social stability, China is now dedicated to advancing the implementation of the strategy of comprehensively building a moderately prosperous society, comprehensively deepening the reform, comprehensively implementing the rule of law, and comprehensively strengthening the Party discipline building. Never in history have we been closer to the goal of the great rejuvenation of the Chinese nation.
Auditing system of socialism with Chinese characteristics	As an institutional arrangement to supervise and restrict power by power, auditing system is an important supervision system of the Party and the State, an "immune system" endogenous within the overall system of national governance, with functions of exposure, resistance, and prevention, and a bedrock and important guarantee for national governance; it plays an important role in promoting the rule of law and improving people's livelihood through reform and development.
	In 1982, the *Constitution of the PRC* stipulated the audit supervision, which marked the establishment of the auditing system of socialism with Chinese characteristics. The *Audit Law of the PRC* implemented in 1995 marked that national audit supervision system embarked on a legal track. The *Constitution*, the *Audit Law* and its *Rules of Implementation*, the *Budget Law*, and other laws constitute a relatively sound audit law system.
	We should improve the systems of inner-party supervision, NPC supervision, democratic supervision, administrative supervision, judicial supervision, audit supervision, social supervision, and public opinion supervision, so as to establish the scientific and effective restriction and supervision system of power exercise and make it more effective. We should improve the auditing system and protect the right to exercise audit oversight independently.
	Auditing shall fully cover the public funds, State-owned assets, State-owned resources and the leading cadres' performance of accountability. We should further play the guarantee and supervision role of auditing, and improve the guarantee mechanism of audit work. Government auditing serves as the bedrock and important guarantee of national governance.

Brief Introduction to the Auditing Systems of 12 Major Countries

Country or Region	Audit System	Audit Responsibilities	Audit Authorities	Audit Reports and Utilization of Audit Results
The United States	1. Auditor General is nominated by the Special Committee of the Congress, examined and approved by the Senate, and then appointed by the President. The term of office is 15 years, and a consecutive term is not allowed. 2. The institutional setting of the U.S. Government Accountability Office is determined by the Auditor General. 3. The U.S. Government Accountability Office reports the audit results, assessment conclusions, audit opinions and legislative proposals to the Congress.	1. Reviewing the duty performance of the federal government. 2. Conducting follow-up audit of the implementation of major diplomatic, military and economic policies; evaluating the validity of policies and proposing the suggestions on improvement. 3. Conducting prospective policy analysis of major risks in terms of politics, economy, society, and national security, and offering opinions and legislative proposals. 4. Evaluating whether the formulation of any regulation complies with statutory procedures in advance. 5. Legally judging the liabilities that federal officials should assume in use of financial funds, and the complaints made by stakeholders involved in bidding/tendering for government procurement projects.	1. Right to examine 2. Right to investigate 3. Right to recommend 4. Right to report	1. The Auditor General reports the work to the Congress every year, and also submits special audit reports and testifies in congressional public hearings. 2. The U.S. Government Accountability Office will generally transfer uncovered problems to the relevant departments for rectification and further action, and transfer any suspected crime to the judicial organ for processing.

	4. The U.S. Government Accountability Office guides, inspects and evaluates the work of the Office of the Inspector General according to law. The Office of the Inspector General implements the audit standards formulated by the U.S. Government Accountability Office. 5. Local audit institutions implement the audit standards formulated by the U.S. Government Accountability Office, and accept its business guidance.	6. Auditing and investigating fraudulent behaviors. 7. Conducting information system security audits. 8. Delivering audit opinions on the financial statements of the federal government and its agencies, annual financial reports, and management of State-owned assets.		
Russia	1. The President of the Accounts Chamber of the Russian Federation, as the first vice premier level officer of the Federal Government, is nominated by a majority vote of Dumas. The term of office is six years.	1. Supervising the preparation of federal budget plans. 2. Auditing the budget implementation of the federal government, government departments, and public institutions. 3. Auditing financial statements, annual financial reports, and disclosure of government debts.	1. Right to examine 2. Right to seal up 3. Right to recommend 4. Right to report	1. The Accounts Chamber of the Russian Federation submits an audit report on the implementation of federal budget plans to the federal parliament every quarter, proposing ways to strengthen budget management.

(continued)

Country or Region	Audit System	Audit Responsibilities	Audit Authorities	Audit Reports and Utilization of Audit Results
2. All federal subjects set up audit institutions according to law, without any leader-member relationship with the Accounts Chamber of the Russian Federation.	4. Auditing the contents relating to the federal financial budget in the draft of federal laws and the rules formulated by all federal departments according to law. 5. Auditing the operation and management of federal state-owned assets (including privatization of state-owned assets). 3. The supervision institutions and relevant internal audit institutions, such as the Federal Anti-Spyware Bureau, Foreign Intelligence Service, Federal Government Information Exchange Center, judicial bodies, the Central Bank, the Ministry of Finance, State Administration of Taxation are obliged to assist the Accounts Chamber of the Russian Federation in conducting audits.	6. Auditing the Federal Central Bank and other banks, and the businesses of other financial institutions relating to the federal budget revenues and expenditures. 7. Auditing the major matters influential to the national safety and the people's livelihood of Russia. 8. Cracking down on corruption and crimes. 9. Conducting the strategic auditing.		2. The Accounts Chamber of the Russian Federation submits a special report to the audited units against the uncovered problems, suggesting them make rectification, compensate for national loss and investigate the liability of relevant persons. 3. The Accounts Chamber of the Russian Federation provides audit information to media, publishes audit announcements, and announces the annual audit work reports. 4. The Accounts Chamber of the Russian Federation is entitled to require audited units to correct errors and supervise their rectification.

Germany				
1. The President of the Bundesrechnungshof (SAI Germany) is nominated by the federal government, and elected by a majority of votes of the federal parliament and federal Senate. The president and vice president of the Bundesrechnungshof are entitled to enjoy the treatment of the Grand Justice of Federal Court. The term of office is 12 years, and a consecutive term is not allowed.	1. Participating in the preparation of federal budgets.	1. Right to examine	1. The Bundesrechnungshof submits annual audit reports on major audit results to the federal parliament and the federal government.
2. The Bundesrechnungshof mainly recruits auditing officers from business backbones of all government departments, and its budgets and final accounts are approved by the parliament.	2. Participating in the discussion of federal budgets.	2. Right to investigate	2. The Bundesrechnungshof submits special reports according to needs, and reports major audit results anytime to the federal parliament and the federal government.
	3. Participating in the implementation of federal budgets.	3. Right to report	
3. The Bundesrechnungshof is not subject to the leadership of the parliament, but takes charge of providing audit results to the federal parliament and suggesting the improvement in the management and use of public funds.	4. Auditing the federal financial statements and annual financial reports.	4. Right to recommend	3. The Bundesrechnungshof offers opinions and suggestions on major financial policies and regulations and legislative proposals to the federal parliament, the federal government, and government departments.
	5. Auditing the management of federal state-owned assets.	5. Right to supervise rectification	
4. The Bundesrechnungshof has no affiliation relationship with the Court of Auditors of 16 states.	6. Auditing social insurance institutions, enterprises or units that accept the federal subsidy or the federal insurance.		4. The Bundesrechnungshof makes a legal resolution according to audit results and suggestions after submitting the audit report on the uncovered problems to the federal parliament.
	7. Offering the consultation and review opinions on financial policies and regulations promulgated by the Federal Government.		

(continued)

Country or Region	Audit System	Audit Responsibilities	Audit Authorities	Audit Reports and Utilization of Audit Results
France	1. The president and senior judges of the Cour des Comptes (SAI France) are appointed by the President upon approval by the Council of Ministers. The president of the Cour des Comptes is entitled to decide the organizational structure and staff appointments. The president and audit judges can be reappointed consecutively until retirement. 2. The Cour des Comptes is not responsible to parliament, but it supervises the acts of government independently according to law, supervises the implementation of financial laws, and submits audit findings and suggestions to the parliament.	1. Conducting regular audits and performance audits on State sectors and public institutions. 2. Auditing budget implementation and draft final accounts. 3. Auditing social security institutions. 4. Providing support for the parliament budget deliberation. 5. Auditing State-owned enterprises and management of state-owned assets. 6. Auditing the private organizations accepting fiscal subsidy (including tax deduction and exemption) or those using public donations. 7. Evaluating public policies formulated by the government.	1. Right to examine 2. Right to investigate 3. Right to report 4. Right to punish 5. Right to recommend 6. Right to decide	1. Publishing audit reports. 2. Publishing comprehensive audit reports on the implementation of fiscal budgets. 3. Publishing reports on public financial position and prospect. 4. Publishing annual audit work reports, mainly including the working conditions of the Cour des Comptes and local audit agencies, main audit findings and suggestions of a particular year, as well as the solution of problems found in the audits of previous years. 5. The Cour des Comptes arouses the attention of the parliament, government, media and the public through submitting and publishing audit reports, and promotes the solution of problems found in audits.

Japan			
1. The leadership organization of the Board of Audit of Japan is the council of auditors consisting of three audit officials. Audit officials are nominated and appointed by the cabinet after the Houses of Congress approve and submit it to the Mikado for signing. Each term of office is seven years, subject to one reappointment.	1. Auditing the monthly revenues and expenditures of public finance.	1. Right to examine	1. The Board of Audit of Japan discloses to the media the audit reports of annual financial statements not involving any secrets and other audit reports
2. The Board of Audit of Japan is entitled to personnel management autonomy, and may decide the employment, appointment and dismissal, rewards and penalties of audit officials, at its discretion.	2. Auditing the annual financial statements.	2. Right to investigate	2. Audited units shall comprehensively implement the requirements and rectification suggestions in a timely manner.
3. Congress deliberates the final accounts according to the audit findings of annual financial statements submitted by the Board of Auditor of Japan.	3. Auditing the assets and liabilities of government.	3. Right to punish	
4. Under the system of separation of powers in legislation, administration and justice, the Board of Audit of Japan belongs to administrative institutions, but it is independent of the cabinet.	4. Auditing the receipts and disbursements of cash, precious metal, and negotiable securities of the treasury or those undertaken by the Bank of Japan on behalf of the state.	4. Right to recommend	
5. The Board of Audit of Japan has no affiliation with local audit institutions. The local audit situation need not be reported to the Board of Audit of Japan, but the Board of Auditor of Japan should have business exchanges with local audit institutions, and train local auditors.	5. Auditing the enterprises whose government investment accounts for over 50 percent of total investment.	5. Right to appraise	
	6. Auditing any local governments, organizations or enterprises that accept the transfer payment and subsidy of State finance or are supported by the state finance, as well as foreign aids and projects.		
	7. Participating in the Congress deliberation on government budget.		

(continued)

Country or Region	Audit System	Audit Responsibilities	Audit Authorities	Audit Reports and Utilization of Audit Results
Republic of Korea	1. The President of Board of Audit and Inspection of Korea is nominated by the President and appointed upon the approval of parliament. Under the direct leadership of the president, the president of Board of Audit and Inspection of Korea ranks fifth after the president, speaker of the House, chief justice, and premier among civil servants, being equivalent to the First Premier. The term of office is four years, and one reappointment is allowed. The age of retirement is 70. 2. Consisting of 5 to 11 members including the president and commissioners, theBoard of Audit and Inspection of Korea conducts panel discussion on any major issues. With the personnel management autonomy, the Board of Audit and Inspection of Korea is fully independent in terms of institutional establishment, recruitment, appointment and dismissal, salaries, and welfare, as well as awards and punishments, and not subject to the limitations of the law on national public servants. 3. The Board of Audit and Inspection of Korea guides the business of the audit and inspection agencies of local self-governing organizations, which in turn shall submit annual audit reports to the Board of Audit and Inspection of Korea.	1. Auditing the financial budget implementation, final accounts and annual financial reports. 2. Auditing the financial institutions, social insurance organizations and State-owned enterprises invested by the government. 3. Auditing the major matters influential to the national security. 4. Auditing the performance of public investment projects. 5. Cracking down on corruption and crimes. 6. Supervising and holding public officers to account for their duty performance.	1. Right to examine 2. Right to investigate 3. Right to report 4. Right to decide the liability for compensation 5. Right to punish or discipline 6. Right to charge rectification 7. Right to urge rectification 8. Right to recommend 9. Right to accuse	1. The Board of Audit and Inspection of Korea discloses audit reports and audit results on the official web site comprehensively. 2. The executive heads of the government must put forward the corresponding corrective measures for the problems found in audits, make public the measures and report them to the Board of Audit and Inspection.

| United Kingdom | 1. Auditing central fiscal budget implementation.
2. Auditing central financial statements and the financial reports of the Central Government.
3. Auditing government performance.
4. Auditing the operation and management of State-owned assets.
5. Auditing the implementation of national policies in key fields. | 1. Right to examine
2. Right to investigate
3. Right to report
4. Right to urge rectification
5. Right to announce | 1. The National Audit Office will submit an audit report to the parliament, which, in turn, will organize a public hearing for the audit report
2. The National Audit Office will conduct the real-time audit on the implementation of corrective measures, and report the results to parliament.
3. The National Audit Office will continue to follow up whether relevant departments have taken remedy measures and put forward suggestions according to law, after finding evidence in major corruption cases and asking for the intervention of the judicial department. |
| | 1. The auditor general is nominated by the prime minister and the parliament, and appointed by the queen. The term of office is 10 years, and a consecutive term is not allowed.
2. The auditor general can independently decide the institutional setting of the National Audit Office of the United Kingdom, and the matters concerning number of employees, way of recruitment, appointment and dismissal, award and punishment, and salary and welfare of employees.
3. The National Audit Office can, after soliciting parliamentary opinion, conduct special financial auditing and performance auditing of public sectors and public institutions according to law, and report the audit results and audit recommendations to the parliament.
4. The National Audit Office is responsible for business instructions and technical exchange with local audit institutions, without any leadership relationship between them. | | |

(continued)

Country or Region	Audit System	Audit Responsibilities	Audit Authorities	Audit Reports and Utilization of Audit Results
Australia	1. The auditor general is nominated by the prime minister upon parliamentary approval and appointed by the governor general. The term of office is 10 years, and a consecutive term is not allowed. 2. The auditor general is entitled to decide the scale and ways of recruitment or employment of auditors, and determine their appointment and dismissal, salaries, awards and punishments. The recruited auditors must have the certificates of academic degree and occupational qualification. 3. The Australian National Audit Office, as a constitutional institution of Australia, is accountable and reports its work to the parliament. 4. All states of Australia set up audit institutions in accordance with local laws with no affiliation with the National Audit Office.	1. Auditing the budget implementation of the federal government. 2. Auditing the financial statements and annual financial reports of the federal government. 3. Conducting performance audit on government agencies and State-owned enterprises. 4. Auditing the operation and management of government departments, State-owned enterprises and State-owned assets. 5. Conducting the real-time audit on the implementation of federal policies.	1. Right to examine 2. Right to investigate 3. Right to report 4. Right to recommend 5. Right to supervise rectification	1. All audit reports are made public, except the contents involving the state secrets and business secrets. 2. The National Audit Office submits an audit report to the parliament, revealing the problems found in the audit, while the Public Accounts Committee and Audit Joint Committee of the parliament are responsible for organizing the hearing, making a legal and valid resolution, and requiring the government, government departments, State-owned enterprises, private enterprises, or individuals to make rectification. 3. The National Audit Office formulates and issues the *Better Practice Guides* to point out the universal problems of these units and matters, and to propose a comprehensive and detailed guide for feasible work improvement.

India				
1. Nominated by the prime minster and appointed by the president, the Comptroller and Auditor General of India is accountable to parliament, with the same level as the Chief Justice of the Supreme Court. The term of office is six years, and reappointment is not allowed. 2. India establishes a uniform audit institutionization system, in which the Comptroller and Auditor General leads the audit and accounting institutions nationwide, and local audit and accounting institutions are the affiliated agencies of the Office of the Comptroller and Auditor General of India. 3. Under the leadership of the Public Accounts Committee and Public Utilities Commission, the Office of the Comptroller and Auditor General performs duties independently in accordance with the Constitution and reports the audit reports to the parliament.	1. Preparing the final accounts and financial reports of all federal and municipal governments and their government agencies. 2. Preparing the final accounts and financial reports of the Federal Government and government agencies. 3. Auditing the budget implementation, final accounts and financial reports of all federal and municipal governments and their government agencies. 4. Auditing the budget implementation, final accounts, financial reports of the federal government and government agencies. 5. Auditing the performance of institutions and projects accepting the funds or government subsidies of the federal government and state governments. 6. Combating corruption.	1. Right to examine 2. Right to interpellate 3. Right to formulate standards 4. Right to recommend revisions of laws and regulations	1. All audit reports of the Office of the Comptroller and Auditor General of India will be made public after the submittals are offered to the president, government, and corresponding legislative institutions, except for matters involving state secrets. 2. The Public Accounts Committee and Public Utilities Commission of the parliament will release deliberation reports and put forward requirements for rectification to the government and relevant audit subjects, after the deliberation in accordance with the memorandum on major issues. The government and related auditees shall report their rectification situation to the Office of the Comptroller and Auditor General and the parliament, and parliament will summarize and release the rectification report.	

(continued)

Country or Region	Audit System	Audit Responsibilities	Audit Authorities	Audit Reports and Utilization of Audit Results
Brazil	1. The Tribunal de Contas da União (SAI Brazil) consists of nine chief justices of auditing who are elected by the federal parliament, of which six are appointed by Congress and the remaining three by the president upon the approval by the Upper House. The chief justices of auditing are appointed for life, and will retire at 70 years. 2. The institutional setting, staffing and budget of the Tribunal de Contas da União are guaranteed in accordance with the *Organic Act of Federal Court of Auditors*, and the budget will be approved by parliament in accordance with specified procedures. 3. Independent of Congress, the Tribunal de Contas da União can decide the contents and ways of audit according to law, and also conduct audits and investigation and make relevant judicial decisions according to the suggestions of the Senate and the House of Representatives. Audit reports are submitted to the Congress	1. Auditing annual government finance reports submitted by the President 2. Auditing the public sector, public, sector entities and State-owned enterprises. 3. Auditing the government-funded projects and conducting investment access examination on foreign capitals and private capitals. 4. Auditing the privatization process, and monitoring the performance of public service outsourcing and public franchising. 5. Auditing the accounts relating to the interests of Brazil among the transnational enterprises that the federal government shares and holds equities. 6. Examining the income and property declaration of public officers.	1. Right to examine 2. Right to investigate 3. Right to punish 4. Right to report 5. Right to recommend 6. Right of jurisdiction 7. Right of special examination	1. The The Tribunal de Contas da União audits the annual financial reports of the government submitted by the President, submits audit reports to the Congress, and also submits the quarterly and yearly audit work reports to the Congress regularly. 2. The auditing and judicial decision results of the Tribunal de Contas da União are made public, except for matters related to state secrets.

4. Local courts of auditors conduct audits in accordance with local laws, without affiliation with the Tribunal de Contas da União, but they should abide by the standards and regulations formulated by the latter.

7. Auditing the employment procedures of managers of public institutions and state-owned enterprises (except those appointed upon the judicial resolution), selection procedures of public servants, and the legality of appropriation for pension and retirement allowance of civilian posts and military personnel.

8. Auditing the tax collection and transfer payment funds appropriated by the federal government to special zones, states, and cities.

9. Issuing a warning when the expenditures and debts of government and its affiliated institutions approximate the limit.

3. The Tribunal de Contas da União orders the responsible persons to indemnify against any loss arising out of auditees' violations, and adjusts the relevant accounts. For persons who violate the laws and regulations on financial control, the Tribunal de Contas da União will impose them a disciplinary action and a fine penalty. Every year, the Tribunal de Contas da União will conduct the real-time audits on the implementation of audit opinions and suggestions in the previous years.

South Africa

1. The Constitution stipulates that the Office of the Auditor-General of South Africa is nominated upon the approval of a majority of votes (60 percent) of the parliament and appointed by the President. The term of office is 5 to 10 years, and a consecutive term is not allowed.

1. Auditing the budget implementation of the Central Government and local governments.

2. Auditing the financial statements and annual financial reports of the Central Government and local governments.

1. Right to examine

2. Right to investigate

1. The Office of the Auditor General submits the audit results of final accounts and annual financial reports of the Central Government and local governments respectively to the parliament and local legislative organizations.

(continued)

Country or Region	Audit System	Audit Responsibilities	Audit Authorities	Audit Reports and Utilization of Audit Results
	2. The Office of the Auditor General takes full charge of audit supervision on behalf of the Central Government and local governments at all levels. The Auditor General is entitled to decide the recruitment, appointment, and dismissal of all auditors and their remuneration. 3. The Office of the Auditor General is accountable and reports its work to the parliament.	3. Participating in anticorruption. The Audit Office is an important force of anticorruption work. 4. Auditing the operation and management of State-owned assets. 5. Auditing institutions in regard to national, provincial or municipal subsidies and funds, and those legally authorized to raise funds for public purposes.	3. Right to report 4. Right to recommend 5. Right to supervise rectification	2. The Office of the Auditor-General offers audit opinions on uncovered problems and reports them to parliament and local legislative organizations, while the latter supervise and urge the audited units to make rectification; if auditing involves serious violations, the Audit Office will transfer the cases to the parliamentary Special Committee on Public Finance.
Mexico	1. The Auditor General is nominated by the Supervision Commission of House of Representatives, and appointed upon the approval of two-thirds of members present. The term of office is eight years, and one reappointment is allowed.	1. Researching and analyzing macroeconomy situation, especially financial conditions. 2. Researching and analyzing the government's economic development plans and the plan implementation of all departments.	1. Right to examine 2. Right to investigate 3. Right to report 4. Right to recommend	1. The Auditoría Superior de la Federación reports the audit results to the House of Representatives via the Supervision Commission of House of Representatives, and the audit reports should be made public after the submission.

2. The Auditor General may determine the organizational structure, scale of staff, way of recruitment, remuneration and treatment, as well as award, punishment, appointment and dismissal of senior auditing officers, and expenditure budget of the Auditoría Superior de la Federación (SAI of Mexico), and offer proposals to the Senate for approval via the Supervision Commission of House of Representatives.

3. The Auditoría Superior de la Federación submits the audit results to the parliament via the Supervision Commission of House of Representatives. The Supervision Commission is responsible for coordinating the relationship between the House of Representatives and the Auditoría Superior de la Federación, and evaluating its work performance

4. Each state of Mexico has its own parliament, government and audit institution. The Auditoría Superior de la Federación has no leadership relationship with audit institutions of all states, which, in turn, conduct auditing independently, coordinate and cooperate with each other at work.

3. Auditing the implementation of federal budget and final accounts.

4. Auditing the federal appropriations and fiscal subsidies to all states, federal districts, State-owned enterprises and private enterprises.

5. Determining the liability of compensation for loss incurred by units and individuals using the federal fiscal funds, and imposing a fine or punishment.

6. Adjusting and revising the public accounts of federal government and federal district.

5. Right to punish
6. Right to supervise rectification

2. The Auditoría Superior de la Federación issues the auditor's opinions on the common problems found in the audit, and requires the audited units to identify responsibilities and implement rectification. Where the problems are serious and involving criminal responsibilities, the Auditoría Superior de la Federación shall transfer the responsible persons to the relevant departments for further action.

Note: This is prepared according to the *Introduction to Foreign Audit Supervision System* jointly compiled by the Scientific Research Institute, Overseas Audit Office, and Department of International Cooperation of the China National Audit Office. Beijing: Modern Economic Publishing House, 2014.

Major References

1. Bai Jingkun, "Analysis on Relationships among Systems, Institutions and Mechanisms." *Management Observer* 5, 2008.

2. Bai Hua, *History of Chinese Political System*. Beijing: China Renmin University Press, 2011.

3. Chen Chenzhao, "Scientific Development and Government Auditing." *Auditing Research* 5, 2007.

4. Chen Taihui et al., *Science of Audit Law*. Haikou: Hainan Publishing House, 2000.

5. Deng Pinsheng et al., *Power Supervision System of Socialism with Chinese Characteristics*. Beijing: Current Affairs Press, 2011.

6. Gong Jun, "Influence and Construction of Audit Cultures." *Internal Auditing in China* 12, 2012.

7. Huang Bailian, "Combating Corruption and Carrying Forward Fine Traditional Cultures." *Way of Seeking* 3, 1992.

8. Jin Taijun, Zhang Jinsong, Shen Chengcheng. *A Study on Political Civilization Construction and Power Supervision Mechanism*. Beijing: People's Publishing House, 2010.

9. Jin Yuelin, *Formal Logic*. Beijing: People's Publishing House, 1979.

10. Compiling Group of Financial and Economic History of Shanxi-Suiyuan-Border Region, Shanxi Provincial Archives Bureau, *Selections of Financial and Economic History of Shansi-Suiyuan Border Region*. Taiyuan: Shanxi People's Publishing House, 1986.

11. Li Jinhua, *Review of 25 Years of Audit Work in China and Prospect*. Beijing: People's Publishing House, 2008.

12. Li, Jinhua, *The History of Audit in China* (Vols. 1, 2, and 3). Beijing: China Modern Economic Publishing House, 2004.

13. Liang Shuming, *Destiny of Chinese Cultures*. Beijing: CITIC Press, 2010.

14. Liu Wei and Zhou Kai, "Comparison and Adoption of Auditing Systems of China and US Governments." *Finance and Trade Research* 1, 2007.

15. Liu Yinglai, "Symposium Overview of Audit Cultural Development." *Auditing Research* 1, 2005.

16. Luo Xucheng, *New Development of Globalization and Marxist National Theory of Modern China—A Perspective of National Governance*. Hangzhou: Zhejiang University Press, 2009.

17. *Marx Engels Selected Works* (Vol. 3). Beijing: People's Publishing House, 1960.

18. Qin Xuan and Liu Yong, "Research on the Categories of Socialist Systems." *People's Tribune* 11, 2010.

19. China Steering Committee of Compiling and Reviewing Cadre Training Materials, *Uphold and Develop Socialism with Chinese Characteristics*. Beijing: People's Publishing House and Party Building Books Publishing House, 2015.

20. Commentary Department of the People's Daily, *Learning and Reading of "Four Comprehensives."* Beijing: People's Publishing House, 2015.

21. Shaanxi Audit Society and Shaanxi Provincial Institute of Auditors. *Audit Work of Shaanxi-Gansu-Ningxia Border Region*. Xi'an: Shanxi People's Publishing House, 1989.

22. Shen Ronghua, *Government Mechanism*. Beijing: National Administration Publishing House, 2003.

23. Compiled by Editorial Committee of Auditing Cadres Professional Education Training Materials under the CNAO, *Interpretation of National Audit Standards*. Beijing: China Modern Economic Publishing House, 2012.

24. Scientific Research Institute, Overseas Audit Office, and Department of International Cooperation of the China National Audit Office, *Introduction to Foreign Audit Supervision System*. Beijing: Modern Economic Publishing House, 2014.

25. Aizhong Shi, "Observations on Audit Culture." *Auditing Research* 1, 2005.

26. Sun Wenxue, *History of Chinese Financial Thoughts* (Vol. 2). Shanghai: Shanghai JiaotongUniversity Press, 2008.

27. Wang Yongqing, "Transformation of Governance Concepts to Systems, Institutions and Mechanisms." *Seeking Truth* 24, 2007.

28. Wang Aiguo, "Resonsideration and Restructuring of Chinese Audit Cultures." *Accounting Research* 3, 2011.

29. Wang Lifeng, *Rule of Law in China.* Beijing: People's Publishing House, 2014.

30. Wang Xiuming, "A Miracle of Audit Culture Construction in New Period—Evaluation on the 'Theory and Practice of Audit Cultures.'" *Finance and Trade Research* 3, 2007.

31. Wei Sen, *Introduction to Economic Analysis of Social Order.* Shanghai: Shanghai Joint Publishing Company, 2001.

32. Wei Liqun, *"Four Comprehensives": New Layout and New Realm.* Beijing: People's Publishing House, 2015.

33. Wen Shuo, *The World History of Auditing* (Revised Edition). Beijing: Enterprise Management Publishing House, 1996.

34. Xiang Huaicheng, *General History of China Finance* (Volume: Contemporary). Beijing: China Financial & Economic Publishing House, 2006.

35. Xiang Junbo, "Auditing System-National Basic Political System." *Audit Research* 5, 2001.

36. Xiao Bin, *Institutional Theory.* Beijing: China University of Politic Science and Law Press, 1989.

37. Xu Jihua, Feng Qina, and Chen Zhenru, *Smart Government—Arrival of the Era of Ruling County by Big Data.* Beijing: CITIC Press, 2014.

38. Xu Yanfu, "Brief Introduction to Audit Culture." *Auditing Research* 5, 2005.

39. Xu Zipei, *Big Data.* Guilin: Guangxi Normal University Press, 2012.

40. Yan Qiang, *National Governance and Policy Changes—Marching to Experience-Based Chinese Political Science.* Beijing: Central Compilation & Translation Press, 2008.

41. Yang Guangbin, *System Forms and the Rise and Decline of Nation.* Beijing: Peking University Press, 2005.

42. Yang Suchang and Xiao Zezhong, "Impacts of Constitutional Thoughts on Auditing System." *Auditing Research* 1, 2004.

43. You Guangfu, *Comparison of Chinese and Foreign Supervision Systems.* Beijing: Commercial Press, 2003.

44. Yu Keping (chief editor), *Country Governance Assessment.* Beijing: Central Compilation & Translation Press, 2009.

45. Yu Zhong, *Context of Power Restrictions in China*. Jinan: Shandong People's Publishing House, 2007.

46. Zhang Xiaojin and Yu Xiaohong, *Promoting the Modernization of the National Governance System and Capacity*. Beijing: People's Publishing House, 2014.

47. Zhang Xukun, "Definition and Classification of Systems." *Zhejiang Social Sciences* 6, 2002.

48. Zhang Yikuan, "On Morality and Code of Ethics of Audit." *Guangdong Audit* 2, 2002.

49. Zhao Baoyun, *A General View on Power Balance Mechanisms of Six Western Countries*. Beijing: Chinese People's Public Security University Press, 2009.

50. Zhao Gang, "Constructing a New Audit Culture." *Journal of Audit and Economics* 2, 2001.

51. Zhao Liwen, "Differentiation of Systems, Institutions and Mechanisms and Their Methodological Significance to Reform and Opening Up." *Journal of the Party School of the Central Committee of the CPC* 13, 2009.

52. China Audit Society and Scientific Research Institute of the China National Audit Office, *Compilation of the History of China's Revolutionary Base Areas*. Beijing: Beijing University of Technology Publishing House, 1990.

53. Drafting Group of Regulations for the Implementation of the Audit Law of the PRC, *Interpretation of New "Regulations for the Implementation of the Audit Law."* Beijing: Law Press China, 2010.

54. Law Department of the National Audit Office of the People's Republic of China, *Interpretation of Revisions of the Audit Law*. Beijing: China Modern Economic Publishing House, 2006.

55. Policy Research Office, CPC Central Committee, *Glorious Achievements and Valuable Experience in the 30 Years of Reform and Opening Up*. Beijing: Research Press, 2008.

56. Zhu Yong (chief editor), *Chinese Law*. Beijing: China University of Politic Science and Law Press, 2012.

57. (U.S.) John Rogers Commons, *Institutional Economics: Its Place in Political Economy*, translated by YuShusheng. Beijing: Commercial Press, 1962.

58. (U.S.) Douglass C. North, *Institutions, Institutional Change and Economic Performance*, translated by LiuShouying. Shanghai: Shanghai Joint Publishing Company, 1994.

59. (U.S.) Michael Chatfield, *A History of Accounting Thought*, translated by Wen Shuo, Dong Xiaobo, et al. Beijing: China Commerce and Trade Press, 1989.

60. (U.S.) Joseph R. Strayer, *On the Medieval Origins of the Modern State*, translated by Hua Jia, Wang Xia, Zong Fuchang. Shanghai: Truth & Wisdom Press, Shanghai People's Publishing House, 2011.

61. (U.K.) Viktor Mayer-Schönbergerand Kenneth Cukier, *Big Data:A Revolution That Will Transform How We Live, Work, and Think*, translated by Sheng Yangyan and Zhou Tao. Hangzhou: Zhejiang People's Publishing House, 2013.

62. (U.S.) Elinor "Lin" Ostrom, David Feeny, and Hartmut Picht, *Rethinking Institutional Analysis and Development*, translated by Wang Cheng et al. Beijing: Commercial Press, 1992.

Postscript

Since the first mention of an auditing system in the Constitution of the People's Republic of China in 1982, the auditing system of socialism with Chinese characteristics has seen more than 30 years' development with great achievements. In order to summarize successful experience and development patterns so as to further enhance the system, a research group was formed to analyze development as well as the primary experience in building the auditing system of socialism with Chinese characteristics. The work, a careful study of the foundations, framework, and features of the system, offered prospects for the further development of the system based on the new situation and requirements of Chinese national governance as well as social and economic development.

After the formation of the overall thinking, basic framework, and writing outline in 2012, Dong Dasheng, Yu Xiaoming, Shi Aizhong, Sun Baohou, Cheng Qiang, Chen Chenzhao, Zhang Tong, Yuan Ye, and Li Xiaozhong offered a number of modifications, participated in the ongoing discussions and put forward valuable opinions and suggestions many times when the first draft appeared. Zhang Ke, Guo Caiyun, Cui Zhenlong, Ma Xiaofang, Jiang Jianghua, Liu Liyun, Peng Xinlin, Wang Gang, Liang Jing, Liu Zhihong, Xiao Zhendong, Zhang Yaoding, Luo Tao, Zou Xiaoping, and Zhang Long took part in the outline discussion, material collection, and writing of the book; Yang Yajun, Zhang Qiang, and Zhang Long offered assistance in the final compiling process. We wish to express hereby our sincere gratitude to all the contributors of the book.

In the process of writing, the book has gone through repeatedly discussion and modification. To all our readers, we would like to present this book as an open thread. Your valuable comments are greatly appreciated.

September 2016

Index